W9-CJD-461

Consumer Reports®

Best
Baby
Products

WITHDRAWN

About this book

Best Baby Products comes to you from CONSUMER REPORTS, the testing and consumer-information source best known for product Ratings and buying guidance. We are also a comprehensive source of unbiased advice about services, personal finance, autos, health and nutrition, and other consumer concerns. Since 1936, the mission of Consumers Union has been to test products, inform the public, and protect consumers. Its income is derived solely from the sale of CONSUMER REPORTS magazine and its other publications and services, and from nonrestrictive, noncommercial contributions, grants, and fees. Only CONSUMER REPORTS has secret shoppers throughout the country who buy all the products we test to be sure that they're the same products you buy. CONSUMER REPORTS accepts no ads from companies, nor do we let any company use our reports or Ratings for commercial purposes.

Other books from Consumer Reports

- Complete Guide to Reducing Energy Costs
- Smart Buyer's Guide to Buying or Leasing a Car
- Consumer Drug Reference
- Consumer Reports Buying Guide
- Electronics Buying Guide
- New Car Buying Guide
- Used Car Buying Guide

Consumer Reports®

Best Baby Products

NINTH EDITION

by Sandra Gordon
& the Editors of CONSUMER REPORTS

CONSUMERS UNION, YONKERS, NEW YORK

Consumer Reports Books

Editor, Books and Special Interest Publications . . . . David Schiff
Author . . . . Sandra Gordon
Contributing Editor . . . . Susan Randol
Coordinating Editor . . . . Robin Melén
Design Manager . . . . Rosemary Simmons
Contributing Art Director . . . . Vicky Vaughn Design
Medical Editor . . . . Marvin Lipman, M.D.
Associate Director, Health and Family . . . . Chris Hendel
Contributing Researcher . . . . Maggie Keresey
Contributing Copy Editor . . . . Donna Boylan
Manager, Content Resource Scheduling . . . . Nancy Crowfoot
Production Associate . . . . Charlene Bianculli
Technology Specialist . . . . Jennifer Dixon
Editorial Associate . . . . Joan Daviet

Consumer Reports

Deputy Editorial Director, Senior Director . . . . Kimberly Kleman
Director, Editorial and Production Operations . . . . David Fox
Design Director . . . . George Arthur
Creative Director . . . . Tim LaPalme
Product Manager, Publications Development . . . . Lesley Greene
Manufacturing & Distribution . . . . Mark Yatarola
Senior Director, Product Safety
 & Consumer Sciences . . . . Don Mays
Program Leader . . . . Joan Muratore
Project Leaders . . . . Rich Handel, Todd Young

Consumers Union

President . . . . James A. Guest
Senior Vice President, Information Products . . . . John J. Sateja
Vice President and Editorial Director . . . . Kevin McKean
Vice President and Technical Director . . . . Jeffrey A. Asher
Vice President, Publishing . . . . Jerry Steinbrink

Pediatric drug information © Copyright, March 2007, American Society of Health-System Pharmacists. Gerald K. McEvoy, Pharm.D. assistant vice president of drug information and editor, AHFS Drug Information. Barbara F. Young, Pharm.D., MHA project editor. Jennifer Meyer Harris, Pharm.D., contributor.

Contents

Introduction
Welcome! Here's how to use this book to get the best values and safest products for your new baby

A-to-Z Guide

Contents

A-to-Z Guide (continued)

Special Reference Section

About the Author

Sandra Gordon writes frequently about health, nutrition, and parenting for books, leading consumer magazines, and Web sites, including Parents, Fitness, American Baby, Family Circle, Clubmom.com, and Babyzone.com. She has appeared on the weekend edition of NBC's "Today" show and as a baby safety expert on The Discovery Health Channel's "Make Room for Baby."

She lives in Connecticut with her husband and their two daughters.

Welcome!

Gearing Up for Your Baby

Congratulations! You have a new baby (or babies!) on the way. Of course, you'll want to welcome your offspring into the world with joy and love, in a secure and nurturing environment. You'll want to select the safest products and find the best values, and *Consumer Reports Best Baby Products* will help you do just that.

One of the first things you'll notice as a new parent is that this stage of life is filled with "stuff": pacifiers, bottles, breast pumps, strollers, car seats, developmental toys, cribs, swings, infant carriers, play yards, and baby gates—not to mention diapers, diapers, and more diapers. (You'll go through more than 2,000 in your baby's first year alone.) Indeed, baby products are a $7 billion industry in the U.S., and hundreds of products are added to the lineup

To test for durability, we put a 40-pound weight in each stroller, then used a machine to walk it over the equivalent of 19 miles of very bumpy pavement.

each year. As you'll soon discover (if you haven't already), stores cater to expectant parents with aisle after aisle of baby gear. Some retailers that once focused solely on adult apparel and merchandise now have divisions—or entire stores—devoted to children and babies. L.L. Bean, Gap, and Pottery Barn are a few prominent examples. Catalogs offer everything from organic cotton diapers to hospital-grade breast pumps. Then there are online venues. Web shopping can be a convenient way to find the information you need about baby products and services and to make purchases—all without having to pack up your baby and the rest of your family and troop from store to store.

All these retailers and manufacturers are smart. They realize that new parents want the best for their baby and that they are willing to shell out for the privilege. In fact, a typical middle-income family in the U.S. will spend an average of $12,673 on baby's first year alone! But you can spend less, get better value, and still buy high-quality, safe products. That's where *Best Baby Products* comes in. We know you want the best for your baby. But you don't necessarily need to spend the most to get it.

To navigate through the world of baby products and stick to your budget, you need to be prepared. Shop with a list and use this buying guide to do your homework before you spend. That way, you'll have a firm idea of what makes and models of products to consider, and which items are a good fit for your lifestyle. If you don't take this strategic route, buying for your baby quickly can become an expensive and overwhelming undertaking, often eliciting more questions than answers. What makes a $250 stroller different from an $800 one? Which car seat is best for an infant? How do you install it, anyway? What's the best sleeping arrangement for a newborn? A crib? Bassinet? Co-sleeper? What's better, the Diaper Genie or the Diaper Dékor? And then there's the overarching question: What do I really need and what's nice but not necessary? True, you'll need some items, but many—as cute or as fashionable as they are—are purely optional. Others, even though they're sold in retail outlets, can be a safety hazard. In *Best Baby Products*, we'll help you determine which is which and advise you on how to spot quality as well as the best brands and models.

Best Baby Products comes to you from CONSUMER REPORTS, the comprehensive source of unbiased advice about products and services, health, and personal finance, published by the nonprofit Consumers Union. Since 1936, the mission of Consumers Union has been to test products, inform the public, and protect consumers. We accept no advertising and buy all the products we test.

Our engineers, market analysts, and editors attend trade shows, read trade publications, and visit stores to spot the latest products and trends. The market analysts query manufacturers about their product lines and update databases of model information.

Stroller brakes are tested on this special ramp.

Then staff shoppers anonymously visit dozens of stores or go online to buy the selected models, just as you would. While shopping for a baby can certainly be fun, we take it very seriously because, let's face it, there's nothing more precious than your newborn.

The products we purchase are put to the test in CONSUMER REPORTS' own labs in Yonkers, N.Y., or at a specialized outside laboratory under the direction of our engineers (crash-testing of car seats, for example). With baby gear, safety is always the key consideration, followed by convenience and usability. The findings of our baby-products experts— based on unbiased, side-by-side testing—can guide you in your search for safe products. *Best Baby Products* also can help you find the best value and tell you when a bigger price tag means better quality—and when it doesn't. We'll even help you decide when you need to buy new, and when used (or hand-me-down) is OK.

How This Book Can Help

Organized in a handy A to Z format, *Best Baby Products* covers a wide range of essential baby (and parent) gear, with an emphasis on quality and safety. We'll help you decide what to buy and what to steer clear

BABY PRODUCTS RECALLS

Dozens of baby products are recalled each year because of violations of safety standards established by the Consumer Product Safety Commission (CPSC). For updated recall information on infant products, consult monthly issues of CONSUMER REPORTS or visit the CPSC's Web site at *www.recalls.gov* or *www.cpsc.gov*. To report a dangerous product or a product-related injury, call CPSC's hotline at (800) 638-2772 or CPSC's teletypewriter at (800) 638-8270, or visit CPSC's Web site at *www.cpsc.gov/talk.html*.

of—dubious products in the marketplace that aren't your safest options. We'll also answer common questions about products that often are not addressed, such as, "We live in the city and take a lot of taxis. What do I do when my baby outgrows her infant car seat?" (See the "Car Seats" chapter on page 97 for our suggestions.) You'll also find a section on keeping your baby safe, a list of recent product recalls, and a guide to using medications for babies.

The baby products marketplace is always changing, of course. New models are frequently introduced and old ones are discontinued. We've tried to make sure that the products listed throughout this book will be available at the time of publication and that the prices will reflect what you'll pay. For the most recent product and pricing information available, be sure to also take advantage of your free 30-day subscription to Consumer Reports Online. If you haven't already registered for your free 30 days, go to *www.ConsumerReports.org/babyoffer*. With this book and the Web, you'll be set to go.

Trend Spotting

Several key trends are influencing the kinds of baby products you'll see in stores, in catalogs, and on the Web right now. Here's a quick peek at what you're apt to find:

More functional designs. Manufacturers, after studying the preferences of parents, have decided that functionality is essential to sales success, and they're right. The best products are not only safe, they're durable, user-friendly, and tailored to your busy lifestyle. You'll find ergonomic strollers with comfort features such as cup holders for parents, built-in containers for baby wipes, and customized storage. Many products today are developed with several uses in mind: dressers that do double duty as changing tables and play yards that function as portable bassinets and changing tables. What product features do you really need? What's nice, but not truly necessary? This book will help you decide.

More stylish choices. Manufacturers have upped the style ante. You'll find products from cutesy to sophisticated, inspired by popular children's characters and television programs ("Dora the Explorer" and "SpongeBob Squarepants"), and chic lines that fit your sense of style. You'll find all-terrain strollers, for example, with chrome or aluminum accents in today's hottest colors—chartreuse, periwinkle, orange, "cognac" and black. You'll also find baby products sold in "montage collections": car seats, strollers, play yards, and swings all in the same French country, camouflage, African, or nautically-inspired Italian-made fabric, designed to blend in with your home décor and satisfy the strong nesting instinct that manufacturers believe pervades today's post-9/11 culture.

What kind of "statement" do you want to make? What "look" can you live with for months or even years? Or does that matter to you? Aesthetics are something to consider before and during your shopping trips because they can play a big role in the price of many products.

Greater attention to safety. Safety is a major concern among product manufacturers, and safer designs continue to evolve while new safety-related products continually are added to the mix. You'll find an array of products—supermarket cart covers, high chair covers for restaurants, and disposable place mats—designed to keep babies safe from germs. Are these safety products really necessary or worth the extra money? Throughout *Best Baby Products*, we'll answer such questions to give you peace of mind.

Overall, products marketed specifically for babies are generally safe, partly because of government regulations. They're approved for safety or certified as meeting safety requirements mandated by federal regulations, or enforced voluntarily by manufacturers. The Consumer Product Safety Commission (*www.cpsc.gov*), for example, regulates baby equipment and oversees recalls. It enforces industry standards that apply to most product categories, as well as mandatory government standards for a few specific categories, such as cribs and clothing.

The U.S. Department of Transportation's National Highway Traffic Safety Administration (*www.nhtsa.gov*) sets mandatory safety standards for the crash performance of child car seats. The U.S. Food and Drug Administration (*www.fda.gov*) regulates baby formula and most baby food, and the U.S. Department of Agriculture (*www.usda.gov*) monitors baby food containing meat, poultry and eggs.

Industry groups such as the Juvenile Product Manufacturers Association (JPMA), a national trade association of 325 companies that make and/or import baby products, administers a program that certifies manufacturers that make products that meet voluntary safety standards. Consumer organizations such as Consumers Union work to refine those standards. CONSUMER REPORTS regularly tests cribs, crib mattresses, car seats, diapers, infant carriers, strollers, play yards, gates, toys, and baby monitors. We often hold products to more rigorous standards than the government requires or that manufacturers and retailers must meet to

New Baby Basics

A master list for moms and dads

Here's a checklist of what you should have on hand before your baby arrives. Many of these products have their own chapters in this book.

Tooling Around

____ **Car seat.**

____ **Stroller.**

Beds and Linens

____ **Crib.**

____ **Crib mattress.**

____ **Bassinet/cradle** (if you don't want to put your baby in a crib right away).

____ **Two to three fitted crib sheets.**

____ **Four or more waffle-weave cotton receiving blankets** for swaddling your baby.

____ **Two mattress pads.**

____ **One to two waterproof liners** (for crib or bassinet).

Diaper Duty

____ **Diapers.** Disposables: One 40-count package of newborn (birth weight under 8 pounds) or of size 1 (birth weight over 8 pounds). Cloth: Two to three dozen, plus six to 10 snap-on, waterproof outer pants, and two to three sets of diaper pins, eight to 10 all-in-ones or diaper system covers; two to three dozen diaper system inserts.

____ **Diaper pail (with refills or bags as needed).**

____ **Diaper bag.**

Dressing Baby

____ **Four sleeping outfits or one-piece** sleepers with attached feet.

____ **Six side-snap T-shirts.**

____ **Four to six one-piece undershirts** that snap around the crotch.

____ **A small baby cap** (although the hospital will probably give you one).

____ **Six pairs socks/booties.**

____ **Two to three soft, comfortable daytime outfits.** Get only a few items in newborn size. Then, go for clothing in the 6-month size—your baby will grow into it quickly. But don't buy baby sleepwear that's too big—it's a safety hazard.

____ **Cotton sweater or light jacket.**

Summer babies:

____ **Brimmed hat.**

Winter babies:

____ **Snowsuit with attached mittens** or fold-over cuffs, or heavy bunting.

____ **Heavy stroller blanket.**

____ **Warm knit hat.**

Feeding Time

If you're planning to breast-feed:

____ **Three to five nursing bras.**

____ **A box of washable or disposable breast pads.**

____ **Breast pump if you expect to use one** (manual or electric).

____ **Four small baby bottles** with newborn nipples for storing expressed breast milk.

____ **Bottle-drying tree.**

____ **Bottle brush.**

____ **Insulated bottle holder for diaper bag** (the hospital may give you one).

____ **Three packs of cloth diapers** or burp cloths.

If you're planning to bottle-feed:

____ **Six 4- to 5-ounce bottles,** plus nipples, rings, and a dishwasher basket if you use a dishwasher.

Bathing/Grooming

____ **Plastic infant bathtub.**

____ **Three soft hooded towels.**

____ **Two packs of baby washcloths.**

____ **Baby body wash that doubles as shampoo.**

____ **Pair of blunt-tip scissors or baby-sized nail clippers.**

____ **Zinc-oxide-based diaper rash ointment.**

____ **Soft brush and comb.**

____ **Mild laundry detergent.**

Medicine Chest Essentials

____ **A pain-and-fever reducer** recommended by your baby's doctor, such as Infant's Tylenol.

____ **Cotton pads/swabs.**

____ **Nasal aspirator.**

____ **Digital rectal thermometer.**

____ **Rubbing alcohol.**

____ **Petroleum jelly.**

Keeping Baby Happy

____ **Pacifiers.**

Extras: Nice but Optional

____ **Baby monitor.**

____ **Changing table.**

____ **A rocker or glider.**

____ **Sling or strap-on soft carrier.**

____ **Boppy, a doughnut-shape pillow** designed to make holding baby during breastfeeding or bottlefeeding easier.

____ **Nursing coverup.** Attaches at your neck and allows for private breast-feeding when you and your baby are in public.

____ **Infant swing.**

____ **Bouncy seat.**

____ **Night-light.**

JUVENILE PRODUCTS MANUFACTURERS ASSOCIATION

CERTIFIED

AN INDEPENDENT TESTING LABORATORY VALIDATES THE MANUFACTURER'S CERTIFICATION OF THIS PRODUCT TO ASTM SAFETY STANDARDS

The JPMA certification seal means a company designed and built a product with JPMA safety standards in mind and had it tested by an independent laboratory. You'll find the seal on bassinets/cradles, bath seats, carriages and strollers, changing tables, full-size cribs, gates and enclosures, hand-held infant carriers, high chairs, infant bouncers, infant swings, play yards/non-full-size cribs, portable bed rails, portable hook-on chairs, soft fabric and backpack carriers, stationary activity centers, toddler beds, and walkers. For more information about products with the JPMA Certification Seal, visit *www.jpma.org.*

comply with voluntary industry standards. You'll find results of our safety tests in specific chapters throughout *Best Baby Products.*

Other children's products may be certified by an independent laboratory as meeting safety standards, or a company may test its own product and vouch that they meet the safety standards. Those products may be just as safe as products certified under the JPMA program, but the JPMA seal is a good guide to safety for consumers—look for it on product packaging.

Registering

Especially if you're a first-time parent, you probably will receive many baby items as gifts. To take the guesswork out of giving for your friends and family, consider registering at baby specialty shops and chain stores, online or in person. If you're having a baby shower, let your shower hostess know where you're registered so she can pass the information along to guests.

Signing up with a registry can help you avoid duplicate or unwanted gifts and may get you coupons and other money-saving offers. But be aware that the information you provide when you register may be sold to other companies for marketing purposes.

When registering, request practical items from the New Baby Basics checklist on pages 14-15. Be as specific as possible, include model numbers and colors, and do just as much homework as if you were paying the tab yourself. For example, test-drive strollers in the store to get an idea of how they handle and practice opening and closing them with one hand (since you may be holding your baby with the other). Using this book will help you select the products that meet all current safety standards and guidelines. If you get things you didn't ask for, aren't sure you'll use, or that don't pass muster safety-wise, don't be afraid to take them back. You can always use the store credit later, when you need specific items (and you will).

What Not to Buy

Baby bath seats. These seats attach to the side of the tub; older models may attach to the bottom with suction cups. Either way, they can give parents a false sense of security. They've been associated with roughly 120 drownings and 160 injuries since 1983. Nearly all those deaths occurred when a parent or caregiver left the baby unattended momentarily. Note that baby bath seats are different from baby bathtubs, which have a steeply angled back or sling insert that helps the parent support the baby during baths. Baby bathtubs are useful, provided caretakers don't leave the child unattended. Consumers Union was among the first organizations to call for a ban on baby bath seats, in 2000. A new design emerged in early 2005; our tests found it to be unsafe. For more on baby bath seats, see page 65.

Soft bedding. The ads in baby magazines suggest that if your crib isn't spilling over with frills and fluff, you're somehow shirking your parental duty. In fact, the safest crib is one that has a firm mattress, a snug-fitting mattress pad, and a fitted crib sheet, and nothing else; no puffy bumper guards, no stuffed animals, no pillows, no quilts. Experts have long recognized that such soft crib bedding creates the risk of suffocation. For bedtime in winter, dress your infant in a one-piece bunting. If you insist on a blanket, keep it at waist height, tucking ends firmly under the sides and bottom of the mattress.

Sleep positioners. These are wedge-shape pieces of foam meant to keep infants in a secure sleeping position. But we believe they're a suffocation hazard and our medical experts don't recommend them.

Changing tables with only three side rails. Changing tables are associated with 2,000 to 3,000 injuries per year, especially ones with only three side rails. The latest industry standard requires flat changing tables to have barriers on all four sides. Buy this type.

Money-Saving Strategies

A new baby can take a surprisingly big bite out of your budget. Here are some ways to save:

Take advantage of freebies and coupons. If you don't mind getting your name on mailing lists, call the toll-free customer-service lines or register at the Web sites of formula, baby-food, and disposable diaper companies for their parenting newsletters and new-parent programs, including coupons and free samples. Even if you don't register, you may get them anyway. Somehow, when you have a new baby, word gets out.

Consider a discount club membership. At places like Costco or Sam's Club, you'll reap discounts on everyday items you'll use a lot, such as disposable diapers, baby wipes, and laundry detergent. Sign on for the loyalty savings card program at your drugstore and supermarket and you'll receive coupons that can rack up savings.

Buy as your baby grows. Except for the basics listed earlier in the chapter, don't buy baby products until you're sure you'll need them. The wait-and-see approach gives you time to check with friends about their experiences with specific baby products and ultimately can save you money. You may be able to borrow some items. Others might not seem necessary once you understand what your baby's needs are.

Stock up in the fall. Fall is prime baby bargain time, since retailers tend to clear their inventory to make room for next year's products, which arrive between November and January.

Shop around. Prices can vary from one shopping venue to another, sometimes dramatically. Megastores and discount chains such as Baby Superstore, Babies "R" Us, Buy Buy Baby, Kmart, Sears, Target, Toys "R" Us, and Wal-Mart often have the lowest prices, although not always the largest selection. For personal attention and informed sales help, smaller stores are a better bet. Another plus: Mom-and-pop stores have more leeway to offer on-the-spot discounts, especially if you're a regular customer. Just be sure to ask, "Is that your best price?"

Keep in mind that salespeople everywhere may have an incentive to push their most expensive wares. And beware of the emotional pull of lines like: "But it's for your baby," and "It's not every day that you have a baby." Unless you're on your guard, it's easy to be persuaded to spend, spend, spend.

Watch for sales. Toys "R" Us, Babies "R" Us, and Buy Buy Baby stores, for example, routinely put out newspaper inserts and in-store fliers with savings of 20 percent or more on brand-name baby items.

Go online. If you shop online, compare prices of bassinets, cribs, changing tables, and hundreds of other baby products quickly by logging on to a shopping Web site such as *www.bizrate.com*, *www.nextag.com*, *www.shopping.com*, or *www.epinions.com*, which also

OFFBEAT BABY GIFTS TO REQUEST

If you're the lucky parent who already has everything—maybe this isn't your first child or you've already had more than one shower—here are several gift ideas to toss out to well-meaning friends and relatives.

• **Diaper service for the first month.** If you're going to use cloth diapers, this will be a big help.

• **Cloth-diapering system.** Again, if you're going with cloth, these diaper-and-cover combos are convenient.

• **A personal chef or a housekeeper for a day, a week, or a month.** Having someone else do the cooking or the cleaning can really help parents get a much-needed break. For more information about a personal chef, contact the American Personal Chef Association at *www.personalchef.com*. National cleaning services can be found online by entering "house cleaning services" in the search function.

• **A birth and/or post-partum doula,** a woman trained to provide emotional, physical, and educational support for women and their families. For more information and to locate a doula in your area, log on to the Web site for Doulas of North America at *www.dona.org*.

• **A gift certificate to a local day spa.** Let someone care for you for a change.

offers product advice from fellow parents. For even more savings online, log onto sites such as *www.couponcabin.com* for a wide selection of the latest online coupons from major e-tailers. But keep tabs on your shipping costs when buying online. They can sometimes wipe out any savings—and then some.

Consider buying used. Gently used baby clothes, bedding, and toys can sometimes be found in thrift stores, online, and at yard sales at a small fraction of their original retail prices. But some items such as car seats and cribs always should be purchased new to ensure they comply with updated safety requirements and have no hidden flaws.

Ask about return policies. A store's return policies can make the difference between being a satisfied customer and being stuck with something you don't want or can't use, so be sure to inquire. It's not unusual for a store to allow returns only up to 30 days after a purchase, which won't help if you're shopping well before your baby arrives.

Weigh warranties. Manufacturers and retailers often replace returned goods that have clear design or manufacturing defects. Hold on to warranty information so you can refer to it if there's a problem. You may find a warranty being used as a sales tool. Some less expensive but adequately firm baby mattresses, for example, offer no warranties, while top-of-the-line models may have a "lifetime guarantee." Is that protection you need to pay for? For a definitive answer, see the "Crib Mattresses" chapter, starting on page 149.

BABY WHERE-TO-BUY GUIDE

The following list is an overview of places to buy and register for baby gear (and, in many cases, products for older kids that you'll need as your baby grows up), from major retailers to more specialized outlets.

Company/Ways to Shop	What You'll Find
AMAZON.COM www.amazon.com Online	You'll find a wide selection of baby products at competitive prices—from diaper pails and car seats to cribs and toys, with comments from fellow parents to inform your buying decisions.
BABIES "R" US www.babiesrus.com 800-888-BABYRUS In store / Online	Babies "R" Us is the baby-outfitting component of the toy superstore Toys "R" Us. You can find almost everything you need to clothe and care for your baby here, except for the fanciest merchandise. Babies "R"' Us offers a baby registry, and an online health/behavior resource guide. The customer service number is listed on the Web site, and you can e-mail for help.
BABY AGE www.babyage.com 800-222-9243 Online	You'll find a wide, though not very deep, range of baby products, from cribs to nursing accessories, at this Web site. It also sells bedding and features an online gift registry.
BABYANT.COM www.babyant.com 866-609-0410 Online One store in California	This Web site sells apparel, toys, and a large variety of gear from well-known manufacturers, such as Aprica, Gerber, and Maclaren. You'll also find a baby registry, baby-care articles, and a "baby gallery" where you can post a photo of your new family member.
BABYBOX.COM www.babybox.com 800-620-5713 Online	This Web-only venue sells high-end infant and toddler apparel, as well as linens and toys. The selection is not very wide.

BABY WHERE-TO-BUY GUIDE

Company/Ways to Shop	What You'll Find
BABY CATALOG OF AMERICA www.babycatalog.com 800-752-9736 Catalog / Online	Savings on pregnancy, baby, and toddler products are available here. There's a closeout page for bargains. Discounts for club members and a gift registry are available.
BABYCENTER www.babycenter.com 866-241-2229 Online	The store component of this information-packed Web site sells a wide range of products for babies and parents, including gear, nursery items, feeding aids, health-care products, clothing, toys, books, music, and videos. There are also products for preconception, pregnancy, and motherhood. Buying guides, a best sellers page with photos, and parents' picks are useful tools offered on the site. There is also a gift registry and tips on throwing a baby shower.
BABY EINSTEIN www.babyeinstein.com 800-793-1454 Catalog / Online	This company sells educational products with an emphasis on language, poetry, art, and music. The line includes videos, music CDs, books, DVDs, puppets, and toys.
BABY DEPOT www.babydepot.com In store (Burlington Coat Factory) Online	Baby Depot is part of Burlington Coat Factory, a nationwide discount chain of stores that carry baby apparel and gear, among other merchandise. There is no phone number, but the customer service e-mail can handle specific questions, such as shipping info.
BABY GAP www.babygap.com 800-427-7895 In store / Online	You'll find a good selection of baby basics (sleepers and T-shirts) as well as mini versions of Gap's trademark khakis, polo shirts, and jeans here. The company also has bedding.
BABY GUARD www.babyguard.com 866-823-2229 Catalog / Online	This company sells a basic selection of latches (for everything from drawers to refrigerators), locks, and accessories for babyproofing your home. It also carries radiator covers, guards for TVs and VCRs, and a wide variety of safety gates.

BABY WHERE-TO-BUY GUIDE

Company/Ways to Shop	What You'll Find
BABYSTYLE.COM www.babystyle.com 877-378-9537 Catalog / Online	This hip-looking Web site offers a large selection of baby and toddler apparel. You must register first to order. It offers free shipping with a purchase of $75 or more.
BABY ULTIMATE www.babyultimate.com 877-724-4537 Online	This Web-only retailer sells all types of apparel, including special-occasion clothing, costumes, and christening outfits. There are also layettes and a selection of toys, mobiles, and photo frames.
BABY UNIVERSE www.babyuniverse.com 877-615-2229 Online	This online superstore sells a wide range of gear, from cribs to high chairs.
BABYWORKS www.babyworks.com 800-422-2910 Catalog / Online	This retailer's focus is on cloth diapering systems, including covers, with a variety of diapers (including unbleached flannel) and accessories. You'll also find a selection of cotton apparel, bedding, and natural skin-care products.
BACK TO BASICS TOYS www.backtobasicstoys.com 800-356-5360 Catalog/ Online	This company, owned by Scholastic, Inc., features a wide selection of colorful toys billed as "non-violent and with enduring play value." The toys are organized by age, price, and type.
BAREFOOT BABY www.barefootbaby.com 800-735-2082 Catalog / Online	You'll find mostly diapers, diaper accessories, toilet-training items, and linens (cleaning cloths, bibs, and so on) from this company, as well as a selection of skin-care items for nursing moms and babies.

BABY WHERE-TO-BUY GUIDE

Company/Ways to Shop	What You'll Find
BJ'S WHOLESALE CLUB www.bjs.com 800-257-2582 In store	This warehouse store often stocks child safety seats, strollers, and other large baby items, as well as a limited, seasonal selection of apparel. You'll find disposable diapers and wipes in big quantities at a discount price here. Membership is required.
BREASTFEEDING. COM www.breastfeeding.com Online	This Web site is primarily an information center for breastfeeding with links to Motherwear and Glamourmom nursing wear as well as a link to Ameda, maker of breast pumps.
BUY BUY BABY www.buybuybaby.com 516-507-3417 In store / Online	Retail outlets of this baby superstore can be found in New York, New Jersey, Maryland, and Virginia. Residents of other states can browse the store's online inventory of car seats, strollers, high chairs, bedding, toys, and more. The Web site lists store locations under Customer Service and has an online registry.
THE CHILDREN'S PLACE www.childrensplace.com 877-752-2387 In store / Online	This nationwide chain sells its own line of casual clothing for kids from infants through size 14. There's a wide selection of layette and infant apparel, including sleepwear and booties.
CONSTRUCTIVE PLAYTHINGS www.constplay.com 800-448-7830 Catalog/Online	This company sells mostly to schools and day-care centers, but anyone can buy from its Web site or catalog. You'll find soft and wooden toys, ride-on toys, puzzles, and games, organized by category.
COSTCO www.costco.com 800-774-2678 In store / Online	You'll find discount prices on disposable diapers and wipes, with occasional good deals on larger items such as child safety seats, carriers, and strollers, at this warehouse-store. You must be a member to shop in the store or online.

Company/Ways to Shop	What You'll Find
DECENT EXPOSURES www.decentexposures.com 800-524-4949 Catalog / Online	Here you'll find 100% cotton baby accessories (some organic), such as caps and bibs, as well as a wide selection of stretchy bras that can be used for nursing.
DISCOVERY TOYS www.discoverytoysinc.com 800-341-8697 Catalog / Online	Toys from this company are sold by representatives in much the same manner as Avon or Pampered Chef products. Discovery Toys has a wide range of high-quality toys and books organized by age group—early years, preschool, and school years. You can preview a selection of toys on its Web site, and can order online through a local sales rep's site.
EBABYSUPERSTORE www.ebabysuperstore.com 866-771-2229 Online	The focus here is on gear, with a very large selection of strollers, play yards, car seats, swings, bouncers, and gates. There's also an interactive "safety center" with suggested items for each room you wish to babyproof. A gift registry is available.
ECOBABY ORGANICS www.ecobaby.com 800-596-7450 Catalog / Online	You'll find a good selection of organic cotton baby items, including diapers, apparel, and bedding. The company also sells nursing tops and toys.
EDDIE BAUER www.eddiebauer.com 800-625-7935 In store / Online	The gear section features a limited selection of diaper bags and car seats.
ETHAN ALLEN KIDS www.ethanallen.com 888-EAHELP1 In store / Catalog	This line from home-furnishings retailer Ethan Allen features cribs and other children's furnishings. Although you can access Ethan Allen Kids on the main Ethan Allen Web site, not much is offered online. Instead, request a catalog (which currently costs $18.95).

BABY WHERE-TO-BUY GUIDE

Company/Ways to Shop	What You'll Find
GYMBOREE www.gymboree.com 877-449-6932 In store / Online	Known for its chain of activity centers offering play groups and music classes for babies and toddlers, Gymboree stores often feature "activity corners," where little ones can catch a video while mom shops within sight. Merchandise includes apparel for newborns to size 10, as well as a Gymboree line of toys, music, and videos.
HANNA ANDERSSON www.hannaandersson.com 800-222-0544 In store / Online / Catalog	This company sells what it calls "European quality" apparel for babies, toddlers and older kids. It has a selection of basics, outerwear, and layettes. Hanna Andersson includes a primer on its Web site to help parents convert its European sizes.
J.C. PENNEY www.jcpenney.com 800-322-1189 In store / Online / Catalog	This department store offers a wide range of baby apparel, gear, and furniture. It sells its own apparel label, as well as other well-known brands. You'll find a good selection of child safety seats, strollers, high chairs, and more. A gift registry is available.
KIDS STUFF www.kidsstuff.com Natural Baby: 800-922-7397 Jeannie's Kids Club: 800-722-5282 Perfectly Safe: 800-898-3696 Catalog /Online	At this online store for infants through age 12, you order products from Natural Baby, Jeannie's Kids Club, and Perfectly Safe catalogs. You can also request a catalog from each retailer.
KMART www.bluelight.com 866-562-7848 In store / Online	The retail outlets of this national chain feature a better selection than the Kmart Web site, though you can find some baby products online, including bedding, car seats, carriers, and infant toys.

BABY WHERE-TO-BUY GUIDE

Company/Ways to Shop	What You'll Find
L.L. BEAN www.llbean.com 800-441-5713 Catalog / Online	Both the catalog and Web site of this outdoor/casualwear outfitter offer bicycle trailers, jogging strollers, a limited selection of bedding, and a good selection of apparel, including outerwear and footwear, organized by gender. There is also some furniture.
LANDS' END www.landsend.com 800-963-4816 Catalog / Online	Both the catalog and Web site offer bedding, apparel, diaper bags, outerwear and footwear.
MACY'S www.macys.com 800-289-6229 In store / Online	Macy's sells baby apparel, including special-occasion outfits, and a good selection of bedding, diaper bags, and shoes.
THE MOMMY MALL www.mommy-mall.com Online	This Web site features direct links to manufacturers, retailers, and e-tailers of baby apparel, furniture, toys, and maternity needs.
NETKIDSWEAR.COM www.netkidswear.com 732-203-9677 Online	Essentially a large online discount store, this site sells name-brand baby clothes and has links to other Web sites.
ONE OF A KIND KID www.oneofakindkid.com 800-276-0054 Online	This Web site features European and American designer baby clothes and children's clothing as well as custom baby bedding, cribs, furniture, and gifts.
ONE STEP AHEAD www.onestepahead.com 800-274-8440 Catalog / Online	This company sells all kinds of baby gear, including diapering systems, potty-training aids, strollers, some clothing, feeding supplies, toys, and bath gear.

BABY WHERE-TO-BUY GUIDE

Company/Ways to Shop	What You'll Find
PEAPODS www.peapods.com 866-WOOD-TOY 866-966-3869 Online	Peapods sells a wide selection of slings, as well as cloth diapers, organic cotton diapers, and diaper covers. It also has toys.
POTTERY BARN KIDS www.potterybarnkids.com 800-993-4923 In store / Catalog / Online	The kids' line of this housewares and home-furnishings retailer features bedding, window treatments, and furniture.
RAINBEE www.rainbee.com 877-724-6233 Online	A wide range of upscale bedding, apparel, furniture, toys, and nursery accessories is offered on this site.
THE RIGHT START www.therightstart.com 888-548-8531 In store / Catalog / Online	This specialty store features a wide variety of clothing, toys, nursery items, and furniture. The Web site offers the same items except clothes. A gift registry is available.
SAFE BEGINNINGS www.safebeginnings.com 800-598-8911 Catalog / Online	This company sells baby-proofing items, baby gear, nursing and feeding paraphernalia, and parenting books and videos. A gift registry is available.
SAM'S CLUB www.samsclub.com 888-746-7726 In store / Online	You'll find discount prices on disposable diapers and wipes, formula, toys, and a limited selection of baby gear, such as portable changing tables. You must be a member to shop in the store or online.

Company/Ways to Shop	What You'll Find
SEARS www.sears.com 800-MY-SEARS 800-697-3277 In store/ Catalog / Online	You'll find the wide range of baby products you'd expect from a department store here. Apparel, furniture, monitors, and more are offered through all of Sears's shopping venues. The Sears Web site has a special baby section, where you can browse its inventory of baby items.
TARGET www.target.com 888-304-4000 In store / Online	Target stocks a huge variety of baby items in-store and online. Furniture, strollers, child safety seats, apparel, and bedding are among the offerings. Its selection of medicine is what you'd expect from a discount drugstore—wide and plentiful.
THIS BABY OF MINE www.thisbabyofmine.com 877-572-6427 Online	This baby-information site also sells diapering systems, nursing apparel and accessories, toys, slings, car-seat covers, shoes, layettes, books, and gifts.
TWINS HELP! www.twinshelp.com 888-440-8946 Online	You'll find twins-related merchandise, novelty items, and some helpful nursery accessories at this very specialized retailer.
USA BABY www.usababy.com 800-323-4108 In store / Catalog	This nationwide chain sells primarily furniture, including nursery ensembles and rockers and gliders, and traveling essentials such as strollers, child safety seats, and play yards. To date, you can't yet purchase directly from its Web site, but you can preview merchandise, find a nearby store, or order a catalog. There's also a baby registry available online.
WAL-MART www.walmart.com 800-966-6546 In store / Online	You'll find what you'd expect at the stores and the Wal-Mart Web site—baby basics at discount prices. The selection of furniture and gear is neither broad nor deep.

1

Autos

Kid-Friendly Vehicles

Whether you're in the market for a new car or evaluating future needs now that you have a baby, here's good news. There's no shortage of vehicles that can be a family car; there are more than 250 models on sale in the U.S. But which one is the best one for you depends on the size of your family, the age of your kids, and your family's activities. "Finding the right family vehicle doesn't have to be a difficult or long process if you invest some time to research your options before you go out shopping," says David Champion, senior director of Consumer Reports Auto Test Division.

Can you get by with a sedan, or do you need the extra passenger space of a minivan, wagon, or a sport-utility vehicle? That, of course, is the $14,000 to $40,000 question.

"Parents need to think about how they'll be using the vehicle, what type of cargo they intend to carry, and how their needs may change during the years they own the vehicle," Champion says.

Shopping Secrets

In general, focus on vehicles with a roomy and versatile interior, plenty of cargo space, ease of access, and windows that make it easy for kids to see outside. "If they can't look out the window, that can trigger boredom and bickering among siblings," Champion says. Four-door sedans and wagons are usually fine for families with one or two children. Bigger families (or familes whose kids have lots of friends), or those that take long trips, should consider a minivan or SUV with a larger cargo area and more seating. All minivans and a growing number of SUVs can seat seven passengers, and some accommodate eight.

Minivans have sliding side doors for easy entry, low floors, easy-to-access cargo areas, and good outward views. SUVs offer roomy interiors and four- or all-wheel-drive to handle bad weather and unpaved roads. But young children may have a tough time getting into SUVs because these vehicles sit high off the ground. Loading groceries, strollers, and other items into the cargo area of a large SUV may be difficult for the same reason. Remember, too, that taller SUVs have a higher center of gravity, which makes them more top-heavy and more susceptible to rolling over than other vehicles. Car-based SUVs, such as the Honda Pilot, may be a family-appropriate choice. No matter what vehicle you choose, make sure it has electronic stability control.

What Kind of Car Should You Buy?

To zero in on a vehicle that's right for your family, consider these questions:

How many people will you be carrying? If you have one or two children, a small or midsized sedan may do fine, while saving you money and offering better fuel economy than a larger vehicle. But remember, kids must ride in the back, away from front airbags, and in appropriate restraints, so if you expect to transport a group—your own kids plus friends—you'll want room to put them all in the back. A roomier choice is a minivan, a seven-passenger wagon, or SUV. All seven-passenger vehicles have a third-row seat that can be folded down or removed when not in use. Third seats in wagons usually face the rear and are best for small children.

Saftey Check: Keep Tires Inflated

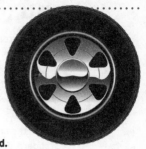

Underinflated tires provide slower turning, faster wear, and run much hotter. Overheated tires can lead to failure. Check the pressure of your vehicle's tires at least once a month, when the tires are cold. Also check the tires before and after long road trips. The recommended tire pressure is found on a label inside the car—usually in a doorjamb, inside the glove-box lid, or inside the fuel-filler lid.

How old are your children? Plan ahead. Young children may not need much room now, but the kids will grow. Also consider how much room you'll need for child safety seats. They can take up a lot of space, and having your seat kicked from the rear gets annoying. If you have older children, consider a car that has as many safety features as you can get and that will be easy to handle as they learn to drive. Small and midsized sedans and wagons are usually good choices; larger vehicles are harder to maneuver.

How much cargo space do you need? The trunk of a sedan may provide enough cargo room for small families. A vehicle with more space may be a better choice for large families and those who travel frequently, have a lot of outdoor activities requiring lots of gear, or need extra room for transporting a stroller, a play yard, or portable infant swing to and from Grandma's. Depending on your cargo needs, your choices range from small wagons to minivans to large SUVs.

How adaptable is the vehicle? Does the rear seat fold down? If so, is it a split design so you can fold one side separately from the other? Does the front passenger seat fold down to accommodate long items? If you're considering a seven-passenger vehicle, check to see if the third-row seat folds flat or has to be removed to enlarge cargo capacity. Remember that vehicles that sit lower to the ground are easier to load and unload.

What conditions will you be driving in? If you'll be driving in rain and very light snow, a two-wheel drive (2WD) vehicle will work fine. Front-wheel drive with traction control is the optimal 2WD configuration for driving in slippery conditions and for navigating treacherous hills. All-wheel drive (AWD) provides additional traction and is a plus for most normal snow conditions or for traveling on dirt roads without high rocks, deep sand, or steep inclines. If you're likely

FAMILY VEHICLE SAFETY CONCERNS

Blind zones. Every year, children are injured and killed because drivers backing up don't see them. According to Kids and Cars, a nonprofit group that works to improve child safety in and around cars, 105 children were killed in back-over incidents in 2005, and 50 children were killed in the first half of 2006. A contributing factor is that some SUVs, pickups, and minivans have much larger blind spots—the area behind a vehicle that the driver can't see—than standard size cars do.

To check a vehicle's blind spot, sit in the driver's seat of the parked vehicle and have someone stand directly behind the car, next to the bumper, and hold out a hand at about waist level. Have the person walk back slowly until you can see the hand through the rear window. This will give you an idea of how big the vehicle's blind spot is. The chart below shows the length of the blind spot for an average-height driver (5 feet, 8 inches) and a shorter driver (5 feet, 1 inch). Some vehicles are now available with an optional rear-view video camera that gives the driver a wide-angle view of much of the area that's usually hidden in the blind spot. The scene appears in an in-dash display. These systems can reduce back-over accidents, but they are typically expensive and usually offered as part of a navigation package that can run well over $2,000. Aftermarket camera systems costing between $200 and $700 that can be installed on any vehicle. Many vehicles are available with a parking-assist system that uses sensors in the rear of the vehicle to alert the driver to solid objects behind the vehicle. Such systems are also available as aftermarket add-ons, priced at $300 to $400. In CONSUMER REPORTS tests, we found that these systems work well as parking aids, but aren't reliable enough to be used as safety aids.

Child safety seats. Child safety seats save lives and should be used until a child is big enough to wear a regular safety belt. The traditional method of attaching a child seat is to use the vehicle's safety belts. However, incompatibilities among the car's safety belts, the car seats, and the child safety seats often have made it difficult, and sometimes impossible, to get a good, tight fit. Vehicles made after Sept. 1, 2002, are required to have the Lower Anchors and Tethers for Children (LATCH) system. It has built-in lower

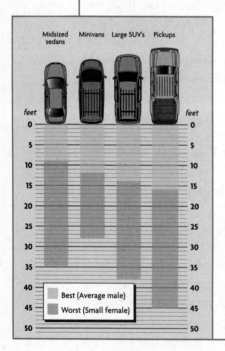

ILLUSTRATION BY TREVOR JOHNSTON

anchors and ready-to-use tether attachment points, so compatible child safety seats can be installed without using the vehicle's safety-belt system.

The system doesn't work equally well in all vehicles. In many cars, the attachment points are obscured or difficult to reach, so it's not easy to use them even with some of the newest child seats. Try your child seat in the vehicle before you buy.

Power-window switches. Small children have suffered injuries or died from accidents involving power windows. Typically, the child is left in the car with the engine running or keys in the ignition. The child leans his head out the window and accidentally kneels on the window switch. The glass moves up forcefully, choking the child. Because the window can quickly crush the windpipe, the child cannot scream for help. Two types of switches are inherently riskier than others if they're mounted horizontally on the door's armrest: Rocker switches move the glass up when you press one end of the switch, down when you press the other; toggle switches work when pushed forward or pulled back. The lever switch, which must be pulled up to raise the glass, is safer because it makes it almost impossible to raise the window accidentally. Switches of any design mounted vertically or on an upswept armrest are harder to activate by accident.

RISKY DESIGNS Horizontal rocker switches (top) and toggle switches (bottom).

Lever switches and autoreverse sensors, which automatically open a closing window if it hits an obstacle on the way up, such as a child's neck or fingers, are common in Europe. But autoreverse is required in the U.S. only in vehicles with remotely controlled windows and auto/one-touch-up windows, which close automatically after the switch is activated once, rather than pressed until the window is completely closed. A safety regulation enacted by the National Highway Traffic Safety Administration in late 2004 mandates that all new vehicles be equipped with safer window switches. Automakers, however, have until late 2008–the 2009 model year–to comply. In the meantime, there are plenty of vehicles that still have the riskier designs. Look for cars with lever switches when shopping for a family vehicle, particularly if you have young children.

SAFER Lever switches have to be pulled up to raise a car window.

to be driving in places where you'll encounter more severe conditions, you should opt for a four-wheel-drive (4WD) vehicle with low-range gearing. If you drive on a lot of snow and ice, switch to winter tires for extra grip and safety, no matter what type of vehicle you have.

How important is fuel economy? As a general rule, the larger the vehicle, the lower the fuel economy. Small, lightweight sedans usually get the best mileage; heavy SUVs get the worst. If you need more cargo room than a sedan can provide, consider a wagon. Some have as much usable cargo space as an SUV, but they usually get better fuel economy.

What safety equipment is included? By law, every new passenger vehicle comes equipped with dual front air bags. But some sophisticated systems have occupant sensors to determine if the air bag should deploy and at what strength. An increasing number of vehicles have head-protection side air bags that deploy to protect occupants in both the front and rear seats. (In general, the safest place to put an infant car seat is in the center rear seat of the automobile, whether or not your car has air bags. For information on installing infant car seats, see the "Car Seats" chapter, page 97.)

Our auto experts also highly recommend a feature called electronic stability control (ESC) especially on SUVs. It's designed to help keep the vehicle under control and on its path during cornering and prevent it from sliding or skidding. Stability control can help prevent SUVs from rolling over.

You Can Get Better Gas Mileage

Don't drive with a cold engine. Engines run most efficiently when they're warm. In our city-driving tests of sedans and SUVs, when we made multiple short trips and started with cold engines, fuel economy was reduced. Engines produce more pollution and wear faster when they're cold. Combine short trips into one so the engine stays warm.

Drive smoothly. In our tests, frequent bursts of acceleration and braking reduced gas mileage by 1 to 3 miles per gallon, depending on the vehicle. The harder you accelerate, the more fuel you use. Unnecessarily hard braking wastes the fuel you use to get up to speed. Also, anticipate the movement of traffic. Use your brakes as little as possible, since every time you hit the brakes, you're wasting fuel. Once you're up to speed on the highway, maintain a steady pace in top gear.

A QUICK FAMILY-FRIENDLY TIP FROM OUR TESTER

"The safety and functional aspects are most important, but the niceties make travel enjoyable. When choosing a new vehicle, look for cup holders in the front and back, storage areas, 12-volt power ports for plugging in games, and rear DVD players, which can keep your child occupied and can help limit distractions, such as sibling squabbles during long drives," says CONSUMER REPORTS auto tester and mother of two Jennifer Stockburger. A good sound system helps, too, since children can be lulled by music. Some systems let your children listen to their music on headphones while you listen to yours.

Smooth acceleration, cornering, and braking not only save fuel but also extend the life of the engine, transmission, brakes, and tires.

Reduce unnecessary drag. At highway speeds, more than 50 percent of engine power goes to overcoming aerodynamic drag. Don't add to that drag by carrying things on top of your vehicle when you don't have to. Even empty racks on the car reduce its fuel economy.

Slow down. Aerodynamic drag exponentially increases the faster you drive. We tested vehicles' fuel economy at 55, 65, and 75 mph. Driving at 75 mph instead of 65 reduced gas mileage 3 to 5 miles per gallon, depending on the vehicle. Slowing down to 55 mph improved the gas mileage by similar margins.

Vehicle Picks

In choosing the best family vehicles, CONSUMER REPORTS looks at a range of factors, including performance, comfort, ease of access, safety, fuel economy, roominess, and reliability. Here are our top picks in several categories. The price ranges were current at the time of publication and may, of course, change. Even so, they'll give you a ballpark idea and are useful for comparison. More detailed car ratings and current pricing information are available online at *www.ConsumerReports.org*. To activate a free 30-day trial membership to the site, see the inside of this book's front cover.

Best Family Sedan: Honda Accord

The Honda Accord is an excellent sedan for families. The Accord V6 is our top-rated family sedan, and the 4-cylinder is close behind. They both have fairly agile handling, and the ride is steady and compliant. The Accord is roomy, quiet, and refined, although some road noise is noticeable. A telescoping steering column allows drivers to find an ideal position. The automatic shifts very smoothly and responsively. The four-cylinder engine is smoother than many V6s. Side and curtain air bags are standard. The V6 model is very quick and relatively fuel efficient. V6 models also get standard stability control for 2006. The V6 hybrid-electric version is even quicker and gets 25 mpg overall, just one mpg better than the four-cylinder, which may not justify its $30,000 price tag. Crash-test results are impressive. Base price range: $18,625 to $31,090 for the sedan FWD VP, LX, SE, EX, and Hybrid.

Best Small Sedan: Honda Civic

The Civic was redesigned in 2006, and the new model is a major improvement over the previous generation. The Civic is now CR's top-rated small sedan. Handling is responsive and secure, and the ride is steady and compliant, but road noise is pronounced. The 1.8-liter, four-cylinder engine is refined, works well with the smooth five-speed automatic, and returned 28 mpg. The hybrid model returned 37 mpg overall. Instruments are arranged into two tiers, and there is a high-mounted digital speedometer. The interior has generous storage space. Standard safety equipment includes an antilock braking system and curtain air bags. Crash-test results are impressive. An ultraclean emissions, natural-gas version, the GX, is available in New York and California. Base price range: $15,010 to $24,590 for the sedan FWD DX, LX, EX, Si, Hybrid, and GX.

Best Three-Row SUV: Honda Pilot

The eight-passenger Pilot has a smooth and quiet V6 engine and an optional full-time AWD system. Fuel economy is good for an eight-passenger SUV. A comfortable ride and secure handling are assets. Although the Pilot is quiet overall, road noise is pronounced. The standard split third-row seat folds flat, creating ample cargo space. Cabin access is easy, and fit and finish is very good. Crash-test results are impressive. Stability control and three-row curtain air bags are standard on all trim lines from 2006. Base price range: $27,095 to $31,945 for the four-door SUV FWD LX, EX, and EX-L, and $28,395 to $33,245 for the four-door SUV AWD.

Best Small SUV: Toyota RAV4

The redesigned RAV4 is our highest-rated small SUV. The V6 version scores at the top, the four-cylinder is second. The RAV4 has a flexible, well-designed interior and agile handling. It is roomier and more substantial than its predecessor, with a quieter interior and a more comfortable ride. Handling is agile and secure with standard stability control. The rear seat is roomy and a third-row seat is optional. The four-cylinder engine feels responsive and returns better fuel economy than in the previous-generation RAV4. The optional 3.5-liter V6 makes the RAV quick and quiet, with only one mpg worse fuel economy than the four-cylinder engine. However, in Limited trim it pushes the price up to $30,000. Side curtain air bags are optional. Base price range: $20,850 to $25,020 for the four-door SUV FWD, and $22,250 to $26,420 for the four-door SUV AWD, for the Base, Sport, and Limited editions.

Best Minivan: Honda Odyssey

The Odyssey outscores the Toyota Sienna by a small margin, and is our top-rated minivan. Interior flexibility and fit and finish are impressive. The third-row seat folds into the floor in sections. Road noise is a bit pronounced. Handling is agile and precise, and the ride is supple and steady. The V6 is smooth and quiet, and on high-end models imperceptibly shuts off three cylinders when cruising to save fuel. The Odyssey is every bit as polished as a midluxury sedan, yet performs minivan duties effectively. Reliability of the 2005 redesign has been average. Crash-test results are impressive. Base price range: $25,645 to $36,895 for the Honda Odyssey FWD LX, EX, and Touring editions.

Best Wagon: Mazda5

This Mazda3-based vehicle has the utility of a small minivan, yet is agile, maneuverable, economical, and affordable. It delivers responsive handling, a comfortable ride, and a relatively quiet interior. Road noise, however, is pronounced. Fuel economy was a decent 23 mpg overall. The 2.3-liter, four-cylinder engine provides adequate performance but lacks reserve power when carrying full loads or climbing hills. Visibility and access are excellent. The vehicle has flexible seating for four passengers and their luggage, or can accommodate six with minimal cargo in a "2+2+2" seating arrangement. But the third-row seat is cramped. Base price range: $17,635 to $21,300 for the Sport Touring and Grand Touring editions.

CHAPTER

2

Baby Bottles & Nipples

E ven if you breast-feed your baby, you may need bottles for pumped breast milk or supplementary formula. After your baby turns a year old and is weaned from formula, whole cow's milk—usually fed by bottle—will likely be a diet staple, possibly with breast milk (although you may decide to transition your baby to a sippy cup at that point). Styles and colors of bottles abound, but you should find bottles that don't cause excessive spit-up, burping, and gas. The bottles should also be easy for your baby to hold and for you to clean.

What's Available

Your main choices are: standard, angle-neck, disposable (drop-ins), and natural-flow. You may also see bottles in shapes like animals or footballs, but they can be hard to clean. We don't recommend them. Bottles and nipples are constantly being improved to reduce the chance of a baby's ingesting air bubbles, which may contribute to colic, spitting up, burping, and gas, and the negative effect of suction, fluid in the ear. Most bottles are made of clear or semitransparent dishwasher-safe polypropylene or polycarbonate plastic, although glass bottles are also available. The main makers of baby bottles are, in alphabetical order: Avent (*www.aventamerica.com*), Dr. Brown's (*www.handi-craft.com*), Evenflo (*www.evenflo.com*), Gerber (*www.gerber.com*), Munchkin (*www.munchkin.com*), Playtex (*www.playtexbaby.com*), Sassy (*www.sassybaby.com*), Second Nature (*www.regallager.com*), and The First Years (*www.thefirstyears.com*). Here's the lowdown on the types of bottles available:

Standard bottles

There are two sizes of this classic shape with straight sides: 4 or 5 ounces for infants and 8 or 9 ounces for older babies.

Pros: These bottles are easy to fill and hold, can be used repeatedly, and allow you to accurately gauge formula amounts. There are many standard bottles and companion nipples, so standard bottles give you more nipple options than disposable bottles. Most breast pumps and baby-bottle warmers are designed to be used with standard bottles, although you can easily transfer pumped breast milk from a standard bottle to a disposable, if you like.

Cons: There's nothing in the basic design that will reduce the amount of air your baby takes in. As your baby drinks, air will replace the liquid and some air may end up in your baby's tummy, creating gas.

SOME LIKE IT WARM

Formula or breast milk is fine right out of the refrigerator, but many babies prefer it warmed up. The best way to heat the bottle is to hold it under a stream of warm water from the faucet or to place it in a bowl of warm water for several minutes. Shake the bottle gently to help distribute the heat.

For about $30, you can buy an electric bottle warmer, which has a chamber you fill with water to produce steam heat. Look for a model with an on/off button and an automatic shutoff to prevent overheating.

For warming on the go, you can buy a bottle warmer that plugs into a car's cigarette lighter. The warming pack fits into any standard cup holder, and a strap-hanger allows you to stow the whole kit in the car when you're not using it. **Price range: $10 to $19.**

Don't use a microwave to heat formula or breast milk. It can cause uneven hot spots you may not be able to detect. It can also destroy the immunological benefits of breast milk. And never put disposable bottles in the microwave—the plastic liner could explode when you take it out, possibly scalding you and your baby.

Price range: $5.99 to $11.99 for a 4- or 5-ounce bottle three-pack; $5.99 to $12.99 for an 8- or 9-ounce bottle three-pack.

Angle-neck bottles

These bottles are bent at the neck, making them easier for you to hold in a comfortable position.

Pros: Their shape causes formula or breast milk to collect at the bottle's nipple end, so your baby is less likely to swallow air. The shape may work well for feeding your baby lying semi-upright; this position may help prevent fluid from collecting in your baby's ear canals, which can lead to ear infections. One type, the Playtex VentAire angle-neck bottle, has a flexible disc at the removable bottom of the bottle. The disk is designed to keep air out of the liquid so your baby drinks virtually bubble free.

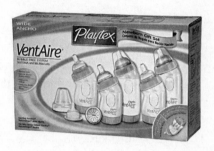

Cons: Angle-neck bottles can be awkward to fill—you must hold them sideways or use a special funnel to pour in liquid.

Price range: $10.99 to $13.49 for a 6-ounce bottle three-pack; $10.99 to $16.99 for a 9-ounce bottle three-pack.

Disposables

In these bottles, a pre-sterilized, disposable plastic pouch, or liner, fits inside a rigid outer holder, called a nurser. The top edge of the liner fits on top of the nurser's rim. You pour in formula or breast milk and hold the liner in place by fastening the lid (a nipple and bottle ring). The liner collapses as your baby drinks, so no air bubbles can form.

Pros: Collapsible liners are designed to prevent air from collecting as your baby sucks. Cleanup is easy. You just throw the liner away, wash the nipple, and you're done.

Cons: You'll need to buy liners continually. "Disposables are expensive when you consider how many liners you need to get you through a day," says Kathy McCann, the mother of an 11-month-old, from Milwaukee, Wis. Still, after trying several brands, she settled on the disposable Deluxe Playtex Nurser, which her son liked and tolerated well.

Price range: Expect to pay about $16 for a starter set with 4- and 8-ounce holders and 10 liners. Liners will run you another $8.95 to $10 for 100 4-ounce or 8-ounce drop-ins.

Natural-flow bottles

These bottles, made by Dr. Brown's, feature a patented internal straw-like vent system that's inserted into the center of the bottle. It's designed to eliminate the vacuum that can form when a baby sucks, so there are no air bubbles, reducing the possibility of colic and gas.

Pros: The patented design may just work. A recent study by the Indiana University School of Nursing of 36 colicky infants found that using these bottles over a two-week period reduced the infants' crying and fussing.

Cons: Compared with other bubble-reducing bottles, such as angle-neck models, these have an extra piece or two to throw into the dishwasher. The straws can be hard to clean. You'll need a tiny bristle brush, which comes with the bottles. Replacement brushes are available where baby bottles are sold, $4.99 for a four-pack.

Price range: $12.99 to $17.99 for Dr. Brown's three-packs and starter kits.

Which Bottle to Choose?
Go with the Flow

Overall, there are no hard and fast rules about how to choose the right bottle for your baby. What works for a friend's baby might not work for yours, which is why word of mouth isn't always helpful. "It seems like there's a different bottle for every baby," says Karin Ochs

. . . .

Nipple safety

Before the first use, boil nipples and accessories, such as the vent on Playtex VentAire bottles, according to the manufacturer's directions—usually five minutes. After each use, wash nipples and accessories in hot, soapy water for about a minute and rinse thoroughly. Silicone nipples are dishwasher safe (top rack only). Some manufacturers advise you to boil nipples and accessories once a week for five minutes. That's a good idea, too.

The Playtex One-Step Kit lets you pump and store breast milk in liners that drop into bottles.

Whichever type of nipple you choose, inspect it regularly, especially when your baby is teething. For safety's sake, replace the nipple at the first sign of tearing, cracking, stickiness, or other signs of excess wear. Your baby could accidentally inhale small pieces, which could cause injury.

Never try to enlarge a nipple hole with a pin. That could cause the nipple to tear and become a choking hazard. For more about nipples, see "The Nuances of Nipples," page 44.

BASIC BOTTLE DO'S AND DON'TS

DO:

• Wash your hands before preparing your baby's bottle.

• Have someone else introduce your baby to the bottle at about four weeks into your nursing regimen if you're breast-feeding but want to begin using a bottle. Your baby may associate mom with breast-feeding and may resist if you try give him the bottle yourself.

• Sterilize your bottles by washing them in the top rack of the dishwasher, or wash bottles in hot tap water with dishwashing detergent and rinse them in hot tap water. If you have well water or nonchlorinated water, or if you simply don't run your dishwasher very often, use a sterilizer or boil bottles in water for 5 to 10 minutes.

• Wean your baby from a bottle by 12 months of age, if possible. By that time, he will be ready to drink from a sippy cup. Prolonged bottle use (after 14 months) can cause your baby to consume too much milk and not enough food, and may delay the development of feeding skills. It can also lead to baby-bottle tooth decay, which is painful, difficult to treat, and can cause problems for permanent teeth.

DON'T:

• Heat formula or breast milk in the microwave. (See "Some Like It Warm" sidebar on page 40 for details.)

• Give your baby a bottle of milk or formula to suck on during the night or at naptime. The habit can cause baby-bottle tooth decay. Give your baby a bottle only at feeding times and don't mix bottles and bed.

• Prop up your baby with a bottle. This feed-yourself practice can lead to choking, ear infections, and tooth decay (yes, again), as well as less cuddling and human contact, which all babies crave.

• Give your baby a bottle to carry around and "nurse." This can lead to tooth decay, drinking too much, and sharing bottles with little friends, increasing the risk of colds and other infections. The contents of the bottle can spoil, which can cause food-borne illness, such as bad tummy bugs, which are no fun for your baby or for you.

from Chicago, the mother of a 7-month-old, who settled on Avent bottles, standard bottles with flexible, "anti-colic" nipples, because her son took to them from day one and they didn't cause too much gas. But that brand didn't work for Joscelyn Willett from San Francisco, the mother of a 5-month-old. Her son didn't like the nipple and gas was a problem. "A combination of trial and error and word of mouth led us to Playtex VentAire bottles," she says, referring to the angle-neck bottles that her son used with success. She likes them too, because they are easy to clean and fill up. Bottom line: Be flexible, and experiment until you find a bottle brand that makes feeding your baby a smooth operation.

The Nuances of Nipples

The bottle you choose is important, but sometimes the nipple, rather than the bottle, makes all the difference to your baby. Some bottles, such as the Second Nature bottle by Regal Lager, are all about the

First Years' Soothie bottle has a nipple that matches the Soothie pacifier.

nipple. This standard baby bottle has a silicone nipple that features a thin membrane with multiple holes. The membrane flexes and the holes open as the baby suckles so the baby controls the flow, which mimics what happens during breast-feeding. The First Years makes the Soothie bottle, which has a nipple that has the same shape and feel as the Soothie pacifier your baby is likely to get in the hospital. (They're distributed through hospitals and sold in retail outlets.) If your baby takes to a Soothie pacifier, you might consider a Soothie bottle. Avent makes the Anti-Colic Nipple, which has an anti-vacuum skirt with a one-way air valve so that less air flows through the bottle. You may have to try one or more nipples until you find one your baby accepts—and there are a lot to choose from.

Shopping Secrets

Most nipples are made of Latex or silicone. Buy silicone nipples only; they're clear or brightly colored, not brownish. Our experts think silicone is safer than Latex, since babies may develop a sensitivity or allergy to Latex. Clear, odorless, taste-free, and heat-resistant, silicone is also less porous than Latex, so a silicone nipple may be better at resisting bacteria, which can settle into any textured material.

What's Available

The major nipple brands are Avent (*www.aventamerica.com*), Dr. Brown's *(www.handi-craft.com)*, Evenflo (Elan nipple, *www.evenflo.com*), Gerber (*www.gerber.com*), Munchkin (*www.munchkin.com*), Playtex (*www.playtexbaby.com*), and The First Years (Soothie nipple, *www.thefirstyears.com*). Nipples are sold with bottles or as part of a feeding-system starter kit, which usually includes 6-ounce and 9-ounce bottles with both slow-flow and fast-flow nipples and an extra nipple or two for good measure. Nurser kits usually include 4- and 8-ounce bottles, disposable liners, a breast-pump adapter ring, sealing disks, and nipple rings. Nipples are also sold separately, usually in packs of two or three, for $2.49 to $9.99.

Features to Consider

Shape. Nipples come in several shapes: the traditional "natural" bell, or dome, shape; a slightly bulbous "orthodontic" design; or a flattened shape. Most nipples are smooth. An exception is the Playtex NaturaLatch, a silicone nipple. Although we recommend silicone nipples, there's also a Latex version of the Playtex NaturaLatch, which has two flow rates. Whether silicone or Latex, the NaturaLatch is slightly textured instead of smooth around the perimeter of the nipple, to feel more like mom. It's intended to promote latch-on and reduce nipple confusion for babies who are both breast- and bottle-fed. The silicone nipple comes in three flow rates: slow, fast, and tri-cut, for thicker preparations, such as infant cereal mixed with formula or expressed breast milk. More on that option just below.

Flow rate. Nipples come in three standard flow variations with different-size holes appropriate for the baby's age: newborn or slow flow (for newborn to 3 months), medium flow (for newborn to 12 months), and fast flow (for babies over 3 months). A nipple should offer some resistance, but not so much that your baby has to struggle to get milk. Generally, younger babies prefer a slower flow; older babies, a faster one (although that's not always the case).

Some bottle nipples, such as Munchkin's Tri-Flow Standard Nipple, are compatible with different brands of standard bottles so you can mix and match, although most bottle nipples are designed to be used with the same brand of bottle. Munchkin's Tri-Flow nipple gives you a choice of three flow rates in one: fast, slow, and medium. A turn of the nipple ring changes the flow rate. Dr. Brown's makes a Preemie Flow nipple for feeding babies born prematurely. Dr. Brown's and other brands, such as Gerber, also offer a Y-cut (a tri-cut or cross-cut) nipple for cereal or thick juices, but the American Academy of Pediatrics doesn't recommend giving a baby "food" through a bottle because it can lead to excessive weight gain. And it's good for a baby to get used to the eating process–taking bites, resting between bites, and setting an eating pace.

Recommendations

There are pluses and minuses with every nipple and baby bottle on the market. Be prepared to try out bottles to find one your baby likes and that is easy for you to use. If you're having a baby shower, register for a variety of starter kits, which have several bottles of various sizes and nipples in one set. Start with, say, Playtex VentAire or Drop-ins, Dr. Brown's, or Avent, and take it from there. You'll know in short order which bottle your baby prefers. If your baby keeps spitting out or battling with a bottle, or is especially fussy after eating, tweak your system; offer a slower or faster nipple, and see if that helps. Some babies are equal-opportunity feeders and will accept any bottle that comes their way. If your baby shows signs of intolerance, such as gas, a rash, persistent vomiting, diarrhea, or any other unusual symptom, talk to your pediatrician. You'll probably need to switch formulas if your baby is formula-fed, not the bottles or nipples.

If you're predominantly or exclusively bottle-feeding, six 4- to 5-ounce bottles will get you off to a good start. If you're supplementing breast-feeding with an occasional bottle, you may need only one or two bottles. Once you settle on a nipple, buy half a dozen so you'll have plenty on hand.

CHAPTER

3

Baby Food

When your baby is 4 to 6 months old and meets some key developmental markers—he sits up with support, holds his neck steady, and shows good head control—a whole new world of tastes and textures opens up. That's when most babies are ready to start mouthing and chewing "solid" food. It's mushy and messy, but it's an important and exciting milestone.

Your baby is ready for a real-food fest when he reaches twice his birth weight. If you eat with your baby at meals, you'll begin to notice entrée envy: He may reach out and grab for the food you're eating. And you'll be able to spoon-feed your baby without resistance. At about 4 months, most babies lose the tongue-thrust reflex, the tendency for an infant to push his tongue against the roof of his mouth when a spoon is inserted. Still, your baby has a way to go before he is nibbling from your plate.

The first solid food your baby will eat is likely to be a soupy mixture of a tablespoon or two of dry infant rice cereal combined with breast milk or formula. Breast milk or formula will be on the menu until your baby is a year old or so and makes the switch to soy, rice, or cow's milk. If your baby doesn't demonstrate an allergic response—rashes, repeated vomiting, diarrhea, or constant fussiness—after three to five days, you can gradually make the cereal thicker. When your baby is 6 months or so, you can begin to introduce, one at a time, yogurt, oatmeal, barley, wheat, and pureed fruits, vegetables, and meats that you buy in jars or make yourself.

When your baby is 7 to 10 months old, you can try bite-size foods, such as Cheerios, pieces of bread, well-cooked pasta, avocado, cheese, and meats cut up for easy chewing. Your pediatrician will be your best source of advice about what to feed your baby and when, and what to do if you hit a snag—if, say, your baby rejects certain foods or suddenly starts eating less (not unusual when a baby is teething). At each well-child visit, starting at about 4 months, you'll probably get a new list of foods your baby can eat and a list of what to avoid, such as peanut butter. (It's generally a no-no until at least age 2.) You may be told to introduce foods one at a time to make sure your baby isn't allergic to them. Always supervise your child when he's eating.

Shopping Secrets

Besides scouring supermarket circulars, joining a food co-op, or buying in bulk at a wholesale price club, try these money-slashing tactics many new parents swear by:

Consider homemade. Although commercial baby food is convenient and has a certain official, "this-is-what-babies-eat" quality about it, except for rice cereal, baby food is something you can make yourself from scratch. All you need is a fork, for example, to mash bananas.

You can process fibrous foods such as sweet potatoes or meat in a baby-food grinder (found in baby stores), food processor, or blender. Before preparing food, always wash your hands and the food thoroughly, and wash your knives and cutting board with soap and water after you've cut meat, to prevent cross-contamination with meat juices.

Buy the freshest fruits and vegetables and use them within a day or two. Remove peels, seeds, and cores. Boil, bake, or steam them until soft, then purée them well. A time-saving tip: Pick one day a week to make a big batch, then freeze individual portions in ice-cube trays. Once they're frozen solid, remove the cubes and store them in plastic freezer bags in the freezer. Frozen fruits and vegetable purees will last three months; pureed meat, fish, and chicken will last up to eight weeks. Good veggies to start with are asparagus tips, avocados, squash, peas, potatoes, sweet peppers, sweet potatoes, and winter squash.

Excellent first fruit choices are apples, apricots, bananas, peaches, pears, plums, and prunes.

Homemade food can go right from freezer to microwave, but make sure it's just barely warm before serving. Add water, breast milk, or formula to smooth the texture, but omit butter, oil, sugar, and salt. And don't use honey as a sweetener for babies under a year old. It can harbor bacteria related to botulism. Give the food a good stir to dissipate any hot spots before serving.

One other caveat: According to the American Academy of Pediatrics (AAP), fresh beets, turnips, carrots, collard greens, and spinach may contain nitrates, chemicals that are rich in the soil in certain parts of the country and can cause an unusual type of anemia (low red-blood-cell count) in infants up to 6 months of age. Unfortunately, you can't solve this problem by buying organic produce. The AAP recommends buying commercially prepared forms of these foods, especially when your child is an infant. Baby food companies screen the produce for nitrates and avoid buying these vegetables in parts of the country where the chemicals have been detected.

Shop outside the baby-food aisle. If you compare the prices of commercial baby foods to the stuff you'd eat yourself, you're apt to find a significant price difference, ounce per ounce. Fresh and canned fruits and vegetables are easy, economical alternatives to commercial baby food. Canned pumpkin, for example, is well puréed, as are many types of applesauce (buy one without added sugar). You can purée the food more at home. Baby-food cookbooks have suggestions and recipes. You might also ask your pediatrician for advice.

Come armed with coupons. In addition to coupons in newspapers and magazines, most major baby food manufacturers post special offers on their Web sites. Recently, Gerber (*www.gerber.com*) offered up to $45 in savings on its products to parents who joined the Growing Up Gerber Club. Beech-Nut (*www.beech-nut.com*) offered shoppers special savings on baby food if they sent in labels from Beech-Nut baby food products or signed up for a free monthly e-newsletter.

Shop online. Shopping online for baby food may not save you money because shipping or delivery charges factor into your total costs, but it can save you time and a trip to the supermarket, which isn't always easy to pull off when you've got a new baby on board. If your local supermarket doesn't offer online shopping, go to the source. Some manufacturers, such as Earth's Best

15 FOODS YOU SHOULD EAT EVERY WEEK

When you're taking care of a new baby and juggling other challenges in your life, it's easy to let your own diet slide. Big mistake. If you don't take care of your nutrition needs, you may not be able to do as good a job of taking care of your baby. You can liken eating right to the principle of the oxygen mask demo on airplanes. Although it feels counterintuitive, parents of small children are instructed to strap on their own oxygen masks before attending to their child's. So feed yourself wisely, as well as your baby. Here are 15 foods that can boost your energy and keep you healthy.

Milk. Just one 8-ounce glass of skim or low-fat milk supplies up to one-third of the calcium you need for strong bones and teeth. A diet rich in calcium may cut your risk of hypertension, colon cancer, and breast cancer, and possibly ease PMS. Milk is a valuable source of vitamin D, vitamin A, riboflavin, niacin, and vitamin B12, says Doreen Chin Pratt, registered dietitian, director of nutrition services at Women & Infants Hospital in Providence, R.I.

Bananas. At about 100 calories each, bananas are a good source of fiber and vitamin B6. They're also loaded with potassium—a mineral that helps regulate blood pressure and is essential to muscle function. Eat one after a workout (when potassium levels may be low due to perspiration loss), mix into smoothies, or add to your cereal for an all-day energy boost.

Orange juice. A stellar source of vitamin C (just one 8-ounce glass supplies more than what you need every day), orange juice is also full of folate, a B vitamin—which may help prevent certain birth defects and colon cancer—as well as potassium. Opt for the calcium-fortified kind to benefit your bones.

Salad. Tossing together a variety of greens (romaine and spinach are rich in vitamin A and folate, and iceberg has fiber), tomatoes, carrots, and cucumbers is a smart way to sneak vegetables into your diet, says Joan Salge Blake, R.D., a clinical assistant professor of nutrition at Boston University.

Studies have shown that getting at least three servings of vegetables a day can reduce your risk of cancer, heart disease, and diabetes. Just be sure to steer clear of high-calorie dressing!

Peanut butter. It's chock-full of protein, fiber, zinc, and vitamin E. It contains mostly unsaturated fat, which helps lower both total and LDL ("bad") cholesterol. Peanut butter and jelly on whole-wheat bread with a glass of milk is a quick, nutritious meal. But don't go for the reduced-fat version. Since the fat is replaced with carbohydrates, you'll get the same number of calories anyway.

Sweet potatoes. These spuds—which are available year-round—should be a staple in your diet, not simply a holiday treat. They're an excellent source of potassium, fiber, and cancer-fighting antioxidants such as beta carotene and vitamin C.

Salmon and fish. This fish is a rich source of omega-3 fatty acids, which can lower your risk of heart disease. Eating salmon once or twice a week may boost your immune system. "If you're pregnant or nursing, the fatty acids in salmon help aid fetal and infant brain and central nervous-system development," says Andrea Crivelli-Kovach, Ph.D., an associate professor of public-health and nutrition at Arcadia University in Glenside, Pa. Government agencies recommend that pregnant or nursing women not eat shark, swordfish, king mackerel, or tilefish. Consumers Union recommends that such women hold off on eating canned tuna, as well.

Broccoli. It's low-cal and rich with vitamins A and C, beta carotene, folate, and fiber—all of which can help reduce your risk of heart disease and protect against certain kinds of cancer. Enjoy it raw or lightly steamed.

Whole-grain cereal. One bowl of whole-grain cereal typically supplies 10 or more vitamins and minerals, as well as complex carbohydrates (for energy), disease-fighting fiber, and phytochemicals—non-nutrient plant ingredients that help prevent disease. Choose cereals with at least 5 grams of fiber per serving.

Lean red meat. Women, especially those who have given birth within the last two years, are at risk for low iron levels, which can lead to a type of anemia. Red meat is an excellent source of iron that's more easily absorbed by the body. Stick with trimmed lean cuts—anything with loin or round in the name—for their low saturated-fat content, and eat no more than one 2- to 3-ounce serving (about the size of your palm) each day.

Vegetable soup. There is a slew of vitamins and minerals in soup loaded with veggies such as carrots, potatoes, and onions. Even better, because it's mostly liquid (and contains fiber), vegetable soup will fill you up on relatively few calories.

Yogurt. A good source of bone-strengthening calcium (an 8-ounce carton contains about a third of your daily needs), low-fat or nonfat yogurt also supplies protein and potassium with less saturated fats. Choose plain yogurt, since the flavored kinds are often high in sugar, and make sure the label says the brand contains "live and active cultures," since these bacteria have been shown to benefit the gastrointestinal tract.

Eggs. They're packed with the protein moms (and dads) need to help build and repair weary muscles. Eggs are also a good source of vitamin D, which helps the body absorb calcium. Still, because egg yolks are high in cholesterol, moderation is key.

Tomato sauce. Tomatoes are loaded with lycopene, a powerful antioxidant that has been shown to help keep arteries clear and reduce the risk of heart disease. Most jarred sauces also contain fiber and vitamins A and C.

Beans. Canned or dried varieties, such as kidney, black, garbanzo, and navy beans, are a low-fat source of protein, iron, and soluble fiber, which can help lower your cholesterol level. "You'll make any meal healthier—from soups and stews to salads and pasta dishes—by adding a can of beans to it," says Blake. However, since canned beans can be high in sodium, rinse them well under cold water or buy the no-salt kind.

(*www.earthsbest.com*), have an online store where you can order baby food directly at prices comparable to what you'd pay if you'd shopped in a brick-and-mortar store.

What's Available

The major brands of baby food are Beech-Nut (*www.beech-nut.com*) and Gerber (*www.gerber.com*), including Recetas Latinas, for the Latin market. The major organic lines are Earth's Best (*www.earthsbest.com*) and Gerber Organic.

Most pediatricians recommend starting your baby on commercial infant rice cereal. It's easy to digest and mixes easily with breast milk or formula. Some cereals have fruit, which is appropriate after your baby has mastered the plain stuff. Commercial makers of jarred baby food usually divide their product line into three stages: beginner (stage 1), intermediate (stage 2), and toddler (stage 3). Stage 1 foods are made for babies just starting on solids. They're usually a single food, puréed for easy swallowing. Beginner vegetables in jars are peas, carrots, green beans, squash, and sweet potatoes. Fruits are applesauce, bananas, peaches, pears, and prunes.

Stage 1 foods have the purest formulations without sauces or flavorings. Sweet potatoes are sweet potatoes and peas are peas. Intermediate (stage 2) foods are for more experienced eaters (at about 7 to 8 months). At this point, the choices are more interesting because foods are combined to improve taste and offer new textures, such as apples and chicken, or turkey and rice—and you don't have to open two jars. Stage 2 foods have a smooth texture, but are not as fine as beginner foods.

Stage 3 foods are for children 9 months and older, babies who are learning to chew and mash. At this stage, chunkier, larger portions, such as Gerber Organic's Herbed Chicken with Pasta, keep up with

growing appetites. Some parents never bother with stage 3 but simply start giving baby normal fare, still mashed and cut up for easy chewing and swallowing. Infant juices are available, but many are no different from the kind marketed for adults. Avoid citrus juice until your pediatrician gives you the go-ahead, usually when your baby is around 6 months old. It can upset little stomachs.

In addition to fruit-juice basics such as apple and

white grape, there are many combinations, some of which contain yogurt and fruit-vegetable blends. Some also have added calcium or vitamin C. Go easy on the juice, though. Too much can cause diarrhea and gas, and contribute to tooth decay. And when babies drink juice, they may take in less breast milk or formula, which contain the nutrients they really need. The AAP recommends limiting fruit juice to no more than 4 to 6 ounces per day from 6 months to 6 years of age, and making it part of a meal, not a snack. The juice your baby drinks should be pasteurized (flash-heated to kill pathogens). Fresh-squeezed juice isn't pasteurized.

Once your baby graduates to cow's milk at the one-year mark, keep in mind that juice fortified with calcium and vitamin D isn't a milk substitute. Milk has a whole package of nutrients, including riboflavin, phosphorus, zinc, and essential amino acids that help form strong bones. Fortified juice doesn't. And don't put your baby to bed with a bottle of juice or milk; that can lead to tooth decay.

The Dish on DHA

Beech-Nut makes a line of baby food, First Advantage, for babies 6 months and older that's fortified with DHA (docosahexaenoic acid), an essential fatty acid naturally found in breast milk and believed to promote mental and visual development. This fortified baby food line tends to cost more than organic baby food. DHA is also being added to some brands of infant formula, as mentioned in the "Formula" chapter. The scientific evidence on the benefits of food fortified with DHA is mounting, but ask your pediatrician for a recommendation. If your pediatrician encourages you to give your baby DHA-fortified

DISHWARE THAT'S NOT FIT TO BE ZAPPED

Besides baby food, you'll need rubber-tipped or plastic spoons and baby-friendly dishwasher- and microwave-safe bowls and plates. Check the label to make sure the dishware is safe for both dishwasher and microwave before you buy—no matter how cute it is. You'll probably use the dishware in the microwave, especially for reheating. If it's not microwave safe and you use it there anyway, chemicals from the plastic could leach into the food. Popular brands of microwave- and dishwasher-safe baby tableware are Primo, Sassy, and The First Years.

foods like First Advantage, you can buy it in stores and online at *www.beech-nut.com.* Some brands of eggs are enriched with DHA, but you can expect to pay as much as 90 cents more per dozen.

Is Organic Better for Your Baby?

You'll find a cornucopia of organic options in the baby food section from two major brands: Earth's Best and Gerber Organic. Natural foods markets often carry their own organic lines as well as specialty brands like Plum Organics, a line of frozen baby food. (For more

information, log on to *www.plumorganics .com.*) Baby food labeled "USDA organic" must meet standards set by the United States Department of Agriculture and be at least 95 percent organic, meaning that all but 5 percent of the content was produced without conventional pesticides and fertilizers. Organic food can't be irradiated (a one-time exposure to radiation intended to kill pathogens such as salmonella, listeria, or E. coli), genetically modified (a technique that alters a plant's DNA), or produced with hormones or antibiotics. Animals used in meat products must be fed organically grown feed.

USDA's National Organic Program accredits certifiers and they, in turn, certify organic producers and processors. Other terms found on food labels, such as "natural," "free-range," and "hormone-free," don't mean organic. Only food that has been certified to meet the USDA organic standards can be legally labeled "organic."

Do organically grown foods contain fewer pesticide residues than conventionally grown foods do? According to our evidence, the answer

is yes. A study published in the peer-reviewed journal Food Additives and Contaminants and co-authored by a senior scientist at Consumers Union showed that organic foods had residues of fewer pesticides that were present at lower levels than those found on conventionally grown foods. In general, foods produced organically or conventionally contain the same kinds and amounts of vitamins and minerals.

Organic for Less

If you buy organic food for your baby, or your whole family, it will cost you. In our informal research, we paid about 25 percent more for jarred organic baby food than for nonorganic versions (about 17 cents

KEEPING BABY'S FOOD SAFE

To keep baby food free of bacteria and other food-borne pathogens that can cause illness:

• Wash your hands with soap and water before handling baby food or preparing formula. Not only will you be keeping your baby safe, but regular handwashing also helps protect you from getting sick.

• Don't feed your baby from the jar (or yogurt container) and then put the uneaten portion back in the refrigerator. Harmful bacteria from your baby's mouth can grow and multiply in the jar. If your baby is likely to eat less than a full jar, spoon a portion into a bowl and put the jar in the refrigerator for later. You generally can keep opened jars in the fridge for up to three days in the case of fruits and vegetables, one day for meats, and two days for meat and vegetable combos. A permanent marker can be handy for dating opened jars so you'll know what went into the refrigerator when.

• Don't leave perishable items out of the refrigerator (without a cold pack) for more than two hours. Throw them away if they've been sitting out longer than that.

• Watch expiration dates on baby food. Listen for the pop of vacuum seals of jarred foods. Don't feed your baby anything that has expired and throw out jars with chipped glass or rusty lids.

• When you're traveling, transport food and filled bottles in an insulated cooler with frozen packs.

• Don't give your baby honey if she is less than a year old. It could contain bacteria associated with botulism, a potentially fatal food poisoning.

• Don't serve your baby or older child raw or unpasteurized milk, which may contain harmful bacteria. And no cow's milk before age 1.

• If you're making homemade baby food, use a brush to clean the blender or food processor blades and parts. Trapped food particles can harbor bacteria.

• To freeze homemade baby food, put the mixture in an ice-cube tray. Cover with heavy-duty plastic wrap and freeze. Later, you can pop the frozen food cubes into a freezer bag or airtight container and date it. Store vegetables up to three months, and meat, fish, and chicken up to eight weeks.

• Use dishwashing detergent, hot water, and a clean rag to wash and rinse all utensils that come in contact with the baby's food, including the can opener. Just wiping them with a paper towel isn't enough. Soap, water, and friction do the trick.

• Don't keep bottles or food in the same bag as dirty diapers unless the food is in its own separate, insulated container or sealed plastic bag.

• When your baby gets to the finger-food stage, which can start as early as 7 months, cut food into bite-size pieces. But don't offer your baby nuts, raisins, grapes, or hot dogs; they're all choking hazards and not appropriate for infants or toddlers.

more on each 2.5-ounce jar of baby food). Still, there are ways to save. Try these thrifty tips:

Supermarket comparison-shop. Check several local grocery stores to find the lowest prices on frequently purchased organic food. We found a 4-ounce jar of organic baby food in the New York area for as little as 69 cents a jar. Also, stock up on sale items. We found 4-ounce jars of store-brand organic baby food on sale for 15 percent off at a national natural foods supermarket. And keep in mind that fresh organic produce is often cheaper in season.

Hit the farmer's market. A USDA study in 2002 found that about 40 percent of these farmers don't charge a premium. Check *www.localharvest.org* for organic growers and market listings.

Join the farm team. Buy a share in a community-supported organic farm. The produce almost always is cheaper than at a farmer's market and often costs less than the same nonorganic items at a super- market. Go to *www.sare.org* for a list of community-supported farms, then contact the farms in your area and ask if they're certified organic. They should be able to produce evidence of certification or, if they sell less than $5,000 worth of produce a year, other documentation that shows they follow organic growing practices, says Barbara Haumann, a spokeswoman for the Organic Trade Association in Greenfield, Mass.

Buy in bulk. Some organic baby food lines, such as Earth's Best, sell packs of 24 2.5-ounce jars at a savings of about 4 cents per jar over single-jar purchases.

Recommendations

Let your pediatrician be your guide about what to feed your baby and when to move to the next stage. Compare the ingredients and nutritional value of commercial baby food and always check expira- tion dates listed on the label or lid. All baby food jars have a depressed area, or "button," in the center of the lid. Reject any jars with a popped-out button—an indication that the product has been opened or the seal broken.

CHAPTER

4

Backpack Carriers

A backpack carrier lets you travel in ways you never thought possible with a baby, including a rugged, back-country hike or snow shoeing. But many parents report that they also use backpack carriers for less exotic trips to the mall, the zoo, or even Disney World.

Backpack carriers are only intended for children old enough to sit up independently, usually at least 6 months old. They can typically be used for a child up to 40 pounds, plus 10 pounds of gear, depending on the model. The weight of the pack itself can add another 4 to 7 pounds to your load, so consider that when choosing a pack. A heavy carrier might make it more difficult to carry your child.

Most backpack carriers have an aluminum or aluminum alloy frame, which together with the waist or hip belt distributes a baby's weight along your back, shoulders, and hips, rather than putting it all on your shoulders and neck as do some front soft infant carriers, especially ones without a waist belt. Although the weight is on your back, "your entire upper torso is supporting it," says Anne Coffman, a physical therapist from New Berlin, Wis., and a member of the

American Physical Therapy Association as well as the mother of two. This tot-toter is a superior choice when your baby approaches 20 pounds, can comfortably sit up by herself, and has full head control. But don't expect a backpack carrier to make your load light. A 25-pound child will still feel heavy after a while, even if her weight is distributed evenly over your hips with maximum padding.

Most backpack carriers come with built-in stands that make loading and mounting easier, but aren't stable enough to be used as baby seats on the ground. Seats and shoulder harnesses are made of moisture-resistant fabric. Many models have multiple positions for the wearer and the child. Carriers usually have densely padded shoulder straps and hip belts, storage compartments, sun/rain hoods, and toy loops. Extras may include a changing pad, a rearview mirror tethered to your shoulder strap so you can watch your baby without removing your pack, and a cell phone pouch or a detachable hip bag.

Backpack carriers, though, can be cumbersome and expensive. Many are designed for the great outdoors, and may be more pack than you need if your idea of an adventure is a trek to the grocery store with your baby on board. Some, such as the Kelty K.I.D.S. Pathfinder (approximately $190), have a substantial aluminum frame that takes up a lot of storage space. Still, some backpacks are now better designed for everyday use. These carriers look more like a regular backpack, but still have a structured frame to support your child. They're less bulky than some of the more traditional backpack carriers and are more packable for short trips that are part of your daily routine.

Shopping Secrets

Bring your baby. When your baby is the right age and weight, take her shopping for a backpack carrier and if she is game, do test runs in the store. Try a backpack with a coat on you and your bundled-up child in the pack if you expect to wear it during colder months.

Practice, practice. With the help of a knowledgeable salesperson, practice putting the carrier on and taking it off. Have your spouse do likewise to make sure it fits you both comfortably. If you and your spouse will be switching the pack back and forth, try adjusting the straps to fit your torso to see if it's easy to do (or not). Walk with the backpack to be sure the frame doesn't hit the back of your head, that it's not too long for your height, that the straps fit properly so they won't slip off your shoulders, and that the frame doesn't start to dig into your lower back after a few minutes. "You should be able to walk comfortably with your arms at your sides," says Coffman. Carrier directions should be clear and easy to follow.

Look for a snug-fitting safety harness. The safest backpack carriers have a harness for the child that connects the shoulder straps with the crotch, torso, and hip restraints for a snug fit. One carrier we tested, the Chicco Smart Support, relies on a lap belt that's separate from the shoulder and crotch straps, leaving openings at the side that could potentially be big enough for a child to slip through. Such slips can sometimes occur when children pull their legs up and subsequently put both feet and legs into one opening; they've been the reason for the recall of several other brands. We consider that style harness inadequate for a small child.

Be wary of second-hand equipment. Many parents pick up a backpack carrier at tag sales. If you decide to buy used, check for recalled brands first at *www.cpsc.gov*. Inspect carriers for excessive wear, which can dangerously weaken straps and seams.

What's Available

Major brands of backpack carriers, in alphabetical order, are Baby Trend (*www.babytrend.com*), Chicco (*www.chiccousa.com*), Deuter (*www.deuter.com*), Evenflo (*www.evenflo.com*), Kelty Kids (*www.keltykids.com*), Macpac (*www.macpac.co.nz*), REI (*www.rei.com*), and Sherpani (*http://sherpani.us*). You'll find the best selection of these major brands at camping/outdoor outlets, specialty Web sites, and catalogs and mass merchandisers, such as Target (*www.target.com*), rather than in baby stores. Prices range from $50 to $320.

As of April 1, 2007, the Juvenile Products Manufacturers Association (JPMA) will begin certifying framed backpack carriers that meet American Society of Testing and Materials (ASTM) requirements, including strength, stability, and leg-opening safety. It may take six months or so to see certified framed backpack carriers on store shelves.

Features to Consider

Two important factors to consider in evaluating backpack carriers are: How much you'll use a backpack carrier and your baby's comfort and safety (not to mention yours). Many models differ by only a feature or two, which can add to the cost (or reduce it). Some features may be more important to you than others. Your best bet is to make a list of must-have features, such as those we cite below, and then try on and compare the various models.

The cockpit. Higher-end backpack carriers tend to offer a roomier ride for a baby and may include stirrups so a baby's feet don't dangle. That support may help reduce the chances your baby's feet will fall asleep as you're plodding along. Padding is key. Some parents say that their children seem happier in a plusher ride.

Fabrics. Backpack carriers are likely to be made of durable nylon

CARRIER CAUTIONS

When using a backpack carrier, follow these safety tips:

* Buckle and tighten all straps at all times so that your child isn't tempted to climb out when you're on the go. Serious injuries, including skull fractures and concussions, can occur when children fall from carriers.
* Keep your baby's fingers away from the frame joints, especially when you're folding the backpack.
* Check on your child from time to time. Children can become overheated in warm weather or be exposed to harmful rays from the sun. See that your child's legs and arms are secure in the leg and arm openings, but also that his circulation isn't impaired in any way.
* Be sure buckles, snaps, straps, and adjustments are secure before each use. Snaps can open and adjustments may be maladjusted, which pose safety hazards.
* Check the backpack periodically for ripped seams, missing or loose fasteners, and frayed seats or straps. Stop using a carrier with frayed seams, which can give way suddenly.
* Bend your knees, not at your waist, to keep your baby from falling out when you're leaning over or reaching for something low.
* Never carry the child in a pack while in a moving vehicle or on an airplane, and never use the carrier as a substitute for a certified child car seat. When you're traveling by car or plane, always secure your child in the appropriate car seat.
* Don't leave your child unattended in a backpack carrier. Your child shouldn't be in a carrier unless the pack is on your back. Don't place your baby in a backpack carrier and then perch her on a kitchen counter or couch, bed or picnic table, even for a moment. Babies can fall or suffocate much faster than you'd think.

similar to what's used in suitcases. Fabrics vary from lightweight to heavy-duty. The material should be sturdy, moisture-resistant, and easy to clean by wiping with a mild detergent. (Let the carrier air out a few days when it gets wet.) Light-reflecting piping or stripes can help drivers see you, but err on the side of caution by keeping a safe distance from traffic.

Fasteners. Carriers have a variety of buckles and fasteners for shoulder and waist straps, and babies' seat. Buckles that hold shoulder and waist straps should be easy to adjust and should hold the straps tightly so they can't work loose when the carrier is in use. Snaps and buckles should be sturdy and difficult for babies to unfasten.

Foldability. A framed backpack carrier that can easily be folded flat to fit in the trunk of your car or in a closet is a plus.

Kickstand. The kickstand should lock firmly in the open position and have hinges with spacers so fingers don't get pinched. When the carrier is on your back, the kickstand should close so it doesn't snag on things as you walk. On one model we tested, the Kelty K.I.D.S. Pathfinder, the kickstand didn't always close fully. It also didn't always automatically open fully to a stable angle. If you didn't notice this, it would pose a slight hazard when unloading a child by yourself. Otherwise, this carrier was rated comparatively high. When the carrier is on the ground with the kickstand open, it should be hard to tip over. However, as we mentioned, never use a carrier with a stand as a baby seat.

Leg openings. These should be fully adjustable to fit snugly around your baby's legs.

Padding. Look for a backpack carrier with padding that covers the metal frame near your baby's face. You'll want padding that's firm rather than mushy.

Seats and seat belts. Look for a seat that adjusts to different baby sizes, so your baby can see over your shoulder from the beginning, but not so high that your child could fall out. The cockpit should be padded for comfort and have enough depth to support your baby's back, and fully adjustable leg openings that are small enough to prevent your baby from slipping out. Check all buckles and other securing hardware and be sure seams won't tear and straps won't slip.

Shoulder, waist, and chest straps. Shoulder-strap padding should be firm and wide. Putting your baby in and strapping the carrier on should be fairly simple. Shoulder straps should have an adjustable chest buckle that keeps straps on your shoulders and prevents chafing at the neck. They should also be adjustable even while you're carrying your baby. Overall, look for as much flexibility in the straps as possible. The chest strap should be adjustable in height and length; the waist belt should be vertically adjustable. But don't be swayed by fancy-looking padding, particularly on shoulder straps, which shouldn't take a lot of stress anyway. Fit and firmness are more important than padding thickness, especially at the shoulder. In the lumbar area, well-made carriers may have a large pad in the middle of the waist strap for adults that helps distribute the baby's weight from your shoulders to your hips and pelvic area, and prevents strain on your lower back. Carrying the weight lower is definitely more comfortable. In the store, fasten the belt to see if it's long enough and neither too high nor too low when the carrier is in place.

Storage pouches. If you can't leave your house without lots of toys, an extra bottle, snacks, and a diaper stash, and want a place to store your cell phone, you'll need a carrier with ample storage, and models differ. The Snugli Cross Country by Evenflo and the Kelty K.I.D.S. Pathfinder, offer the most storage of the models we tested. Some models have only a small pouch for a cell phone or bottle. Others are loaded with pockets, pouches, and toy loops, with handy ones built into the waist belt. Zippered pouches or ones with a Velcro closure are better because things can't fall out. Plastic-lined pockets are good for damp items. Some heavy-duty carriers for serious hiking have removable pouch accessories so you can choose what to add or remove. But be mindful not to exceed the weight maximum of the carrier you choose.

Sun/weather shield. Since a baby's eyes and skin are sensitive, you'll need to protect her from the sun and bad weather. Most backpack carriers come with a sun/weather shield or offer them as an accessory. If the carrier you select doesn't come with a shield, buy one separately on the spot. (As we mentioned, "soft" carriers don't offer this feature.) Not all sun/weather shields are created equal. The better shields are "hoods" that provide full coverage. And be sure to cover any part of your baby's skin that's showing with baby-appropriate sunscreen, starting at 6 months of age, according to the American Academy of Pediatrics.

Recommendations

Before buying a backpack carrier, think about how much you'll use it. That will help you determine what to spend. Price, however, isn't necessarily a reliable indicator of quality. Our top-rated model, the Snugli Cross Country, for example, cost $70, compared to the lowest-rated model, Chicco's Smart Support, which retails for approximately $95. Consider sharing with neighbors if you expect to use a backpack carrier only occasionally. If you plan longer or more frequent outings with your baby, consider models that will have more storage features, better padding, and a more comfortable fit.

As we mentioned, don't use a backpack carrier until your child can sit up unassisted (usually at 6 months) and has full head control. And even though a child carrier can give you the freedom to venture where a stroller can't, don't use one in areas where you won't have firm footing, such as hiking on wet rocks, big boulders, icy terrain, or wet, leafy trails. Many children are injured when adults fall. Also, don't leave your child unattended while he's in the carrier, use the carrier as a seat, or put it on an elevated surface, such as a table or bench, with your child in it, even for a minute. And check on your child periodically as you're walking to make sure he's still comfortable and secure. Before you venture out, become familiar with your backpack carrier. If the directions are unclear about, for example, how to secure your child in a carrier seat, how to use a carrier seat's lap belt, or assemble an accessory, such as a rain hood, call the manufacturer. Don't wing it. Unclear directions and a lack of understanding can be dangerous since both your and and your child's safety depend on setting up a backpack carrier and adjusting the straps properly. Be sure to send in the registration card so you'll be notified in the event of a recall.

Finally, before doing a lot of walking with a carrier, be in good physical shape. It's easy to underestimate, but you'll need a strong back, hips and quadriceps to lug around a baby. Stay within the recommended weight limits. When your child outgrows the backpack carrier, stop using it.

Ratings • Backpack Carriers

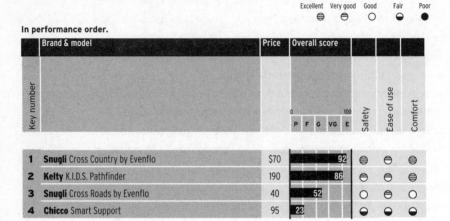

In performance order.

Excellent	Very good	Good	Fair	Poor
⊜	⊖	○	◐	●

Key number	Brand & model	Price	Overall score	Safety	Ease of use	Comfort
1	**Snugli** Cross Country by Evenflo	$70	92	⊜	⊜	⊜
2	**Kelty** K.I.D.S. Pathfinder	190	86	⊜	⊜	⊜
3	**Snugli** Cross Roads by Evenflo	40	52	○	⊖	○
4	**Chicco** Smart Support	95	23	◐	◐	◐

Guide to the Ratings

The upper child weight limit for frame-type carriers is 40 pounds. Child weight range is as stated by the manufacturer. **Overall score** is based mainly on safety and judgments for ease of use as well as comfort for parents. Parameters were evaluated using standard test methods and measurements and judgments of parent panelists. **Ease of use** is an aggregate of judgments on how well the carriers fit the adult and fit the child, as well as overall bulk and weight of the carrier. **Comfort** was assessed based on measurements and judgments of padding and positioning of straps and seating. **Price** is approximate retail.

Bathtubs

Forget about the towel-lined sink you were probably bathed in as a baby. Although that's certainly still an option, there are plenty of portable bathtubs on the market these days that make bath time a whole lot easier—and more fun for both of you. A baby bathtub provides an appropriately compact place for bathing. It can be placed in a sink, in a regular bathtub, on a counter or kitchen table, or right on the floor. However, no matter where you bathe your baby, be sure to keep a hand on her at all times to prevent her from sliding underwater. Babies and baby bathtubs—especially in regular tubs with a nonskid surface on the bottom—have a way of slipping and sliding.

Many tubs have a removable mesh or fabric inner cradle so a baby can't move around inside too much. Others have a foam-lined contoured interior that allows a baby who can't sit up yet to relax in a semi-upright position. In any case, you'll use a

WHAT NOT TO BUY: A BABY BATH SEAT

Baby bath seats, almost all of which stick to a bathtub with suction cups, have been blamed for about 120 drownings and at least 160 injuries since 1983. For that reason, in July 2000, Consumers Union (the nonprofit publisher of CONSUMER REPORTS) and other consumer organizations petitioned the Consumer Product Safety Commission (CPSC) to ban the seats. So far, the only reform is a revision of a voluntary industry safety standard, which took effect on Feb. 1, 2005. However, seats using suction cups are unlikely to adhere to the nonskid surface in new tubs and may tip with less force than the revised standard allows. The CPSC therefore advises parents who have a tub with a textured or nonskid bottom not to use a bath seat.

But, in our opinion, that's not good enough. Bath seats can tip over when suction cups fail, and babies and toddlers can become trapped underwater. And despite warning labels, the seats can induce a false sense of security, leading parents to think they can turn their back on the baby for a short time. In many of these tragic cases, parents had left the room momentarily, and in at least one case, an adult was present.

Avoid using any baby bath seat, including the latest hybrid models. The Safety 1st Deluxe 4-in-1 Bath Station ($20), for example, converts from a bathtub to a bath seat with a support bar for the baby to straddle in the tub itself. Still, our tests show that the tub could slide if it's used in seat mode in a regular bathtub with a non-slip surface. Although the User Guide warns parents to use the bath station only on smooth (not nonskid) surfaces, it's too easy to ignore. If the tub is mounted in a regular bathtub with a non-slip surface, a child could tip in the bath seat and possibly hit her head on the adult bathtub. We don't recommend using this product in the seat mode because of the possibility of injury.

The Juvenile Products Manufacturers Association (JPMA) certifies two brands of bath seats: Safety 1st and The First Years. Still, given the troubled history of baby bath seats, we continue to believe parents should avoid this product for the time being. To date, there is an existing American Society for Testing and Materials (ASTM) standard for bath seats and a draft, preliminary standard for infant bath tubs. We tested three infant bathtubs to the draft of the standard and the Safety 1st 4-in-1 Bath Station (a hybrid tub) to the bath seat standard also. See page 72.

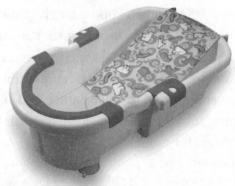

In our tests, the
Safety 1st Deluxe 4-in-1 Bath
Station was not recommended in
the bath seat mode.

baby bathtub for less time than you may think. At about 6 months, when your baby can sit up, she'll probably be too big to be bathed in an infant tub that sits in the sink. Although there are tubs on the market that are supposedly designed for babies from newborn to toddler or 0 to 25 pounds, she'll probably outgrow this style baby bathtub too, once she's about 9 months old. Then it's time to move your baby to a regular bathtub that contains only a small amount of water.

Bath Basics

Before we get into the specifics of what's on the market, here are a few bath-time tips. For starters, don't worry about giving your baby an official bath right away. Except for sponge baths, bathing doesn't start until the stump of your baby's umbilical cord falls off (between one and three weeks post-delivery). After that, you can give your baby a bath every day if you like, although two to three times a week is better because daily bathing can dry out a baby's tender skin. In addition to the tub, you'll need a soft towel (preferably hooded to cradle your baby's head), a baby washcloth, and baby body wash that doubles as shampoo.

There are a variety of baby bathtubs on the market. Keep in mind that just about any tub you buy will be awkward to use at first, mainly because bathing a wiggly baby—who may dislike temperature changes and being put in water—is awkward and daunting for even the most experienced parent. "When my son was a newborn, we were so nervous about giving him baths that we couldn't really judge if one tub was better or worse than any other," says Amy Yelin from Arlington, Mass., the mother of a now 8-month-old. In other words, at first you'll just want to get the job done—and fast. Expect your baby to protest the first time or two. After that, she will probably grow to enjoy bath time—and so will you. But remember, when your baby is in the bath, you should always have a hand on her.

MAKING THE MOST OF TUB-TIME FUN

By the time your baby is 9 to 10 months old, she'll begin to understand the notion of object permanence—that if you or an object is out of sight, you or it still exists. To reinforce that concept and add an element of surprise, try this take on peek-a-boo: "During bath time, have toys disappear under a washcloth, then magically reappear," suggests Stacy DeBroff, author of "The Mom Book: 4,278 Tips for Moms." Or cover your face with a towel, then uncover it—again and again.

BATH TUB SAFETY TIPS

In addition to *not* buying a bath seat, follow these bathtub safety tips:

• Never leave your baby unattended during bath time, even for a second, even when you're just filling the tub with water. (To play it safe, stay within arm's reach of your child when he's around water, whether he's in an adult or toddler tub. If your baby can't sit up on his own yet, always keep a hand on him at bath time, too. Plan ahead. Make sure you have everything on hand before you start the bath. You don't want to have to scurry for a washcloth or towel while your baby is in the tub.

• When bathing your baby, fill the tub with as little water as possible. Two inches is a good amount.

• Be careful about scalding water. The water should feel warm, not hot. Before you put your baby in the tub, test the temperature with your wrist, elbow, or the back of your hand. Don't rely on a tub with a temperature indicator, such as a drain plug that changes color to indicate too hot, too cold, and just right. If you're using a thermometer with a read-out, baby bath water should be between 90 and 100 degrees. But again, use your wrist, elbow, or the back of your hand as your main guide.

• If you need to leave the bathroom, take your baby with you. Don't rely on older children to watch the baby for you. If the phone rings, let the answering machine or Voice Mail pick it up. If there's a knock on the door, ignore it. Make that rule as stringent as strapping your baby into her car seat every time you drive.

• When using a baby bathtub in the sink or in a regular tub, always turn the hot water off first and watch out for hot metal spigots. Get a cover for the bathtub's spout to protect your child from its heat-conducting metal and hard edges. Some covers are soft plastic in the shape of an animal, such as a moose or an elephant. Others are inflatable plastic. Swoosh tub water around with your hand so that any hot spots even out. To play it safe, reduce the setting of your hot-water heater to 120° F. An infant's skin burns much more easily than an adult's.

• Always empty the bathtub immediately after bath time. Babies can drown in as little as one inch of water.

• When your baby graduates to a regular bathtub, attach rubber strips to the bottom of the tub to prevent slipping.

• Remind caregivers, your spouse, and the baby's grandparents about these safety tips. Better yet, if they're new to bath time, tell them not to give your baby a bath while you're away if that's possible.

What's Available

Major brands of baby bathtubs are, in alphabetical order: Evenflo *(www.evenflo.com)*, Fisher-Price *(www.fisher-price.com)*, Juvenile Solutions *(www.juvenilesolutions.com)*, Kel-Gar *(www.kelgar.com)*, Munchkin *(www.munchkin.com)*, Primo *(www.primobaby.com)*, Priva *(www.priva-inc.com)*, Safety 1st *(www.safety1st.com)*, Summer Infant *(www.summerinfant.com)*, and The First Years *(www.thefirstyears.com)*. You'll see basic tubs that are flat on the bottom, tubs with contoured interiors or inserts that help position a baby's head above water, and tubs with supportive, internal nylon mesh slings featuring padded headrests that cradle newborns. You'll also see inserts that don't include a tub; they're little more than a sling that can be used in both a baby tub and a sink to prop your baby up.

You'll also find tubs designed to fit in the sink initially, then convert to a tub that can be placed in a regular bathtub when your baby can sit up. You can even find tubs with many of these features that fold for more compact storage. Bathtubs range from $9.99 to $40.

Bath seats designed to be used in a regular tub by a baby who is able to sit up are available, but we don't recommend them. (See "What not to buy," page 66.) There are also inflatable tubs that fit inside a regular bathtub to give your baby a padded space to bathe but we don't recommend those either because they can be dangerous.

Features to Consider

Contoured design with padded lining. In lieu of a sling, a contoured design is a must for keeping a baby from sliding around too much.

A drain with an attached plug. This can make the tub easier to empty. A large drain plug allows for quicker post-bath cleanup.

Temperature indicator. Some models of bathtubs, such as the Summer Infant Newborn-to-Toddler Bath Center and The First Years Sure Comfort Deluxe Newborn-to-Toddler Tub, have temperature indicators—a temperature strip or a drain plug that change color when the water is too hot for a baby. In our tests, we found these features to be impractical. The Summer Infant temperature strip was too slow to react to temperature changes, and The First Years color-changing plug was even less specific. It's too difficult to keep track of a temperature strip or the shade of a plug when you're bathing a baby. Don't look for these high-tech extras when you're shopping.

Two tubs in one

One end of the EuroBath is designed to accommodate your newborn; the other end is for older babies.

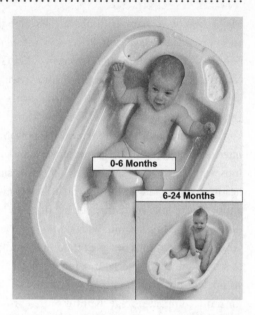

0-6 Months

6-24 Months

Instead, test water with your elbow, the inside of your wrist, or the back of your hand before putting your baby in the tub or rinsing him off.

Convertibility. Some tubs, such as the Fisher-Price Aquarium Bath Center and Primo's EuroBath, are made to last from newborn to toddler. The Aquarium Bath Center includes a hammock-like padded infant cradle that you take out when your baby can sit up unassisted. The Eurobath is molded to support a baby under both arms; a crotch post keeps babies from slipping forward in the water. With this model, babies can be bathed in a reclining position from birth to 6 months. Then, from 6 to 24 months, they sit upright facing the other direction; the older baby end of the tub has less infrastructure and more wiggle room. "I used the Primo EuroBath until I felt comfortable putting my daughter in a regular bathtub," says Robin Kelman from Lafayette Hill, Pa., the mother of a 16-month-old who was happy with the unit. A convertible tub, though, probably won't last you as long as manufacturers claim. As we mentioned, a convertible tub will probably buy you three more months or so, but not much more.

Foldability. Some tubs, like the Safety 1st Fold-Up Tub, fold in half for easy storage. To make sure a foldable tub won't leak, practice at first with a small amount of water. The downside? This style can be compact; your baby may bust out of it quickly. "My son grew out of his foldable tub really fast, which meant that I had to put him into the big tub a little before I was comfortable," says Emily Carlton from Long Beach, Calif., the mother of an 8 month old.

An internal mesh sling/cradle. It's cozy and supportive, especially for a newborn. Some models, like the Mother's Touch Large Comfort Bather by Summer Infant, come with a two-position backrest for added comfort. Some fabric slings have steel rods that support the infrastructure. We think steel rods might become uncomfortable when your baby kicks his legs or moves from side to side. Other slings are hammock-like and don't have steel rods. Look for those.

Fresh-water rinse. Some tubs, such as the Newborn-to-Toddler Bath Center and Shower by Summer Infant, feature a separate, battery-powered shower unit that lets you rinse your baby with fresh water from the sink instead of using bath water. But some parents, such as Heidi Suppelsa from Saint Louis, Mo., the mother of a baby boy, found this feature unwieldy. "I thought I'd use it all the time, but it ended up being too cumbersome when my husband or I were bathing our son solo. I needed one hand on the baby, another to wash him, then two additional hands to use the shower feature," she says. In our tests, we found that the shower head delivered water too slowly to get the job done fast and efficiently. There are also shower units that sit inside the tub, but some parents report that these units get in the way, crowding their baby's leg room. They ended up using the spray attachment from the sink or a plastic cupful of water at rinse time, which can be the best way to go anyway, in our opinion.

Easy storage. Some models have a handle or hook on the back to hang the tub up for draining or storage. That's a feature to look for if space is tight. Hang the tub upright from its hook in your shower, so water doesn't drip on the bathroom floor.

A smooth, overhanging rim. This feature makes it much easier to carry a heavy, water-filled tub (without your baby in it) from the sink to another location.

Nonskid surface. Some models have a nonskid surface on the bottom to keep the tub from sliding in a regular bathtub.

Recommendations

For a baby 6 months or younger, buy a bathtub that has a contoured design or an internal sling that cradles the baby in the water. A mildew-resistant, padded foam lining is also a plus, although to prevent mildew and soap-scum buildup, you'll still have to clean the tub and dry it after each use. If you're short on space, buy a unit that folds. You can also buy one that doesn't fold and can be stored in your shower (ideally) or a closet.

Don't buy an inflatable bath tub or a bath seat, even if your pediatrician recommends it. (One new mom we know of even tried out a bath seat at the pediatrician's office.) And be consistent and a stickler when it comes to bath time safety. Follow the safety guidelines we outline every time your baby takes a bath.

BATH SEATS AND TUBS

MODEL	PRICE	PROS	CONS
The First Years Sure Comfort Deluxe Newborn-to-Toddler Tub	$17	A hammock-like sling for newborns. Padded contoured backrest to position your infant. Built-in basin for rinse water or bath supplies.	Small size probably not good past six months old. Unreliable color-changing temperature plug.
Summer Infant Newborn-to-Toddler Bath Center and Shower	27	Larger size probably good till 9 months. Padded seat.	Battery powered showerhead has weak spray. Steel rod supported sling might be uncomfortable for newborns. Temperature strip is slow to react.
Safety 1st 4-in-1 Bath Station	20	Larger size probably good till 9 months.	Not recommended in seat mode. Backrest has no contours or padding. Steel rod supported sling might be uncomfortable for newborns. Has difficult-to-clean areas.

6

Bicycle-mounted Child Seats & Trailers

A - B - C

Hauling the laundry basket up and down stairs and chasing around a toddler-wannabe certainly qualify as exercise. Still, if you get the feeling it's not enough, a bicycle-mounted child seat or a bicycle trailer can help you cover some ground in the name of fitness and fresh air without having to hire a babysitter.

Bicycle-mounted seats are mounted behind or in front of a cyclist's seat and can transport one child age 1 to 5 or so. In both seats, the child faces forward. They're potentially less safe than trailers, which have two bicycle-type wheels and a long hitching arm that fastens to a bicycle from behind and rides low to the ground. In an accident, a child would fall about three feet from a mounted bike seat, compared with a fall of about a half a foot from a trailer. With the added weight of a little passenger at the back or front, a bicycle with a mounted seat might be harder to handle, which can be unnerving or just annoying, depending on your cycling experience. Getting on and off a bike with a baby in a mounted seat can also be difficult.

Trailers attach to the rear axle or frame of a bike, and can carry children from

CERTIFICATION

There is no certification program by an independent organization for these products, although the American Society for Testing and Materials (ASTM) has developed a voluntary standard for rear-mounted bicycle child carriers and bicycle trailers designed for people. A manufacturer may test to the requirements of that standard and certify that the product meets it. Our advice is to buy a trailer or a rear-mounted seat that meets all ASTM standards.

age 1 through 6 or so. They provide some protection to passengers since children are seated, strapped in, and usually enclosed in a zippered compartment. Trailers have a rigid frame enclosed in durable fabric, which offers some protection for young passengers if the unit rolls over. But children still must wear a bike helmet. (For our helmet ratings, see page 79.) As we mentioned, because a trailer is closer to the ground, it's potentially safer than a bicycle-mounted seat in a fall. Some designs have a hitching arm that allows the bike to fall without affecting the trailer.

Still, trailers pose safety problems because their low profile makes them difficult for motorists to see, especially in limited light. They should have a 3½- to 7-foot-tall, high-visibility orange flag. Trailers are also wider than the bike, so they take up more of the roadway. If you're riding on the shoulder, the trailer can stick out into the road if you're not careful. And trailers can tip over if you turn abruptly or turn when one wheel is going over a bump. As you speed up, braking becomes harder, especially on wet surfaces. Trailers can become snagged on bushes or other objects.

Shopping Secrets

Take a trailer or a bicycle-mounted seat for a test ride. Put some weight in it if you test it at the store. Don't test-drive it with your child in it. Save that for home, after you've selected a seat, installed it according to the manufacturer's directions, and feel comfortable with it. Bring your child along when you shop, though, to see if the seat is a good fit. If you can't test-drive at the store, borrow a friend's bicycle trailer or mounted bicycle seat and take it for a spin with weight in it, such as a sack of potatoes (not your child).

Buy for *your* bike. In our tests, some bicycle trailers couldn't be mounted on bicycles with disc brakes, and some bicycle-mounted seats couldn't be used on bicycles with oversize tubes. The Wee Ride 98055, for example, a seat that mounts in the center front of an adult bike, could be mounted only on bikes with a small head tube, the metal tube between the bicycle frame and the front forks. So keep compatibility in mind when you're shopping.

Avoid buying a trailer or bicycle-mounted seat that you're not able to examine carefully, such as one sold exclusively over the Internet. Keep your receipt and the trailer or mounted seat's packaging in case you discover a fitting problem when you get home.

What's Available

The major brands of mounted bicycle seats are, in alphabetical order: Bell (available at retailers and e-tailers such as *www.rei.com* and *www.target*
.com), Fisher-Price (*www.fisher-price.com*), Kettler (*www.kettlerusa.com*), Topeak (*www.topeak.com*), and Wee Ride (*www.weeride.com*). Prices range from $23 to $160. Some mount behind the bike's seat, while others mount in front, accommodating one child from 40 to 50 pounds (it varies by manufacturer).

The major brand of bicycle trailers are, in alphabetical order: Burley (*www.burley.com*), Chariot (*www.chariotcarriers.com*), InStep (*www.instep.net*), and Schwinn (*www.schwinnbike.com*). Prices range from $90 to $785 for one- and two-passenger models, and the trailers can hold up to 100 pounds.

Features to Consider

Assembly. If you plan to buy a bike trailer or a bicycle-mounted seat and put it together or install it yourself, you'll need clear instructions because assembly and installation can be a challenge. If you need help, call the company or consult your local bike shop.

Convertibility. Some manufacturers offer conversion kits that allow you to turn a trailer into a jogging stroller or a cargo carrier. That's an attractive, expense-saving, two-for-one option.

Cross bars. Some bicycle-mounted seats have a cross bar that goes across the lap in addition to a five-point harness, which is an added safety feature in case of a fall—and gives children something to hold onto, which may make them feel more secure.

Protection from the elements. Many trailers come with a plastic shields, which protects against sun, wind, and rain. A zippered front shield will keep water or mud from splattering your child. But if the shield encloses the entire cabin, make certain there's ventilation, such as breathable mesh windows. Your kids may appreciate tinted windows, which aren't available on all models. They protect your child from sun glare, and keep the "cockpit" cool.

Folding mechanism. Some trailers feature quick-release wheels and fold easily for storage (even in a hall closet), which can be an advantage if you don't have a garage.

Frame. Trailer frames generally are made of steel, but in more expensive models they may be aluminum alloy, which is lighter. The frame should be sturdy. Better models offer a roll cage—a perimeter frame—to better protect passengers in the event of a rollover. Keep in mind that these roll cages are not strong enough to protect against a collision with a vehicle.

Harness. With either a bicycle-mounted seat or a trailer, a padded, adjustable five-point harness is ideal: two straps over the shoulders, two for the waist, and a crotch strap, much like the restraints on a child's car seat.

Hitching arm. A trailer's hitching arm should have a backup to prevent the trailer from breaking loose. Check the wheel mounting to be sure that it will hold. Look for a universal hitch, which can be used with almost any bicycle. Some hitching arms are designed to help keep the trailer upright even if your bike goes down.

Reflectors. Some trailers and bicycle-mounted seats have side and/or rear reflective strips or reflectors, which are good even if you're not planning to ride at twilight—and we don't recommend riding at twilight or at night.

The Burley Solo features accessories that let you walk it, jog it, or tow it behind your bike.

Safety flag. If you're buying a trailer, a safety flag—a high-visibility pennant on a whip tall enough (3½ to 7 feet) to make it visible to drivers—is a must.

Seating. The interior of a trailer should offer comfortable seating with adequate legroom and good back support. The seat's protective cavity should be free of protrusions. Roominess is a plus, as are storage pockets for toys and such. At the higher end of the price range, you'll find seats that recline, cushier padding, and, on two-passenger trailers, a seat divider. On bicycle-mounted seats, look for a padded seat cushion for a smoother ride. Seats with a reclining backrest and an adjustable foot and headrest are common at the top of the price range.

Seat location. If you're shopping for a bicycle-mounted seat, consider whether you want a seat that mounts in the back or the front. In our tests, with an 18-month-old and a 30-month old, the kids seemed to prefer riding up front, and we found the tested front-mounted seat did not affect the bike's handling as much. However, our parent testers had to bow their knees out slightly to avoid rubbing against the seat or the occupant, which isn't necessarily a safety issue, but it can be uncomfortable. A front rider can grab the handlebars while using this seat, which could cause an accident.

Side protection. Some bicycle-mounted seats offer side protectors, which help shield a child in the event of a fall.

Wheels. Trailer wheels usually are made with steel rims, which can rust, or aluminum ones, which don't. The wheels should also have one or more reflectors. Look for high-quality rubber tires. Also, consider wheel size. In our tests, larger wheels rolled over bumps better, but smaller wheels made maneuvering easier.

Recommendations

Don't buy a bicycle trailer or a bicycle-mounted seat until your baby is at least 1 year old. We don't recommend bicycle trailers and bicycle-mounted seats for children younger than that because they may not be physically equipped to withstand the forces they'll be exposed to when riding in a bicycle seat or trailer. And when they're younger than age 1, they can't support their head properly with a helmet on, which all riders should wear.

Choose based on your needs, riding ability, and where you are riding. Trailers are "off-road vehicles"; use them only in parks and on safe, smooth trails where there's no risk of encounters with cars. Follow the manufacturer's recommendations regarding the maximum weight, which is usually up to 100 pounds.

The better bicycle trailers have sturdy construction, tinted windows, a comfortable interior, and a wide wheel base. But before you buy, ask yourself if you will use the trailer enough to justify the price. If you think you'll use it only occasionally, buy the most durable trailer you can find at the low-end price. Also, consider how much weight you'll tow. If the weight of the bicycle trailer plus the passenger or passengers exceeds 50 pounds, you may start to feel like a beast of burden.

Pedaling uphill can be especially difficult. At that point, maybe it's time for riders to get their own bikes.

Take your cycling ability into consideration. If you opt for a bicycle-mounted seat, you might find a rear-mounted seat with a child in tow unnerving and exhausting to operate. If you're a novice or not in top shape, you'd probably be better off with a front-mounted seat. If you go with a bicycle trailer, ride with only one child at a time if you're an infrequent rider. Finally, have your child wear a lightweight, well-fitting bike helmet, and never leave a child in the seat with the bike on the kick stand, which isn't made to support the weight.

Ratings • Bike Helmets

A helmet that fits properly helps protect your child from injury. A well-designed and properly fitted bike helmet can prevent up to 88 percent of bicycle-related brain injuries, according to an industry estimate, so of course you'll want to make sure everyone–yourself as well as your child–is protected with a properly fitted helmet whenever you ride.

Before you buy a helmet, try it on your child in the store–preferably a bike shop or a store where the sales-

A bike helmet should sit level on your head (left), not tilted back like a hat.

person can help you choose the right size and adjust the helmet to your child's head (or your head, if you're also shopping for one for yourself). A helmet should fit snugly and sit level on your child's head, not tilt back like a hat. Not all helmets match all heads, and your child will resist an uncomfortable helmet, or one he doesn't like, so pick a color or design he approves of.

After an accident, replace any helmet that has done its job by absorbing impact. Some manufacturers will knock something off the price of a replacement.

To be sure the helmet you choose for your child is safe, look for a label inside the helmet that states that the helmet meets the Consumer Product Safety Commission's mandatory safety standard.

All of these bike helmets passed our impact and strap-retention tests. If possible, try the helmet on at the store for fit and comfort. Otherwise, make sure that you can return it.

	Excellent	Very good	Good	Fair	Poor
	⊖	⊖	○	◒	●

Within types, in performance order.

Key number	Brand & model	Price	Overall score	Impact absorption	Retentions system	Ventilation	Ease of use
	Similar models in small type comparable to tested models.		0 ——— 100 P F G VG E				
	ADULT						
1	**Bell** Citi **CR Best Buy**	$45	79	⊖	⊖	⊖	⊖
2	**Bell** Slant **CR Best Buy**	50	79	⊖	⊖	⊖	⊖
3	**Specialized** Aurora	100	77	⊖	⊖	⊖	⊖
4	**Bell** X-Ray	100	68	○	⊖	⊖	⊖
5	**Giro** Atmos	190	68	○	⊖	⊖	⊖
6	**Giro** Havoc	60	68	○	⊖	⊖	⊖
7	**Specialized** Air-8	60	67	○	⊖	⊖	⊖
8	**Trek** Interval 2 Sport	60	66	○	⊖	⊖	⊖

			Excellent	Very good	Good	Fair	Poor
			⊖	⊖	○	⊖	●

Within types, in performance order.

Key number	Brand & model **Similar models** in small type comparable to tested models.	Price	Overall score 0 — 100 P F G VG E	Impact absorption	Retentions system	Ventilation	Ease of use
	ADULT						
9	**Trek** Vapor 3 Sport	50	66	○	⊖	⊖	⊖
10	**Serfas** Cosmos Plus	35	65	○	⊖	⊖	⊖
11	**Louis** Garneau Equinox	35	64	○	⊖	⊖	⊖
12	**Bell** Metropolis	70	63	○	⊖	⊖	⊖
13	**Louis** Garneau Chrono	90	48	○	⊖	⊖	⊖
	NOT ACCEPTABLE						
14	**Trek** Anthem C Elite Anthem C Elite WSD	125					
	TODDLER						
15	**Bell** Boomerang	30	63	⊖	⊖	⊖	⊖
16	**Giro** Me2	30	51	○	⊖	⊖	⊖
17	**Louis** Garneau Babyboomer X	30	46	○	⊖	⊖	⊖

Guide to the Ratings

Overall score is based primarily on impact absorption, retention-system strength, ventilation, and ease of use. **Impact absorption** refers to how well the helmet absorbed the forces of an impact; it's based on tests at various impact speeds and on various impact surfaces. **Retention system** refers to how well the helmet's straps, buckles, and other hardware met our strength criteria. **Ventilation** is our evaluation of vent design and how well air flows through the helmet to provide cooling while riding. **Ease of use** is our judgment of how easy the various buckles and adjustments were to use. **Price** is approximate retail.

CHAPTER

7

Bouncer Seats

B abies like to be where the action is. A bouncer seat—also called a "bouncy" seat—gives an infant a place to hang out near you and the rest of the family during his first six months or so, or until he reaches the weight or age limit. It's typically 18 to 30 pounds or 6 months old, depending on the model.

For babies who need a little help falling asleep, a bouncer seat that vibrates can be invaluable because it imitates a lulling car ride. (Keep in mind, however, that the safest place for a baby to sleep is on his back in a crib on a firm mattress.) A bouncer seat generally consists of a lightweight frame made from metal wire, tubular metal, or heavy-gauge plastic, though the Svan Bouncer by Svan/Scandinavian Child ($120) has a frame made from bent birchwood. Covered with a soft, removable, washable pad that conforms to a baby's shape, bouncer seats are somewhat springy and bounce or rock when your baby moves to keep him relaxed and amused. The fabric seat is rounded to support a baby's still-fragile spine, and a semi-upright tilt gives him a view of the surroundings. Many parents report that their babies love to nap in a bouncer seat. The sitting angle also appears to be more comfortable for some babies than lying in a flat crib after they've had a big meal.

Most models have a detachable, bent-wire play bar (sometimes covered with padding) or an overhead mobile of plastic toys for your baby to kick, bat, and chew. Some models have a set of colorful lights and sound effects that respond to a baby's movements and/or vibrate at two or three speeds to lull the baby to sleep. Some simulate nature sounds or a heartbeat or play computer-chip-generated classical music. Others transform your child's smallest movements or your fancy footwork (they have a foot-bounce you step on to activate bouncing) into a soothing rocking motion, sans batteries. The latest versions on the market, such as the Graco Travel Lite Folding Bouncer ($39.99), fold compactly for travel.

The Svan Bouncer by Svan/ Scandinavian Child provides a stylish alternative to traditional bouncy seats.

Shopping Secrets

Buy either a bouncer seat or a swing. Don't buy both, especially if space or budget is a consideration. Many parents report that it's overkill since both provide a secure and soothing place for your baby to relax and stay occupied while you get some hands-free time to catch up on things around the house. If your baby doesn't like the motion of a swing (some don't), go with a bouncer. If your baby seems to need more motion than a bouncer provides, opt for a swing. If space is an issue or you'll be traveling often, a travel swing or a bouncer is a good options since they both take up much less floor space than a traditional infant swing.

Do test rides. If you can, try your baby out in a friend or relative's swing and bouncer or test store models, if possible, to gauge what your baby prefers.

Keep this product's short life span in mind. Even though some manufacturers say their products can be used up to age 3, your baby will probably use a bouncer for only five or six months—tops. Once he can sit up unassisted, he'll likely move on to more interesting things, like playing and rolling. With that in mind, an inexpensive, lightweight model (provided it's stable), such as the Cover 'n Play Bouncer by Fisher-Price ($20), may serve you as well as a top-end design like the Maclaren Activity Baby Rocker ($80). In general, more money will get you a seat that's made to last (from durable wood, such as the Svan Bouncer) and one that may be decked out with toys, reclining and vibrating features, realistic (not tinny) music, plush fabric, and the ability to rock as well as bounce. Still, more isn't always better. Parents report product satisfaction at both ends of the price spectrum.

What's Available

The major brands of bouncer seats, in alphabetical order, are: Baby Björn (*www.babybjorn.com*), Combi International (*www.combi-intl .com*), Delta Enterprise (*www.deltaenterprise.com*), Fisher-Price *(www .fisher-price.com)*, Graco (*www.gracobaby.com*), Kolcraft (*www.kol craft.com*), Maclaren *(www.maclarenbaby.com)*, Safety 1st *(www.safety first.com)*, Svan *(www.svanusa.com)*, and Summer Infant (*www .summerinfant.com*). Prices range from $20 to $120. Many require AA, D and/or C batteries (not included).

Features to Consider

Cushiness. Seat padding can vary from basic to extra-thick. Because wet diapers are bound to come in contact with the fabric covering, upholstery should be removable and machine washable (check the label). There also shouldn't be any loose threads or gaps in the seams.

Frame. When you're in the store, give the various display models a "bounce." Bring your own batteries, in case the display models don't have them. A bouncer seat should have a wide, stable base and be springy. If it seems stiff, it probably won't bounce with your baby in it.

Foldability. Some models fold nearly flat, which is handy if you'll be traveling with your bouncer seat.

Canopy. Some models have a canopy to block light. The canopy can be a sunshade if your baby spends time in it outside, but be sure to position the bouncer in the shade so the baby won't become overheated or get sunburned.

Music and vibration. Some bouncers can play up to 10 songs, with additional sound effects, to stimulate your baby's sense of hearing. These models usually provide a vibration feature along with music since both features are often packaged in the same mechanism. Vibration simulates the motion of a soothing car ride.

Rockability. Some bouncers are designed to rock as well as bounce, but most infants aren't strong enough to self-generate a rocking motion—so if a bouncer just rocks, there won't be much movement until your baby is several months old. Some rocker-bouncers, like one we tested, the Baby Einstein Discovering Water Rocker Seat, come with a kickstand, so you have the option of keeping the bouncer from rocking. In this mode, however, we found that the Water Rocker Seat didn't bounce much at all. Moreover, when this seat was in the bouncer position (the kickstand wasn't engaged), it failed to meet two test requirements of the American Society for Testing and Materials (ASTM) safety standards for bouncer seats. The seat was difficult to assemble, which is another reason for its low score. For the results of our bouncer seat tests, see the Ratings on page 86.

Seat belts. Most models have a soft fabric three-point crotch strap as a restraint; others have a five-point harness, which is ideal for newborns because they tend to list to the side or slide to the end of the seat. Check all fasteners on models with three-point or five-point harnesses to see that they're strong, secure, and easy for you to work, and that

BOUNCER-SEAT SAFETY

Nearly 2,000 infants are injured each year in bouncy seats. Here's how to protect your newborn:

• Stick to the weight limit. Manufacturers suggest an upper weight limit, usually from 18 to 30 pounds. A child who is over the weight limit can make the seat tip.

• Never use a bouncer seat as a car seat.

• Stop using a bouncer seat as soon as your baby can sit up unassisted if the bouncer is not designed for toddlers (some are); check the manufacturer's recommendations.

• Put the seat on the floor. Never use it on an elevated surface, such as a table, where the baby's movement could rock it to the edge, or on a soft surface, such as a bed, sofa, pillow, or cushion. The seat may tip and soft surfaces are a suffocation hazard.

• Don't carry your baby while he's in the bouncer, even if it has a carrying handle, and never use the toy bar as a handle.

• Always keep a close eye on your baby, even if you think he's completely safe and secure in the bouncer seat.

• Make sure the bouncer you select doesn't have any sharp edges.

• Always secure your baby with the bouncer's 3- or 5-point safety harness.

• Don't use a bouncy seat that's damaged or broken.

• Don't park your baby in a bouncer. The American Academy of Pediatrics says babies who spend excessive time in bouncers (or car seats) may be prone to positional plagiocephaly, also called flattened head syndrome, a persistent flat spot in the back or on one side of the head. The AAP doesn't say how much is too much, so use your best judgment. No more than 30 minutes at a shot seems reasonable to us. Don't substitute a bouncy seat for cuddle time.

CERTIFICATION

Of all the brands of bouncy seats on the market, seven have been certified by The Juvenile Products Manufacturers Association (JPMA) as meeting the safety standards set by the American Society for Testing and Materials. These include Delta Enterprise, Dorel Juvenile Group (Safety 1st), Fisher-Price, Graco, Kolcraft, Svan/Scandinavian Child (Svan chair), and Summer Infant. The industry's voluntary standard covers structural integrity as well as stability, restraint system, slip resistance, and safety instructions, which should be on some form of permanent label or stamped directly on the product. As is the case with all products for children, bouncers are also covered by the federal safety standards for small parts, lead paint, and hazardous sharp points and edges.

Some models of infant bouncer seats have been recalled in recent years. Problems have included seats with an unstable base, kickstands that may not hold the seat stationary, toys or parts that may break off from the toy bar, and toy bars that suddenly come loose, causing cuts and bruises.

they won't poke your baby. They should be stiff enough to be safe without being so rigid that they pinch or are difficult for you to operate.

Head support. Seats with an adjustable, removable cushioned head support are ideal for newborns.

Seat fabric. Fabric patterns range from kid-friendly to sophisticated solid color combos, such as chocolate and orange, black and watermelon. But foremost, a seat cover should be removable and machine washable.

Seat positioning. Some bouncer seats recline more than others. At least two seatback positions—upright and recline—are a definite plus. The recline feature is necessary for infants, since they don't have the head control that sitting, even on a slight incline, requires.

Toy bar. Besides watching you and your family from the sidelines, your baby may enjoy the sensory stimulation of toys, sounds, and lights that many bouncer seats come with. A toy bar isn't necessary in the early months, since your baby may not want to play with the toys all the time or even know what to do with them. Toy bars come into play around 4 months of age, though music and vibration features will likely be appreciated well before then. Toys usually are suspended from a removable play bar, although some models, such as the Sensory Selections Bouncer by Fisher-Price ($50), feature a swing-away motorized mobile, which suspends toys in front of a baby in mobile fashion. Look for spinning, squeaking toys and teethers in bright or contrasting colors. Some models have toys that are pastel, which won't make as dramatic an impact on your baby as brighter colors will. If your baby can't reach the toy bar, position it so he can kick at it. Most bouncers allow you to take the play bar off and use just the seat for snoozing and quiet time. Not all models have toy bars, though many parents believe they're a must-have, especially starting at around the 4-month mark. Don't use the toy bar as a carrying handle.

Recommendations

Make safety your primary concern. You'll want a bouncer seat with a base or rear support that's wider than the seat itself for steadiness. Test the stability of models in the store. When you press down on a bouncer from different positions, it shouldn't tip sideways. When you rock it front to back, it should stay in place. The bottom of the base should have rubber pads or other nonskid surfaces that really work.

If you're buying a seat with toys attached to a toy bar, squeeze and tug them to make sure they won't break off. The bar should stay in place when you bat at it.

Ratings • Bouncer Seats

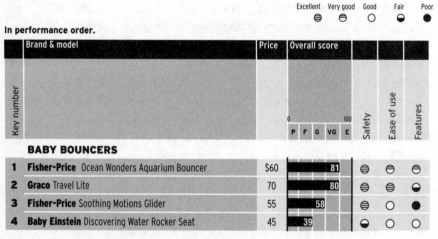

	Excellent	Very good	Good	Fair	Poor
	⊖	⊖	○	⊕	●

In performance order.

Key number	Brand & model	Price	Overall score		Safety	Ease of use	Features
			0	100			
			P F G VG E				
	BABY BOUNCERS						
1	**Fisher-Price** Ocean Wonders Aquarium Bouncer	$60	81		⊖	⊖	⊖
2	**Graco** Travel Lite	70	80		⊖	⊖	⊖
3	**Fisher-Price** Soothing Motions Glider	55	58		⊖	○	●
4	**Baby Einstein** Discovering Water Rocker Seat	45	39		⊕	○	○

Guide to the Ratings

Overall score takes into account safety, ease of use and features. **Safety** is based on ASTM tests. **Ease of use** assesses ease of assembly and portability. **Features** include music, sound, and lights, foldability, whether it has a canopy, etc. **Price** is approximate retail.

CHAPTER

8

Breast Pumps

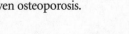

A s you probably know, these days, "breast is best." The American Academy of Pediatrics, as well as a number of leading professional organizations, including the Academy of Breastfeeding Medicine and the World Health Organization, recommend breast-feeding for the first six months of a baby's life, unless there's a medical reason not to do so, without supplementing with water, formula, or juice.

If you want to continue breast-feeding nonexclusively after that, these groups say all the better. That's because breast milk—custom-made nourishment specially formulated by Mother Nature—offers so many benefits: It boosts your baby's immune system, promotes brain development, and may reduce your child's risk of Sudden Infant Death Syndrome (SIDS) as well as diabetes, some types of cancer, obesity, high cholesterol, and asthma later in life. Breastfeeding helps moms return to their pre-baby weight faster, and may decrease the risk of breast and ovarian cancer, and even osteoporosis.

Breast-feeding is convenient—there are no bottles to prepare and warm—and it's free! There's no formula to buy, which can run you up to an average of $124 per month, depending on the type of formula you buy. But unless you plan to take your baby with you wherever you go and the process always goes smoothly, you'll probably need a breast pump. In fact, a pump can be indispensable for nursing mothers in a number of scenarios: You want to continue breast-feeding but return to work; you need to formula-feed your baby temporarily for medical reasons but want to resume breast-feeding when you get the go-ahead from your doctor; or you need to miss a feeding occasionally because you're traveling or otherwise away from your baby.

A breast pump may come in handy during those first few days after you've delivered, when the breasts can become so full that a baby may have trouble latching on. Things can be sailing along in the hospital, but when you get home, supply can outpace demand. The solution is to express some milk with a breast pump—and to have one on hand before your baby is born, so you're ready to go as soon as you return home after delivery. A breast pump also allows you to store milk (in bottles or storage bags) for later, then bottle-feed it to your baby or mix it with a little in cereal when she reaches the "solid" food stage at around 6 months.

You can refrigerate breast milk safely for 24 hours, or freeze it for three to six months. A housekeeping note: Date it when you freeze it and store it in the back of the freezer, not on the door. That's a warm spot that can prompt thawing every time the door is opened. When the time comes to use it, thaw breast milk in warm water. Don't boil or microwave it; both of those heating methods can destroy valuable immunological components that make breast milk the liquid gold it is. Microwaving can create uneven "hot spots" that can scald a baby's mouth and throat.

There are several types of breast pumps available—from large, hospital-grade pumps and midweight personal-use automatic pumps to small, lightweight, and easily portable manual models that work one breast at a time. You'll want a pump that's appropriate to your particular situation. Pumping can be time consuming and just one more thing to do, but it shouldn't be painful or frustrating. Choosing the right pump can make the difference between meeting your breast-feeding goals and having to stop short.

A baby's natural sucking rhythm is 40 to 60 cycles per minute (one pull per second or a little less). Hospital-grade and personal-use automatic pumps typically operate at 30 to 50 cycles per minute. Other pumps are usually less efficient. As a general rule, the more suction and releases per minute a pump provides, the better it will be at stimulating your milk supply. Efficiency is especially important if you plan to save a large quantity of milk. If you're returning to work, for example, you'll need to have much more breast milk on hand than if you stay home with your babies or are supplementing breast milk with formula.

Once you find the right pump, using it will take a little practice. You'll need to learn how to position it correctly and adjust the suctioning to get the best results. Don't worry—with the right pump, you'll soon get the hang of it. Pumps require some assembling and disassembling for cleaning. Wash any parts of the pump that touch your breasts or the milk containers in the dishwasher, or with hot, soapy water. Drain them dry before each use.

Shopping Secrets

Consider renting. To save money (midweight, personal-use automatic pumps can retail for as much as $350), think about renting a pump. "I rented one from a medical supplies store near my home," says Elisabeth Elman Feldman, the mother of one from Old Bridge, N.J., who breast-fed for three months for a total cost of $150. If you plan to breast-feed longer than three or four months, however, buying is the way to go. But check with your rental vendor. Many offer a price break the longer you rent. For information on pump rentals in your area and referrals to lactation consultants who can advise you on the type of pump you need and where to rent it, contact the International Lactation Consultant Association (*www.ilca.org*) or La Leche League (*www.lalecheleague.org*). The hospital where you delivered your baby may have a lactation consultant on staff.

Shop around. You can find deals on new breast pumps online, and at hospital birthing centers. You also can consult a La Leche League leader in your area (check the group's Web site for a leader near you). A little research reveals that there are deals to be had in the online breast pump marketplace once you know what kind of pump you want. (Not sure where to start? Simply type in "breast pump" on a search engine like Google.)

Browse at the hospital. Many hospitals and birthing centers are now in the breast-pump business, offering competitive prices on a variety of pumps, plus advice that can help ensure success. You can

WHAT NOT TO BUY: A USED PERSONAL-USE BREAST PUMP

Tempted to borrow your best friend's breast pump, or pick up a preowned one online or at a yard sale? Think again. Buying a used electric personal-use pump or borrowing a friend's can put your baby's health at risk because breast milk can carry bacteria and viruses. These potential contaminants can travel through the tubing and lodge in the pump's internal mechanism—the part that connects to the tubing—which can't be removed, replaced, or fully sterilized. With each suction and release, these contaminants can be microscopically blown into the milk you're expressing and possibly infect your baby, says Nancy S. Mohrbacher, a lactation consultant with Hollister Incorporated in Arlington Heights, Ill., the maker of Hollister and Ameda breast pumps. That's why manufacturers encourage nursing moms to think of a breast pump as a toothbrush or lipstick—like any personal use item you wouldn't share with a friend.

However, hospital-grade rental pumps, such as Hollister's Elite, SMB, and Lact-e Electric Breast Pumps and Medela's Symphony, Classic, and Lactina, are designed for many users and are built to last for years. They may prevent cross- and self-contamination with a special collection filter that prohibits milk from entering the internal diaphragm. Or they're designed so that the milk comes in contact only with the bottles and tubing that attach to the pump, so there's no cross-contamination.

The Purely Yours Breast Pump by Ameda is the only personal-use pump on the market to date that features a patented silicone diaphragm that provides a barrier so there's no air exchange between the pump tubing and the breast flange—so you never have to clean the tubing. The diaphragm protects expressed milk from contamination that may exist in the pump and protects the pump from any contamination in the milk. It also prevents self-contamination, which can occur when moisture and/or milk particles enter the pump tubing and organisms, such as bacteria and mold, grow there and get blown back into the milk. (The risk of self-contamination is why most other brands of pumps will instruct you to examine the tubing after every pumping and to clean or replace tubing if you see milk or moisture there.) Still, even with its unique milk collection system, the Ameda Purely Yours Pump isn't marketed as a multi-user pump because it's much lighter and more portable than Ameda's rental pumps. These have the same internal diaphragm as its personal-use pumps, but with a heavier-duty, "industrial-strength" motor, says Mohrbacher.

also get a recommendation from your hospital's lactation consultant as to the right type of pump for you.

What's Available

Now that breast-feeding has made a comeback (some hospitals organize human breast-milk banks for babies who, for some reason, can't physically breast-feed), the options in breast pumps are dizzying. The major brands, in alphabetical order, are: Ameda (*www.amedababy.com*), Avent (*www.aventamerica.com*), Dr. Brown's (*www.handi-craft.com*), Evenflo (*www.evenflo.com*), Medela (*www.medela.com*), Playtex (*www.playtexbaby.com*), The First Years (*www.thefirstyears.com*), Whisper Wear (*www.whisperwear.com*), and Whittlestone (*www.whittlestone.com*).

Breast pumps come in these basic types: large, hospital-grade, dual-action models, which typically aren't available for sale (you rent them from the hospital where you deliver or from a lactation or rental center); midweight, personal-use, automatic models that are comparable to hospital-grade pumps and can travel with you; small electric or battery-operated units that double- or single-pump; one-handed manual pumps; and "hands-free" pumps that you wear in your bra that pump while you work or do errands.

Here's the lowdown on each:

Hospital-grade breast pumps

These electric powerhouses are about the size of a car battery and can weigh 5 to 11 pounds. Manufactured for users in hospitals and for those who choose to rent, they have sensitive controls that allow you to regulate suction rhythm, intensity, and pressure. Some have a pumping action that's almost identical to a baby's natural sucking, which can help build and maintain your milk supply. A hospital-grade pump can cut pumping sessions in half—to just 15 minutes with a dual pump, which empties both breasts at once. These are expensive to buy, but you can rent them from hospitals, medical-supply stores, lactation consultants, drugstores, and specialty retail stores.

Pros: They're fast and efficient. Many are also light, comparable to a midweight, personal-use automatic pump.

Cons: Even though some come with a rechargeable battery and an adapter for use in a vehicle, many don't come with a discreet carrying case. You wouldn't want to lug one to and from work every day because they can be awkward and heavy.

Price: Expect to pay around $45 a month to rent one. You may also need to purchase your own breast shields, containers, and tubing, which can run an additional $35 or so.

Choose this option if: Nursing is difficult because your baby has trouble latching on; you're not sure how much you'll need a breast pump, but you want one on hand just in case; you plan to pump for three months or less; you must dramatically increase your milk supply and need the power of a hospital-grade pump.

Top brands/models to consider: the Elite Electric breast pump by Ameda (*www.amedababy.com*); Medela's rental line: Symphony, Lactina, or Classic breast pumps (*www.medela.com*); Whittlestone Breast Expresser (the rental version, *www.whittlestone.com*).

Midweight, personal-use, automatic breast pumps

Usually no bigger than a briefcase and weighing around 8 pounds or less, these electric breast pumps typically are lighter and slightly less efficient than the hospital-grade models. Like a hospital-grade pump, a personal-use automatic can slash pumping time because it has a powerful motor and serious suction. Many personal-use automatic pumps have suction that mimics a baby's natural sucking, which typically begins with rapid, high-frequency suction and changes to a slower, suck/swallow pattern. They're designed to mimic a baby and thereby foster faster milk flow, although some use a constant vacuum, with self-adjusting suction settings. Intermittent action better imitates a baby than a constant vacuum—and it's probably easier on you, too.

The Medela Advanced Pump in Style Metro Bag features "2-Phase Expression" technology, which has two pumping patterns–a rapid cycle followed by a second, slower mode. It's portable, and it's stylish.

Many models come housed in a black microfiber tote bag or backpack, which is ideal if you're working outside your home. They're often equipped with an adapter for your car's cigarette lighter or a battery pack for times when you're not near an electrical outlet. Most come with all necessary attachments, including removable cooler carrier and cooling element, battery pack, AC adapter, and collection containers, lids, and stands.

Pros: This is a quick and portable way to double-pump and fill up a bottle in minutes.

Cons: It's probably more than you need if you plan to pump only occasionally.

Price: $195 to $350 to buy.

Choose this option if: You'll be returning to work full- or part-time and you need to pump throughout the day to maintain your milk supply and express milk for missed feedings.

Top brands/models to consider: Ameda Purely Yours Electric breast pump *(www.amedababy.com)*; Avent Isis IQ Duo or Uno *(www.aventamerica.com)*; Evenflo's Elan Feeding System *(www.even flo.com)*; Medela Pump in Style Advanced or Original, *(www .medela.com)*; Playtex Embrace Electric Double Breast Pump *(www.playtexbaby.com)*, Whittlestone Breast Expresser (the personal-use version, *www.whittlestone.com*).

Small electric or battery-operated units

Using widely available AA or C batteries or household current, these lightweight, compact devices can fit discreetly in your purse or briefcase. They're relatively quiet, but the suction can be sluggish, although the vacuum on some models can be regulated for maximum comfort. Others, though, have a constant vacuum that can cause nipple discomfort.

Pros: They are relatively inexpensive and portable. With the battery pack, you can pump anywhere, anytime.

Cons: If you use this pump more than occasionally, you may find that pumping takes too long. Consider one of these for occasional use only.

Price: $65 (single pump) to $130 (double pump) to buy.

Choose this option if: You need to pump only occasionally because you'll be away from your baby now and then, for a night out or a couple of hours during the day.

Top models/brands to consider: Medela Single or Double Deluxe breast pump *(www.medela.com)*.

Manual breast pumps

With these small pumps, you produce the suction yourself by squeezing a bulb or lever or by manipulating a syringe-style cylinder. There are many designs of manual pumps on the market. Cylinder, or piston-style, pumps usually allow you to control pressure and minimize discomfort. Some manual models can be operated with one hand. They're easier to use than those requiring one hand to hold, one to pump.

Pros: They're less expensive than electric models and don't need an

THRIFT TIP

Some electric breast pumps come with a manual breast pump, so you get two for the price of one.

electrical source or batteries, and often are compact enough to fit in a tote or purse.

Cons: Manual pumps often are markedly slower than other pumps. We recommend these only for occasional use, such as when you're traveling.

Price: $35 to $50 to buy.

Choose this option if: You're a stay-at-home or work-from-home mom and you need to miss only a rare feeding because of a night out; you're traveling or you have plugged milk ducts or sore nipples. A manual pump is also ideal for pumping on the go, in places where electricity may not be available. Look for one with an ergonomic handle, not a bulb, though any small pump could tire your hand and arm and cause repetitive strain injuries if you use it frequently.

Top brands/models to consider: Medela Harmony (*www.medela .com*); Avent's Isis manual pump (*www.aventamerica.com*); Dr. Brown's manual breast pump (*www.handi-craft.com*).

Hands-free pumps

Placed inside your bra, this battery-operated pump, which is no bigger than a bagel and comes with an AC adapter, mimics the feel and sucking pattern of a baby. Milk travels through a flexible stem and collects in a self-sealing, spill-proof bag.

Pros: You don't have to drop everything you're doing. You can pump while you're reading, working, or talking on the phone. It's the ultimate in multitasking.

Cons: Some women report that you need a super-tight bra and must position the pump exactly to work this pump. Otherwise, milk won't collect properly. Since you place the pump inside your bra, your chest size will expand considerably, so you may need to wear a large sweater or blazer to camouflage the fact that you're pumping, if you do so in public. We also hear this option isn't quiet, so you'll probably want to pump in private. Moreover, the milk collection is relatively slow. It takes three to five minutes for milk to begin collecting in the bag. In the world of breast pumping, that's an eternity.

Price: $110 (for a single pump) to $200 (double pump) to buy.

Choose this option if: Your schedule is hectic and you'll be pumping only occasionally.

Top brands/models to consider: Whisper Wear (*www.whisperwear .com*) is the only brand of hands-free pump we know of on the market.

Features to Consider

Suction settings. The best pumps mimic a baby's natural nursing rhythm by automatically pumping in two distinct modes: rapid, to simulate a baby's rapid sucking to begin fast milk flow, and slower, to simulate a baby's deeper sucking to produce the most milk flow. Together, the two phases offer a more authentic breast-feeding experience with greater comfort, increased milk flow, and quicker nursing time. "Closer to Nature" brands/models on the market that purport to pump more like a baby include Medela's Pump In Style Advanced shoulder bag or backpack, its hospital-grade Symphony, and its Harmony manual breast pump. Others, such as Avent's Isis iQ Duo and Isis iQ Uno electronic dual and single breast pumps, allow you to automate the pumping rhythm, speed, and suction at the touch of a button instead of relying on pre-set controls.

Warranty. If you'll be using your personal-use breast pump every day, look for a pump that has at least a one-year warranty on the motor. A generous warranty typically is a sign of quality and durability.

Adapter/batteries. If you're pumping on the road or you don't have access to an electrical outlet (say, for example, you don't have a pumping room at work and you're relegated to a restroom stall), look for a pump that can run on batteries or that includes an adapter that can attach to your car's cigarette lighter. However, even if you have a "hands-free" model, we don't recommend pumping while driving because pumping can be distracting.

Double-pumping. If you'll be pumping at work or pumping often, get a double hospital-grade or midweight, personal-use, automatic pump. By expressing both breasts at once, you can complete a pumping session in 10 to 15 minutes. Besides being fast, double pumps are better for milk production. Double-pumping increases levels of prolactin, the hormone responsible for milk production. Smaller pumps or a single pump may not be able to maintain your milk supply long-term and can quickly become frustrating to use.

Carrying case. If you'll be commuting or traveling, a professional-looking pump "briefcase" or sporty backpack is the way to go. Most models, other than the hospital-grade ones, come in a chic, black microfiber case with a shoulder strap. Some models, such as Evenflo's Elan Feeding System and Medela's Pump in Style Advanced, also feature a removable cooling compartment and pump motor, so you can lighten your commute by leaving a section at work.

Insulated storage compartments. Look for compartments in the pump's carrying case if you'll be pumping on the go and need to store your milk for later. But be sure to keep an ice pack or two with your breast milk in the storage compartment.

LCD display. Some breast pumps have gone high-tech, such as the Evenflo Elan, offering an LCD panel that displays speed and suction settings as well as the time and length you last pumped—even which breast you pumped last.

Recommendations

Consider renting a hospital-grade breast pump if you're not sure how long you'll need to use a pump or if you know you'll need to pump for only a short time and you plan to be home with your baby. If you expect to use a breast pump regularly, especially if you plan to return to work, buy a top-quality midweight, personal-use, automatic model at the best price you can find. This caliber of pump will help you get a significant volume of milk in a given time and will be your best bet for maintaining your milk supply. If you plan to use a breast pump only occasionally, a manual pump or a small electric or battery-operated one will probably be all you need. They're appropriate and made for occasional use only.

Since using a breast pump can be tricky, most manufacturers now supply informational brochures with their units. You also can call manufacturers' customer-service lines if you encounter problems with a specific pump. Many manufacturers offer a 90-day warranty on parts and will repair or even replace a product without charge. But keep your receipt or the printout from your baby registry as proof of purchase.

There's a host of information on the Internet about breast-feeding in general and specific guidance on such issues as how to get into a pumping routine after you return to work. The La Leche League, at *www.lalecheleague.org*, is a good place to start. This Web site offers a breast-feeding bulletin board, an online community of other mothers you can turn to for ideas on how to overcome breast-feeding obstacles, answers to your most pressing questions, and podcasts on breast-feeding and parenting.

CHAPTER

9

Car
Seats

A child car seat should be high on your to-buy list. You'll need one to bring your baby home from the hospital and for every car trip with your baby thereafter. In fact, hospitals and birthing centers generally won't let you leave by car with your newborn if you don't have one. Every state requires that kids up to 4 years of age ride in a car seat; most require booster seats for older children.

What's Available

The major brands of car seats you're likely to encounter are, in alphabetical order: Baby Trend (*www.babytrend.com*), Britax (*www.britaxusa.net*), Chicco (*www.chiccousa.com*), Combi (*www.combi-intl.com*), Compass (*www.compass baby.com*), Cosco (*www.coscojuvenile.com*), Eddie Bauer (*www.djgusa.com*), Evenflo (*www.evenflo.com*), Graco (*www.gracobaby.com*), Peg-Pérego (*www.pegperego.com*), and Safety 1st (*www.safety1st.com*). There are also car beds for preemies and other very small newborns if there's a concern that a car seat may not provide a secure fit or that it may exacerbate breathing problems. In addition, there are specially designed car seats for children with physical disabilities. Ask your pediatrician for a recommendation or visit the Automotive Safety Program at *www.preventinjury.org* (or call 800-543-6227). Every model of car seat sold in the U.S. must meet federal safety standards. These are your basic choices:

Infant seats

These rear-facing seats are for babies up to 22 pounds. They allow infants to recline at an angle that doesn't interfere with breathing and protects them best in a crash, compared to a convertible car seat (page 101). Many strollers are now designed to accommodate infant car seats, or you can purchase an empty stroller frame that will accept many infant car seats. For more information on infant car seats and stroller frames, see Strollers, page 261. All infant car-seat models come with a handle, a convenience that lets you remove the seat and use it as a carrier. And nearly all have a base that secures to your vehicle with LATCH connections or a vehicle safety belt. LATCH, which stands for Lower Anchors and Tethers for Children, includes belts that hook the base to metal anchors in the car. You can strap most infant seats into a car without a base, using the vehicle safety belts, and some people continue to do so.

Infant seats have either a three-point harness—two adjustable shoulder straps that come together at a buckle in the shell or a crotch strap—or even better, an adjustable five-point system—two straps over the shoulders, two for the thighs, and a crotch strap. The vast majority of infant car seats have five-point harnesses, but there are a few three-point models still around—though we recommend the five-point version.

The handle on infant seats usually swings from a position behind the seat's shell when in the car to an upright position for carrying. When using as a carrier, be sure the seat is reclined so that your baby's head doesn't fall forward and inhibit his breathing. Also, never place the seat on an elevated surface.

Slots underneath most seats help them attach to the frame of a shopping cart, but the American Academy of

Pediatrics (AAP) doesn't recommend using them this way, and neither do we. (For more on shopping cart safety, see page 239.)

Pros: With an infant car seat, you can move your baby from car to house or vice versa without waking him up—a plus for both of you. Extra bases are available so you can keep a secured base in each of your vehicles.

Cons: Your baby may outgrow an infant car seat quickly and become too heavy for you to use it as a carrier. As a result, you may find yourself having to buy a convertible car seat after your baby is 6 to 9 months old. However, our advice is still to start with an infant seat before moving up to a convertible seat because it's more secure and compact for infants. We consider them the safest way to transport the youngest babies.

Price range: $50 to $250 for the seat and base; stroller frame sold separately. At least one brand of seat, the Orbit, is sold as a system—car seat base, infant car seat, and exclusive coordinating stroller frame. We have not tested the Orbit infant car seat system, which retails for $900.

HOW TO TOTE AN INFANT CAR SEAT

If you opt to use your infant car seat as a carrier, realize that it can be a killer on your wrists, elbow, lower back, and neck if you tote it by the handle or if you string it on your forearm like a handbag. "The greater the horizontal distance from the weight you're carrying to your torso, the more stress on your joints, discs, ligaments, and muscles," says Mary Ellen Modica, a physical therapist at Schwab STEPS Rehabilitation Clinic in Chicago, Ill. "It's equivalent to walking around with three or four full paint cans in one hand—something most people wouldn't do, but yet, they'll carry a car seat that way."

Instead, "Carry the car seat in front of you so that you have both hands on the handle," advises Diane Dalton, orthopedic clinical specialist at Boston University's Sargent College of Health and Rehabilitation, in Boston, Mass. With the weight of the seat and your baby centered and close to your trunk, the force on your body will be reduced, Dalton says. Another option: Leave the infant seat in your car and transfer your baby to a soft infant carrier (more about those on page 245) or a stroller (see page 261), or use a travel system (see next page).

Or simply carry your baby in your arms, and your child will benefit. Infants transported that way use their head, neck, and shoulder muscles and establish stronger trunk stability "Those upper muscles may develop sooner in babies who aren't carried around in a car seat," says Patrice M. Winter, a physical therapist and consultant in northern Virginia.

Travel systems

A travel system offers one-stop shopping: It consists of an infant car seat, a car-seat base for your car, and a separate stroller all in one. With these systems, you create a carriage by snapping an infant car seat into a stroller. The snap-on car seat is generally positioned atop the stroller so the infant rides facing you—the person pushing. Once your baby can sit up, she can ride in the stroller seat. Many car-seat manufacturers offer these combination strollers/infant car seats. And many stand-alone strollers are now designed to accommodate infant car seats from various manufacturers.

Pros: A travel system allows you to move a sleeping baby in the infant car seat undisturbed from car to stroller and vice versa.

Cons: Some travel-system strollers can be used only with a car seat from the same company. A way around that is to choose a stroller that accepts car seats from a number of different manufacturers. Travel systems can also be bulky, so if you're a city dweller who negotiates more subway stairs than highways or if the trunk of your car isn't too roomy, you may be better off with a separate car seat and a compact stroller that's appropriate for a newborn.

For more information on travel systems, see Strollers, page 261.

Price range: $130 to more than $600.

A Look at the LATCH System

Many infant seats sold in Europe include a "foot" to help stabilize the base.

Since Sept. 1, 2002, all child car seats with an internal harness (three- or five-point safety belt) and nearly all passenger vehicles sold in the U.S. have been required to include equipment designed for simpler buckling. This system, called LATCH (Lower Anchors and Tethers for Children), consists of child car-seat connections that attach to anchor points in the vehicle—two lower attachments and an upper tether on a child safety seat that anchor and connect with lower anchors usually found in the crease of the vehicle rear seat, and a top tether built into a vehicle's back seat. LATCH eliminates the need to use a vehicle's safety belts to install the seat. You can still use safety belts to install a LATCH-equipped child

A Tight Fit

When installing a LATCH car seat, attach the lower anchor **(A)** and the tether **(B)**. A secure car seat shouldn't be able to move more than 1 inch forward or sideways.

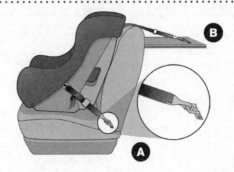

car seat—for example, in an older car that lacks LATCH anchors.

We think you are more likely to get a secure connection with LATCH. However, the system is not without its problems. We believe that infant car seats might be better secured if their bases were attached to floorboard anchor points in addition to existing LATCH anchors. Another improvement would be for the U.S. standard to allow for car-seat bases similar to many sold in Europe. They include a "foot" that adds stability in a frontal crash.

Another problem with LATCH is that anchors in many cars are hard to access. And most vehicles don't have LATCH anchors in the safest seat in the car: the center rear. It can also be hard to adjust safety belts to a car seat located in the center rear. General Motors vehicles are an exception; many have center LATCH anchors. And some Ford models allow parents to use the inner two LATCH anchors from the outer seats to install a child seat in the center rear. A big advantage of LATCH is that once you access the car anchors, the car seat typically fits securely. A tight fit is a major factor in crash protection. With LATCH, our testers are able to get child seats to fit tightly in almost all cars. With vehicle safety belts, a secure fit is hard to achieve in some cars.

Down the Road

Here are more seating options for children riding rear or front-facing.

Convertible seats

With a convertible seat, your child faces rearward as an infant, then toward the front of the vehicle as a toddler. The seat can function as a rear-facing seat for infants up to 30 or 35 pounds, depending on the

DON'T DO THE TWISTED-CAR-SEAT LIFT

Lifting your toddler in and out of a forward-facing car seat can put stress on your knees, lower back, neck, shoulder, elbows, and wrists, leading to injury over time. That's especially true if you twist and lean into the car with both your feet on the ground. You'll probably catch yourself doing this unhealthy stretch once you become aware of it.

A better idea: If your car seat is near the door, put one leg into the car and face the car seat as you're putting your child in it, advises Boston University's Diane Dalton You'll take pressure off your back. If your car seat is in the middle of the back seat, climb in and face it as you lift your child in. Of course, positioning yourself properly can take a few extra seconds you may not always feel you have.

Still, "it doesn't have to be perfect all the time," says Dalton, "But the more often you lift correctly, the better you're able to tolerate it when you don't."

One other safety tip: Use the curb side (rather than the traffic side) when putting a child into your car or taking him out.

model, and as a front-facing seat for toddlers generally up to 40 pounds (a few have a 65-pound limit). Models typically have an adjustable five-point harness system—two straps over the shoulders, two for the thighs, and a crotch strap between the legs. A convertible car seat can be a money saver, taking your child from infancy to kindergarten and maybe even beyond. But we advise starting with an infant seat first, though, as mentioned earlier, then switching to a convertible car seat when your baby outgrows his infant car seat.

Use a convertible car seat in the rear-facing position until your baby is at least 1 year old and weighs 20 pounds or more provided the seat can handle that weight. If your baby weighs 20 pounds before her first birthday, she should remain rear-facing until she turns 1. Convertible seats aren't compatible with strollers, so you will have to transfer your baby from the convertible car seat to a carriage or stroller when you're ready to set out on foot. Such jostling can wake a sleeping baby, a problem if you need to take your child on frequent shopping expeditions or other errands.

Price range: $60 to $300.

Toddler/booster seats

Looking like large versions of convertible seats, these front-facing seats are used with an internal harness (three- or five-point safety belt) for toddlers 20 to 40 pounds, for most models. Some models, however, can be used with the internal harness at higher weights. The SafeGuard Child Seat, for example can be used with the harness for kids up to 65 pounds when attached with vehicle seat belts.

Toddler/booster seats are either LATCH-attached or can be secured using the vehicle belts and tethers. When kids reach 40 pounds, the seat becomes a belt-positioned booster seat (see below), which children can use until they're 80 pounds, although some models of toddler/booster seats go as high as 100 pounds.

Price range: $80 to $270.

Belt-positioning booster seats

These are generally for children weighing 40 to 80 pounds. Belt-positioning booster seats use the vehicle's own safety belts to restrain the child.

Price range: $20 to $130.

Built-in seats

Some U.S. and foreign automakers offer on select cars and minivans an integrated, forward-facing child seat that has a harness and accommodates toddlers weighing more than 20 pounds. There are also some booster-seat versions. Built-in seats must meet the same performance standards as add-on child seats. However, they offer little or no side protection and they're usually located next to a door, instead of the safer center position. You may also need proper child restraint for when your child travels in other vehicles.

Shopping Secrets—For Convertible Car Seats and Beyond

Make sure the seat is compatible with your car. Check the fit of any models you're considering in your own car. Even before that, though, we suggest placing similar-looking models side by side in the store to compare features. Place your child in the seat to get a sense of the ease of buckling and unbuckling. Then, if possible, bring the floor model to your car for a mock installation. Be aware that some vehicle seats are too short, indented, or excessively sloped to allow a good fit of a child car seat.

Evenflo Triumph Deluxe convertible car seat, $140.

If you live in a city and you take lots of cabs, what do you do when your baby outgrows his infant car seat?

Any time a child rides in a car, he needs to be restrained in a car seat or, in the case of older children, about age 8, at the very least a properly fitting seat belt, says Sandy Sinclair, a highway safety specialist with the National Highway Traffic Safety Administration, in Washington, DC. Never hold a baby on your lap; the force of an accident may tear her from your arms or your own body may crush her. Likewise don't strap your child in with you in a seat belt; this too could result in injury. In lieu of lugging around a standard convertible car seat, consider buying a portable car seat for taxis and travel. Check out the Sit 'n' Stroll by Tripleplay Products *(www.tripleplayproducts .com)*, which converts from a stroller to a car seat. It works as a rear-facing restraint up to 30 pounds and a forward facing seat up to 40 pounds. "For short strolls and jumping in and out of cabs, it's fantastic," says Dave Frankland of New York City, the father of a 2-year-old and a 10-month-old. We have not tested this seat.

The Sit 'n' Stroll combination car seat/stroller by Tripleplay Products, $220

Try the floor model of a convertible seat in both the rear- and front-facing positions. Check out the harness release button in the rear-facing position; in some models it may be too low to reach comfortably. If the store won't let you take the seat out to your car to try it, make sure you can return any car seat you buy—or go to another store.

Check the store's return policy. If you're not happy with a particular car seat for whatever reason, it's important to know that you can return it and try again with another model. Be aware that a badly soiled or damaged seat may not be exchanged.

Features to Consider

Fabric. Today's car seats cater to every possible taste—plain colors, plaids, animal and paw-print motifs, and patriotic red, white, and blue.

Remember that, style aside, babies tend to be messy, so washable fabric is a plus, especially if your car seat will be with you beyond the first year, when sippy cups and eating on the go can kick into high gear. Car-seat upholstery from some leading brands, however, requires hand washing and line drying. Most coverings are rigged through the harness-strap system and are held in place with elastic so they

Graco Backless TurboBooster, $20.

can be removed for laundering, but in some cases extracting the fabric from the seat can require extensive dismantling. Check the seat's manual for how-to's.

Extras. Add-on seat covers ("boots"), thicker padding, and adjustable head-support cushions may offer greater comfort. But buy them only if they are sold by the same maker as the seat and for that specific seat. Some models have elastic side pockets for toys, bottles, or snacks. As your baby grows, they can come in handy, but they're not absolutely necessary.

Harness slots. Look for seats with more than one harness slot so your baby has room to grow. The harness fits properly in rear-facing seats when it's at or below your child's shoulders and in forward-facing seats when it's in the slots at or above your child's shoulders.

Recline adjustment. When used rear-facing, some convertible seats recline to up to five positions, which come in handy for when your child decides to nap in the car.

Snack accessories. Many convertible and booster seats come with cup holder and snack trays. These are nice, but not necessary, especially if your car is equipped with cup holders in the back seat.

Recommendations:
Convertible and Other Car Seats

Pay close attention to the height and weight limits of the seat you buy. As mentioned, we recommend starting out with a infant seat because that is the most secure seat for very young babies. Next, use a convertible seat in the rear-facing orientation up to the seat's limits in that mode, then switch the convertible seat around, and use it front-facing until your toddler reaches the next height and weight limits. After that, use a booster seat until your child is tall enough to use the car's safety belts, typically at least 57 inches and between 8 and 12

years old. Even with a seat belt, all children under the age of 13 should ride in the back seat.

Installation: Getting It Right

When installing a seat for the first time, give yourself a good half-hour. If you can recruit a helper, even better. Here are a few pointers for making installation easier.

Read all about it. Consult the instructions that come with the seat so you're familiar with the seat before you try to install it. Also, check your vehicle owner's manual for information on how to use your car's LATCH anchors or safety belts with that car seat. Some car manufacturers also have a free how-to brochure or video that can help. Keep these instructions handy for future reference.

Position the seat. As we've mentioned, the center rear seat is the safest spot. You may have to place the seat next to a door if you have more than one small child; if there isn't a shoulder belt in the center (for use with a booster seat); if your LATCH-compatible vehicle lacks lower anchors in the center rear position and you don't want to use the center-seat vehicle belt; or if using the center rear seat would make the child seat unstable, among other reasons.

Secure the seat. Use your weight to push the child seat into your vehicle's seat (you may want to use a knee) while pulling the slack out of the car'sLATCH strap or safety belt. With a rear-facing seat, adjust the angle as directed by the manufacturer, using the level indicator or other means to get the backrest of the car seat close to a 45-degree incline. With a front-facing seat for a toddler up to 40 pounds, use the top tether of the car seat. If the top tether is not in use, such as with a toddler/booster seat used as a booster, remove the top-tether strap or secure it so it doesn't fly around and injure your child in a crash. When you're securing an infant or toddler seat with a car's safety belt, you may need a locking clip so the lap belt remains tight. See the manufacturer's instructions for details.

Check the seat every time you use it. Whenever you buckle your child in, try shifting the car seat from side to side and back to front. It shouldn't move more than an inch in either direction. Make sure the harness straps fit snugly. Your overall goal: The seat must be buckled tightly into your vehicle and your child must be buckled snugly into the seat at all times.

Double-check with the experts. After you've installed the seat, make sure it's correct. You can find a free car-seat inspection station near you by visiting *www.nhtsa.gov*. The NHTSA site also has detailed instructions with photos for seat installation.

MORE TIPS FOR SAFER SEATING

Always use a car safety seat and make sure your child is buckled up every time you drive, even if it's just down the street or criss-crossing a parking lot.

Keep your child's convertible seat facing the rear of the vehicle until he reaches the weight and height limits specified by the manufacturer. Don't switch the convertible car seat to a front-facing orientation for a child younger than 1 year and weighing 20 pounds or less. That can result in death or serious injury in a crash. Some children ride rear-facing beyond their second birthday.

Location, location. The safest place for a child is in your vehicle's rear-center seat. The car seat should never be installed on a front seat that has an air bag. Two exceptions: If your car doesn't have a back seat, or if your child has a medical condition that requires constant monitoring, you can have an on/off switch installed for the front-passenger air bag or have it disconnected so the child's car seat can go next to the driver. But to have that done you'll need a letter of authorization from the National Highway Traffic Safety Administration (NHTSA). To obtain one, contact the agency via its Web site, *www.nhtsa.gov*.

Insist on new. Although there are many baby items you can borrow or buy secondhand, don't make a car seat one of them if you can avoid it. A used seat may have been in a crash or recalled. The manufacturer's instructions may be missing. If, for some reason, you must use a secondhand seat, avoid those with an unknown history or that are older than 6 years. In the world of car seats, a 6-year-old model is a relic—and risky. You'll also want to avoid recalled models. You can check for recalled models at *www-odi.nhtsa.dot.gov/cars/problems/recalls*.

Send in the registration card that comes with new car seats. That way, you can be notified by the manufacturer if the car seat is recalled You can also find recall information at the NHTSA Web site *(www.nhtsa.gov)* and monthly recall reports at *www.ConsumerReports.org*. If you have a car seat that attaches to a stroller, you can sign up for the Consumer Product Safety Commission's e-mail subscription list at *www.cpsc.gov/cpsclist.asp*. Updated recall information on all infant products will be sent directly to your e-mail in-box.

Replace the seat after a crash. Although NHTSA now says that parents can be confident that a child car seat will continue to do its job after a minor crash—with "minor crash" defined as the seat has no visible cracks or deformation caused by the crash; the crashed vehicle can be driven; no one in the car was injured; the door nearest the car seat was not damaged; and air bags did not deploy—we believe you should err on the side of maximum safety and replace the seat even after a "minor" crash.

WHICH CAR SEAT FOR AN OBESE CHILD?

Certain models are better if your child exceeds the typical weight

Childhood obesity has safety implications beyond the obvious health risks. For one thing, parents of obese children may find it difficult to find a car safety seat that is appropriate for their child's age and development yet will accommodate their weight or size.

A study in a recent issue of Pediatrics, the journal of the American Academy of Pediatrics, projects that there are nearly 300,000 children whose age-weight combinations place them at risk for difficulty in obtaining an appropriate child safety seat. Three-year-olds who weigh more than 40 pounds are the largest group affected, the study says. In all, about 1 percent of children up to 6 years old are affected, according to the study.

The problem: Children between 1 and 4 years old typically ride in the forward-facing position of a convertible child safety seat, which usually accommodates children who weigh 20 to 40 pounds. Some obese children exceed 40 pounds or otherwise don't fit in these seats.

Belt-positioning booster seats typically accommodate children more than 40 pounds, but they're not intended for kids younger than 4 or for very active children because boosters typically rely on vehicle shoulder belts to keep children in place. Those belts don't prevent children from leaning forward or placing the shoulder belt behind their back or under their arm.

The answer: Parents can do one of two things, depending on their child. Some forward-facing car seats can be used with their internal harness for children up to 65 pounds. At right, we've listed numerous seats that claim to accommodate heavier children.

The other option for parents is to use a toddler-booster seat with a five-point harness. Many such seats are sold with harnesses. CONSUMER REPORTS recommends that any child younger than 4 years of age, even children who exceed the 40-pound limit, should not use a booster seat without a harness system.

Booster seats should be used until children are 4 feet 9 inches tall and are able to safely use an adult safety belt.

Recommendations

• Parents of all children, but particularly obese ones, should pay strict attention to weight and height limits on car seats. If you're considering a booster seat, make sure your child is strapped in the booster seat with a harness and the vehicle belt until he reaches the weight limit for the harness.

• When possible, the car seat should be positioned in the center of the back seat, the safest place in a vehicle, even if that means attaching the car seat with the car safety belt instead of the LATCH system. Read the user manual very carefully for how to install the seat in your vehicle as your child reaches different weight ranges.

CAR SEATS FOR OBESE CHILDREN

The following seats are appropriate for obese children according to their manufacturer's specifications as most can be used with a harness and vehicle belt up to 65 pounds, or in two cases, 80 to 105 pounds.

Brand & model	Price	Type	Rear-facing restriction	Front-facing restriction with harness with LATCH	Front-facing restriction with harness with vehicle belt	Front-facing restriction in BPB-mode (using vehicle lap/ shoulder belt)
Britax Marathon	$270	Convertible	5-33 lbs. lbs.	48 lbs.	65 lbs.	NA
Britax Decathlon	$285	Convertible	5-33 lbs. lbs.	48 lbs.	65 lbs.	NA
Britax Boulevard*	$300	Convertible	5-33 lbs. lbs.	48 lbs.	65 lbs.	NA
Sunshine Kids Radian 65	$200	Convertible	5-33 lbs. lbs.	48 lbs.	65 lbs.	NA
Britax Regent	$270	Youth	—	48 lbs.	80 lbs.	NA
Snug Seat/Britax Traveller Plus	$625	Youth	—	48 lbs.	105 lbs.	NA
SafeGuard Child Seat	$430	Youth	—	48 lbs.	65 lbs.	NA
Safety 1st Apex	$130	Toddler/ Booster	—	40 lbs.	65 lbs.	100 lbs.
Britax Parkway	$100	Booster	—	—	—	100 lbs.

* There was a recall on the E9L57 model of this seat in 2006 due to possible tether failure.

Preparing Your Baby for a Safe and Comfy Ride

Once you have correctly installed a car seat, follow these tips to sure your child is correctly secured in the seat:

Have your baby ride rear-facing. Babies should ride rear-facing until at least one year of age and at least 20 pounds. If your baby outgrows his infant car seat before age 1, install a convertible car seat in the rear-facing position. Don't place an infant seat in a forward-facing position; it always stays rear-facing.

Take off the wraps. If you need to keep your baby warm, place blankets or thick coats over her after you strap her into an infant or convertible car seat. Don't wrap your baby up in a blanket, thick coat or other bulky garment and then strap her into a restraint system. That may affect the restraint's integrity.

Position the harness. The harness chest clip should be fastened and positioned at your child's mid-chest or armpit level, which keeps the shoulder straps from slipping. Harness straps should be snug and straight (not twisted). If a harness is properly snug, you should not be able to insert more than one of your fingers behind it. Position rear-facing harness straps at, or slightly below, your child's shoulders. (On forward-facing convertible and booster seats, harness straps should be positioned at, or slightly above, your child's shoulders.)

CHAPTER

10

Changing Tables & Dressers

You can diaper a baby just about anywhere you have room and where the baby is safe from falling, even on the floor. But since you'll change 2,000-plus diapers in your baby's first year alone, your back will benefit from something made for the task—either a standard changing table or a dresser that doubles as one.

You'll be able to diaper your baby at a comfortable level (most changing tables stand 36 to 43 inches high), and have diapers within easy reach. Unlike the crib or the floor, changing tables also have shelves, baskets, and/or drawers you can use to store other essentials, such as wipes, rash ointment, and a toy or two to keep your baby busy. A vinyl changing pad is usually included, but covers are sold separately, available in a variety of colors and patterns.

Another option you may see in stores is a removable changing pad

Furniture Straps

In an average year, nine children, usually younger than 5, are killed when household furniture tips onto them, and an estimated 8,000 to 10,000 people, mostly children, are hurt. Toppling furniture can cause broken bones, bruising, and death from suffocation. But furniture straps can help keep your child safe. They secure a dresser, armoire, or bookcase to the wall to prevent it from tipping over when a child grabs it to balance himself or tries to climb. You'll need to find a stud in the wall to drive the screws into. If installed properly, furniture straps are effective protection up to about age 4.

Several manufacturers make furniture straps. We judged the Parent Units Heavy Duty Topple Stop Furniture Fastening System, $14 for two, the best model of the three furniture straps we tested (www.parentunits.com). Installing the straps requires many steps involving screws and adhesive, and none of the required tools is included. When installing the straps on furniture made of particleboard instead of solid wood, it might be necessary to first attach pieces of solid wood to the furniture.

Other products we tested were the KidCo Anti-Tip Furniture Strap, $6.99 for two (www.kidco.com), and Safety 1st Furniture Wall Straps, $4.49 for two (www.safety1st.com). These fabric straps must be screwed into both the wall and the furniture (or into wood attached to the furniture). The length is adjustable.

that simply affixes to the top of a regular dresser. If you decide to go this route, which is the least expensive ($15 to $35), look for a changing table pad with at least two opposing contoured sides with a baby restraint strap, such as the Contour Changing Pad by Simmons (*www.simmons kids.com*). With that style changing "table," you simply remove the pad (sold separately) when your baby grows out of the changing table stage (usually around age 2) and the changing table becomes a full-time dresser.

There are wooden, retractable changing tables, such as the Bellini Slide Top Changer (*www.bellini.com*), which sits on top of a Bellini dresser and attaches to the back of it with hidden L brackets. This mini-changing table usually has a flat changing surface. But to comply with the most recent industry safety standards, a flat (not contoured) changing table must have barrier protection on all sides. Because the retractable (or slide-top) style has protection on only three sides, we can't recommend it at this time.

Shopping Secrets

Consider storage. Most changing tables have open shelves that make it easy to reach diapers and clothing, either stacked or in decorative wicker baskets, but some have drawers or a combination of drawers and shelves. Having at least one drawer, preferably right under the table, can help you quickly retrieve the supplies you need, though some parents prefer open shelving. A drawer offers an advantage over open shelving because it can hide diaper supplies, which look like a treasure trove to the curious toddler your baby will become before you know it.

Look for barriers on four sides. A traditional changing table is usually surrounded by a restraining barrier made of rails or solid wood. According to the latest American Society for Testing and Materials (ASTM) safety standards, changing tables with a flat surface must have a barrier on all sides, as noted earlier. If only two or three sides are protected instead of four, don't buy it. Changing tables with a contoured changing surface need barriers on only two opposing sides to comply with the latest safety standards.

Go for girth. If you're planning to use a dresser as your changing table, think short and fat, not tall and thin. A dresser that's wider and lower to the ground will be less likely to fall forward when you place your baby on top. If you end up with a taller dresser, mount it to the wall with furniture straps so it won't tip over.

What's Available

Major makers of changing tables and dressers that can be used as changing tables are, in alphabetical order: Ameriwood Furniture (available via *www.amazon.com*), Angel Line (*www.angelline.com*), Badger Basket (*www.badgerbasket.com*), Bellini (*www.bellini.com*), Child Craft (*www.childcraftindustries.com*), Da Vinci (can be found online at e-tailers such as *www.babyuniverse.com*), Delta Enterprise (*www.deltaenterprise.com*; available at retailers and e-tailers such as *www.target.com* and *www.toysrus.com*), Jardine Enterprise (available online at *www.toysrus.com*), J. Mason (*www.jmason.com*), Nursery Smart (*www.nurserysmart.com*), Pottery Barn Kids (*www.potterybarnkids.com*), Relics (*www.relicsfurniture.com*), Scandinavian Child (*www.scichild.com*); Sorelle (*www.sorrellefurniture.com*), Stokke (*www.stokke.com*), Storkcraft Baby (*www.storkcraft.com*), and Young America Collection (*www.youngamerica.stanleyfurniture.com*). Most models have wooden frames, but you may find some made of wicker.

A safety belt—a single strap with a wide buckle—is usually included with the changing pad. If there isn't one, buy a changing pad with a safety belt and attach the pad to the table according to the manufacturer's directions.

Changing tables range from $15 to $35 (for a simple changing table pad you attach to a dresser top) to over $1,300 for solid wood models that convert to a flat-top dresser with drawers/enclosed shelving. For $70 to $130, you can buy an adequate changing table with open shelving and possibly one drawer, but quality is a factor. At the low end, parents have reported drawers that stick, changing pads with plastic that cracks in short order, and lesser-quality wood (typically laminated particleboard). Still, tables in this lower price range may be sufficient, depending on your situation. If your baby spends part of the time in daycare, for example, the table may hold up well. You'll probably have to assemble the table yourself, which can be tricky if you're not handy, and the table you select has a drawer that requires installing. At the high end of the price range, changing tables may be custom finished in the paint color of your choice. Drawers, solid-wood construction, and convertibility drive up the price.

Features to Consider

Safety strap. The changing table you're considering should have a pad that affixes to the table and a safety strap. Changing pads are also sold separately, but use a pad in a size the changing table manufacturer recommends.

Sturdiness. A changing table or dresser shouldn't wobble when you give it a light shake. Test the floor model in the store, if possible.

Wheels. Some tables come on wheels and are designed to be moved from room to room. If you buy a table with wheels, make sure it has brakes that lock so you can keep the table stable when you park it.

Diaper direction. On most changing tables, you have to change your baby from the side. But on a few, such as the Natural Diaper Corner Baby Changing Table by Badger Basket, $135, (*www.badgerbasket.com*), which features a contoured pad, you can change your baby from head to toe, which some parents find a more comfortable position.

Wood. Depending on how much you'll use a changing table, you may want one with a good pedigree. Pricier changing tables tend to be sturdy and constructed from solid birch, beech, and maple rather than particleboard with a wood finish. If this is your first baby, and you plan a larger family, it may make sense to pay more. It's also worth spending a little more if you plan to convert the changing table into a media center, bookcase, or desk (an option with the Stokke Collection, *www.stokke.com*). In any event, look for wood surfaces that are smooth and splinter-free.

This changing table by Badger Basket can be converted into a media center or storage shelf once your baby is out of diapers.

Height. As we mentioned, changing tables vary in height. Some are as low as 36 inches; others as high as 43 inches. If you're tall, go with a taller table or dresser and secure it to the wall to reduce the risk of tipping. If you're short, aim lower.

Recommendations

Before you buy, consider all the furniture you plan for the nursery. You may decide that you don't need a changing table or simply don't have room for one. If you're tight on space or budget, consider using a dresser as a changing table; buy a contoured changing pad with a safety strap and affix it to the dresser, according to the manufacturer's installation directions. If you think you would like a more traditional changing table, try before you buy. Test the table in the store, as if you were changing a baby. If you see a backache in your future because that changing table is too low, try another. Check drawers and cabinets. The operation should be quiet and smooth. The unit should seem sturdy. Look for a changing table with safety straps to help prevent your baby from falling—and use the straps every time you change your baby's diaper. If the table comes with a pad, use only the pad that's provided by the manufacturer. Don't use a changing table that's damaged or broken. Stop using your changing table when your baby reaches the manufacturer's age or weight limit, which is typically age 2, or 30 pounds.

If you buy a cloth changing pad, make sure it has a waterproof layer on the underside, which helps the changing table stay clean and sanitary. Vinyl changing pads can be wiped clean with soap and water. Purchase two or three covers so you can throw one in the wash and have at least one on hand.

More Tipping Points: Armoires, Book Cases, Dressers and TV Stands

If there are young children in the house, it's a good idea to attach any potentially unstable furniture to a wall with tip-over straps or restraints, and keep heavy objects like TVs off dressers. This added step is necessary even though ASTM has a tip-over standard for chests, armoires, and dressers, and Underwriters Laboratories has one for TV stands. Childhood injuries and deaths from falling furniture and television sets are a growing problem, according to Consumer Product Safety Commission statistics.

The ASTM tip-over standard for chests, armoires, and dressers requires that an empty unit can't tip when any doors are open and all drawers are open two-thirds of the way or to the stop, whichever is less. It also can't tip when one drawer is open two-thirds of the way (or a door is opened fully) and a 50-pound load (to simulate a child's weight) is applied to the center front of each drawer. (ASTM is currently working on a revised tip-over standard.)

The tip-stability section of the UL standard for carts and stands for A/V equipment mandates that the unit can't tip when holding a load that weighs as much as a television set (using the largest TV size

QUICK-CHANGE ARTISTRY

Before changing your baby's diaper, be sure any products you need—diapers, wipes, or the wipe warmer—are within arm's reach and place the diaper pail adjacent to the table. Never leave your baby alone on a changing table—even for a moment, even if you're using the safety straps, and even if you're sure your baby is secure.

specified by the manufacturer) and placed on a plane inclined 10 degrees from horizontal. However, those standards are voluntary, and many manufacturers don't even claim to meet them. Our tests revealed that furniture often doesn't meet the standards, and that the standards are inadequate in any case.

We tested dressers, armoires, bookcases, and TV stands in two ways: against applicable standards and then while using the furniture the way you might—with drawers full of clothes and fully opened, and with carpeting underneath, for example. Most of the tested furniture is typical of that found in children's rooms and is sold through retailers that include *www.babydepot.com*, *www.burlingtoncoatfactory.com*, *www.ikea.com*, *www.jcpenney.com*, *www.kidkraft.com*, *www.pottery barnkids.com*, *www.sears.com*, *www.target.com*, and *www.walmart.com*.

One of five dressers failed the ASTM test, another broke, and three others passed but tipped when drawers were opened all the way (farther than the two-thirds required by ASTM). Three of five armoires failed the ASTM test. One TV stand failed the UL test even when empty. The following chart provides specifics.

Ratings • Furniture

Brand & model	Price	Meets standard?	Comments
DRESSERS Covered by voluntary ASTM tip-over standard.			
South Shore Blueberry 5-drawer Chest (Sears.com)	$120	Yes	But tipped with all drawers open all the way.
Kendall Drawer Chest Dresser (Pottery BarnKids.com)	600	Yes	But tipped when 50-lb. weight was applied to drawers opened all the way.
Creative Interiors Reflections Dresser (Sears.com)	160	Yes	But tipped when 50-lb. weight was applied to clothing-filled drawers opened all the way.
Bassett Mission Natural Five Drawer Chest (BurlingtonCoatFactory.com)	220	No	Tipped when 50-lb. weight was applied to empty drawers opened 2/3 of the way.
South Shore 5-drawer Chest (Burlington-CoatFactory.com)	120	–	Did not survive test. Some drawers broke when 50-lb. weight was applied to edges, side panels pulled away slightly.
ARMOIRES Covered by voluntary ASTM tip-over standard.			
Storkcraft Traditional Nursery Armoire (JCPenney.com)	$270	Yes	Also passed our tests on carpet, with drawers and shelves loaded.
Berkeley Armoire (PotteryBarnKids.com)	1,000	Yes	Also passed our tests on carpet, with drawers and shelves loaded.
Diktad Wardrobe (Ikea.com)	200	No	Tipped when 50-lb. weight was applied to door.
Prepac White 3-Drawer Wardrobe (Target.com)	200	No	Tipped when 50-lb weight was applied to door.
Quebeko Q-Bik Blonde Maple Armoire (Target.com)	200	No	Tipped when we applied 50-lb. weight to top drawer, which fell to floor. Rails bent or broke.
BOOKCASES Not covered by ASTM; may be added shortly.			
Madison Tall (PotteryBarnKids.com)	$300	NA	No problems.
Kidkraft Avalon 3-Shelf (Kidkraft and Target.com)	110	NA	No problems.
Avery Triple Shelf (PotteryBarnKids.com)	700	NA	Unit did not tip, but adjustable shelves tipped down when 50-lb weight was applied.
TV STANDS Covered by tip-stability section of voluntary Underwriters Laboratories (UL) standard.			
Sauder TV/VCR Cart (Walmart.com)	$20	Yes	With 27-inch TV, TV tilted but unit did not.
Markor TV Storage Unit (Ikea.com)	250	No	Failed with 135-lb. weight. 27-inch TV tilted; unit did not.
Linon Home Decor Beadboard Entertainment Center (Target.com)	400	No	Tipped on 10-degree plane even when empty.
Quebeko Pablo Mobile TV/Audio Cart (Target.com)	120	No	Tipped with 70-lb. weight on top shelf. With 27-inch TV, unit tipped.

Clothing

Warning: It will take every ounce of willpower not to load up at checkout with mini Levi's, teeny-tiny sailor suits, floral sundresses, peasant smocks, and rompers in every color. Baby clothes, trendier than ever and oh-so-scrumptious, are as irresistible to parents (and friends and relatives) as a pool on a scorching day. Everyone wants her baby to be well-dressed, and manufacturers have responded with micro styles that appeal to our adult fashion sense.

Not that your baby cares. All she wants is to be comfortable. And that's important to keep in mind. The basic necessities—even if they're "preowned"—will keep your little cutie content. Still, you may not want to dress your baby in just any old thing.

Shopping Secrets
Expect to get clothes as gifts. During your first forays into the baby department, buy only a few items in newborn size, such as one or two sleepers. Depending on how

large your baby is at birth, she may outgrow this size within a few weeks. You'll want to focus on 6-month-size clothing—your baby will grow into it quickly. Even then, try to hold back and fill in after you've reaped the birth-announcement bounty. Clothes from generous friends and relatives may get you through the first year. Rest assured that knowing gift-givers, such as friends who are already parents, grandmothers, and aunts, will buy in bigger sizes, understanding how fast babies grow.

Watch for sales on brands you like. Sales are everywhere—in stores, in catalogs, and online at the end of each season and in between. Major chain stores that sell baby clothes have regular promotions, sometimes weekly. If your baby is a newborn, resist the urge to stock up, since most babies whiz through this size range. Don't shop too far in advance on larger sizes, either. Infants can have sudden growth

THE WELL-DRESSED NEWBORN BABY

Here's a review of the Baby Basics list from the Introduction. Use your own judgment on how much you want to buy yourself, and what you can expect as gifts.

Basics

____ Four sleeping outfits or one-piece sleepers with attached feet. Sleepers and sacks are preferable to covering a baby with blankets, which can be a suffocation hazard. Snug-fitting cotton and flame-resistant sleepwear are the safest choices. Loose-fitting sleepwear that's not made of flame-resistant material is a fire hazard.

____ Six side-snap T-shirts.

____ Four to six one-piece undershirts that snap around the crotch.

____ A small baby cap (the hospital will probably give you one).

____ Six pairs of socks/booties.

____ Two to three soft, comfortable daytime outfits.

____ Cotton sweater or light jacket.

Summer babies

____ Brimmed hat with elastic chin strap to keep your baby from batting it off.

Winter babies

____ Warm knit hat with elastic chin strap.

____ Snowsuit.

spurts that throw off your sizing forecasts. A winter coat you snag for your baby in August may be too small by December.

Consider used. If you've never bought anything secondhand, start now. You can easily get away with it, especially when your child is an infant. "My biggest money saver was the local moms' group sale," says Laura Winblade of Bellevue, Wash., mother of a preschooler and a first-grader. "In my area, there's one for mothers of multiples, and they have a sale twice a year. Babies go through clothes so quickly, the small stuff is always in good condition. But I found that as my children got older, it was harder to find quality used clothes."

Winblade has a point. As babies become toddlers, and messy activities such as fingerpainting come into play, clothing gets more wear and tear. But infant clothing is another story; it's not unheard of to pay 50 cents for a near-perfect pair of pants that would cost you $12 or more new. Secondhand shops are prime real estate for special-occasion baby and toddler clothes such as christening and holiday outfits and fancy party duds that have been worn only once or twice (if at all). You'll likely pay a fraction of the retail cost.

Check local tag or garage sales, try browsing Web sites such as *www.eBay.com* and *www.craigslist.com*, and put the word out among parents you know. You may get quite serviceable clothes delivered by the box load to your front door. But inspect hand-me-downs carefully for unraveling thread, loose buttons or snaps, or scratchy appliqués and elastic bands. Don't dress your child in anything that's not as good as new or that appears unsafe to you.

What's Available

You'll find " boy" and "girl" baby clothes in every imaginable pattern, color (besides pink and blue, think mocha, powder, buttermilk, safari, camouflage, silver, avocado, Bordeaux, and pistachio), style, and fabric. Cotton, which is soft and absorbent, is still the most common fiber. Organic cotton children's clothes are coming into their own as the trend toward "green" takes hold outside the health food store. Many garments are made of cotton/polyester blends, which dry quickly and resist wrinkles, or cotton/spandex for maximum give. You'll also find thick, soft knits and fleece made of microfiber.

At specialty boutiques, you'll see high-maintenance fabrics that require ironing or dry cleaning, such as linen and cashmere, as well as hand-knit items.

Major brands of infant wear can be found in leading department stores and retail chains across the country, online, and in catalogs. They include, in alphabetical order: Baby Gap (*www.gap.com*), Baby Lulu (*www.babylulu.com*), Baby Style (*www.babystyle.com*), Bunnies by the Bay (*www.bunniesbythebay.com*), Carter's (*www.carters.com*), First Impressions Baby, (available at *www.macys.com*), Flapdoodles (*www.flapdoodles.com*), Good Lad (*www.goodlad.com*), Gymboree (*www.gymboree.com*), Halo Innovations (for sleep sacks, also known as wearable blankets, *www.haloinnovations.com*), Hanna Andersson (*www.hannaandersson.com*), Lands' End (*www.landsend.com*), Little Me (*www.littleme.com*), Mulberribush (*www.mulberribush.com*), Old Navy (*www.oldnavy.com*), Pumpkin Patch (available at *www.nordstrom.com*), Ralph Lauren (*www.polo.com*), Talbots Kids (*www.talbotskids.com*), and Tommy Hilfiger (available at *www.macys.com*). Many of these brands can also be found at major retailers and e-tailers such as *www.target.com*, *www.babiesrus.com*,

FOOTWEAR FOOTNOTES: LOSE THE SHOES

Shoes complete the outfit for kids, but wait until your child begins walking—usually at 10 to 14 months—before buying her first official pair of shoes. That's when a child really needs them. Jane Andersen, D.P.M., a spokeswoman for the American Podiatric Medical Association, recommends picking a first shoe with flexibility, which helps the foot develop its arch. "Try to bend the shoe in half," she says. "If it bends easily, it's a good shoe." The best shoes also have traction on the bottom so your baby won't slip easily. A shoe doesn't have to be expensive to be flexible, but in Anderson's shopping experience, the most flexible shoes are higher-ticket brands. In our opinion, that might include Merrell (available at *www.shoes.com*), Nina Kids (available at leading e-tailers such as *www.zappos.com*), Pediped (*www.pediped.com*), Stride Rite (*www.striderite.com*), and Umi (*www.umishoes.com*). And, adds Andersen, stores that sell higher-ticket brands generally have experienced sales help to make sure you buy the right size. You'll want some room at the toe, but not so much that your child will trip. Also, keep in mind that toddlers kick off anything and everything, so look for flexible shoes that lace. They're harder to take off than shoes with Velcro closures.

To keep your prewalker's feet warm outside on cool days, look for soft, elasticized baby socks or booties that cling to the feet so your baby can't kick them off. You don't have to buy the leather baby shoes you'll see everywhere, which can easily run you $25 per pair or more, and which your baby will outgrow quickly.

www.buybuybaby.com, and *www.babyuniverse.com*. As with adult clothing, prices run the gamut.

Sizing Demystified

Confused about what size clothes to buy for your baby? Here's help. Baby clothing sizes are usually based on age: preemie, 0 to 3 months (newborn), 3 to 6 months, 6 to 9 months, 9 to 12 months, 12 months, 18 months, and 24 months. However, one manufacturer's 6 to 9 months may be quite different from another's because there are no standard sizes in the industry. Every brand of baby clothing has its own size specifications. A general rule, "Double your baby's age," says Vivian G. Reisman, president of Baby Steps, a children's clothing manufacturer based in Closter, N.J. For example, if you're buying for a 3-month-old, buy a 6-month-old size; if you're shopping for a 6-month-old, buy a 12-month-old size, and so on. Even though that doubled size may seem a little big at first, your baby will grow into the clothing quickly and you'll have leeway for shrinkage.

You don't always have to double the size, though. It depends on the manufacturer, so experiment. "I've found that some brands, like the Gap and Old Navy, run true to a child's age," says Michelle Dyson, a mother of two, from Boulder, Colo.

The age-doubling formula ends at around age 2 anyway, says Reisman. Then, buy one to two sizes up, depending on your child's size. For example, an average-size 2-year-old (a toddler in the 50th percentile for height and weight) can probably wear a size 3. But a large 2-year-old (say, in the 95th percentile) would wear a size 4, she says.

Read the weight and length charts found on the back of many garment packages or consult a size chart, which many baby-clothing stores keep on hand, especially those that sell garments in European sizes. But be sure to know your baby's height in inches—that's key to converting your baby's size to centimeters.

Features to Consider

Your primary concerns should be dressing ease, softness, durability, and safety, then style. Since most babies dislike having anything pulled over their headu, look for garments that are easy to take off and put on, with front-opening or side-snap tops. Snaps are easier (and faster) than buttons. Quick access to the diaper area is essential, so opt for snap-open legs or loosely elastic waists. Velcro closures are quick and convenient. Before washing, close them so that they don't fill up with lint and threads and lose their holding power.

Comfort. Check the seams on the inside of the garment. They should be smooth, not rough, and lie flat rather than sticking out. Don't buy clothes with tight elastic bands on arms, legs, neck, or waist. They can irritate your baby's skin and restrict circulation. Bypass anything that could be scratchy—unpainted metal zippers, appliqués, or snaps with rough or uneven backings. If an appliqué is made of heat-welded plastic, check for rough edges on the back. Give sequins, buttons, and snaps a quick tug to make sure they can't easily come off, posing a choking hazard. But don't pull so hard that you weaken the attachment in the process. And recheck after each washing.

Fabric. Labels on baby apparel must state fiber content and care instructions. All-cotton knits may look large when new, but they can shrink as much as 10 percent with repeated washing. Polyester/cotton blends are less expensive than pure cotton or organic cotton and more resistant to wrinkles and shrinking. Avoid thin, semitransparent items or garments with poor finishing such as unclipped thread. Although babies grow fast, you'll need clothing that's durable enough to last several months or more.

Safe Sleepwear

Fabric and fit are important safety considerations for your baby's sleepwear. For infants to children's size 14, Consumer Product Safety Commission regulations dictate that sleepwear must either be made of flame-resistant fabric, or fit snugly. Flame-resistant fabric must not ignite easily and must self-extinguish quickly when removed from a flame to meet government flammability requirements. Sleepwear that fits snugly does not trap the air needed for fabric to burn and reduces the chances of contact with a flame. Flame-resistant fabrics may be worn either loose or snug-fitting; they're often made of polyester, but cotton can be treated so that it's flame resistant. When you're shopping for sleepwear, keep these ground rules in mind:

• Don't buy oversize sleepwear that's not flame-resistant (look for a label on the garment indicating flame resistance).

• Don't allow your baby to sleep in loose T-shirts, sweatshirts, or other apparel made from non-flame-resistant fabrics.

• Don't buy snug-fitting sleepwear a size or two larger so your baby has growing room. That defeats the purpose of the garment and puts

REMOVE DRAWSTRINGS

When your baby reaches size 2T (not uncommon around his first birthday), the Consumer Product Safety Commission recommends removing neck drawstrings from all outerwear, including hooded jackets and sweatshirts. Strings can get caught on playground equipment or other things like school bus doors. They are a strangulation hazard.

Also, check the drawstrings at the waistbands and bottoms of children's outerwear in sizes 2T to 16. The strings should extend no more than three inches from the garment when it's expanded to its fullest width. A waist drawstring should be sewn to the garment at its midpoint so the string can't be pulled to one side, making it long enough to catch on playground equipment.

Purchase children's jackets and sweatshirts that have snaps, buttons, Velcro, or elastic at the neck and waist. Finally, remove toggles or knots at the ends of all drawstrings, which can also invite trouble.

your baby at risk. Snug-fitting sleepwear looks tight, but it stretches. It must have a prominent warning on the label that states: Wear snug-fitting, not flame resistant.

For infants, we recommend a wearable blanket, or sleep sack, to replace loose blankets in your baby's crib. Sleep sacks don't fit snugly; there's plenty of kicking room. They're typically made of flame-resistant fabric, but check the garment's label to be sure. For more on sleep sacks, see the "Crib Bedding" chapter, page 143.

Recommendations

When stocking up on basics before your baby arrives, purchase very little in newborn size. Your baby will outgrow these tiny garments fast—sometimes in less than a month. It's more practical to buy in the 3- to 6-month or 6- to 9-month size. If saving money is your mission, do most of your shopping post-baby showers and after friends and relatives respond to your birth announcement. Then fill in any gaps in your baby's wardrobe and buy as she grows.

Consider safety. Be wary of tiny buttons, hooks, snaps, pompoms, bows, and appliqués. They can be choking hazards. Routinely check clothes and fasteners for these loose items. Avoid loosely knitted clothes—sweaters, booties, or hats—that look like they might trap a baby's tiny fingers or toes. Cut all dangling threads before your baby wears a garment and avoid clothing that has seams with very few stitches per inch.

Before you put socks or booties on your baby, turn them inside out to look for small threads that could capture toes.

Low-price and mid-price garments often have soft but sturdy fabrics, competent workmanship, and plenty of fashion flair. And they're usually machine washable—a definite plus. Upscale baby clothes cost more (sometimes amazingly more) than standard garments, without a proportionate increase in quality and durability. If you buy such clothes, you're doing it for style. High-fashion clothes may require hand laundering, even dry cleaning. (Air out any dry-cleaned clothes before your baby wears them.) Remember that your baby will quickly outgrow anything you buy. And no matter how carefully you monitor, he will spill on everything as he becomes more mobile.

Recall Reminder

Baby garments are occasionally recalled because of safety hazards such as snaps that come off or sleepwear that's marketed as flame-resistant when it's really not. For updated recall information on infant products, consult monthly issues of CONSUMER REPORTS or visit the Consumer Product Safety Commission's Web site at *www.recalls.gov* or *www .cpsc.gov*. To report a dangerous product or a product-related injury, call CPSC's hotline at (800) 638-2772 or CPSC's teletypewriter at (800) 638-8270, or visit CPSC's Web site at *www.cpsc.gov/talk.html.*

CHAPTER

12

Cribs

O f all the items on your baby-shopping list, a crib probably will be among the most challenging to select. There's a vast array of cribs on the market, ranging from economy and midpriced models to high-end cribs with hand-painted details and European influences that up the style ante. Whether your baby sleeps in a crib from the get-go or starts with a bassinet or cradle (an alternative for your baby's first four months or so), you'll want a crib that's durable and safe and matches your tastes and budget.

Basic Is Best

When you're crib shopping, you may be tempted to buy the showiest model, and bumper guards and coverlets that say your nursery is fit for a prince or princess. Resist the temptation. The safest cribs are basic; they have simple lines and no scrollwork or finials—infants can strangle if their clothing gets caught in such detail work. Heeding this advice will get you a safer crib and it will save you money.

According to the American Academy of Pediatrics, the best sleeping arrangement for a newborn is a full-size crib or safety-approved bassinet or cradle; it advises keeping your baby's crib, cradle, or bassinet in your bedroom until she's at least 6 months old. After that, it's fine to move the crib to the nursery. But we think full-size cribs, which are federally regulated, are better than bassinets and cradles, for which there are only voluntary standards (see "Crib Alternatives" chapter, starting on page 137).

Shopping Secrets

Buy new. If possible, avoid buying or accepting a used crib. Older models may not meet current safety standards or may be in disrepair. If you must use an older crib, avoid those built before 2000, about a year after the latest voluntary standards for slat-attachment strength took effect. (Check the manufacture date on the crib label, which is required by law.) Currently, 12 states have laws banning the sale of unsafe used cribs or prohibiting their use in child-care facilities. Your state may have such a law.

Decide about drop sides. Do you want a crib with both sides that drop so that you can get your baby from either side, a crib with one side that drops, or one with stationary sides? Deciding first about drop sides will narrow the selection and make shopping easier. If you're considering a crib with no drop sides—the most stable approach—be sure to test models in the store. Cribs with stationary sides have less hardware (less chance of missing or broken parts), but if you are not tall, it can be hard to get your baby. Use the mattress' lowest setting to see how easy it is for you to bend in and pick up your baby.

If you're shopping for a crib with drop sides, operate them in the store to make sure they raise and lower smoothly and quietly. Models that open with a lift-and-leg-press action or those with a lift-and-foot-release mechanism (see "Features to Consider," on page 132) can usually be operated with one hand—an advantage when you've got a baby in the other. Still, you'll probably raise and lower the side of the crib only during the first few months. Once babies get bigger and stand up in the crib, many parents pick them up without lowering the side. So a crib that doesn't have the best drop-side mechanism but is satisfactory in other ways can still be a good option. Of course, if the crib will be against a wall, you'll have no use for a second drop side.

Check construction and workmanship. The simplest in-store test is to shake the crib slightly to see if the frame seems loose. But be aware that display models aren't always as tightly assembled as they could be. Without applying excessive pressure, try rotating each slat to see if it's well secured to the railings. You shouldn't find loose bars on a new crib.

Look for the JPMA sticker. Manufacturers in the Juvenile Products Manufacturers Association certification program are required to adhere to voluntary and mandatory standards. Look for the JPMA sticker on the crib or packaging. JPMA currently certifies the following full-size cribs brands: Astro Child, Avalon Products, Baby's Dream Furniture, Bassett Furniture Industries, Bella D'Este Ltd., Bellini, Child Craft, Delta Enterprise, Dorel Juvenile Group, Evenflo, Ever Bright International, Homelegance by Topline Furniture, Jardine Enterprise, NettoCollection, Pt. Domusindo Perdana, Simmons Juvenile Furniture, Simplicity, Stork Craft, Young America, and Yu Wei Co. Ltd. For the very latest JPMA certified full-size cribs, log on to *www.jpma.org* and click on "Certification Program" under the "Consumer" heading.

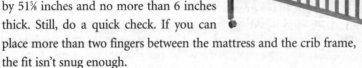

Buy the mattress at the same time. In the store, pair the mattress and crib you plan to buy to make sure they're a good fit. (Mattresses typically are sold separately.) By law, a mattress used in a full-size crib must be at least 27¼ inches by 51⅝ inches and no more than 6 inches thick. Still, do a quick check. If you can place more than two fingers between the mattress and the crib frame, the fit isn't snug enough.

What's Available

Major brands of cribs include, in alphabetical order: Angel Line (*www.angelline.com*), Bellini (*www.bellini.com*), Bonavita (*www.bona vita-cribs.com*), Child Craft (makers of Child Craft and Legacy cribs, *www.childcraftindustries.com*), Da Vinci (can be found online at e-tailers such as *www.dreamtimebaby.com* and *www.babyuniverse.com*), Delta Enterprise (*www.deltaenterprise.com*), Dorel Juvenile Group (*www.djgusa.com*, also at Cosco), Nursery Smart (*www.nurserysmart.com*), Simmons Kids (*www.simmonskids.com*), Simplicity (*www.simplicityforchildren.com*), Sorelle (*www.sorellefurniture.com*),

WHAT NOT TO BUY OR USE

Heirloom cribs. According to the Juvenile Products Manufacturers Association, approximately 50 babies each year suffocate or strangle after becoming trapped between broken crib parts or in cribs with older, unsafe designs. The JPMA advises consumers to buy a new crib rather than use an heirloom or a secondhand one, even if your budget is tight—or the crib has been in your family for three generations. Old or heirloom cribs can also have lead-based paint.

Co-sleepers. These beds allow infants to sleep near their parents for bonding and nursing. The Bedside Co-Sleeper by Arm's Reach Concepts, $200, for example, attaches to an adult bed with belts, giving a mom easy access to her infant. But the Consumer Product Safety Commission hasn't established safety standards for these products, so the American Academy of Pediatrics doesn't recommend them. In general, the AAP advises against co-sleeping and bed-sharing. If you bring your baby into your bed for nursing, return him to his own bed when he's done.

Sleep positioners. These wedge-shape pieces of foam (below) are designed to help babies sleep on their backs. Pediatricians and child safety experts caution against putting anything cushioned in a crib because soft materials could close off the child's air passages, causing suffocation. Don't believe store displays for these products. They give the wrong message. The AAP says that while various devices have been developed to maintain sleep position or to reduce the risk of rebreathing (inhaling exhaled carbon dioxide rather than fresh air, which increases the risk of Sudden Infant Death Syndrome), such devices are not recommended because none has been tested sufficiently to show efficacy or safety.

Soft bedding. The safest crib is one that has a firm mattress, a snug-fitting mattress pad, and a fitted crib sheet—and nothing else; no puffy bumper guards, no stuffed animals, no pillows, no quilts. Experts have long recognized the suffocation risk inherent in such soft crib bedding. If you insist on a blanket, keep it at waist height, and tuck the ends firmly under the sides and bottom of the mattress. There should be no loose blankets in your baby's sleep area. If that sounds tough to manage (babies have been known to kick off their blanket), dress your baby in a footed sleeper, with layers underneath, such as a lighter-weight sleeper for warmth, or put your baby to sleep in a wearable blanket (left), such as the Halo SleepSack, $29.95 (*www.halosleep.com*), or the Kiddopotamus BeddieBye sleep blanket, $15 to $20 (*www.kiddopotamus.com*). If you decide to use crib bumpers, they should be thin, firm, and securely tied. Mesh bumpers are a very good option.

Stanley Furniture (*www.stanley furniture.com*), Stokke (*www.stokke usa.com*), Storkcraft (*www.storkcraft .com*), and Westwood Design (*www.westwoodbaby.com*). Crib prices range from $100 for economy models to over $3,000 for convertible custom models. While good values can be found, cribs are getting more expensive. In general, paying more will get you better quality in the finish, wood, design, and operating mechanism. Still, price and quality don't necessarily correlate. You can find good-quality cribs at the lowest end. Here's more on what you'll get at the various price points.

Economy cribs ($100 to $199). Models at the low end of the price scale can be adequate. Prices are low because manufacturers use less expensive materials and simpler finishes and designs. These models tend to be lighter than top-of-the-line cribs. White or pastel paint or shiny lacquer-like finish may cover wood defects, such as knots and variations in shading. You may notice minor finishing flaws, such as poorly sanded rough spots, uneven patches of paint, and the heads of metal brads or glue residue at the base of the slats. On a low-priced model, typically only one side of the crib can be released. The metal mattress support hooks at each corner may be loose. The springs supporting the mattress are lighter in construction than those in pricier models. When you shake the crib, make sure it is sturdy, not rattly.

Midpriced cribs ($200 to $499). At this price level, it becomes increasingly difficult to discern quality differences from brand to brand. You'll find a lot in this price range. These models are sturdier and more decorative than economy models. They come in an array of wood finishes, from Scandinavian-style natural to golden maple and oak shades, reddish-brown cherries, and deep mahoganies. End boards may be solid and smoothly finished, and many models have slats on all sides. The gentle curves of the end boards are well finished with rounded edges. Slats are thicker than those of economy models and may be

HOW LONG SHOULD YOUR BABY SLEEP IN A CRIB?

For safety's sake, monitor your child's development closely and stop using a crib as soon as your toddler can climb out. At that point, consider a bed with child railings or put the mattress on the floor. Don't put your child back into the crib after the first "escape," regardless of his age. A child attempting to climb out of a crib can fall and be seriously injured.

round or flat, with rounded edges. The mattress supports on these models tend to be sturdy, the springs heavier. These cribs have single, double, or no drop sides. Locking wheels or casters (sometimes optional) provide stability. There may be one or two stabilizer bars—metal rods that extend between the two end rods—running underneath for greater rigidity. The best-made cribs in this category have recessed guides—a grooved channel in each end board for the drop side, no exposed brads or glue residue where the slats are fastened to the rails, and a uniform finish. They may have extra-high posts, canopies, or a storage drawer underneath.

In this price range you'll find cribs that convert into other configurations. One type, typically called a 3-in-1 crib, converts to a daybed and to a full size bed. You'll also find 4-in-1 cribs that convert to a toddler bed, a daybed, and a full-size bed. The most versatile cribs can become a toddler bed, a full-size bed and a love seat.

High-end cribs ($500 and up). These models, many of them imported from Europe, have hand-rubbed, glazed, or burnished finishes. You'll see round cribs (still a novelty, though they've been around awhile), sleigh styles with curved end boards and hand-painted details, and models handcrafted from wrought iron. These cribs may have single, double, or no drop sides. On some with drop sides, the hardware is recessed and may be so well hidden that it's difficult to tell if the side lowers. The mattress is supported by heavy-gauge springs and heavyweight metal frames and may adjust to four heights. These cribs may include a drawer and convert to a daybed/toddler bed or other nursery furniture. At the highest end, you'll find custom-made regular and convertible cribs that may be sold as part of a nursery suite; a fairy-tale canopy may be part of the ensemble.

Features to Consider

Convertibility. Consider buying a crib that converts to a toddler bed only if you don't plan to have more children soon. Otherwise, you'll need the crib for your next baby and never get the chance to convert it. Consider buying a convertible crib if you don't mind ending up with a toddler bed that's very crib-like. Many convertible cribs can be switched to a "big girl" or "big boy" bed simply by removing one drop side; the basic look of the crib remains. On the other hand, some parents report that the change from a crib to a toddler bed is so small that toddlers have an easier time making the transition. Finally, keep in

Check all crib hardware from time to time and replace anything that's loose. Missing and loose parts are a leading cause of accidents and death because they can create gaps where a baby can wedge his head and neck, and suffocate or strangle. Tighten all nuts, bolts, and screws. Check mattress support attachments regularly to make sure none is bent or broken. If you move a crib, double-check that all support hangers are secure.

mind that some convertible beds require parts that typically aren't included in the original purchase, such as bed rails, stabilizing rails, or support rails (for converting to a full-size bed).

The Stokke Sleepi (*www.stokkeusa.com*) is a crib that grows with your child. It converts to a toddler bed, and can be extended to accommodate kids up to age 7. After that, the bed can be transformed into two stylish chairs for kids, tweens, and teens.

Bottom drawer. Some models include a drawer or two under the mattress support structure. Under-crib drawers usually are not attached to the crib frame. Some are freestanding and roll out from under the crib on casters. Some cribs have a set of drawers attached to the short end of the unit. Before buying, pull any drawer all the way out to inspect its construction. You may find that it has a thin, cardboard-like bottom that could bow and give way when loaded with linens or clothing. A drawer bottom made of a harder material, such as fiberboard, is more likely to hold up.

Drop sides. The newest cribs with drop sides have relatively quiet releases that require you to lift the rail while you push the release with your leg. The older design requires you to lift the side while pressing a metal lever or tab under the railing with your foot. The foot maneuver is awkward because you have to stand on one leg to do it. Metal components often rattle and squeak. A third, though rare, type of release mechanism has latches at each end of the top rail that must be pulled out at the same time. Federal regulations require that lowering mechanisms be built to prevent accidental release by a baby or sibling.

Finish. Cribs with dark wood finishes are available,

LOCATION, LOCATION, LOCATION

Place your baby's crib well away from windows, window blinds, wall hangings, curtains, toys, and other furniture so that an adventurous baby can't get at anything dangerous.

although cribs in lighter stains such as natural wood, oaks, and maples tend to be more popular. White, however, remains the most common crib color. Other painted colors include off-whites, washed whites (revealing the wood's grain), and pastel green, blue, pink, or yellow. A little roughness in the finish isn't a problem as long as there are no serious defects such as splintering or peeling paint.

Mattress height. All full-size cribs have at least two mattress height positions; more expensive models have three or four. To prevent your baby from falling out of the crib, adjust the mattress support to its lowest height as soon as she can sit or pull up, usually between 6 and 8 months of age. Many models don't require tools for adjusting mattress height; in some models, screws or bolts are hard to reach.

Mattress supports. Most mattress supports consist of a metal frame with springs. In some cribs, the mattress support is a one-piece board; in others, it's a grid with wood slats. The mattress supports are adjustable so the mattress can be raised or lowered, depending on the size of the child. Mattress supports need to be held securely in place so they aren't dislodged when you're changing a crib sheet or when another child or large pet pushes up from underneath.

Sides and railings. Crib sides are constructed by fitting bars (or spindles or slats) into holes in the top and bottom rails, then securing each bar with glue and one or two metal brads. The small holes made by the brads are usually filled and covered with a finish so they're invisible. A mandatory safety standard requires that crib slats be no more than 2⅜ inches apart, so slat spacing shouldn't be an issue. Corner posts or finials should be no higher than 1/16 inches.

Structural integrity. Sturdiness is a sign of construction quality. One or more stabilizer bars—metal rods fastened to both end boards beneath the crib—help make the frame more rigid.

Teething rails. These are smooth, plastic coverings for the top of the side rails to protect the crib and a gnawing baby's gums. The voluntary industry standard says teething rails should be built to stay in place and not crack or break.

SAFER SLEEPING

To reduce the risk of Sudden Infant Death Syndrome (SIDS)—the sudden, inexplicable death of an infant under 1 year of age—always place your baby to sleep on her back (unless your pediatrician advises otherwise) at naptime and nighttime in a crib that meets all safety standards and has a firm, tight-fitting mattress. Children who sleep on their stomachs have the highest likelihood of SIDS. In fact, since the beginning of the "Back to Sleep" campaign in 1992, which recommended that babies sleep on their backs with no soft bedding in the sleep area, SIDS rates have dropped by more than 50 percent. Some studies suggest that breast-feeding also appears to decrease the risk of SIDS. Here are other ways to keep your baby safe during a snooze:

- **Don't dress your baby too warmly.** Overheating may be a contributor to SIDS. Keep the temperature in your baby's room between 68 and 72°F. Your baby shouldn't feel hot to the touch.
- **Consider using a pacifier at naptime and bedtime.** If your baby is breast-fed, wait to introduce a pacifier until 1 month of age, after breast-feeding is firmly established. But if your baby doesn't want a pacifier, don't force him to take it. Begin weaning your baby off the pacifier after his first birthday.
- **Replace loose crib blankets with a wearable sleep sack.**
- **Ban smoking around your baby and don't smoke while you're pregnant.** Exposure to cigarette smoke in the womb and after your baby is born increases the risk of SIDS.
- **Don't put your baby to sleep on a waterbed, sofa, sheepskin, quilt, soft mattress, pillow, or bean bag chair.** The fluffy bedding materials and soft surfaces can allow a dangerous buildup of carbon dioxide from the baby's own breathing. Rebreathing exhaled carbon dioxide has been identified as a potential cause of SIDS.
- **Remove all soft, fluffy, or loose bedding and other items from your baby's crib,** including decorative pillows and stuffed animals.
- **Don't let your baby share your bed.** In addition to the risk that you might roll onto your baby, adult beds pose other hazards. Your baby could get trapped between the bed and a wall, headboard, bed frame, or other object. Accidental suffocation in soft bedding is another danger, or the baby could fall off the bed. If you breast-feed your baby in bed, be sure to return her to the crib afterward.
- **Position the crib away from windows, window blinds, wall hangings, and draperies.** Children can strangle on the cords.
- **Don't use an electric blanket, heating pad, or even a warm water bottle to heat your baby's crib.** An infant's skin is highly heat-sensitive and can be burned by temperatures comfortable to an adult.
- **Buy a new crib; a safe crib doesn't have to be expensive.**
- **Don't use a crib with loose, broken, or missing slats, spindles or finials,** or hardware, cut-out designs in the headboard or footboard, cracked or peeling paint, splinters or rough edges. And don't try to repair the crib yourself, or jimmy-rig it with string or shoe laces.
- **Educate your parents and other caregivers** who may be with your baby at naptime or nighttime about these safe sleeping tips.

Wheels/casters. Plastic or metal crib wheels can be standard rollers or round, multidirectional, ball-shape casters that swivel and make it easier to haul a crib from one room to another. Not all cribs come with them, which isn't an issue if your crib won't be venturing out of the nursery. If your baby's crib will be on bare wood or tile floors and you choose a crib with wheels, make sure they lock to prevent the crib from "walking" across the room—and the other children from taking baby on a joy ride when your back is turned.

Recommendations

Buy a new, full-size crib made after 2000 that is JPMA-certified or certified to meet the American Society for Testing and Materials (ASTM) voluntary standards (ASTM F-1169 and ASTM F-966). Certification assures you that the crib conforms to the latest federal and voluntary safety standards. Still, be on the lookout for safety hazards. Even when you're buying new, take along a soda can when you shop. If you can pass the can between the slats, they're too far apart. Check for sharp edges and protruding screws, nuts, corner posts, decorative knobs, and other pieces that could catch a baby's clothing at the neck. Buying new will help protect your baby from hidden dangers such as drop sides, slats, or hardware that may have been weakened by rough use, or excessive dampness or heat during storage. By law, the production date of the crib has to be displayed both on the crib and on its shipping carton.

Cribs are shipped unassembled, so if you're not certain you can put a crib together correctly (typically a two-person job that requires a full hour—from unpacking to complete assembly), ask the retailer to send a qualified assembly crew to your home. This can cost an extra $70 or more unless assembly is included in the retail price, but it can give you valuable peace of mind. Besides saving tempers and fingers, having the store assemble the crib allows you to inspect it on the spot—and reject it if you discover flaws.

If you assemble the crib, put it together where your baby will be sleeping initially, such as in your bedroom (recommended for your baby's first six months). Once it's put together, the crib may not fit through a small door, and you may need to dissemble and reassemble it again in your baby's nursery six months later. That's not convenient, but you'll have the reassurance that your baby is sleeping in the safest possible place.

13

Crib Alternatives

For the first four to five months of your baby's life, you have some alternatives to a crib, including bassinets, Moses baskets, co-sleepers, cradles, and portable cribs (play yards). They seem to offer a cozy nest near a parent's bed, as a newborn or young infant might seem more at home in a compact space than in a large, airy crib. But as we mentioned in the "Cribs" chapter, we think the best beds for babies are full-size cribs, which are federally regulated, which means they're subject to mandatory safety standards that manufacturers must follow when making cribs.

If they don't comply, the product can be recalled from the market under the Federal Hazardous Substances Act. There are also American Society for Testing and Materials (ASTM) voluntary safety standards for full-size cribs, which most manufacturers also use as a guideline.

Bassinets and cradles are subject to an ASTM voluntary safety standard (juvenile products that don't comply with a voluntary standard can be recalled if the Consumer Product Safety Commission considers them a safety hazard), but are not subject to any mandatory federal safety standards. That's why we advocate full-size cribs over bassinets and cradles, which are the products we'll focus on in this chapter.

A bassinet is a compact baby bed made of fabric, wicker, or woven wooden splints; some come with wheels and can usually be moved easily from room to room. Many have a rigid hood that can be attached on one end to block light.

Cradles are bassinets that rock from side to side. Both types of baby beds take up little space. As we mentioned in the "Cribs" chapter, the American Academy of Pediatrics (AAP) recommends sharing a room, not a bed, with your baby for his first six months. A full-size crib could go in your bedroom initially, but if you're short on space, a bassinet or cradle (some do double duty) is your next best bet. A bouncer seat, a swing, or a play yard with a bassinet insert are acceptable for an impromptu snooze, provided none has any loose fabric, which is a suffocation hazard. And don't add loose fabric, such as a blanket, comforter, or any type of pillow or stuffed animal.

A co-sleeper is an infant bed that attaches to an adult bed. Because safety standards for co-sleepers haven't been established, the AAP doesn't recommend them, and we don't either. And because there are no safety standards for Moses baskets—a basket with a bottom pad and puffy fabric sides with handles, designed so you can easily tote your baby from room to room—we don't recommend Moses baskets either.

Shopping Secrets

Look for the Juvenile Products Manufacturers Association (JPMA) seal. Bassinets have had some safety issues—rough, sharp inside edges and soft sides that can trap a baby. (The soft, thin mattress found in most models is designed to reduce the hazard of suffocation.) The hinged legs on folding bassinets have been known to give way accidentally. Fortunately, safety standards were updated by ASTM in 2006, and are the basis of JPMA certification, which signals that a product meets those voluntary safety standards. Buy new and look for the following manufacturers, which carry the JPMA certification seal: Amby Baby, Kolcraft, Scandinavian Child, Simplicity for Children, and The First Years.

If you opt for a cradle, go with one that barely rocks.
Cradles with a pronounced rocking motion can press a tiny baby against the side of the unit, which can pose a safety hazard. Look for a model with a frame suspended on hooks, or with locking hardware to stabilize the rocking motion so the cradle won't tilt too much.

Consider a bassinet or cradle as only a quick fix. Once your baby begins to push up on his hands and knees or reaches the manufacturer's maximum weight (usually 15 to 18 pounds, but sometimes as high as 25 pounds), whichever comes first, it's time to move him to a crib. Although you won't believe it when you bring your baby home, he'll soon be busting out of his bassinet; some babies run out of leg and headroom in just three quick months. So factor that into your budget and buying decision.

What's Available

Major brands of bassinets and cradles are, in alphabetical order: Amby Baby (*www.ambybaby.com*), Badger Basket (*www.badger basket.com*), Eddie Bauer (*www.djgusa.com*), Kolcraft (*www.kolcraft .com*), Posh Tots (*www.poshtots.com*), Scandinavian Child (*www .scichild.com*), Simplicity for Children (*www.simplicityforchildren.com*), and The First Years (*www.thefirstyears.com*). Prices range from $40 for basic bassinets to $800 (and more) for custom-made deluxe bassinets decked out with elegant, flowing bed skirts and decorative ruffles and bows, or intricate wooden or ornate iron cradles. In general, you'll find a lot to choose from in the basic to slightly upgraded range—$70 to $175.

The hammock cradle, also known as a motion bed, by Amby Baby ($238), which is certified by JPMA, can be used for babies up to 25 pounds. Its angled, slightly upright sleeping position is designed to help babies suffering from colic and reflux.

Features to Consider

Convertibility. Most bassinets convert into impromptu changing tables and many include pockets or storage underneath for diapers, wipes, and so on. Simply fold down the canopy so you have the entire bed to use as a changing surface; the sides protect your baby from rolling. Some bassinets can be converted into cradles with a quick-release latch and retractable wheels, allowing the unit to rock. Others can become a co-sleeper that attaches to an adult bed, but again, we do

BASSINET AND CRADLE SAFETY

Here are more safety considerations to keep in mind:
• Say no to an heirloom cradle or bassinet. It's a quaint idea to use one that's been in the family for generations, but chances are it isn't up to today's safety standards.
• Don't leave your baby unattended in a rocking cradle. Use the hardware to stop the rocking motion before your baby's bed and naptime, and around pets and toddlers.
• If you carry or move a bassinet or cradle, do it without your child in it.
• Use only the mattress or pad provided by the manufacturer and only the fitted sheet made for the bassinet, and put your baby to sleep in a wearable blanket (swaddle sack) instead of covering him with a blanket. For more information on sleep sacks, see "Crib Bedding," page 143.
• Don't add any bedding, such as a mattress, pillow, comforter, or padding, to your baby's bassinet or cradle.
• Don't let strings, toys suspended from a mobile, or window blind or curtain cords hang into the bassinet. Position the mobile so your baby can't reach it. Don't worry; it will still stimulate him. And don't add any suspended toys on your own. Use only those provided with the product. Shorten window blinds by cutting the looped cords in half and keep them out of your baby's reach.
• To reduce the risk of Sudden Infant Death Syndrome, place your baby on her back in a cradle or bassinet, just as you would in a full-size crib.

not recommend that option. Some bassinets even morph into other useful items, such as a toy box, when your baby has outgrown the bassinet function.

Portability. Some bassinets have a handle so you can carry it from room to room, to keep your baby nearby. Others have functioning wheels so you can roll the entire unit around.

Toys. You may also find bassinets/cradles with a detachable mobile or a canopy with attached toys to amuse your baby and stimulate his sense of sight.

Sound effects, vibration, light. Music or nature sounds with volume control and vibration are also popular features that can be embedded in a mobile and activated by remote control or the touch of a key pad. These extras can soothe a fussy baby—or not. "Vibration just seemed to annoy my baby, so we didn't use that, and the sound didn't last long enough—only five minutes—to get our baby to sleep," says Jennifer Hancock of Ellenton, Fla., the mother of one. But all was not lost. Her son, who is now 1, slept in a bassinet for his first two months and Jennifer is still using it as a changing table. Some bassinets feature a soft-glow night-light so you can peek on your baby without disturbing him. That's a plus. These extras usually run on AA batteries (not included).

Shape. Most bassinets and cradles are rectangular, but at least one manufacturer we know of (Badger Basket) makes an oval bassinet. We're not sure this shape offers any advantages, except as a style statement or conversation piece.

Bedding. Most bassinets/cradles have a mattress pad—which, according to the voluntary industry standard, should be no thicker than 1½ inches—and a fitted sheet. Most bassinets also have fabric lining. You'll pay more for bassinets with a liner with an attached pleated or ruffled hood, or a bed skirt that cascades to the floor. At the highest end, these extras can be custom made. Popular bassinet and cradle bedding fabrics are toile, vintage florals, gingham, white eyelet, and colorful checks and plaids. No matter what look you go for, choose bedding that's machine washable.

Canopy. A canopy can help block light—so you can read before bedtime, for example, without waking your baby. It may be retractable or removable, which creates more usable space if you'll be changing your baby in the bassinet.

Storage. A bottom storage basket is useful for stashing a change of clothes, booties, toys, diapers, and wipes. A flowing bed skirt can block access, so get a bassinet with a short skirt.

Recommendations

First, decide whether or not you truly need a bassinet or cradle. If the crib you've selected fits in your bedroom, consider having your baby sleep in that from day one, then shift the crib into the nursery when your baby is 6 months old or so. If you do want a bassinet or cradle, consider how you'll use it and how portable you'll need it to be. If you just want a place for your baby to sleep nearby at night, buy a basic model, preferably one that's JPMA certified. (View other bassinets and cradles with some caution. Most likely they're also in compliance with the voluntary safety standard, but unless they've been officially JPMA certified, you can't be sure.)

Look for a model with a sturdy bottom and a wide, stable base. There should be no sharp points or edges on the inside or outside, or small parts that could be a choking hazard. If the bassinet or cradle is made of wood, it should be free of splinters. Check any folding mechanisms.

If the legs or frame collapse for storage, make sure they lock into place when the unit is set up. Make sure the mattress and padding are smooth and extra firm, and fit snugly. The mattress pad should be no more than 1½ inches thick.

Use only a fitted sheet provided by the manufacturer or one specifically designed to fit the dimension of the mattress. Buy at least three fitted sheets so you have one to use, one for the wash, and one as a backup. Don't use a pillowcase or another size sheet as a substitute. If you need any parts, get them from the same company that made the cradle or bassinet. To order, check the instruction manual.

Abide by the manufacturer's weight and size specifications and stop using the product when it's time. There are usually warnings on the product, sometimes a lot of them. A note about assembly: Some bassinets have as many as 13 parts, and you may need a Phillips screwdriver and a good half hour to put the puzzle together. Bassinets and cradles have a short life span. If budget is a consideration, it doesn't make sense to splurge on this item. Cradles and bassinets, especially those embellished with a flowing skirt and bows, can pull on your heartstrings but dent your pocketbook. Such window dressing is nice, but definitely not necessary.

CHAPTER
14

Crib Bedding

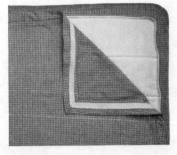

Right up there on the excitement scale with creating your list of baby names is pondering the endless possibilities for making your baby's room special. Some expectant parents even learn the gender of their baby ahead of time just so they can get an early start on decorating! Making a big deal out of the baby's room is part of the fun of parenthood (although you can certainly be low-key if you wish). From a fantasy room that clearly stands apart to a subdued space that blends with the décor in your house, your baby's nursery can be anything you want.

A logical place to start in designing your baby's room is with the crib bedding, blanket, and crib skirt. Then choose paint or wallpaper and other accessories, such as the fabric for your rocking chair, based on those colors and patterns. It's often much easier to start with the crib linens and then paint or wallpaper. But as you know from the Cribs chapter, to guard against suffocation, we recommend keeping your baby's crib simple—just a tight fitted sheet, and maybe a crib skirt/dust ruffle for a touch of style. If you want to use a bumper, make sure it's thin, firm, securely tied and meshy, not puffy or padded. Instead of blankets or quilts, we recommend dressing your baby in a one-piece bunting. If you use a blanket, keep it at waist height and tuck ends firmly under the sides and bottom of the mattress.

A fitted sheet and a crib skirt aren't much to work with, but they can get your creative juices flowing. Colors and styles of fitted crib sheets and crib dust ruffles run the gamut—from bears, boats, barnyard animals, and bunnies, to prints, checks, florals, toile, and stripes in bold and muted tones. Consider coordinating them with the window treatments. Besides conventional fabrics like 100 percent traditional cotton, you'll find fitted sheets in soft, organic cotton, cotton fleece, flannel, and T-shirtish cotton knit.

Though they often come in sets or "collections," crib linens are also sold individually, though you may have to look for these separates. And if anything but a "fully loaded" crib (with luxurious, cushy bumpers and so on) leaves you feeling decoratively deprived, think of how you'll rest easier knowing your baby is sleeping in a safe place.

CHEAT SHEET

Warning: Changing a fitted crib sheet, even it's not in the middle of the night after a leaky diaper debacle, falls into the category of *who knew it would be this hard?* There must be an easier way–and we're happy to report there is, but it will cost you slightly more than conventional sheets.

The QuickZip crib sheet by Clouds and Stars (*www.cloudsandstars.com*) is designed to the make sheet changing hassle-free. This fitted sheet completely encases the mattress. A removable top panel zips onto the base with a single, covered zipper. To change the sheet, just unzip and change the top panel. The QuickZip Sheet Set retails for roughly $34.99 on the Clouds and Stars Web site (there are periodic sales). The sheets are also available at specialty retailers such as Buy Buy Baby (*www.buybuybaby .com*). Top sheet panels, sold separately, start at $12.74.

WHAT NOT TO BUY

Remember, bare is best. The safest crib is one that has a firm mattress that meets the federally mandated measurements of 27¼ inches by 51⅝ inches and is no more than six inches thick. It has a snug-fitting mattress pad and fitted crib sheet—and nothing else. Don't buy puffy or padded bumper guards, stuffed animals, pillows, quilts, or a duvet for your baby's crib. Experts have long recognized the suffocation risk inherent in such soft crib bedding.

If you choose to use a crib bumper, make sure it's meshy, thin, firm, and securely tied. Be sure to remove a bumper as soon as your baby can pull up to a standing position so he can't use it as a stepping stool to climb out. The bumper should fit around the entire crib and tie or snap securely in at least six locations. Bumper ties should be no more than 7 inches long.

What's Available

Major brands of crib sheets and dust ruffles, and retailers that sell them separately (not part of a set), are, in alphabetical order: American Baby Company (*www.ababycompany.com*), Amy Coe (*www.amycoe.com*), Babylicious (*www.babylicious.ca*), Baby Martex (*www.martex.com*), Baby Style (*www.babystyle.com*), Basic Comfort (*www.basiccomfort .com*), Carter's (*www.carters.com*), Clouds and Stars (*www.cloudsand stars.com*), Halo (*www.halosleep.com*), Kidsline (*www.kidslineinc.com*), The Land of Nod (*www.landofnod.com*), Laura Ashley (*www.lauraashley.com*), Pottery Barn Kids (*www .potterybarnkids.com*), and Shabby Chic (*www.shabbychic.com*). Prices for fitted crib sheets range from $5.99 to $70. Prices for crib dust ruffles range from $16 to $120.

Bedding 101

Here's a rundown of what you'll need to outfit your baby's crib:

Mattress pad. Buy two waterproof mattress pads so you can have one as a backup. These quilted pads should be thin—one inch or less in thickness. They're usually made of cotton or a synthetic material and should cover the mattress securely. Most, like fitted sheets, have elastic all the way around. Never use a plastic bag as a mattress cover. Plastic is a suffocation hazard.

Fitted sheet. Most crib sheets have fitted corners, which keep them secure. Fabrics range from woven cottons and cotton blends to lightweight flannel. Two to three should get you off to a good start.

IT'S TUMMY TIME

Even though you shouldn't use a coverlet (blanket) or comforter in your baby's crib, a blanket or comforter can come in handy as a play mat or exercise pad for tummy time under your watchful supervision. Tummy time—the time your baby spends on the floor during the day doing "push-ups"—helps your baby develop upper body coordination and posture and neck strength, prerequisites for crawling and other physical skills.

Don't use fitted sheets that are loose or bunchy; they should fit your baby's crib mattress like a skin.

A swaddle wrap. This sleep sack is made for infants as an alternative to a receiving blanket (a very thin blanket typically made of woven cotton used for swaddling), though that's also an option. A swaddle wrap slips over a regular sleeper or diaper and has plenty of room for little legs to stretch and kick. Use a swaddle wrap or receiving blanket to swaddle your newborn during nap and nighttime for the first few months. Buy a half-dozen waffle-weave receiving blankets made of 100 percent cotton for good absorbency (or put them on your shower gift list), or four swaddle wraps. Leading swaddle wraps are the 2-in-1 SleepSack Swaddle by Halo (*www.halosleep.com*), $29.95, which is recommended by First Candle/SIDS Alliance (an organization that provides information on Sudden Infant Death Syndrome and ways to reduce the risk of infant death), and the Original 2-in-1 Swaddler & Sleep Sack by Swaddleaze (*www.2virtues.com*), $25. Both brands convert to a conventional sleeveless sleep sack when your baby no longer needs swaddling. Look for flame-resistant fabric, such as polyester. Use it instead of a crib blanket (not recommended).

Wearable blanket. After your baby outgrows his swaddler, he'll be ready for a regular sleep sack, a wearable blanket that goes over a regular sleeper or diaper, with lots of leg room for stretching and kicking. Popular brands are the Halo SleepSack, which usually retails for $20 (and is recommended by the First Candle/SIDS Alliance, *www.halosleep.com*), the Back to Sleep Sack by Prince LionHeart ($21.99, *www.princelionsheart.com*), and the BeddieBye wearable blanket by Kiddopotamus ($15 to $20, *www.kiddopotamus.com*). Look for flame-resistant fabric.

Crib skirt. It's not necessary, but it does add design flair to the crib and your baby's room.

NURSERY DECORATING DOS AND DON'TS

Don't limit yourself to linens. A crib skirt or fitted sheet can set the style and tone for your baby's nursery. But you can also pull a color scheme from a patterned rug, which, incidentally, helps camouflage stains and spills. A piece of artwork can be your creative catalyst, and it doesn't have to be a pricey oil painting. An inexpensive poster will do. "Or, if you have older children, involve them in decorating the baby's room by having them paint or draw a picture that you mat and frame," suggests Suzanne Morrissey, the editor of *Kids' Rooms Etc.* "If you have your heart set on certain colors, just give them those colors of markers or paint to work with."

Do design the nursery to fit your taste. "Don't be afraid to depart from pastels," says Serena Dugan, co-CEO and designer of Serena & Lily, a Sausalito, Calif., company that manufactures luxury bedding and furnishings for nurseries and children's rooms. "Creating a memorable nursery means stepping outside of what's predictable." Instead of using whimsical wallpaper or a painting the room a babyish blue or pink, consider a paint hue that your child won't grow out of so quickly, such as yellow, lime green, or lavender for girls, or navy, red, or Kelly green for boys. Then just change the accessories to update.

Do consider convertible furniture. Furniture that morphs—a crib that converts to a toddler bed, a changing table that changes into a desk—can help you go the distance so that when your baby moves onto the "big boy" or "big girl" stage, the room doesn't need a design overhaul.

Don't forget the ceiling. "Babies spend a lot of time looking up, so consider painting the ceiling an inspiring color and apply whimsical appliqués, or hang an interesting chandelier, such as one with jewels of different colors," suggests Suzann Nordstrom, a mother of twins and an interior designer on the faculty of the Illinois Institute of Art-Schaumburg.

Do secure chests or tables. Growing toddlers will climb on the furniture, so bolt high bookcases and chests to the wall so they won't tip if your child climbs on them. Or choose furniture that's wide and low to the ground. For more on furniture safety, see "Changing Tables and Dressers," page 111.

Don't place your baby's crib near windows, draperies, toys, blinds, wall-mounted decorative accessories with long cords, or other furniture so an adventurous baby can't reach anything dangerous. Stencils on the walls are a safe alternative to wall hangings.

Do arrange furniture so it's safe for you, too. Position furniture and toys so you'll have a clear path when you enter the room at night. Any area rug or throw rug should have a nonskid backing or be secured to the floor with double-faced tape so no edges stick up.

Don't wait until the last minute to paint. Paint the nursery at least one week before your baby's arrival. That allows time for fumes to subside before your baby comes home. If possible, use a paint that's labeled low-VOC (volatile organic compounds), chemicals that can vaporize into the air and may be irritating to a baby (and to some adults). Wear a respirator or mask when applying low-VOC or any paint. To reduce other fumes, air out new furniture and anything made of plastic or wood.

Recommendations

Whether you decorate your baby's room lavishly or simply, make safety your main concern. Ignore those inviting retail nursery displays and buy your linens separately—the crib skirt/dust ruffle and the fitted sheet, rather than an entire collection. Purchase tightly fitting sheets, then recheck the fit after each laundering, since washing can cause shrinking or weaken the elastic. Check for loose threads that could catch a baby's head or neck. Launder sheets twice before the first use to remove any chemical residue from the fabric-treatment process and to ensure correct fit. Consider using a mild liquid or powder laundry detergent, such as Dreft, a specially formulated laundry detergent for infants and toddlers. Remember, bare is best. Follow the suggestions in the "Cribs" chapter (page 127) for safe sleeping, such as putting your baby to bed on her back.

CHAPTER

15

Crib Mattresses

When you're shopping for a crib, you'll also need to choose a mattress, which typically is sold separately. Don't underestimate this purchase; a mattress is as important as the crib. After all, your baby will spend a lot of time snoozing—up to 18 hours a day initially—so it's essential to select the best-quality mattress you can afford. Size and firmness are the main concerns. If a mattress is too small, it can leave gaps in the crib that could trap and endanger your baby. If a mattress is too soft, it can conform to your baby's shape, causing a risk of suffocation or Sudden Infant Death Syndrome (SIDS).

There are two general types of crib mattresses: foam and innerspring. Either is an acceptable choice. Both types—if they're good quality—will keep their shape well and provide excellent support for infants and toddlers. There are differences, though. Foam—made from polyurethane—tends to be lighter. The densest foam mattress usually weighs 7 to 8 pounds,

compared with the 15 to 23 pounds of an innerspring mattress. So, although you're probably just lifting a corner at a time, changing your baby's sheets may be easier with a foam unit. Foam is also less springy and therefore less likely to encourage your child to use the mattress as a trampoline. Still, innerspring mattresses remain the most popular because they are what most adults sleep on in the U.S.

Mattresses are a "blind" item, meaning that almost everything that matters is on the inside, where you can't see it. A crib mattress can feel great in the store, but begin to falter once your baby starts to use it. We've learned that you can't depend on sales staff, even at reputable retail outlets, to give you accurate information. One salesperson told us, quite convincingly, that innerspring mattresses were better than foam because foam tends to "break down" after 18 months. Twenty-five years ago that may have been true, but not anymore. "A top-quality foam crib mattress will hold up just as long as an innerspring crib mattress, with normal use," says Dennis Schuetz, director of marketing for Colgate Kids, a manufacturer of juvenile mattresses, in Atlanta. That's because foam crib mattresses have become much more durable.

Features to Consider
The best foam mattresses

If you decide to go with foam because it's lightweight, density is the most significant sign of quality.

Dense foam. The best foam mattresses are firm and heavy and resilient—they bounce back quickly when you squeeze them in the

WHAT NOT TO BUY

Buy a new crib mattress, if possible. That way, your baby will be protected by the most current flammability safety standards. Buying new also ensures that the mattress you buy is sanitary. If you buy a used mattress, you don't know how it was cared for or stored. Mold can grow within improperly stored crib mattresses, and bacteria can fester on the surface from liquids (diaper leakage, spit-up) that weren't properly cleaned up. So buy a new mattress, especially for your first baby. If you take care if it and it stays firm, you can save it for your next child.

center and the edges with both hands. To assess foam quality, compare the weight of different models. That's not always easy to do in a store, but if you're able to lift several mattresses, do it. In general, the heavier the foam mattress, the denser (and better) the foam. You can give the mattress a squeeze test in the center by pressing your palms into both sides at once. A dense mattress won't allow you to press very far.

The best innerspring mattresses

If you decide on an innerspring mattress, follow this general rule: the more layers and the better quality of those layers, the better the mattress.

High coil count and low steel gauge. "Coil count," the number of springs or steel coils a mattress contains, is a popular marketing point. But a generous coil count doesn't always mean a firmer mattress. The cheapest innerspring baby mattresses may have fewer than 80 coils and more expensive models may have more than 280 coils, but a model with 150 coils could be firmer than one with 200. How? The gauge of steel in those 150 coils may be thicker than the steel in the 200-coil mattress. Steel gauge for mattress coils ranges from 12.5 to 19; the lower the number, the thicker the steel. Thicker is stronger. So look for a moderate to high coil count—135 to 150 coils is a good midrange—*and* a lower coil steel gauge, 15.5 or below.

Coir fiber or wrap pad as the insulator pad. On top of the coils is an insulator pad that keeps the coils from poking through a mattress' cushioning layers (see below) and bothering your baby. The best insulator pad is made from coir fiber—shredded and woven coconut shell—but fiber wrap pad, also called "rag" or "shoddy" pad, which is made from miscellaneous and pressed scraps of cloth, is also good. Coir fiber is more expensive than fiber wrap pad, but either works well. The lowest quality insulator pad is made from woven

SHOULD YOU BUY A CONVERTIBLE MATTRESS?

If you're planning to convert your baby's crib to a toddler bed, "dual firmness" convertible mattresses are available at the top end (in the $260 range). These mattresses are designed to go the distance. They're extra firm for infants on one side, and they're cushier, with standard foam or springy, "viscoelastic" memory foam for toddlers on the other. (You can flip the mattress after your baby's first birthday, when the risk of SIDS decreases.) But put this added feature in the "not necessary" category. Your baby will still be happy with a firm mattress when he becomes a toddler. If he's exposed to a more forgiving mattress, he probably won't want to go back. So if you buy a dual-firmness mattress, be sure not to flip it too soon.

polyester. Because it tends to form pockets over time, becoming concave where most of the baby's weight rests, it's less durable.

Foam or cotton cushioning layers. The next layer in the mattress sandwich is the cushioning, which may be made of foam, cotton, or polyester. Foam and cotton are signs of quality, though they contribute to the price. Polyester, which is less expensive and increasingly pervasive because the cost of foam to manufacturers has been rising, isn't ideal because of its tendency to form pockets.

Border rods. They go around the perimeter of the mattress top and bottom, and are the thickest pieces of steel a mattress contains. Don't buy innerspring mattresses that don't have border rods. Border rods provide extra firmness, durability, and edge support so a mattress won't sag when your baby stands or walks near the edge. Consider border rods a must-have.

Cover. Encasing the entire mattress is a fabric or vinyl cover. Fabric breathes more than vinyl, but ventilation holes in a vinyl covering help air circulate. The more vents the better. A thicker or layered vinyl covering better resists leaks, stains, punctures, and tears, so go with vinyl over fabric. Look for at least a triple laminated ("3-ply") covering, which will give a mattress a tougher shell, adding to its longevity. Unlike a cloth cover, vinyl also acts as a barrier to dust mites.

Shopping Secrets

Check for firmness. Buy the firmest, heaviest mattress you can find. Don't worry that it may feel too firm. "If it feels good to you, it's too soft for your baby," Schuetz says. Most babies will get used to sleeping on anything after a day or two. Press on the mattress in the center and at the edges. It should snap back readily and should not conform to the shape of your hand.

Test the fit. By law, all full-size crib mattresses must be at least 27¼ inches by 51⅝ inches and no more than six inches thick. Shop in a store that displays crib mattresses and check the fit before you buy by pairing the mattress with the crib you choose. If you can squeeze more than two fingers between the mattress and the crib, the mattress is too small.

Know quality—then find it. Don't buy a mattress from a manufacturer or a retailer that doesn't reveal, with in-store information or displays, what the mattresses is made of, or the components of each layer.

Don't worry about warranties. Some mattresses offer a one-year, a seven-year, or even a lifetime warranty. Don't be swayed by a long warranty, and don't pay extra for a mattress with a warranty. "Warranties are mostly a marketing tool to entice the consumer to spend more," says Schuetz. In general, you can expect any quality crib mattress to last as long as you're going to use it, provided that the cover hasn't become ripped or torn and that it's been used properly (for sleeping, not for toddler tumbling).

What's Available

The major brands of foam and innerspring crib mattresses are, in alphabetical order: Colgate (*www.colgatekids.com*), Da Vinci (available at retailers and e-tailers such as *www.babyuniverse.com*), Dream on Me (*www.dreamonme-usa.com*), Kolcraft (*www.kolcraft.com*, which offers a number of brands, including Baby Prestige, Pediatric, and Sealy), Moonlight Slumber (*www.moonlightslumber.com*), and Simmons Kids (*www.simmonskids.com*).

IS A WATERPROOF MATTRESS COVER NECESSARY?

It's a good idea, even if the mattress you select is leak proof, because a mattress cover will make your baby's sleeping surface cozier. Without it, the chill of the mattress's vinyl cover is apt to come through, no matter what the thread count is of the fitted sheet. A waterproof cover will protect the surface of your baby's mattress from diaper leaks, absorb the liquid, and wick it away from your baby's skin. But it's still a good idea to wipe down a crib mattress with a damp cloth and mild soap any time the mattress gets wet or soiled.

SAFER MATTRESSES

All mattresses sold in the U.S., including crib mattresses, must meet current federal flammability standards. One standard, 16 CFR Part 1632, which has been in place for more than 30 years, covers the mattress' ability to resist ignition from a cigarette. A new performance standard, effective nationally July 1, 2007, requires that all mattresses pass an open-flame test. The standard is designed to retard the flammability of mattresses from open flames, such as lighters and matches, reducing the severity of mattress fires and buying you time to get your family out of your home safely in the event of a fire. The new standard is expected to save as many as 270 lives and prevent up to 84 percent of the injuries that occur each year from fires that start in mattresses.

Mattress manufacturers don't have to use flame-retardant chemicals. According to the Consumer Product Safety Commission (CPSC), many fibers—including rayon, acrylics, wool, and some polyesters currently used in crib mattress foams, fillings, barriers, and ticking—are flame-resistant enough to meet both standards. Those fibers may be used in every component of a mattress or even just one to meet the new standard. But even if flame-retardant chemicals are used, they're safe. "The CPSC has extensively tested mattresses for any health problems associated with flame retardant chemicals and the risk has been proven to be insignificant," says Patty Davis, a spokesperson for the CPSC, in Bethesda, Md. If you're still concerned, however, buy a crib mattress with a vinyl covering rather than cloth. "Vinyl acts a barrier to flame-retardant chemicals used in the mattress," Davis says.

You don't have to spend a fortune to get a good-quality mattress, but don't skimp, either. A mattress that costs between $90 and $200 will generally serve your baby well. Prices for foam and innerspring mattress are comparable, ranging from $50 to $530 (for mattress constructed with tufted organic cotton), but you can't go wrong if you spend in the range of $90 to $200. Low-priced models (less than $90) tend to be mushy and flimsy. Higher-priced models tend to be firmer, and therefore safer.

With an innerspring, the number of layers, what each component is made of, and the quality of the covering add to the price and increase comfort. The cheapest foam and innerspring mattresses have thin vinyl coverings and edgings that can tear, crack, and dry out over time. As prices go up, coverings become thick, puncture-resistant, reinforced double or triple laminates. The weight also tends to increase because the innerspring mattress contains more or better-gauge steel and better-quality cushioning while the foam mattress is made of denser, better-quality foam. Reversibility, the presence of ventilators, and thickness are factors that differentiate models.

Diapers

You'll change thousands of diapers by the time your child is 2 to 3 years old and ready for the potty. Fortunately, diaper quality is better than ever, which makes the task easier. Your first major decision in the diaper department will be between the cloth or disposable kind. Both kinds have their benefits and drawbacks. On the one hand, disposable diapers are undeniably convenient, but they're also costly: You can expect to spend $1,500 to $2,000 or more on disposables by the time your baby is out of them.

Cloth diapers are less expensive than disposables, especially if you do the laundering yourself. All-in-ones and cloth "diapering systems" that close with snaps or Velcro, are almost as easy to use as disposable diapers. But you still have to wash them. Despite a resurgence in the popularity of cloth diapers, disposable diapers remain the most popular choice among today's parents, as well as day-care centers and hospitals. A disposable diaper is an absorbent pad sandwiched between two sheets of nonwoven fabric. The pad contains chemical crystals that can absorb up to 800 times their weight in liquid and hold it in gel form. This helps keep liquid away from your baby's skin, so you can leave him in one longer than in a cloth diaper without causing him discomfort.

The quality of disposable diapers has improved in recent years. They're generally less leaky, feel less moist when they're wet, and provide a better fit. All the diapers we tested absorb far more liquid than a child is likely to produce during the time a single diaper is worn. Diapers are often sized according to a baby's weight, beginning with preemie and newborn and progressing to sizes 1 through 6. Some store brands are marked simply small, medium, large, and extra large, and weight ranges are listed on the package. The biggest diapers fit children 35 pounds and over. As the sizes increase, you get fewer diapers for the same price. A large package might give you 72 diapers in size 1, but only 40 in size 6. As with many things, buying the largest packages can still reduce your per-diaper costs.

All disposables are not the same, however. You'll see differences from brand to brand in fit, absorbency rate, and leakage control. For this book, we tested seven models of disposables, supplying 14 families with an infant or toddler with enough diapers of each model for 10 days. The children in the test wore diapers in sizes 3 to 6 and were evenly divided by gender. Pampers Cruisers and Pampers Baby Dry with Caterpillar Flex prevented leaks best and scored Excellent for leak prevention. Kirkland Signature (Costco's brand), Huggies Supreme with Natural Fit, and White Cloud (Wal-Mart) were in the middle of the pack, rating Very Good for leak prevention. Runners-up Luv's Ultra and Huggies had Good leak prevention. Overall, the families reported more often that Pampers and Huggies-brand diapers fit well, compared to other the brands tested. For Ratings, see page 162.

DISPOSABLE DIAPERS
What's Available
Major brand names of disposable diapers are Huggies (*www.huggies babynetwork.com*), Luvs (*www.luvs.com*), and Pampers (*http://us .pampers.com*).

Store brands include Cottontails (Stop & Shop brand, available at Stop & Shop supermarkets; not available online), CVS (*www.cvs.com*), Kirkland Signature (Costco), Little Ones (Kmart's brand; not available online), Simply Dry (another Stop & Shop brand; not available online), Target brand (available in Target stores only), and White Cloud (Wal-Mart; not available online). We found prices of our tested diapers varying from a low 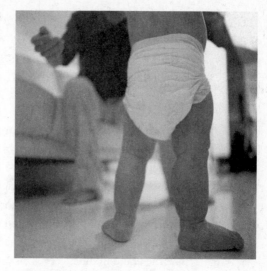 of 17 cents to a high of 24 cents when buying them in the largest-size package available. Although our tests show that the top-rated diapers are name brands because overall they tend to be more absorbent and fit better, you may find store brands more than adequate—and a cost cutter. In our informal research, we calculated a savings of 4 cents per diaper when we compared the cost of size 1 CVS-brand diapers with Pampers Baby Dry, also size 1, from the same store. Discounting pennies per diaper may not seem like much, but with, for example, 10 changes per day, which is reasonable with an infant, you'd bank about $12 per month and $144 per year using the size 1 store brand diapers as an example.

Features to Consider

Fasteners. The type of fastener varies from brand to brand. Most now have Velcro fasteners, which, unlike tape, don't lose their sticking power when they come in contact with baby creams or powders. In our tests, there were no problems with the closures on Pampers Baby Dry and Huggies Supreme, but parents reported more difficulties with the closures on Luvs Ultra.

Contoured fit. Many diaper brands have elastic around the waist, legs, and thighs to help prevent leaks.

Lotion. Many diapers have a lotion in the liner that is supposed to protect baby's skin. But keep diaper cream on hand for the inevitable outbreaks of diaper rash.

Stretch sides. These sides help the diaper do a better job of molding to each baby's contours, which can help stop leaks. Diapers with stretch sides may be more comfortable, too.

Ultra-absorbent core. Many diapers have materials in the crotch padding that enhances absorbency.

Recommendations

Plan on using plenty of diapers for your newborn, but don't load up on the newborn size. Babies with higher birth weights may not fit the smallest size at all. Buy by weight. Start with one package of 40-count newborn diapers if your baby weighs less than 8 pounds at birth. If your baby weighs 8 pounds or more, start with a package of size 1s, then buy in volume after you find the brand you like best. Use our Ratings as a guide, but don't be afraid to experiment. You'll find a favorite brand in time.

In general, purchasing the largest-count package you can find is the way to go. Buying the "Mega" versus the "Jumbo"-size package, for example, could save you up to 10 cents per diaper. You'll save the most money if you buy store-brand diapers in economy-size boxes (which come in counts of 68, 80, 92, and 144), but you can also find competitive deals on name-brand diapers on sale, in various size packages.

Also, don't be too quick to jump to the next size diaper. Selecting the smallest diaper your baby can wear comfortably will save you money in the long run because a larger diaper costs more. Manufacturers usually charge the same amount per package regardless of the actual size of the diapers, but they will put progressively fewer diapers in the package as the size gets larger. In addition, a larger diaper may allow leaks.

Diaper sizes vary from brand to brand. One brand's size 1 may fit children from 8 to 14 pounds, while another's fits those 8 to 18 pounds, combining size 1 and 2 into one package. A brand's weight ranges usually overlap: Size 2 in one brand covers 12 to 18 pounds; size 3, 16 to 28 pounds; and so forth.

Stores often put disposable diapers on sale as "loss leaders" to induce parents to shop there, so watch for specials and stock up when the time comes. Take advantage of freebies and coupons, and consider joining a warehouse club, such as Costco or Sam's Club.

You can also find good deals on name-brand and some store-brand diapers at *www.amazon.com*, *www.drugstore.com*, or *www.cvs.com*, and save yourself a trip to the store. You might also call the toll-free customer-service lines of disposable diaper companies, or register at the Web sites, for their new-parent programs, which often include coupons and free samples. But keep in mind that your name may get on mailing lists.

In our tests, Pampers Baby Dry diapers with Caterpillar Flex performed almost as well as the top-rated Pampers Cruisers and cost less, making them a good deal. But if your budget is tight, try store brands. In our tests, two store brands, Costco's Kirkland Signature and Wal-Mart's White Cloud, rated Very Good for leak prevention.

CLOTH DIAPERS
What's Available
Cloth diapers are made from absorbent cotton fabrics: terry (like towels, but softer), bird's-eye (similar to old-fashioned tea towels), gauze (thin and lightweight), and flannel (similar to the material used in flannel sheets and pajamas, but denser and thicker). Flannel is the softest against the skin, and the most absorbent. A combination of terry and flannel is also quite absorbent.

All-in-ones (a diaper and a protective cover as one unit) and diapering systems (a moisture-resistant cover into which you insert a diaper) are superior to plain diapers for absorbency, fit, and leak control and spare you the hassle of safety pins. But they are also more expensive. Major brands of cloth diapers, all-in-ones, and cloth diapering systems are Bum Genius (*www.bumgenius.com*), Bumkins (*www.bumkins.com*), Dundee (available at *www.buybuy baby.com*), Fuzzi Bunz (*www.fuzzibunz.com*), Gerber (*www.gerber childrenswear.com*), Kushies (*www.kushiesonline.com*), and Swaddlebees (*www.swaddlebees.com*).

Cloth diapers and diapering systems are available at baby and toy stores, via mail-order and through diaper-specific Web sites (such as those above). Cloth diapers cost from $1 to $3 (or more) each, and waterproof pants cost $2.50 and up. All-in-ones and diapering systems have higher start-up costs. You'll pay in the range of $7 to $12 apiece for all-in-ones and $24 to $36 for a system of five cloth diapers and a moisture-resistant wrap that the diapers fit into. But you'll use both types again and again, which can make them a cost-effective option.

DIAPER-WASHING BASICS

Wash cloth diapers two dozen at a time every two to three days. Presoak first, using your washer's highest water level and the hottest water. Launder with a hot wash and cold rinse. Any detergent labeled free of perfume or dyes will work fine. Don't use soap. It leaves a build-up. As long as you presoak, you don't need to use chlorine bleach, which shortens diaper life. To remove stains, use chlorine-free bleach or washing soda. If your baby is prone to diaper rash, rinse diapers twice, adding three-fourths of a cup of white vinegar to the second rinse.

Don't use liquid fabric softener or dryer sheets. Your baby may have an allergic reaction to the fragrance. Fabric softener can also leave a waxy buildup on diapers, making them water-repellent instead of absorbent.

Features to Consider

Cloth diapers are easy to use, but less convenient than disposables because of the laundry involved. If you don't use a diaper service, you have to soak the soiled diapers in a "wet" diaper pail or rinse them and store them in a "dry," plastic-bag-lined diaper pail between laundry loads. And the demands of a new baby can make keeping up with diaper washing a daunting proposition. Cloth diapers are easier to deal with if you use a diaper service, although you can wind up paying as much as you would for disposables. For that reason you may want to drop hints with friends and relatives that you'd welcome a diaper service as a shower gift.

Diaper types

There are five types of cloth diaper: unfolded or flat, prefolded, fitted or shaped, all-in-one, and diapering systems, sometimes called "pocket" diapers.

Unfolded diapers are rectangles of flat fabric that you fold to fit your baby's shape, holding them in place with diaper pins.

Prefolded diapers are also rectangular, but because of the way that they're folded, they have extra layers in the center. Like unfolded diapers, they also require pinning.

Fitted or shaped diapers are contoured more like disposables, with a narrow crotch and wide wings that wrap around a baby's waist. Some require diaper pins, but others have Velcro fasteners or snaps. They may also have elastic at the waist and legs, and a more absorbent layer in the center. With shaped diapers, you have to buy different sizes as your baby grows.

With all of these first three diaper types, you'll also need to use waterproof pants.

All-in-ones combine the diaper and the outer waterproof cover into one piece so cloth diapering is a one-step procedure. They're convenient for quick changes on the go and, with an extra diaper inside, can work well overnight. However, they're bulky and thick, so they may not dry quickly after laundering. And you have to buy larger sizes as your baby grows.

Diapering systems, sometimes called "pocket" diapers, are the most expensive cloth option. They include a moisture-resistant covering of nylon or polyester into which you insert a folded diaper or a disposable or washable liner. The outer covering comes in a range of sizes to accommodate a baby's growth. Velcro fasteners or several rows of snaps (for different fits) keep the covering closed.

Recommendations

The type of cloth diaper you choose (as well as whether you go with cloth at all) is a matter of personal preference. If you choose cloth diapers, you will need two to three dozen to begin with, plus six to ten waterproof outer pants. If you go the all-in-one-or diapering-system route, having eight to 10 on hand should be adequate. Buy two or three dozen diaper inserts for the system. Browse online to find the most competitive prices.

Ratings • Disposable Diapers

	Excellent	Very good	Good	Fair	Poor
	⊜	⊖	○	◑	●

In performance order.

Key no.	Brand and Model	Monthly Price	Overall score	Leakage prevention	Design
	DISPOSABLE DIAPERS				
1	**Pampers** Cruisers	37	96	⊜	⊜
2	**Pampers** Baby Dry with Caterpillar Flex	29	88	⊜	⊜
3	**Huggies** Supreme with Natural Fit	35	79	⊖	⊜
4	**Kirkland** Signature	29	73	⊖	○
5	**White Cloud**	29	64	⊜	◑
6	**Huggies**	34	48	○	○
7	**Luvs** Ultra	26	37	○	●

Guide to the Ratings

Overall score is mainly based on leakage prevention. **Leakage prevention,** as reported by our panelists, takes into account the severity of leaks. **Design** takes into account closure reliability, absorption rate, and how well the diapers fit the panelists' children. **Monthly price** is based on the cost of 155 size 4 diapers (five a day for a month) purchased in the largest-size package available.

CHAPTER
17

Diaper
Bags

W hen you're on the go, a diaper bag probably will be
your constant sidekick—your
changing table away from
home as well as a baby entertainment center
and portable food court, since many bags
have separate compartments where you can
stash toys, bottles, and snacks. It might also double as
your purse. So consider size, style, comfort, and durability, just as
you would with any handbag or tote you carry frequently. Any bag
will work, of course, even a classic canvas duffel.

But chances are you'll be happier with one that's specifically designed for baby gear.
You'll need compartments to keep things organized, and that's what many diaper bags
have to offer that generic carry-alls don't.

Diaper bags have come a long way from the traditional rectangular, pastel-colored
bags adorned with Pooh and other characters (although these diaper bags are still an
option). In the past few years, there's been an explosion of styles, colors, designs, and
functions. Manufacturers recognize that today's parents are active and that Dad,

who may be taking on a bigger parenting role, may want his own bag. The trend is to unisex family diaper bags that both parents can use, ones that can be handed from Mom to Dad without embarrassment.

Many of the newest diaper bags are designed to double as an adult

backpack or a satchel for your laptop. Bags aimed at dads come in guy-friendly, rugged fabrics, such as camouflage and faux suede. Other diaper bags are designed purely for moms' sense of style. They look like a purse—you'd never know there were diapers and bottles inside—and feature fun details such as pompom trim; classy colors including raspberry, lilac, olive, and black; and floral or mod prints.

Features such as "parent" pockets for your iPod, wallet, cell phone, and day planner; insulated bottle pockets and compartments for baby wipes; and lightly padded shoulder straps are now standard so you don't have to carry two or three bags. Ditto for a large, wipe-clean, detachable changing pad.

Shopping Secrets

Consider how you'll use your diaper bag. There are many styles available: backpack, messenger, and tote are three of the most popular. To decide which is right for you, think about how you'll be using your bag. Do you expect to be a heavy packer, prepared for anything, with extra diapers, changes of clothes, and favorite toys? Do you bottle feed? Do you want to attach the diaper bag to the back of the stroller? (There are stroller diaper bags designed specifically for that.) Will your spouse be the one who carries it? Do you need a diaper bag that blends in, so you feel comfortable carrying the same bag from work to day care? Will you be using your diaper bag on lots of day trips? Do you consider a diaper bag an accessory, like a chic pair of pumps? And perhaps most important, what's your budget? The answers to these questions can help you decide how roomy your bag needs to be, the number and types of compartments you should look for, the style that's likely to work best for your lifestyle, and aesthetic decisions, such as color and type of fabric.

"Test drive" models in the store. You'll be carrying your bag for a while, perhaps more than two years if you carry it until your baby is potty-trained. So, even if you buy online, it's a good idea to go to a

STOP DIGGING THROUGH YOUR DIAPER BAG

If the diaper bag you select—or that's given to you—doesn't have compartments, compartmentalize it yourself by placing similar items in small plastic Ziploc bags or see-through cosmetic bags. "Put toys in one bag, your baby's pacifier in another, and designate another just for baby wipes," says Elizabeth Hagen, a mother of five and a professional organizer from Sioux Falls, S.D. If your diaper bag has a zippered side pocket, designate that area as a home for your keys and cell phone. Then, to find these important items faster, get into the habit of putting them away right after you use them. "Taking that split second to put things where they belong saves you time and frustration later," Hagen says.

store to try on some bags for size, look, and feel. Load up the bags with baby stuff you bring from home. Consider where you'd put diapers, a change of clothes for your baby, wipes, the changing pad, an insulated lunch bag, your keys and wallet, and whatever else you typically carry with you. Bring the baby bottles you use (or plan to use) to make sure the bottle holders on contender diaper bags accommodate that size and type of bottle. Try unfolding the changing pad with one hand; you may be holding your baby in the other. It should be easy to use. Functionality is key—so is comfort.

Don't think bigger is necessarily better. You want a good-size diaper bag, yes. As your baby grows, bigger diapers take up more diaper bag space. But you don't want one that's so roomy that you're constantly losing things in its caverns or bumping into people. A weekender or deep hobo-style diaper bag, for example, may be too big for your everyday needs unless you have more than one child's things to carry with you. And even if you don't have a lot of stuff, there's a tendency to fill the void. Before you know it, a large diaper bag can easily outweigh your baby.

Look for extra compartments. Babies are a demanding lot. Trying to find a pacifier, for example, when your baby starts howling can feel like an emergency. Internal and external zippered pockets, toy loops, key clips, and bungee cords offer speedy access to pacifiers, toys, baby wipes, and your keys. Everything should be within easy reach. You want to be able to grab and keep going, without having to break stride or put your baby down to find what you need.

Watch for sales. Since diaper bags have become as trendy as purses, brands, styles, and fabrics constantly make their debut on the market. To make room for new inventory, retailers often offer sales to move the perfectly good bags that didn't get snatched up. That's especially true on high-design bags that make a style statement or cater to the seasons. We scanned the Internet and found diaper bags up to 50 percent off their original prices. The Internet offers an efficient way to window shop and compare prices.

What's Available

Major brands, in alphabetical order, include: Amy Michelle (*www.amymichellebags.com*), Baby Einstein (*www.babyeinstein.com*; available at retailers and e-tailers such as *www.target.com*), Baby Sherpa (*www.babysherpa.com*), Bumble Bags (*www.bumblebags.com*), Caden Lane Baby (*www.cadenlaneco.com*), Dad Gear (*www.dadgear.com*), Daisy Gear (*www.daisygear.com*), Diaper Dude (*www.diaperdude.com*), Eddie Bauer (*www.eddiebauer.com*), Fleurville (*www.fleurville.com*), Kate Spade (*www.katespade.com*), Lands' End (*www.landsend.com*), OiOi (*www.oioi.com.au*), O Yikes! (*www.oyikes.com*), Petunia Pickle Bottom (*www.petuniapicklebottom.com*), Reese Li (*www.reeseli.com*), Skip Hop (*www.skiphop.com*), Timi & Leslie (*www.timiandleslie.com*), and 2 Red Hens (*www.2redhens.com*).

Fabrics and patterns run the gamut from classic Pooh to sophisticated solids, florals, geometrics, checks, plaids, and stripes in rugged nylon and microfiber as well as dry-clean-only rayon/silk. Designs include backpacks, tote-style bags that could pass for briefcases, deep hobo bags, handbags with shoulder straps, fanny packs that resemble tool belts, ultra-hip urban slings, and messenger bags. Some diaper bags are made to attach to the back of the stroller, and can easily make the transition from stroller to shoulder. Diaper bags range from $12.99 for a low-end fabric or vinyl model to $350 or more for well-appointed designer bags.

Features to Consider

Changing pad. Most bags come with a rectangular changing pad that folds up and fits in the bag and can be wiped clean. Many pads fold to fit into a designated pocket. Some have a semirigid interior that helps maintain the pad's shape. But some are cushier than others. Cushy is better.

Construction. Look for wide, padded, adjustable shoulder straps, well-reinforced seams (tug on them to make sure they're strong) and quality hardware—heavy-duty plastic or metal zippers and sturdy closures. Zippers, rather than magnetic closures, ensure that your stuff won't fall out if your diaper bag tips over.

Handles vs. hands-free. The handles of a tote-style bag should be short enough so that the bag doesn't drag on the ground when you carry it like a suitcase, but long enough so it can be slung over your shoulder or worn on the diagonal. Wide or well-padded straps are more comfortable. A backpack, messenger, or sling-style diaper bag keeps your hands and arms free. A backpack's shoulder straps should be adjustable for proper fit, and a sternum strap, which connects the shoulder straps at the upper chest, helps redistribute the weight to make lugging baby gear more comfortable.

Fabric. Bags made of quilted fabric or silk are often favored by gift givers, but heavy-duty, moisture-resistant nylon or microfiber is more practical, especially if you're planning to have more than one child and you want the bag to go the distance. Beware of vinyl bags if you live in a cold climate. They can crack when the temperature dips. And you'll want a diaper bag that's washable inside and out.

Color. Some manufacturers continue to offer "baby colors"—pastels and light-colored prints. But dark shades are less likely to show stains.

And if you go for a more adult look, you can consider using the bag for other purposes when diapering days are over, assuming it has held up well enough. Still, make sure the interior is a light color. Otherwise, you will find yourself digging for items in a black hole.

Storage. Easy-to-access, zippered interior and exterior compart-ments, which can function as a wallet and as storage for things you constantly need such as baby wipes, pacifiers, and your cell phone, are a convenient plus. Make sure the zippers are heavy-duty so they'll hold up. Clear vinyl or mesh pockets inside can hold diapers, wipes, and other baby gear. If you'll be taking lots of outings or doing lots of traveling with your baby, look for a bag with an insulated cooler section. Bottle pockets are handy, but make sure they fit your brand of baby bottles or your favorite bottled water or juice for older babies. Always keep bottles and food away from dirty diapers.

QUICK! GRAB A BABY WIPE

You'll use lots of baby wipes and sometimes you just can't find them fast enough. To solve that problem, the Messenger Bag by Dad Gear features an "easy-access wipes window" that fits most brands of travel baby wipes. You simply attach the wipes on the inside of the bag with a strip of Velcro. At the lift of a small flap, you can retrieve wipes one at a time without having to open the bag and dig inside.

Recommendations

Opt for a bag that leaves your hands free, such as a backpack or messenger-style diaper bag with a diagonal strap. Another option is a stroller bag, which easily straps to a stroller's handlebars. Many messenger and tote baby bags now have a stroller-bar feature. That way, you won't have to balance your baby in one hand and a bag in the other. A hands-free bag also makes it easier to keep up with an energetic toddler (your baby, in no time). And it's healthier for your neck and shoulders, too, when your torso bears the brunt of the weight you're carrying. Loading up one shoulder can lead to neck and back strain. Be careful of overloading your diaper bag. Don't place too heavy a bag (more than 5 or 6 pounds) on stroller handlebars; it may cause the stroller to tip.

If value is what you're after, midpriced models (in the $35 to $100 range) offer the best mix of sound construction and generous storage. Low-end models (in the $20 to $35 range) skimp on quality and durability, leaving you with a bag that may tear, fray, or get stained or sticky and soon have to be replaced. If you expect to have more than one child, spending a little more will get you a good-quality bag that will last through several siblings.

Designer diaper bags are a class unto themselves. If you want a certain look or designer label, you'll pay for it. You're apt to get a good-quality bag, too. But make sure it's made of a roadworthy fabric and has all the features you're looking for.

Diaper
Pails

Changing diapers, of course, is the least glamorous aspect of taking care of a baby. But it must be done many times a day, and the right diaper pail can make the job easier. That's especially true if you have more than one baby at a time in diapers—twins or triplets or children close in age.

The type of pail you'll want depends on whether you're using cloth diapers or disposables. Cloth-diaper users now favor a "dry" pail, a plastic-lined pail you put rinsed diapers in until wash time. "Wet" pails—a plastic pail for soaking diapers before laundering—were once the standard, but are not used as much anymore. The typical disposable-diaper pail is also plastic, and it may be rigged with special liners that lock in diaper odors at the twist or flip of a handle, or with regular garbage bags.

What's Available

Cloth. Wet pails for cloth diapers are strong enough to hold a considerable amount of water but easy to carry, have a comfortable handle and a spout for pouring out soaking solution. A dry pail can be any sturdy plastic model with a liner, such as the Safety 1st Easy Saver *(www.safety1st.com)*, which can also be used for disposables.

Disposables. For disposable diapers, the major models of pails are, in alphabetical order, Baby Trend Diaper Champ (*www.babytrend.com*), Diaper Dékor (*www.regallager.com*), Diaper Genie and Diaper Genie II (*www.playtexbaby.com* or *www.DiaperGenie.com*), and Safety 1st (*www.safety1st.com*). Prices range from $9.99 to $40.

The Diaper Genie (approximately $19.99), the veteran of the bunch, twists each diaper in an individual pouch, which forms an odor-blocking seal. To operate it, you press the safety latch and open the lid; insert a rolled diaper between the securing clips; close the lid, making sure the safety latch snaps shut; turn the twist cap two times to seal the diaper in place. To empty the pail, close the lid and safety latch; turn the twist cap two times; then, while pressing the cutter button on the lid, turn the twist cap one half-turn counterclockwise. Hold the pail over a garbage can and push a button to open the bottom. You don't have to touch the liner; the diapers come out automatically.

Parents have complained that the Diaper Genie can be complicated to use. For easier diaper disposal, try the Diaper Genie II Advanced Disposal System (approximately $30). It's easier to operate because you skip the diaper-twisting step. Just lift the lid, insert a tightly rolled diaper through the clamp opening, close the lid and you're done. Installing a refill cartridge, which contains the plastic that forms the bags, is simpler, as well. Another plus: You can open and close the disposer one-handed, which helps when you're holding a baby in the other.

Strong competitors to the Diaper Genie and Diaper Genie II are the Diaper Champ and the Diaper Dékor. They're simple models that require no twists or turns. Like the Diaper Genie II, the Diaper Champ can be opened and closed with one hand. The Champ has a handle that flips back and forth. The Diaper Dékor has a hands-free design. You step on a pedal to open the lid, and then throw a diaper through flapper doors. It's available in a plus-size model, the Diaper Dékor Plus, which claims to hold up to 46 diapers instead of the usual 25 to 30, but 25 is more realistic for the Diaper Dékor Plus and 19 for the Diaper Genie, according to our tests.

Unlike either the Diaper Genie or the Diaper Dékor, the Diaper Champ can be used with any type of bag, including regular trash bags or plastic grocery bags. The others require specially made tubular bags specific to each that you have to purchase. Refills range from $5.99 (for a single pack for the the Diaper Genie) to $21.99 for a Diaper Dékor Plus Liner Refill Value Pack (three full-size refills).

The Diaper Genie can be used with two types of bags: stage one for infants and stage two for toddlers. The Dékor and Dékor Plus and the Diaper Genies have built-in cutters to cut the tubular bag when it's filled. You then knot the filled bag and throw it away. Knot the end of the plastic film to create a new bag and start over.

Features to Consider

Capacity. Diaper pail makers claim pails hold between 24 and 46 disposable diapers, although our tests show that capacity is often overstated. We were able to put 19 wet diapers in the Genie, which purports to hold up to 30 diapers, and 25 in the Dékor Plus, which is said to have a diaper capacity of 46. The Diaper Champ doesn't make any claims; its holding capacity depends on the size of the bag you use. When we used a large, plastic department store bag, we were able to put 30 wet diapers in it. Keep in mind that diaper-pail capacity decreases as your baby grows into bigger diapers.

Child-resistant lid. Look for a disposables pail with a lid that has a child-resistant locking button or a mechanism that makes it difficult for a child to break in, such as a step pedal opener. For cloth diapers, you'll need a standard wet pail, or a dry waste-basket-type diaper pail that can be used for either cloth or disposables, with a securely locking lid to prevent your baby and other curious children from falling in.

Comfort. If you're going the cloth route and choose a wet pail, pick one with a pouring lip and comfortable handles.

Ease of use. Some diaper pails require more than two steps; you have to open the lid, then shove the diaper into the plastic-bag insert, then twist. Others can be operated with one hand or have a hands-free pedal and are only a two-step process. All the diaper pails we tested were relatively easy to use. The Diaper Genie though, required three steps to dispose of a diaper. The Diaper Champ and the Diaper Dékor Plus were the easiest to use. We didn't test the Diaper Genie II, although its new, simple disposal system might make it a contender.

Liners or bags. Some pails require special plastic liners, which add to the cost of diapering, while others use regular garbage or plastic bags. The cost of refills will depend on the brand of diaper pail you choose. Liners for the Diaper Dékor Plus, for example, cost $3 per month and refills for the Diaper Genie range from $6 to $12. See our chart below for the cost comparison of refills.

Recommendations

Of the three diaper pails we tested—the Diaper Dékor Plus, the Diaper Genie, and the Baby Trend Diaper Champ—the Diaper Champ, which uses any type of plastic bag for diaper disposal, contained odor well, but slightly less so than the diaper pails that require their own bags. But if a little odor doesn't bother you and you're looking to cut costs, consider the Diaper Champ. The Diaper Dékor Plus contains odors well and is easy to use. The Diaper Genie we tested contained odors well, but was more difficult to use. Each diaper pail, however, had its pros and cons, which we list, below. Take those into consideration when making your buying decision.

DIAPER PAILS

RANK	MODEL	CAPACITY (wetted diapers)	PRICE FOR PAIL	MONTHLY COST **	PROS	CONS
1	Diaper Dékor Plus	25	$40	$3	Contains odors well. Large opening. Two easy steps to dispose of diaper.	Can tip up when used on carpet when activated. Directions could be more detailed.
2	Diaper Genie	19	$20	$6/ Stage 1 $12/ Stage 2	Contained odors well. Large opening.	Need to push diaper down into pail. Three steps to dispose of diaper.
3	Baby Trend Diaper Champ	30* *Using large department store-type bag	$30	na ** to dispose of 155 size 4 diapers	Large opening. Two easy steps to dispose of diaper. Can use any type of bag.	Does not contain odors as well as others. Children might be drawn to play with rotating handle.

CHAPTER
19

Digital Cameras

L ights! Camera! Action! From your baby's birth to all of those firsts—first smile, first tooth, first step—each day is a photo opportunity that can make you run for your camera. Now's the time to get ready to capture the memories you'll enjoy for years to come.

Still shooting with that trusty old film camera? The arrival of your new baby may be the perfect time to switch to digital technology. Prices have dropped as digital cameras have become an everyday product for millions.

Digital cameras are perfect for shooting tiny, squirmy, uncooperative subjects because snapping away costs nothing—instead of paying a photo processor to print everything on a roll of film, you choose which images you want to print. You can e-mail photos to Grandma and Grandpa and the rest of the family, and let them print what they want to tack on their fridges.

Plus, digital cameras give you extraordinary control over the images you choose to print. You can transfer images to your computer, then crop, adjust color and contrast, and add textures and other special effects. You can make prints at home on a color inkjet or snapshot printer; drop off the memory card at one of a growing number of photofinishers; use a self-service kiosk at your local drugstore to select, edit, and print pictures instantly; or upload images to an online photofinisher. Final results can be e-mailed, made into cards or T-shirts, or uploaded to a photo-sharing Web site for storage, viewing, and sharing with others. Or you can display copies of digital photos on your desk using a single "digital picture frame." Like camcorders, digital cameras have liquid-crystal-display monitors for composing shots or viewing ones already taken. Many digital cameras can also shoot video with sound. Some camcorders can shoot still photos, but a typical camcorder's resolution is no match for a good still camera's.

What's Available

The leading manufacturers of digital cameras include, in alphabetical order: Canon (*www.usa.canon.com*), Fujifilm (*www.fujifilm.com*), HP (*www.hp.com*), Kodak (*www.kodak.com*), Nikon (*www.nikon.com*), Olympus (*www.olympus.com*), and Sony (*www.sony.com*).

Digital cameras come in various sizes. **Subcompacts**, which weigh 5 to 8 ounces, can fit in a pocket. Price: $200 to $500. Too big to pocket, but small enough for most handbags and glove boxes, are **compacts**. They typically weigh 7 to 14 ounces. Price: $150 to $400. Subcompacts and compacts are often equipped with scene modes to make shooting easier and large LCD monitors for composing and reviewing shots. Many now have a 6-megapixel or greater resolution. They're suitable for making 5x7 or larger prints, as well as snapshots.

Advanced compact cameras are typically larger and heavier than compacts, with versatile controls and long zoom lenses. Price: $250 to $800. **Super-zoom cameras** have a very long zoom range—10x or greater. They're usually larger and heavier than compacts, but a few new models are designed to be smaller and lighter than older models. Price: $220 to $700. **SLR,** or single-lens reflex cameras, the largest and heaviest, have the most versatility and power and interchangeable lenses. Price: $600 to $2,000. These bigger, serious cameras provide more zoom, better image control, and greater speed than compacts and subcompacts. But if you're just looking to get good shots of your family, they're probably overkill.

They're best suited for challenging lighting, nature, sports, or artistic photography.

Shopping Secrets

Choose your time and place. Digital camera prices don't fluctuate seasonally, but most new models reach the market during two periods—March through May and September through November. During those times, many older models are replaced by more capable ones that often cost about the same. Buy between May and August or November and February. During these periods, older models may be discounted before they disappear. (You can tell that a camera isn't long for this world if the manufacturer offers a limited-time rebate.) Scrutinize too-good-to-be-true offers. Some dealers use them to unload refurbished cameras. If you're comfortable with refurbished and the price is right, fine. But keep in mind that the latest model, even without a steep discount, may be as good a value because it has more capabilities.

Go online to find the best price. Compare prices by using an Internet shopping "bot," which gathers prices from a number of retailers, such as *www.MySimon.com, www.BizRate.com, www.shopping.com, www.nextag.com, www.pricescan.com,* and *www.shopper.com.* Another source is the Shop Online feature for subscribers to *www.ConsumerReports.org.* If models you're researching are available from a walk-in retailer near you, visit the store to try out the camera. In the latest subscriber survey conducted by the Consumer Reports National Research Center, online retailers fared well, but if you want personal service, shop in brick-and-mortar stores.

Features to Consider

Camera size. Virtually all digital cameras take decent pictures these days. First decide if your priority is small size or extra photographic power and flexibility. Compacts are the mainstream cameras, and have the capabilities most people need, for as little as $200 for a fine performer. Choose a subcompact if you're willing to pay extra, and can accept a few compromises, to be able to carry it in your pocket. Get an advanced compact if you want lots of control over exposure and the image but prefer a built-in lens. Go for a super-zoom if you want to shoot closeups of distant subjects. Spring for an SLR if you must have it all, are willing to lug around that much weight, and can afford separate lenses.

Resolution. Most cameras now offer at least 5 megapixels of resolution, though a few older, 4-megapixel models may linger in stores. Buying more than 5 megapixels costs less than it used to, but you'll still pay $30 to $50 per additional megapixel for a basic compact camera and a bit more for a higher-resolution subcompact. More megapixels usually translate into more picture detail. But beyond 5 megapixels, you're unlikely to see the difference unless you crop images heavily or make poster-size prints. Even in the 8x10 prints we use for our tests, high resolution doesn't assure high overall print quality, since other factors, such as lens quality, affect the score.

A 5-megapixel camera should provide all the resolution most people need. If you want to crop or blow up your images into posters, get at least 7 megapixels. If you need both high resolution (greater than 5 megapixels) and impeccable quality, focus on advanced compacts and SLRs.

Zoom range. Another feature to consider carefully is a zoom range that's greater than the 3x found on most cameras. (A zoom lens' range is the ratio of its highest, telephoto focal length to its lowest, wide-angle length. For example, a zoom lens that's considered equivalent to a film camera's 35-mm to 105-mm lens has a range of 3x.) The wider the range, the greater the flexibility you have for composing shots. A few compacts and subcompacts now feature ranges as high as 5x, enough to make a distant figure fill the frame. But you shouldn't pay extra—financially or in size and weight—for a zoom range greater than 3x unless you often shoot distant subjects, such as wildlife and sporting events.

Reliability. Overall, digital cameras have been among the most reliable products in our subscriber surveys; fewer than 10 percent of those purchased needed repair or had a serious problem. That said, our latest survey found small differences in reliability between point-and-shoot cameras and same-brand SLRs. And reliability by brand differs somewhat and might help you fine-tune your buying decision. Olympus has been among the more repair-prone brands of SLR. Overall, it doesn't pay to buy an extended warranty for a digital camera. Check whether your credit card provides coverage. Such plans, often found on gold and platinum cards, may lengthen the original warranty by up to one year.

Recommendations

Going digital makes it easy to take photos of your baby and share them with friends and relatives who are computer users. When choosing a digital camera, check out *www.ConsumerReports.org* and take both our Quick Picks and Ratings into consideration, weighing all the factors we mentioned in this chapter. The Ratings list models by overall performance. Quick Picks are the choices our experts recommend, after balancing more than a dozen factors.

TAKING BETTER BABY PHOTOS

Babies and toddlers make challenging subjects for photos. After all, they don't necessarily smile when you want them to, or look at the camera, and they've been known to wiggle right out of a shot. Here are some things you can do to get better baby shots.

"Get into your child's environment," urges Bob Watts, owner of Enterprise Photo, a professional photography business in Kimberly, Idaho. If your baby is playing on the floor in the living room, you (the photographer) should get down there, too. "You don't want to be standing up, shooting from above," says Watts. Your baby will think, "What's Mommy or Daddy doing now?" That may yield a confused or fearful expression.

Respect your baby's personality. Don't expect a baby to turn into a ham just because you have a camera in hand. "You want to capture your baby's personality so that later you'll say, 'I recognize that look or that attitude,'" Watts says. If your child is shy, you might want to click the shutter when his chin is down a bit. If your baby is a spark plug, you want to capture those bright eyes and big smile.

Recruit an assistant. Have your spouse, a sibling, friend, aunt, or uncle play with your baby while you wield the camera. "You'll get a more natural shot if your baby is doing something rather than simply looking at you," Watts says.

Use the power of persuasion. When you want your baby to look at the camera (while playing with a toy, for example), "say, 'Show that toy to me,' or 'Show it to Mommy,'" Watts suggests. But don't hold the toy yourself because babies tend to reach for whatever you have. "You'll get hands in the picture," Watts says.

Schedule picture time when your baby is happiest. That could be right after meals rather than immediately after a nap.

Keep a camera handy for spontaneous moments. In addition to a digital camera, you might also have several disposable cameras strategically located around the house—on the mantel, on top of your refrigerator, and in your bedroom, for those impromptu shots.

Practice, practice, practice. If you aren't a veteran photographer, take lots of pictures until using the camera becomes second nature. "That way, when you get that magic moment, you're not fumbling around, trying to figure out how to turn the camera on," Watts says.

Engage toddlers and older children in make-believe. If you're trying to get a shot of them in their Halloween costumes, initiate a game of trick-or-treat in which you ring the doorbell and have them hold out their candy sacks. "And have them say their names instead of cheese," says Watts. "I don't know why it works, but right after children say their names, they usually smile."

Based on our judgments of uncropped 8x10-inch prints, all the cameras produced images that were excellent. But if we had used only a small portion of the original image and enlarged it to 8x10, the higher-megapixel cameras would have produced better results than the others. The advanced compact and superzoom models have features demanding photographers will appreciate, such as manual controls, especially long battery life, and a next-shot delay no longer than two seconds.

CAMCORDERS: DIGITAL WINS

If you're in the market for a camcorder, you can do a lot more with videos of your youngster shot on digital or analog camcorders than play them back, unedited, on your TV. You can edit and embellish them with music using your computer, then play your productions on your DVD or PC. Or send them to friends or family via e-mail. Digital camcorders, now the dominant type, generally offer very good picture quality, along with very good sound capability, compactness, and easy handling. Analog camcorders, now a small part of the market, generally have good picture and sound quality and are less expensive.

WHAT'S AVAILABLE

Sony (*www.sony.com*) dominates the camcorder market. Other top brands are Canon (*www.usa.canon.com*), JVC (*www.jvc.com*), Panasonic (*www.panasonic.com*), and Samsung (*www.samsung.com*). Most digital models come in the MiniDV format, but there are also disc-based DVD-RAM, DVD-R, and DVD+RW formats. Newer models record to flash memory or a hard drive.

MiniDV. Don't let their small size deceive you. Although some models can be slipped into a large pocket, MiniDV camcorders can record very high-quality images. Expect to pay about $6.50 for a 60-minute tape. Price: $350 to more than $1,000.

Disc-based. Capitalizing on the popularity and capabilities of DVD movie discs, these formats offer benefits that tape can't provide: long-term durability, compactness, and random access to scenes, as with a DVD. Disc prices range from about $4 to $20. Price: $600 to $1,000.

Analog. Most analogs now use the Hi8 format; VHS-C and Super VHS-C are disappearing from the market. Blank tapes range from $3.50 to $6.50. Picture quality is generally good, though a notch below digital. Price: $200 to $300. For the latest Ratings, visit *www.ConsumerReports.org*.

CHAPTER

20

Formula

As the parent of a newborn, you'll have a million things to do. But planning gourmet meals for your baby won't be one of them. Until your child is about 6 months old, breast milk or formula will take care of breakfast, lunch, dinner, snacks, and those middle-of-the-night wake-up calls. That's all your baby needs to grow healthy and strong. Then you can begin adding so-called solid food to the mix—continuing to breast-feed and/or supplement with formula—until your baby's first birthday or so, when cow's milk becomes an option.

As we mention in the "Breast Pumps" chapter, nursing is good for babies and moms. Even the infant-formula companies will tell you, as Nestlé does on its Web site, "Breast milk is best for babies." Breast milk contains a uniquely superior mix of carbohydrates, amino acids, fatty acids, hormones, immunity-enhancing antibodies, vitamins, minerals, and enzymes that work to give your baby the best possible start. It's Mother Nature's liquid gold that commercial formula can simulate, but not equal. Breast-feeding may reduce the risk of Sudden Infant Death Syndrome and a range of infectious diseases, including bacterial meningitis and

If you decide to supplement breast-feeding with formula, consult your pediatrician about how best to proceed. So your milk supply won't run out, you'll probably be advised to breast-feed at regular times each day, such as your baby's breakfast and again at bedtime.

diarrhea, as well as respiratory, urinary tract, and ear infections. It may also enhance your baby's brain power and visual acuity. According to the American Academy of Pediatrics (AAP), babies who are breast-fed rather than formula-fed may have less risk of asthma, obesity, diabetes, and certain forms of cancer through adulthood. It's good news for moms, too, since breast-feeding reduces a woman's risk of breast and ovarian cancer as well as bone-weakening osteoporosis.

Financially, breast milk is a bargain. The cost of formula, however, can add up. In fact, if your baby is consuming only formula, you're likely to shell out about $1,500 by her first birthday, depending on her nutritional requirements and the type of formula you choose. There's also the money you may spend on doctor bills. One study found that breast-fed infants had fewer hospital admissions.

Still, the decision about whether to go with breast milk or formula (or both) can be complicated, depending on your work situation and lots of other factors. The short answer: Try breast-feeding if you can. The AAP recommends breast-feeding exclusively for a baby's first six months. If you can't breast-feed or if you decide to wean your baby before age 1, you'll need to give him formula. Usually derived from cow's milk, formula provides a wide range of nutrients but not all the crucial components of breast milk. If your baby is exclusively formula-fed, he will probably drink 2 to 3 ounces of formula every three to four hours during the first few weeks. By six months of age, he may be up to 6 to 8 ounces every four or five hours.

Shopping Secrets

Shop at mass merchandisers. Formula sold by mass merchandisers, such as Wal-Mart, Costco, and Sam's Club, costs 16 percent less than formula sold in supermarkets, according to a U.S. Department of Agriculture report. And formula sold in drugstores cost 19 percent more than in supermarkets, so shop there only as a last resort. Generally, milk-based formula tends to cost less than soy-based formula, so don't buy soy or another type of special formula unless your pediatrician recommends it.

Join the club. Some formula companies, such as Similac, have a membership club you can join for free by filling out an online form. After you enroll, you're eligible for exclusive offers and savings.

Buy online. Many retailers, including many mass merchandisers, don't sell formula through their Web site, so you'll have to go shopping, and then schlep the stuff home. But you can purchase formula online at *www.amazon.com*. The site offers Enfamil, Similac, and Nestle Good Start, and free shipping on some quantities. The site also has some organic brands, such as Babys Only and Bright Beginnings. You can sign up for Amazon Prime, which entitles you to unlimited "free" standard and two-day shipping on eligible items, as well as other benefits, for an annual membership fee of $79. Another option is to buy formula online from the manufacturer's Web site. Enfamil (*www.enfamil.com*) and Similac (*www.welcomeaddition.com*) offer this convenient option. If you buy three or more cases at a shot from the manufacturer, you may get a reduced price and standard shipping may be included. By checking around online, we found this

STORAGE GUIDELINES

Don't leave breast milk or formula out for more than two hours. If you do, throw it away. And never put an unfinished bottle of breast milk or formula in the refrigerator for another time. To protect your baby from potentially harmful bacteria, toss it and start fresh.

To make sure the formula and breast milk you feed your baby are safe, follow these Food and Drug Administration tips for storing these liquids in the refrigerator and freezer.

Liquid	Refrigerator	Freezer	Special Instructions
Expressed breast milk	24 hours	3 to 6 months	Label it with the date you put it in the freezer
Formula	Don't pre-mix batches and refrigerate; prepare it as your baby needs it	Not recommended	For unopened cans of formula, observe "Use by" dates printed on the container.

to be a good deal, and, unlike at Amazon, there's no membership fee.

Use powder, if possible. Powdered formulas are the least expensive option. The USDA reports that liquid concentrate formulas, though more convenient and easier to mix than powder, tend to cost more.

Buy big. Across brands, larger cans of formula, whether it's in powder or liquid form, cost less per reconstituted ounce than smaller cans. Buy the largest cans you can find.

Consider a store brand. You'll find store brands of formula at major retailers such as Kmart and Wal-Mart, and the savings can be substantial. We found that the store brand of formula at a local Wal-Mart (Parent's Choice) cost 50 percent less per ounce than a leading

PREPARING FORMULA AND BREAST MILK SAFELY

When preparing formula, follow label directions exactly and instruct caregivers to do the same. The Food and Drug Administration says to boil cold tap water for a minute before mixing with formula, but whether boiling is necessary is controversial. Your best bet is to follow the formula manufacturer's instructions exactly, and to ask your pediatrician which type of water to use. Your pediatrician may say it's OK to use sterilized bottled water (check the label to make sure it says it's sterile). All bottled water must meet strict standards for tap water established by the Environmental Protection Agency. But if the bottled water doesn't say sterile, you'll probably need to boil it.

If you're using powder, the FDA now recommends reconstituting immediately before feeding your baby rather than making several bottles at once, although some manufacturers' instructions will tell you that prepared bottles are fine as long as they're consumed within 24 hours. You may want to get your pediatrician's take on this as well. For liquid concentrates and ready-to-feed products, the FDA advises consumers to follow manufacturer's storage instructions.

If you use different brands of powdered formula, don't mix up the scoopers. They may hold different amounts.

Don't heat breast milk or formula in the microwave, which can create dangerous hot spots. Instead, warm up bottles under running hot water or in a pan of water that's been heated on the stove for a few minutes. Shake the bottle before serving to even out the temperature, and test the formula or breast milk on the back of your hand. If it's lukewarm, it's ready for your baby, although your baby may be fine with cold breast milk or formula, too.

Never try to stretch formula with extra water. Improperly diluted formula can cause malnutrition and water intoxication, which is can be life-threatening. On the other hand, too little water can cause diarrhea or dehydration and will give your baby more calories than she needs.

WHY BABIES DON'T NEED WATER

You may wonder if it's OK to give your baby water, or if your baby needs it, especially in the summer. The answer is no. During the first year of a baby's life, you don't need to supplement formula with bottles of water—even on hot days. In fact, giving infants water can be dangerous because they can easily suffer from water intoxication, a condition in which their developing kidneys can't excrete water fast enough. As a result, water builds up in the body and dilutes the electrolyte balance of the blood, which can cause seizures, coma, or even death. Give your baby a little extra breast milk or formula instead of water if you sense that she's thirsty on especially hot days.

national brand (Enfamil). "With our second baby, we were much more relaxed parents and used the store-brand formula rather than the name-brand right away. It saved us a lot of money with the same results," says Dawn Glossa, from Oak Park, Ill., the mother of two. That's to be expected. According to the FDA, all formula marketed in the U.S. must meet the same nutrient specifications, which are set at levels to fulfill the needs of infants. Although infant-formula manufacturers may have their own proprietary formulations, brand-name and store-brand formula all must contain at least the minimum levels of all nutrients specified in FDA regulations, without exceeding maximum levels, where those are specified.

Check the "use by" date. When buying formula, look for the "use by" date on the label, which is required by the FDA. Until that date, you can be sure the formula will contain no less than the amount of each nutrient declared on the product label and will be of acceptable quality.

Be brand loyal. Although major brands of formula are roughly equal, it's generally recommended that you stick with the brand your baby gets used to. It's fine to use liquid and powder interchangeably.

Features to Consider

DHA/ARA. Many brands of formula are now fortified with DHA (docosahexaenoic acid) and ARA (arachidonic acid), synthesized versions of the essential fatty acids that are naturally found in breast milk; the natural versions of DHA and ARA are also concentrated in the cells of the brain and eyes. The fortified formulas tend to cost a bit more than standard formulas, and whether you should spring for them is debatable. Some evidence supports the hypothesis that supplementing formulas with DHA and ARA benefits infants; other studies refute this. What to do? It may depend on whom you ask. "In light of the current science, as a father and a pediatrician, I would consider it unethical not to give a baby formula supplemented with DHA/ARA because for some babies, formula is the sole source of nutrition for the first six months of life," says William Sears, M.D., co-author of "The Healthiest Kid in the Neighborhood." Your pediatrician may have an opinion, which is worth seeking. And keep in mind that even formulas with DHA and ARA aren't a perfect match for breast milk because the exact chemical makeup of breast milk still isn't known.

Iron. The formula that you buy should be fortified with iron unless your pediatrician says otherwise. Although there are low-iron formulas available, the AAP strongly discourages using them because they can increase the risk of infant iron deficiency.

Organic. To date, at least one manufacturer, Similac, offers an organic version of its milk-based formula, which includes iron, DHA, and ARA. We expect others may follow suit shortly. Organic formula costs slightly more than nonorganic, but it's something to consider. Using organic formula is a matter of personal preference.

What's Available

The major brands of formula are, in alphabetical order: Enfamil (*www.enfamil.com*), Nestlé Good Start (*www.verybestbaby.com*), and Similac (*www.welcomeaddition.com*). Formula comes in three versions: powder, concentrated liquid, and ready-to-feed liquid. Besides standard formula, which is cow's milk-based, there are special formulas, such as lactose-free and lactose-reduced for babies who have problems

digesting lactose, a natural carbohydrate found in milk. Soy and protein-hydrolyzed formulas are available for babies with a cow's milk protein allergy. Hydrolyzed formula may be prescribed for babies who are allergic to soy, and for other reasons. Soy formula is an option if you prefer that your baby have a vegetarian diet. There are also specific formulas to reduce spit-up, and for pre-term and low-birth-weight babies, older babies, and toddlers.

Your pediatrician is the best source of advice on

FORMULA COMPLAINTS AND CONCERNS

If you have a general complaint about a food product, including infant formula, contact the Food and Drug Administration via its Web site, *www.fda.gov/opacom/backgrounders/problem.html*. If you think your infant has suffered a harmful effect from an infant formula, call your pediatrician and ask that it be reported. Your pediatrician can do so via the FDA's MedWatch hotline at 800-332-1088 or online at *www.fda.gov/medwatch*. The MedWatch program allows health-care providers to report problems possibly caused by FDA-regulated products such as infant formula.

what to feed your baby. But your baby's preferences and nutritional needs will affect the choice, too. Sometimes it simply comes down to trial and error.

Powdered formula
Pros: It's the least costly.
Cons: With both powders and concentrated liquids (see below), you must carefully measure the added water to be sure that your baby gets the right concentration of nutrients. And as we mentioned, according to the FDA, it's best *not* to prepare several bottles at a time, so that's a lot of mixing.

Concentrated liquid formula
Pros: It's slightly faster to prepare than powdered because you don't have to mix a solid with a liquid.
Cons: It's more expensive than powder, and you still have to boil water, if that's what your pediatrician recommends. (As we mentioned, the FDA says yes to boiling.)

Liquid formula
Pros: It's convenient. The water is already mixed in, so you're good to go. It doesn't require mixing.
Cons: It's the most expensive.

Recommendations
If you're planning to use formula, ask your pediatrician for a recommendation, but don't buy much of it until after your baby is born. Many companies are generous with free samples, and the hospital may load you up with samples when you go home. If you register at a baby

store for gifts or word gets out that you're expecting, you may receive unsolicited samples from formula companies in the mail right around your due date. That's another place to start.

Your baby may prefer one type of formula or may be able to tolerate only a particular brand, so be prepared to experiment. No matter what brand you settle on, if your baby shows signs of intolerance, such as gas, a rash, persistent vomiting, diarrhea, or any other unusual symptom, consult your pediatrician. You may need to switch brands, or change to a hydrolyzed or soy-based formula.

21

Gates

G-H-I

With an active baby on the loose, it can seem that every time you turn around, you're opening or closing a gate. But a gate or two can actually make your life a little easier and your child a lot safer by keeping her contained and away from hazards, such as stairs. You can also use a gate to keep a pet away from a child (and vice versa). Child safety gates are intended for children between 6 months and 24 months of age, not for older children.

All the gates CONSUMER REPORTS tested (see page 194 for test results) can be opened and closed by an adult, but have various designs to prevent children from opening them. Child safety gates come in two basic types, based on the method of installation.

Hardware-mounted or Permanent Gate

This type of gate requires screws for installation in a doorway. You drill holes in a door frame or stud behind the wall and attach the gate with brackets and screws. If properly secured to the doorjamb or between two walls, hardware-mounted gates are the most secure choice, although no gate can be guaranteed to keep a child in or out. Many hardware-mounted gates are made with vertical wood, enamel-coated steel, or aluminum tubing slats and top and bottom rails.

Where you'll need it: At the top of the stairs. Hardware-mounted gates are intended for stair locations. Most will swing open only one way—such as away from the stairs—for maximum safety. Some brands allow you to choose in which direction it swings (for example, if you decide to install the gate at the bottom of stairs).

Installation: You must drill holes into the door frame or, if the opening doesn't have a wood door frame, you must drill through the drywall or plaster into the wood framing behind. (You can fill in the holes later with wood putty or wall-patching compound when you no longer use the gate.) You can remove many of these gates from the mounting hardware when you want the doorway or opening free.

Pressure-mounted Gate

A pressure-mounted gate is held in an opening by pressure against the door frame or walls. Pressure-mounted gates can have two sliding panels that adjust to make the gate fit the opening. (You remove the panels or slide them to the side to walk through.) A pressure bar or some other locking mechanism then wedges the gate into place without hardware. A swing-style pressure-mounted gate, which has a gate door that swings open, is also an option. Pressure keeps it in place and installation doesn't require drilling. Like hardware-mounted gates, pressure-mounted gates are often made with vertical wood, enamel-coated steel, or aluminum tubing slats and top and bottom rails. They may also be made of plastic, wire, or nylon mesh or plastic-coated wire, which may be framed with end tubes and top rails of either wood or coated metal. A few are made with transparent plastic center panels.

Where you'll need it: Pressure-mounted gates are suitable for less hazardous locations, such as between rooms. They're useful in areas where falling isn't a major concern, such as in a doorway separating two areas with same-level flooring; you might use one, for example, to cordon off your kitchen so you can make dinner

without a crawling baby underfoot, or at the bottom of a stairway to discourage your little climber from venturing upstairs. We recommend that you *not* use a pressure-mounted gate at the top of stairs. Take that recommendation seriously.

Installation: To set one up, you adjust it to fit the opening by squeezing it in place. A pressure bar or other locking mechanism wedges the gate in place, leaving no permanent holes, although it may mar the door frame or wall. Basic pressure gates fit openings between 26 and 38 inches, give or take a few inches, depending on the model. Many houses and apartments have wider door openings, so manufac-

WHAT NOT TO BUY: OLD-FASHIONED ACCORDION-STYLE GATES

Avoid old-fashioned, accordion-style wooden gates with large "V"s at the top and diamond shape spaces between the slats; they can trap heads and necks. You may run across them at tag sales, thrift stores, and at other second-hand markets. If you have this type of gate, replace it with another model. Although there are newer accordion-style gates on the market that meet current American Society for Testing and Materials (ASTM) safety standards—which include smaller openings to reduce the risk of trapping heads and necks—if the gate doesn't have a top crossbar, there still will be protrusions at the top of the gate that might snag clothing or necklaces, which concern us. Overall, we recommend avoiding those newer models also.

turers offer wider models—some as wide as 62 inches. Some models have optional extensions you purchase separately.

Shopping Secrets

Decide where you'll use it. A hardware-mounted gate is harder to dislodge than a pressure-mounted gate. That's why it is the only choice anywhere security is paramount, such as the top of a stairway. For less hazardous areas such as between rooms, a portable pressure-mounted gate may do the trick.

Size up the slats. Avoid gates with horizontal slats; they're an invitation for a child to climb. Luckily, there don't seem to be many on the market. Some gates have enough space between their vertical slats to let adventurous toddlers get a foothold on the gate's horizontal bottom rail. They won't be able to climb up the gate, but they may be able to hop onto the bottom rail and go for a ride, which could be unsafe, perhaps even dislodging a pressure gate, or strain the gate's integrity. So look for narrow spaces between the vertical slats. Vertical slats or bars should be less than 3 inches apart to prevent head entrapment, but try to find slats even closer together.

Check construction. Look for sturdy construction and an even finish. Wood surfaces should be smooth, splinter-free, and fashioned with rounded rather than sharply squared edges. Metal is more durable than wood. Some metal gates have a support bar that

CERTIFICATION

Located on the frame or packaging, a certification sticker shows that the gate meets the minimum requirements of the American Society for Testing and Materials (ASTM) voluntary standard and that its manufacturer participates in the certification program administered by the Juvenile Products Manufacturers Association (JPMA). The standard addresses issues including the size of openings, such as the distance between the bottom of the gate and the floor (so that a small torso can't pass through and there's minimal risk of head and neck entrapment), gate side height, the strength of the top rails and framing components, the integrity of the latching mechanism, and the configuration of the uppermost edge. The following brands of gates bear the JPMA seal: Cardinal Gates, Dorel Juvenile Group (Safety 1st), Evenflo, GMI, Kidco, Kunshan E-Tech Industrial Co., Mommy's Helper, North States Industries, Inc., Regal Lager, Retract-A-Gate/Creative Frontier, Simplicity for Children, Summer Infant Products, and The First Years.

crosses the floor beneath the gate, which could cause tripping when the gate is open.

Do your homework. Bring width measurements of doors or openings with you when you shop, and try to avoid gates that will need to be at their maximum width to fit; they may wobble.

Try it before you buy. Most tested models have a dual-action latch that can be opened with one adult hand. Try to test models in the store to make sure they're easy for you to use.

What's Available

The major brands of child safety gates are, in alphabetical order: Cardinal Gates (*www.cardinalgates.com*), Evenflo (*www.evenflo.com*), GMI (*www.gmigates.com*), KidCo (*www.kidco.com*), Lascal (*www.regal lager.com*), Mommy's Helper (*www.mommyshelperinc.com*), North States Industries (*www.northstatesind.com*), Regalo (available at *www.walmart.com*), Safety 1st (*www.safety1st.com*), Simplicity (*www.simplicityforchildren.com*), Summer Infant (*www.summer infant.com*), and The First Years (*www.thefirstyears.com*). Prices range from $12.56 to $134.99.

Features to Consider

Gate safety depends on solid construction, reliable hardware, and the absence of entrapment hazards.

Height. To discourage an adventurous child from climbing over, a gate must stand a minimum of three-quarters of the child's height. Most gates measure 22 inches or more from top to bottom. If your child is tall for his age, go with a higher gate. Some stand as high as 32 inches. When a child is taller than 36 inches or weighs more than 30 pounds (usually at about 2 years of age), a gate is no longer adequate or safe.

Installation flexibility. Many gates can be mounted to odd areas, such as stair balusters, angled banisters, and into drywall where there is no wood framing behind. You may, however, need to purchase a specific installation kit for these areas, and adjust to fit openings as wide as 62 inches. Kidco has an installation kit for mounting its gates even to wrought iron. Some hardware-mounted gates can be slid out of their wall mountings, which is a bonus when, say, you're entertaining and don't want the gate in the way.

Latches. Many gates have a dual-action latch that can be opened

with one hand by an adult. Try different types of latches in the store to make sure they're easy to use. A gate with a squeezing mechanism opens by compressing parts of the gate, but this type of latch can be uncomfortable to use, so test it in the store. Other options are a pressure-release handle, which can be lifted with one hand to open the gate. Some models have a foot pedal that requires strong pressure to release.

The latest models, such as the Evenflo SimpleEffort and Simple-Effort Plus, both pressure-mounted gates, unlock at the push of a button on a wall console or remote control, though with the SimpleEffort model we tested, we had to wait about 6 seconds to be able to relatch the gate. To open the gate, you won't have to put your baby down. But you still have to push the gate open (your knee can do the job) and close the gate manually. Nine-volt and 4 C batteries are required (not included). The Auto-Close Gate by North States Industries, which can be either pressure- or hardware-mounted, closes and locks automatically with a little shove. Plus, it can be opened by an adult with one hand.

Sound and color. Many gates audibly click when they're shut, signaling that they're doing their job. Others, such as the Perfect Fit Gate by Safety 1st and the Evenflo SimpleStep Gate, have a color indicator showing when the gate is locked.

Let there be light–on the stairway. At least one model we know of, the Smart Light Stair Gate by Safety 1st, features a motion sensor night-light that glows when you approach it—an added safety and convenience feature around stairs for when you're parenting on the night shift.

Travel. Some pressure-mounted models are marketed for temporary situations, such as travel, and come with a carrying case, like the Kidco Gateway to Go G14. They can make a hotel room or a relative's home more child-friendly.

Recommendations

Whether you choose a hardware- or pressure-mounted gate, look for one that's JPMA-certified and install it according to the manufacturer's directions. Never use a pressure gate or the pressure-mount option on a gate that can be installed either way at the top of stairs—no matter how much you want to avoid drilling holes into your woodwork. Choose a gate with a straight top edge and closely spaced, rigid vertical slats or a mesh screen. Avoid accordion-style gates without a top filler bar (with open spokes at the top) and gates with horizontal slats or similarly tempting footholds. If you choose a model with mesh panels, look for a fine weave—wide-holed mesh may provide a foothold for climbing or could trap fingers.

Follow mounting instructions carefully. Allow yourself a good hour for installing hardware-mounted gates. If you suspect your gate-installation skills aren't up to snuff or you don't have an electric drill, which is usually required, recruit a handy friend or relative. After you've installed a gate, frequently check hardware where it attaches to the gate and wall. Loose hardware not only makes a gate less effective but may be a choking risk if it falls off, or your baby pulls it off. Pressure-mounted gates can also be surprisingly easy to dislodge. Even the most stable pressure-mounted gate will work loose over time, so inspect it often. Keep large toys, such as stuffed animals or riding toys, away from the gate so they can't be used as a step stool for climbing over the gate.

Always close the gate when you leave the room or use the stairs. Finally, remember that a gate is only a deterrent, not a replacement for adult supervision. You'll still have to keep a close eye on your child.

Ratings • Gates

Excellent ⊜ Very good ⊖ Good ○ Fair ◑ Poor ●

Within types, in performance order.

Key number	Brand & model	Fits openings (in.)	Weight (lbs.)	Installed height (in.)	One-hand open & close	Can be used on uneven surfaces	Price	Overall score 0 P F G VG E 100	Security	Design safety	Convenience
HARDWARE MOUNTED											
1	**The First Years** Simple & Secure Stair Gate	29.5-44	10	29	Yes	Yes	$60	87	⊖	⊖	○
2	**Safety 1st** Lift and Lock Security*	30-42	7	28	Yes	No	20	81	⊖	⊖	○
3	**Kidco** Safeway Gate G20	25-43.5	7	31	Yes	Yes	70	77	⊖	⊖	○
4	**North States** Auto-Close*	29.5-38	13	30	Yes	Yes	80	76	⊖	○	⊖
5	**Cardinal Gate** Stairway Special SS-30A	27-42.5	6	30	Yes	Yes	80	61	⊖	◑	○
PRESSURE MOUNTED											
6	**KidCo** Gateway G11	30-36	10	30	Yes	Yes	70	74	○	⊖	⊖
7	**North States** Auto Close*	29.5-38	13	30	Yes	Yes	80	66	⊖	○	⊖
8	**Kidco** Gateway to Go G14	28-36	5	29	Yes	Yes	70	53	◑	⊖	⊖
9	**Evenflo** Simple Effort Hands-Free Metal	28-37.5	14	29	Yes	Yes	50	40	◑	○	⊖
10	**The First Years** Hands-Free Gate 3600	29-34	11	31	Yes ①	Yes	60	28	◑	○	⊖
11	**Safety 1st** Lift and Lock Security*	28-42	7	27	No	No	20	13	●	⊖	○

① Hands-free open & close also   * Gate could be mounted with hardware or pressure.

Guide to the Ratings

Overall score is based primarily on security. **Security** indicates how well the gate resisted being dislodged. **Design safety** reflects the gate's adherence to the ASTM standard for gates. **Convenience** reflects features and versatility. **Price** is the approximate retail.

22

High Chairs

F eeding a hungry baby in a high chair isn't always a picnic. But the right high chair can help contain mealtime madness and make the whole experience a lot more enjoyable, for you and your baby. A high chair usually consists of a frame of molded plastic or metal tubing and an attached seat with a safety belt and a footrest.

There are still a few old-fashioned wooden high chairs out there with a removable tray, or arms that lift the tray over a baby's head. They're not always as comfortable or cushy for babies as the modern, form-fitting models on the market now, and many of them may not be certified to meet the latest safety standards. We say don't use them.

Some chairs are loaded with features, such as adjustable trays with dishwasher-safe inserts that make cleanup a cinch and seat backs that recline to multiple positions. Others are basic models that don't even fold. A few hybrid units can convert into other types of gear, such as a table and chair for an older child. At the very least, you'll want a stable, sturdy high chair that can stand up to spilling, kicking, and regular cleaning for at least a year. You'll probably use a high chair for less time than you'd think. Although high chairs are intended for infancy up to about age 3, some babies can't bear to sit in a high chair once they become adventurous toddlers.

For our Ratings, which begin on page 203, we tested 19 high chairs ranging in price from $25 to $575. Throughout this chapter, we'll include insights from our tests that can you help decide which high chair is right for you.

Shopping Secrets

Take a hands-on approach to buying a high chair. We suggest visiting the baby store near you that has the broadest selection. Then do the following:

Open and close the fastener on the seat's safety harness. Try it one-handed to make sure it's easy to use. If it's not, you might be tempted not to use it every time your child is in the seat—which is a must. Although the voluntary industry standard developed by the American Society for Testing and Materials (ASTM) does not call for a five-point harness (waist and crotch restraint with shoulder straps), a three-point harness (waist and crotch restraint) is required for certification. On some chairs, you can convert a five-point harness to a three-point harness, but we don't recommend it. Five-point harnesses are safer because they can prevent a child from standing up in a high chair and possibly falling.

Test the tray. It should be easy for you to engage and disengage, but not for your baby. Ideally, tray latches shouldn't be accessible or visible to your baby.

Check for a crotch post. The voluntary industry standard requires that high chairs have a passive crotch restraint, which is usually a fixed crotch post that may be attached to the tray or the seat of the chair. The crotch post prevents a child from sliding out of the chair and under the tray. In our tests, we found one high chair, the Mozzee Nest ($575), that didn't have a passive crotch restraint. For this reason and others, including its failure in ASTM stability tests, the chair was rated Not Acceptable. For more on the crotch post, see "Features to Consider."

CERTIFICATION

Acertification sticker on a high chair's tray or frame shows that the model meets ASTM voluntary standards, and that its manufacturer participates in the pass/fail certification program administered by the Juvenile Products Manufacturers Association (JPMA). Certified high chairs are required to have a passive restraint, such as a crotch post; a locking device that prevents accidental folding; secure caps and plugs; sturdy, break-resistant trays; legs wide enough to increase stability (but not so wide that you trip over them); and no springs or dangerous scissoring actions that could harm little fingers. Safety belts have to pass force tests. High chairs are also covered by the federal safety standard for small parts.

JPMA-certified high chairs include Baby Trend, Chicco, Classy Kid Inc., Dorel Juvenile Group (Safety 1st), Evenflo, Fisher-Price, Graco, J. Mason, Kolcraft, Peg-Pérego, Scandinavian Child (Svan), and Stokke.

Adjust the seat height to see how well that mechanism works. Not all chairs have this feature, but some come with as many as eight possible heights. Adjustable seat heights can accommodate parents of varying heights and allow the high chair to be used at the level of your dining table, so your baby can eat with the rest of the family.

Assess the seat cover. Look for a chair with upholstery made to last. It should feel substantial, not flimsy. Make sure upholstery seams won't scratch your baby's legs. Seat covers should be wipe-clean (preferred) or machine washable.

Make sure wheels can be locked. If you're buying a model with wheels, they should lock or become immobilized by the weight of your baby in the seat.

Watch out for rough edges. Examine the underside of the feeding tray to make sure there's nothing sharp that could scratch your baby. Look for small holes or hinges that could trap little fingers.

Check for small parts. Make sure the caps or plugs that cover the ends of metal tubing are well secured. Parts small enough for a child to swallow or inhale are a choking hazard.

Try folding it. If you plan to fold up your high chair as often as every day, practice in the store. Some chairs that claim to be foldable can have stiff folding mechanisms. Technically they may be foldable, but they're not user-friendly.

What's Available

Major brands of high chairs are, in alphabetical order: Baby Trend (*www.babytrend.com*), Chicco (*www.chiccousa.com*), Combi (*www.combi-intl.com*), Dorel Juvenile Group (Cosco, Disney, Eddie Bauer, and Safety 1st, *www.djgusa.com*), Evenflo (*www.evenflo.com*), Fisher-Price (*www.fisher-price.com*), Graco (*www.gracobaby.com*), Kolcraft (*www.kolcraft.com*), Peg-Pérego (*www.pegperego.com*), Stokke (*Stokkeusa.com*), Svan (*www.svanusa.com*), and Zooper (*www.zooper.com*). There are three general price categories:

Basic High Chairs

High chairs at this end of the price range (under $50) are simple, compact, and generally work quite well. These models are essentially plastic seats on plastic or steel-tubing legs, and may or may not have tray and height adjustments. They tend to lack bells and whistles, such as wheels; and they don't fold for storage or recline, a feature you may not use unless you're bottle-feeding. The seat is usually upholstered with a wipe-clean vinyl covering or bare plastic, and the pad may be removable and washable. Some have a towel rack to store bibs, towels, and wash cloths. In our tests, some basic models scored higher than some bigger-ticket high chairs, indicating that price isn't necessarily correlated with safety or ease of use.

Pros: A basic high chair can serve you and your baby well, but it pays to comparison shop because some brands may suit your needs better than others. This kind may be a good choice to keep at Grandma's house.

Cons: Avoid chairs in this price range with grooves in the seat's molded plastic (a mess magnet); cotton seat pads rather than vinyl, which don't hold up as well; and trays with side-release buttons that are accessible to your baby. Some parents report that their babies can remove these trays—food and all—as early as 9 months of age. Be on the lookout for chairs with protruding legs. Three in our tests—Baby Connection Convenience ($25), Cosco Beginnings Simple Start ($30), and the Kolcraft Recline 'n Dine ($30)—had such widely spaced legs that we consider them a tripping hazard to parents and siblings.

TIPS FOR SAFER SEATING

Always use a high chair's safety restraints, even in a reclining position. Never depend on the tray alone to do the job because it doesn't prevent your child from standing up and possibly falling out of the chair. According to the latest Consumer Product Safety Commission figures, more than 7,000 children suffered injuries related to high chairs in 2005. Deaths also can occur. Most of the injuries resulted from falls when restraining straps weren't used and/or parents turned their backs. The restraints aren't failsafe, and they can provide a false sense of security, which is why your child should always be in view when he's in a high chair. A child can stand in the chair and topple it. He can also slip under the tray and strangle when his head becomes trapped between the tray and the chair seat. Here are some other safety tips:

* On chairs that fold, be sure the locking device is engaged each time you set up the chair.
* Don't let older children hang onto a chair or its tray, play around it, or climb into it, especially when your baby is in it. The chair could tip over.
* If your chair's seat is adjustable, don't raise or lower the seat height with your child in the chair.
* If your high chair seat reclines, don't adjust it while your child is seated in the chair.
* Don't use the seat's recline feature for infants who weigh more than the maximum (usually 20 pounds).
* Don't lift or move a high chair with your child in it.
* Keep the chair away from a table, counter, wall, or other surface from which your child could push off with feet or hands. That can lead to tipping.
* Inspect the chair often. After your baby has been using the chair for a while, check to make sure it's still in good shape. You'll want to be sure the seat belt buckles and the wheel locks are secure, the chair and its reclining mechanism still lock into place, and any small parts remain firmly attached.

Midpriced High Chairs

In this price range ($50 to $200), you'll find chairs with many convenience features, including multiple tray and chair heights; casters for mobility, with a locking feature for safe parking; a reclining, padded seat for infant feeding; a one-hand removable tray; a dishwasher-safe tray insert for easy cleanup; flip-out organizer compartments on the tray that hold utensils, dishes, or baby food jars; easy folding for storage; and a five-point harness instead of a three-point harness. Most have vinyl seat pads that can be removed for cleaning, although you may see models with cloth covers in this price range; those are a challenge to keep clean. Frames and seats are usually made of molded, rigid plastic or steel.

Pros: Generally, these chairs are sturdier and have more usable features. Chair fabric patterns tend to be more muted and sophisticated, with names like "Pebblestone" and "Livingston." If you're looking for a high chair that fits your home décor, or at least isn't covered with teddy bears or nursery figures, you should have lots of options. There's a lot to choose from in this price range.

Cons: If you're looking for a simple chair that doesn't fold, with a wipe-clean cover, chairs in this price range probably will have more features than you may need.

High-End High Chairs

In this price range ($200 to $575) are European imports and traditional solid-wood, custom-made high chairs, some that lack a passive crotch restraint. Chairs at this end of the market tend to have a sleek, upscale appearance. Many have fewer features, though, than midrange models and a much higher price tag. Some, on the other hand, go all out to justify their price tag. The Peg-Pérego Dondolino ($230), for example, is a deluxe high chair with seven height positions and four angles of seat recline; it has a padded insert to support younger babies. But what really sets it apart is that it plays music and can function as a rocking high chair.

Pros: Top-dollar high chairs may mean top quality, which is important to consider if you want the chair to last for another baby or more. But that doesn't mean a midpriced high chair won't last, too. High-end high chairs tend to be stylish, but don't make looks your deciding factor.

Cons: Chairs in this range aren't necessarily the safest option. In our tests, the Svan Chair ($230), for example, a wooden high chair by Scandinavian Child, passed all ASTM safety tests except one for forward stability. We determined that a child seated in this chair, or a sibling pulling on it, might be able to tip the chair over, possibly causing serious injury. The Mozzee Nest ($575) failed the stability test, as well. We found the Mozzee Not Acceptable because of this and other failures to comply with standards.

Features to Consider

Crotch post. To prevent a baby from slipping under the tray and getting his head caught between the tray and the chair, high chairs must have a fixed center crotch post to comply with the voluntary ASTM safety standard for high chairs. The post is not meant to replace the safety belt, though. Check the leg openings that form between the tray/passive crotch restraint and the sides of the high chair. Children have been known to maneuver both legs to one side. The leg openings on the high chair shouldn't be large enough for a child to fit both legs in one.

Foldability. Some high chairs fold for storage. If that's important to you because your home is space-challenged, make sure there's a secure locking system to prevent accidental folding while your child is in the chair or being put into it. Such a system should engage automatically when you open the chair.

Safety belt. As we mentioned, this is an important feature. Most high chairs have an adjustable three-point harness, but a five-point harness is safer. The shoulder straps it provides could keep a tenacious, on-the-go baby from climbing out and falling.

Seat adjustment. Seats can move up or down to as many as eight height positions on some chairs. They may also recline (in case your baby falls asleep right after eating). However, except for bottle feeding, don't use a seat in the reclining position while feeding your baby— that's a choking hazard. On a height-adjusting chair, the seat slides along the chair frame, locking into various positions. Height options range from nearly floor level to standard high-chair level; the middle height is low enough so the seat (with the tray removed) can be pushed up to a dining room table.

Bon Appetit, Baby

Restaurant high chairs are notorious for having broken safety restraints and other defects. One option: Bring your own portable hook-on chair (keep one in your trunk just in case). The Graco Travel Lite Table Chair *(www.gracobaby.com)*, which retails for around $34.99, is the only portable table chair on the market certified by JPMA (CONSUMER REPORTS has not tested it, however). Its locking mechanism provides a secure fit on most standard table tops—but not with a tablecloth.

Toys. Some high chairs have toy bars or toys that attach to the tray, an option your baby will likely enjoy, although to keep your baby busy, you can certainly buy toys that fasten to high-chair trays. But do not use strings to attach them because strings and cords are a strangulation hazard. Make sure the toys are securely fastened and have no small parts that could become detached.

Tray. You'll want a lightweight tray you can take off with one hand or that swings to the side when not in use. Many high chairs have a dishwasher-safe tray insert that snaps on and off for easy cleanup. Some trays have compartments to hold utensils, dishes, or jars of baby food. Those are nice, but not necessary.

Upholstery. Most models have seat coverings—or entire seat panels—that can be wiped clean, or come off for more thorough cleaning. Opt for a seat cover with a pattern rather than a solid color; patterns are better at concealing stains. Vinyl is easier to spot-clean than cloth.

Wheels. Wheels may make it easier to move the high chair around, which is important if you'll be scooting the high chair from the kitchen to the dining room. On the other hand, wheels can be a nuisance because they may allow the chair to move as you're trying to pull a tray off or put your baby in. Older children may be tempted to take the baby for a joyride when you turn your back. If you decide on a wheeled model, look for locks on the wheels, preferably on all four.

Recommendations

Use our Ratings as a guide, and look carefully at the high chairs you're considering to make sure the one you want will suit your needs. Midpriced high chairs generally are the best value and have the best combination of useful features, so start there. The top-rated Graco Contempo 3800, for example, has many convenience features and the slimmest fold of any of the models we tested. It also did well in our Safety tests, and it was extremely easy to use. This chair comes out of the box fully assembled, a real plus. At $100, it's a bit expensive, but we think it's worth the cost. You can always look for sales at baby goods stores or find the best price online.

The Evenflo Expressions Plus is a less expensive choice, at $60, and it has many of the same safety and convenience features as the top-rated

Graco Contempo 3800. Most of the other high chairs scored Very Good and, depending on the selection of features you're looking for, might be fine for your needs. You may not know what high chair will suit you best until you try using one. Keep your receipt, or if you register for one, ask for a gift receipt to be included so you can return the chair if it doesn't suit you. Some high chairs have as many as 26 parts. If you're not handy, consider buying a high chair that comes fully assembled.

Ratings • High Chairs

Excellent ⊖ Very good ⊖ Good ○ Fair ◑ Poor ●

In performance order.

Key number	Brand & model	Price	Overall score (0–100) P F G VG E	Safety	Ease of use	Weight (lbs.)	Projected footprint (sq. in.)	Folded size (cu. ft.)	Harness type	Seat cushion material/how to clean	Reclinable seat/ # positions	Adjustable seat height/ # positions
HIGH CHAIRS												
1	**Graco** Contempo 3800	$100	92	⊖	⊖	20	858	4	5-pt to 3-pt	vinyl / wipe clean	Y / 3	Y / 6
2	**Evenflo** Expressions Plus	60	88	⊖	⊖	19	792	10	3-point	vinyl / wipe clean	Y / 3	Y / 7
3	**Evenflo** Majestic Discovery	90	84	⊖	⊖	26	894	15	3-point	vinyl / wipe clean	Y / 4	Y / 8
4	**Sesame** Beginnings Deluxe SP001-SBH	50	80	⊖	⊖	17	959	-	3-point	vinyl / wipe clean	Y / 3	No
5	**Disney** Every Day with Pooh	50	79	⊖	⊖	19	740	-	3-point	vinyl / wipe clean	Y / 3	No
6	**Chicco** Polly Notting Hill	120	79	⊖	⊖	24	718	5	5-point	fabric / wipe clean	Y / 3	Y / 7
7	**Graco** Harmony 3935	80	79	⊖	⊖	16	818	14	5-pt to 3-pt	fabric / wash	Y / 4	Y / 6
8	**Eddie Bauer** Wood 03033	100	76	⊖	⊖	22	615	-	3-point	fabric / wipe clean	---	No
9	**Baby Connection** Convenience	25	76	⊖	⊖	10	793	-	3-point	vinyl / wipe clean	---	No
10	**Kolcraft** Recline'n'Dine KH001-BPA	30	75	⊖	⊖	13	825	-	3-point	vinyl / wipe clean	Y / 3	No
11	**Peg Perego** Prima Pappa Diner	170	75	⊖	⊖	23	710	7	5-point	vinyl / wipe clean	Y / 4	Y / 7
12	**Cosco** Beginnings Simple Start	30	75	⊖	⊖	11	827	-	3-point	vinyl / wipe clean	Y / 3	No
13	**Combi** Transition	120	75	⊖	○	24	614	-	5-point	vinyl / wash	Y / 3	No
14	**Baby Trend** Trend Malawi	90	71	⊖	⊖	20	616	6	5-point	vinyl / wipe clean	Y / 4	Y / 6
15	**Fisher-Price** Easy Clean	80	63	⊖	○	19	805	13	5-pt to 3-pt	vinyl / wipe clean	Y / 3	Y / 7

	Excellent	Very good	Good	Fair	Poor
	⊖	⊖	○	◔	●

In performance order.

Key number	Brand & model	Price	Overall score 0____100 P F G VG E	Safety	Ease of use	Weight (lbs.)	Projected footprint (sq. in.)	Folded size (cu. ft.)	Harness type	Seat cushion material/how to clean	Reclinable seat/ # positions	Adjustable seat height / # positions
	HIGH CHAIRS											
16	**Svan** Chair	235	55	◔	○	16	407	-	3-point	fabric / wipe clean	---	Y / sliding
17	**Fisher-Price** Space Saver	48	55	○	○	10	349	-	5-pt to 3-pt	vinyl / wash	Y / 3	Y / 3
18	**Stokke** Tripp Trapp	200	41	○	◔	16	356	-	5-point	fabric / wash	---	Y / 5+
19	**Mozzee** Nest	570	27	●	○	19	361	-	5-point	none/wipe clean	---	No

Guide to the Ratings

Overall score is based primarily on safety and ease of use. **Ease of use** is based on trained panelists' assessments of harness use, folding and unfolding, removing and replacing the tray, adjusting seat back and height where applicable, removing and replacing the seat cover. **Safety** for each high chair was assessed by testing for compliance with ASTM F-404-04, a voluntary standard; the standard includes stability and dynamic load assessments as well as many other tests. Models that failed to comply with the ASTM standard were judged Not Acceptable. **Price** is approximate retail. **Weight** is the weight of the chair (with tray in place) in pounds. **Projected footprint** is the amount of floor space, in square inches, that the chair requires while in use. Folded size is the volume (in cubic feet) that the folded chair occupies. **Harness type** is 5-point, which we strongly recommend, or 3-point. **Seat cushion material/How to Clean** is just that—with the manufacturer's suggested method of cleaning everyday spills. **Reclinable seat/# positions** indicates whether or not the chair has a reclinable seatback, and if so, how many positions are available. **Adjustable seat height/# positions** indicates whether or not the chair's seat height is adjustable, and, if so, the number of positions available.

23

Humidifiers

When your baby has a cold or cough, the moist air a humidifier produces can help loosen congestion, which will help him breathe and feel better. Your doctor might recommend a humidifier if your baby is diagnosed with croup, a contagious wintertime viral infection, or bronchiolitis, an infection of the tiny lower airways in the lungs that is common in babies and toddlers. "Almost all kids will get a bout of bronchiolitis by age 3," says Susanna McColley, M.D., division head of pulmonary medicine at Children's Memorial Hospital in Chicago.

A humidifier can help ease itchy skin and other problems associated with dry air. Ideally, indoor humidity should be 30 to 50 percent. But that level can drop significantly in winter, since cold air holds less moisture, and heating makes it even dryer.

Humidifiers come in three major configurations: small tabletop models, which can humidify one room; large stand-alone console models with substantial tanks that can humidify multiple rooms; and in-duct systems that are used in forced-air heating systems to humidify a whole house. In this chapter, we'll focus on table-top models that can be placed right in your baby's room and used during nap and bedtime to ease congestion—and let you breathe easy, too.

Tabletop humidifiers include evaporative models, also called cool-mist models, which use a fan to blow air over a paper wicking filter. When air from the fan blows across the filter, the water in the filter evaporates into the air. Warm-mist models are another option. They use a heating unit to boil water before cooling the steam, but the American Academy of Pediatrics doesn't recommend them for use with children because of the risk of accidental burns or scalding. A curious baby or toddler might touch the unit or knock it over.

What's Available

Major humidifier brands are Crane (available at leading retailers such as *www.walmart.com*), Holmes (*www.holmesproducts.com*), Kaz (*www.kazstore.com*), Sunbeam (*www.sunbeam.com*), and Vicks (*www.vicks.com*). (Crane, Holmes, Kaz, and Vicks are the most popular brands you'll find in baby stores and pharmacies.) Most tabletop humidifiers have small tanks that need to be refilled frequently. Evaporative models are noisy; warm-mist models are costly to run. Prices range from $20 to $100.

Shopping Secrets

Be the queen (or king) of clean. Before buying a humidifier, be sure you're willing to take the trouble to clean and disinfect it regularly to prevent mold and mildew. Germs thrive wherever there's standing water. To make cleaning easier, look for easy-to-use controls and for a removable tank that fits beneath faucets. The filter should be a cinch to replace. For cleaning tips, see "Recommendations" on the next page.

Aim for automation. Some portable models can be programmed to turn on automatically, and turn off by themselves if the water runs dry. That's a plus—and one less thing you have to remember.

Keep a warm-mist humidifier away from your baby. Warm-mist humidifiers tend to be quieter than cool-mist models; some make little or no noise except mild boiling and hissing sounds. But if you choose this option, and your pediatrician is OK with it, make sure you put the humidifier in a spot where your baby can't reach or touch it, or accidentally knock it over. The water in it gets hot.

Features to Consider

Be sure it has a humidistat. Whether it's dial or digital, a humidistat controls humidity levels and shuts the humidifier off when the set level is reached. Humidistats that display room humidity levels and settings are best. Models without a humidistat can allow humidity levels to rise too high. Overhumidification can lead to mold and bacteria growth.

Consider your water. Some humidifiers have lower output with hard water. Fortunately, that can be easily remedied. If you have hard water, use distilled water, which has a lower mineral content than most tap water and can help boost your humidifier's efficiency.

Recommendations

No matter what brand of humidifier you buy, clean it regularly. The more you use it, the more vigilant you need to be. Mold can grow within 48 hours on wet surfaces, and mold in the tank or in the water then can be transferred into the air, causing itchy eyes and worsening any breathing troubles your baby may have. For the best results, follow these tips:

Change the water daily. Empty the tank, dry all interior surfaces, and refill with clean water. Don't be swayed by tank size. Generally, the larger the tank, the longer your table-top humidifier can run without running dry. A one-gallon tank may run up to 11 hours; a 1.5 gallon tank may operate up to 20 hours without refilling. But no matter how large the tank, you should change the water daily, so buying a humidifier with a larger tank won't save you a step.

Descale your humidifier often. Although some parts may be washable in the dishwasher, they still need to be descaled (demineralized) with vinegar to reduce water-mineral buildup, which can decrease a humidifier's output, especially if you're not using distilled water. They also need to be disinfected with bleach. Completely dry all parts between descaling and disinfecting. And after disinfecting, carefully rinse the tank to avoid breathing harmful chemicals. Follow the manufacturer's directions and schedule for descaling and disinfecting parts and replacing filters, wicks, and the like.

Clean it before you store it. And clean it again when you take it out of storage.

CHAPTER

24

Monitors

Baby monitors are an extra set of ears—and, in some cases, eyes—that allow you to keep tabs on your sleeping baby. There are two basic types: audio and video/audio. Both operate within a selected radio frequency band to send sound from the baby's room to a receiver. Each monitor consists of a transmitter (child unit) and one or more receivers (parent units). Video/audio monitors have a small wall-mounted or tabletop camera to transmit images to a video monitor.

A baby monitor's challenge is to transmit recognizable sound (and/or images) over a distance with minimal interference—static, buzzing, or irritating noise—from other electronic products and transmitters, including cordless phones that share the same frequency bands, cellular phones, appliances, and even fluorescent lights. Interference can also be hearing someone else's conversation, which makes it difficult, if not impossible, to decipher the sounds coming from your monitor. Interference can also mean fuzzy reception in video monitors. Overall, interference is probably the biggest complaint parents have about baby monitors.

Shopping Secrets

Feel free to skip this purchase. Some parents are reassured by the constant surveillance of a baby's every whimper and movement. Others find it nerve-racking and feel like they have to be hypervigilant. Decide which category you're in before you go shopping. A monitor isn't a must-have. If you live in a small house or apartment or want a break when your baby is sleeping—which is legitimate—it's OK not to have one.

Consider your home and lifestyle. You may appreciate a monitor with both sound and lights, so you can "see" your baby's cries. The louder he cries, the more the monitor lights up. If you'll be taking business calls during naptime, for example, it can be helpful to turn the sound down low and rely on the lights. A video monitor can serve the same purpose, though we believe an audio monitor with lights can suffice. Similarly, if you live in a large house, you may want a monitor with two receivers rather than just one. In general, look for monitors with features that are easy to move about, such as a compact parent unit that clips onto your belt. Try it on before buying, if possible; antennas have been known to poke the wearer.

Factor in your phone. To minimize the possibility of interference, choose a baby monitor that operates on a different frequency band from other wireless products in your home. A 2.4GHz cordless phone and a 2.4GHz monitor can interfere with each other. The 2.4GHz frequency band is widely used for cordless phones.

Consider digital if you have nearby neighbors with babies. If you want to be sure the sounds transmitted by your monitor are heard only by you and not by neighbors who might have a similar model (or a cordless phone using the same frequency band), go with a digital monitor, not an analog one. This will also ensure that the sounds you hear are coming from your baby and not the neighbor's. Analog monitors operate on a particular frequency band, much like a radio, sending signals from monitor to receiver in a straight shot. Digital monitors, on the other hand, encode the signal as it travels between the monitor and the receiver, making it nearly impossible for the sounds to be heard by others, and reduces the possibility of running into interference from other electronic devices.

Learn the return policy. Before you buy or register for any wireless product, such as a baby monitor, be sure the store will let you return or exchange it, in case you can't get rid of interference problems. If you receive a monitor as a baby shower gift and know where it was purchased, try it before the retailer's return period (usually 30 days) runs out.

What's Available

The major brands of baby monitors, in alphabetical order, are: Evenflo (*www.evenflo.com*), Fisher-Price (*www.fisher-price.com*), Graco (*www.gracobaby.com*), Mobicam (*www.getmobi.com*), Philips (*www.hearmybaby.com*), Safety 1st (*www.safety1st.com*), Sony (*www.sony.com*), Summer Infant (*www.summerinfant.com*), The First Years (*www.thefirstyears.com*), and Unisar BébéSounds (*www.bebesounds.com*). Prices range from $15 to $200 for audio monitors, $100 to $200 for audio/video monitors. The higher the price, the more features and frills.

Features to Consider

Frequency band. As we mentioned, the closer your monitor's frequency is to that of another device, such as a cordless phone, the more likely you'll hear static or cross talk. One manufacturer, Philips Electronics, has addressed the interference issue by using a new frequency band: 1.9GHz. The new frequency, reserved exclusively for voice-only applications by the Federal Communications Commission, is called DECT technology, for digitally enhanced cordless telecommunications. The Philips SCD 589 baby monitor ($200) is the only one we know of that uses the 1.9GHz frequency band. And as far as we know, there's only one cordless phone that uses the 1.9GHz band, also made by Philips. In our tests, the Philips monitors and its brandmate cordless phone, didn't interfere with each other. Overall, the 1.9GHz frequency band is lightly used, at least for now, and can improve your chances of privacy and no interference.

Multiple channels. Some monitors offer only two channels; others, as many as 60. Multiple channels can be an advantage. If you're getting interference, you can change channels and try to get rid of it. Some models use an "auto-select" feature to automatically find a free and secure channel, which is handy.

Sound lights. With this common feature, a monitor's lights turn on when the baby makes a sound; the louder he cries, the brighter the lights get. Consider this a must-have. It's helpful in a noisy room, plus it lets you turn the volume down and still know when your baby is crying.

Out-of-range indicator. This common feature is a light or beep that lets you know you've reached the range limit of the monitor. Models that lack this feature may let you know you're out of range with static, but that's not as definitive as an out-of-range indictor.

Low-battery indicator. Look for a monitor with a light or an icon on an LCD display that lets you know the batteries in your parent unit are running low.

Extra parent unit. If you have two parent units, you can keep one receiver near your bed and carry the other around with you during the day, or both you and your spouse can listen for your baby at the same time.

Nice but Not Necessary

Walkie-talkie. You'll find this feature in models with more than one parent unit. It lets you talk to each other via the receivers.

Talking remotely to your baby. At least one monitor we tested, the Philips SCD 589 baby monitor, has an "intercom" that allows you to speak to your child in his crib by pushing a button on your parent unit.

Auto playback or music. Some baby monitors, such as the Sony BabyCall ($50), let you record a voice message for your baby or play lullabies or other soothing music.

Expandability. Some monitors let you add more cameras, a VCR, or webcam so the system covers more areas in your house. Other models have additional parent units you can buy.

Definitely Not Necessary

Attaching the monitor to your baby's crib. All of the monitors we tested could easily detect baby's sounds from 5 or more feet away, so there's no need to put the monitor directly on the crib rail.

Works Better in Theory

Pager or parent-unit finder. If you've lost the parent unit, you can press a button on the child unit to make the parent unit beep.

Unfortunately, the parent unit must be turned on for this feature to work, and if you leave the parent unit on, the batteries may go dead before you find it.

Recommendations

Among the models we tested, the digital baby monitors are top-rated. Short of DECT technology, there's no guarantee against interference with either digital or analog monitors, although digital monitors are less susceptible and more private. One digital model in particular, the Philips SCD 589, is loaded with features, and since it operates in the fairly lightly used, for now, 1.9GHZ frequency band, it's unlikely to pick up interference. However, at $200, it's pricey.

If you anticipate interference and want to spend less than $200, buy a less-pricey digital model that's not in the same frequency band as other wireless products in your home, and consider models with more than two channels. The other digital monitors we tested were very good: The Graco iMonitor ($90) has two parent units; a similar version with one parent unit is available for $60. The Summer Infant Secure Sounds ($50) is a good choice for privacy, though, like the Graco iMonitor, it has fewer frills than the Philips SCD 589.

We suggest avoiding the Evenflo WhisperConnect Sensa ($50). It has a Pet Sensor, which is designed to alert you to any unusual movement around your baby's crib—a cat or other animal climbed in, say. That feature worked well, but you can easily keep animals away from the crib by closing the door to your baby's room. And one of the three samples we tested had an annoying problem: The "out of range" alarm would go off at random. This happened over and over again with that particular sample, and once or twice with one of the other two samples we used for testing.

The audio/video monitors we tested have small color screens, and unlike earlier models, reasonably good pictures. However, we found them to be susceptible to interference, particularly from microwave ovens in use. Some models, such as the MobiCam ($190), let you tape to a VCR or watch your monitor on the television set. But overall, we don't see much need for a video baby monitor.

Ratings • Baby Monitors

We tested 11 audio monitors and three video/audio monitors, ranging from $35 to $200. The monitors were rated based on convenience, sensitivity, interference, and battery life. We tested for interference in three home settings: an apartment in a congested area, with buildings spaced close together; an average-size private house (1,800 square feet), and a larger private house (3,500 square feet). Each of these residences had one or more of the following: cordless phone, cell phone, wireless computer network, and microwave oven. Overall, there were far fewer problems with interference than expected with so many wireless devices in relatively small areas. The monitors ranged from Excellent to Good for the basic job of listening to, or, in the case of video monitors, seeing and hearing, a baby.

Excellent	Very good	Good	Fair	Poor
⊜	⊖	○	◒	●

Within types, in performance order.

Key number	Brand & model	Type	Price	Overall score	Convenience	Sensitivity	Interference	Battery life
	AUDIO							
1	**Philips** Digital SCD 589	1.9 GHz digital	$200	91	⊜	⊜	⊜	○
2	**The First Years** Digital	2.4 GHz digital	50	78	⊜	⊜	⊜	⊜
3	**Graco** imonitor 2795DIG	900 MHz digital	90	77	⊜	⊜	⊜	◒
4	**Summer Infant** Secure Sounds	2.4 GHz digital	50	77	⊜	⊜	⊜	○
5	**Sony** BabyCall NTM-910	900 MHz analog	50	75	○	⊜	⊜	⊜
6	**The First Years** Attachable	900 MHz analog	40	75	○	⊜	⊜	⊜
7	**Evenflo** WhisperConnect Pro	900 MHz analog	35	68	◒	⊜	⊜	⊜
8	**Safety 1st** Home Connection Monitor System	900 MHz analog	130	68	○	⊜	⊜	●
9	**Fisher-Price** Private Connection with Dual Receivers	900 MHz analog	50	67	◒	⊜	⊜	○
11	**Graco** Respond 2M06	900 MHz analog	50	66	◒	⊜	⊜	○
10	**Evenflo** WhisperConnect SENSA	900 MHz analog	50	64	◒	⊜	⊜	○
	VIDEO/AUDIO							
12	**Safety 1st** Color-View 08047	2.4 GHz video/audio	190	56	○	⊜	◒	◒
13	**MobiCam** 70001	2.4 GHz video/audio	190	53	◒	⊜	◒	◒
14	**Unisar** Bebesounds Portable Video and Sound TV872	2.4 GHz video/audio	190	51	○	⊜	◒	◒

Guide to the Ratings

Overall score is based on the convenience, sensitivity, susceptibility to interference, and the battery life of the tested models. **Convenience** includes the type of technology the monitor uses (digital versus analog), battery type (rechargeable or disposable), and other features that may make a monitor easier to use. **Sensitivity** reflects the ability to pick up low levels of sound. **Interference** is based on the models' susceptibility to interference from other electronic products in our tests. **Battery life** ranged from 1.5 to as much as 28 hours. **Price** is approximate retail.

Nursing Bras

I f you decide to breast-feed, you won't necessarily need bottles, a bottle sterilizer, or formula. But you will need a nursing bra. It will be your key piece of equipment to get the job done quickly and easily.

Nursing bras look like regular bras, but the cups open or lower from the front when you unsnap, unzip, or unhook the closure. You should be able to open the cup for nursing quickly and simply with one hand. (You'll be holding your hungry baby with the other.) If you can close it one-handed, too, even better. Most manufacturers have several nursing-bra lines, including models that are comfortable for sleeping or lounging; traditional, seamless "soft cup" and underwire styles; and super-supportive sports nursing bras that can take a pounding on the tennis court. The latest generation is nursing bras that are built into nylon/Lycra tank tops and T-shirts; discreet zippers offer quick breast-feeding access.

Whatever style you choose, proper fit is the key to breast-feeding success, says Lynne Andrako, R.N., clinical education specialist for Medela, a breast pump and nursing-bra manufacturer. Andrako is also a certified bra fitter and lactation consultant. A poorly fitting bra not only will be uncomfortable but also may increase the risk of plugged ducts and/or mastitis, a breast infection. An ill-fitting bra can put pressure on milk ducts, which may cause them to become plugged, and a magnet for infection-causing bacteria. Andrako estimates that 80 percent of women buy the wrong size nursing bra. Where do they go wrong? To accommodate their changing breasts (even early on, breasts enlarge and become heavier), women often increase their bras' band size but go up only one cup size.

Andrako says the rib cage can enlarge a bit during pregnancy, but generally not enough to warrant increasing the band size you normally wear. You can easily accommodate any increase by adjusting the hooks in the back. So if you're a 34 before pregnancy, chances are you'll be a 34 during and after, she says. But if you wore a C cup pre-pregnancy, you may go up to an F—or higher. Cup sizes usually go from A through D, then DD, DDD, F, G, H, and I.

ARE NURSING CLOTHES NECESSARY?

You can buy special nursing shirts and nightwear that have strategically placed slits and flaps that give you fast access to your nursing bra, making breast-feeding ultra-convenient. Although nursing clothes make breast-feeding easy, they're not essential. A button-down blouse, stretchy T-shirt or sweater, and two-piece pajamas—in other words, your regular clothes—can work just as well. Regular clothes can be even more discreet, if that's important to you. Because of their front flaps, which consist of two extra pieces of fabric, nursing shirts tend to advertise the fact that you're nursing, although no one, except other mothers, may notice.

The newest generation of nursing wear—clingy tank tops and T-shirts—have a built-in nursing bra so you don't have to wear both a nursing bra and a nursing top. Still, like traditional "nursing" shirts, they're an added expense, and their life span tends to be brief. Many moms, especially those who plan to breast-feed for a while, abandon the nursing duds in short order and breast-feed in whatever they throw on that day.

The Easy-Zip Tank Top by Second Nature does double duty; it's a tank top with a built-in nursing bra.

BEST FOR BREASTS

Tempted to use your regular bra for nursing instead of a nursing bra? That's not a good idea. Regular bras aren't designed for nursing and may not give you the extra support you need. Lifting your regular bra up over your breast to nurse can put a lot of pressure on breast tissue, increasing the risk of infection.

Shopping Secrets

Get fitted by a certified bra fitter. Yes, there's a certification program for bra fitting. When you're a nursing mother, getting a properly fitting bra is more important than ever. You'll want comfortable nursing bras that provide the right support—ones that don't bind, pinch, hike up in the back or front, or irritate breast tissue. Breasts change dramatically during pregnancy and lactation, when they enlarge even more. For optimum size and fit, go bra shopping no sooner than four weeks before your delivery date—your breasts will be nursing size by then. Your size may change again after you give birth, if only temporarily; that's why it's important to buy a bra with plenty of give. Shop at a maternity store and ask the saleswoman if there's a certified bra fitter on staff. This service is usually free of charge. If a certified bra fitter isn't available, a lactation consultant, perhaps one affiliated with the hospital where you'll deliver, can usually help. Many lactation consultants are also certified bra fitters.

When you're being fitted, you'll be measured under your arms. The tape will also be wrapped around your torso at the fullest point of the bust. The difference between the two measurements is your cup size. Once you get your official, post-measurement size, you can find a style you like and feel comfortable in. Don't be put off by the size the fitter recommends, which could be much different from what you normally wear. Keep an open mind and try it on before you decide whether it's right for you. Once you realize the difference in not only support and comfort but appearance (a properly fitting bra will make you look much better!), you won't be hung up on letters of the alphabet. You may not end up with the bra size you thought you'd wear, but the bra probably will fit well.

Once you're confident you've got the right size, buy online from that manufacturer or from a catalog, if you want to. If you're buying a bra you haven't tried on, double-check the retailer's instructions for measuring since brands may be sized differently, and make sure you can return it just in case. Or play it safe by buying all your nursing bras at the maternity store where you were measured.

Buy three to five bras. That should be enough to meet your needs, allowing you to have a couple of bras on deck and one or two in the wash. Plan to buy a sleep/loungewear bra for the early days of nursing when you'll want to wear your nursing bra and pads 24/7 for leakage control.

Shop as early as four weeks pre-delivery, as we mentioned, but no earlier. By then, your breasts will be nursing size, so you can be sure you'll get the correct size bra. Your breasts may enlarge even more after your milk comes in, so look for bras with cups that stretch. If you're still not comfortable, you may need to be fitted again.

If you're especially large-breasted, you may need to shop around. If the bras available in your local maternity store aren't large enough, try a specialty lingerie or "foundation" store instead. These shops usually can meet your needs and even custom-make bras in your size, if necessary.

Think twice before buying an underwire nursing bra. The pressure from the underwire support may contribute to breast maladies, such as clogged milk ducts. If you want to go this route, the same rules apply: Don't go by looks alone. Make sure the underwire bra you select is flexible and fits properly.

What's Available

Some of the major brands, in alphabetical order, are Bravado (*www* *.bravadodesigns.com*), Elle Macpherson Intimates (available at retailers such as Nordstrom, *www.nordstrom.com*), Fancee Free (*www.fanceefree mfg.com*), Leading Lady (*www.leadinglady.com*), Medela (*www.medela .com*), Motherhood (*www.motherhoodnursing.com*), Playtex (*www.play texbras.com*), and Second Nature (*www.regallager.com*). Major maternity retailers, such as A Pea in the Pod (*www.apeainthepod.com)* and Mimi Maternity (*www.mimimaternity.com*), have their own brand of nursing bras. Nursing bras range from about $4.99 (just the basics) to about $62 (designer bras with decorative lace).

Accessories

In addition to nursing bras, you'll need disposable or washable cotton pads that you can tuck inside to absorb any leakage. The disposable types are usually made of super-absorbent material that wicks moisture away from the skin. They're higher-tech than cotton nursing pads, but also more expensive. Both kinds prevent clothing stains and skin irritation and are invisible to the outside world.

You may also need adjustable bra strap pads that attach to any bra to relieve strap pressure and special bra shells that can protect sore nipples from irritation or help draw out inverted nipples.

You can find nursing pads, bra strap pads, and bra shells at drugstores; specialty maternity shops, such as Mimi Maternity, and baby product stores; and on Web sites such as *www.medela.com.*

Features to Consider

Support. In the world of nursing bras, support is queen. You'll need it now more than ever, just to feel comfortable. The best nursing bras open in the back but have flaps in the front for access. They also have strong side and undercup support and an extra wide back for a forming fit that doesn't feel tight. Straps should be adjustable. Soft cup styles usually feature a "no-roll" band, which is a plus. If you're extra ample, you may be a candidate for bras with extra wide, padded shoulder straps. But be sure to try them on before you buy, to see if they're comfortable.

Closures. How you open and close the flaps on your nursing bra is important. The front flap on many nursing bras attaches at the top, near the shoulder strap. Other nursing-bra flaps open and close between the two cups. Go with whatever type is easier for you to unclasp discreetly one-handed (without having to put your baby down). If you can close your bra one-handed, all the better. Squeeze or push-type latches are easy to operate one-handed, compared with snaps, which usually take two hands to close. Practice in the dressing room at the store.

Adjustability. Near the end of your pregnancy and in the early

WHAT NOT TO BUY: A HIGH-MAINTENANCE NURSING BRA

There are nursing bras available that require hand-washing, so check the maintenance tag before you buy. Who has time for that? You won't. Because your baby will be high-maintenance enough, you don't want to spend any downtime you have on this laundry detail.

weeks of nursing, your breasts may enlarge dramatically, then return to a smaller size once breast feeding gets established. For greatest comfort, you'll want a nursing bra that "grows" with you and springs back again throughout the day—before and after feedings. After you've found your correct bra size, look for brands made with Lycra, which adjusts to changing breast size and fullness. Or opt for 100-percent cotton bras with stretch cups and with three to four hook adjustments in the back so you can change the band size as needed throughout the day.

Color and style. Nursing bras once came only in white, beige (taupe), or black. Times are a changin'. Though white is still the norm, you'll now find nursing bras in red, black, pink, polka dot, florals, and animal prints, some with lace and ribbon.

Recommendations

The best nursing bras are stretchy, absorbent, and don't bind the breasts in any way that could interfere with milk flow. Look for bras that are 100 percent cotton or a cotton-Lycra blend or other stretchy synthetic. Since the right size bra is so important to getting breast-feeding off to a good start and reducing the risk of complications, such as clogged milk ducts, shop at a maternity store or visit a lactation consultant/certified bra fitter for at least your first bra. To find a lactation consultant in your area, contact the hospital or birth center where you'll deliver, or log onto the International Lactation Consultant Association at *www.ilca.org*. A professional fitting will ensure a comfortable fit and the correct size. Try on bras for size and feel, and practice with nursing pads in place. After you've bought one properly fitting bra, order more online or from a catalog. Many Web sites offer competitive deals. But stick with the manufacturer and style you were fitted with, or be fitted again, if you'd like to try a different style or brand.

CHAPTER
26

Pacifiers

A pacifier, a latex or silicone nipple mounted on a wide plastic shield, can be a sanity saver, especially when your baby is fussy. "The sucking action will calm babies and can even help some of their jaw muscles develop properly," says Julie Barna, a doctor of dental medicine and spokeswoman for the Academy of General Dentistry. Pacifiers also may reduce the threat of Sudden Infant Death Syndrome (SIDS). In fact, the American Academy of Pediatrics recommends that babies up to age 1 use pacifiers at bedtime and naptime because pacifiers appear to substantially cut that risk.

If you're worried that pacifiers can interfere with breast-feeding or damage teeth, consider this: The latest AAP guidelines say there's little evidence that pacifiers harm teeth before age 1 or cause infants to lose interest in breast-feeding. However, the AAP recommends waiting until your breast-fed baby is 1 month old before introducing a pacifier to ensure that breast-feeding is firmly established.

You can give your baby a pacifier at bed or naptime during his first year or so, when the risk of SIDS is greatest. Using pacifiers at other times of the day probably doesn't

Thumbs Down on Thumb-Sucking

A pacifier is healthier for your baby than thumb-sucking. Why? As a baby sucks on her thumb, she pushes the top jaw forward and bottom jaw backward, which can cause jaw misalignment and malformation over time. And a baby's thumb can be dirty, which introduces bacteria into the mouth that could cause illness. It can also be a tough habit to break because a baby's thumb is always handy. You might want to discourage the habit by giving your child a pacifier whenever you catch him with his thumb in his mouth. Babies tend to thumb-suck when they're tired, which is another reason to have a pacifier ready at bedtime and naptime.

harm your child, provided she stops by age 2, when the practice may cause protruding front teeth and an improper bite, and prevent the jaw from forming properly.

For some parents, a pacifier is a godsend. For others, it's a waste of money because some babies, especially those who are breast-feeding, don't like pacifiers and will repeatedly spit them out, no matter which brand or type you try. Will your baby crave a pacifier or be satisfied with the breast or bottle? You'll know soon enough.

So Many Pacifiers, So Little Time

If you find yourself in the pacifier aisle, you'll see a large variety—from angled pacifiers with a wide tip, frequently called "orthodontic," to a basic, round-tipped pacifier, advertised as "most like mother." "Orthodontic means that your baby's top and bottom jaw are in a correct position when he's sucking on it," Barna says. That position doesn't interfere with normal jaw growth and development and, in fact, may promote it. According to Barna, most pacifiers sold in the U.S. are orthodontically correct, whether or not they're labeled "orthodontic." But look for the American Dental Association Seal of Approval on the pacifier package just to be sure. Pacifiers come in several sizes and are classified by age on the package, so it's easy to see which size to buy.

Shopping Secrets

Check for recalls before you shop. Recently, the Consumer Product Safety Commission announced a recall of Baby 2 Pack pacifiers because the nipple could become detached from the guard or shield, posing a choking hazard. For recent recalls, check the CPSC Web site at *www.cpsc.gov.*

Be sure the base has ventilation holes. In the highly unlikely event that a baby sucks her pacifier into her mouth, ventilation holes will admit air. Pacifiers are required to have at least two ventilation holes in the shield, but check just to be sure.

Don't buy models with strings or anything else attached. Never give an infant a pacifier with a string, even if it's short. It's a strangulation hazard.

Buy silicone pacifiers only. Babies can develop an allergy or sensitivity to latex.

What's Available

Major brands of pacifiers include, in alphabetical order: Avent (*www .aventamerica.com*), Evenflo (*www.evenflo.com*), Gerber (*www.gerber .com*), Mam (*www.sassybaby.com*), Playtex (*www.playtexbaby.com*), The First Years (*www.thefirstyears.com*), maker of the Soothie, popular among hospitals), Tigex (*www.tigexusa.com*) and Tommee Tippee (*www .tommee tippee.com.au*). Pacifiers range from $3.79 to $6.50 for a package of two. Novelty pacifiers, such as those that play music, may cost $6.99 or more apiece.

Features to Consider

Handles. Some pacifiers have knobs on the back; others have rings. Babies don't care either way, though some parents do. Ring handles make pacifiers easier to retrieve from the bottom of a diaper bag and other locations where pacifiers land, but they can give your baby a "charging bull" appearance.

Snap-on caps. Some pacifiers, like the Avent brand, have a snap-on cap. It's one more thing to keep track of, but it can help keep your baby's pacifier clean when you're out and about and it's not in use. Don't let your baby play with the cap, though; it's a choking hazard.

Illumination. Some pacifier handles glow in the dark, which helps you find the pacifier in the crib in the middle of the night.

Carrying cases and clip-on ribbons. Carrying cases and short, clip-on ribbons that attach the pacifier to clothing and prevent it from ending up on the floor or the street are available separately. As noted in Shopping Secrets, we don't recommend using clip-on ribbons.

Sound. Some pacifiers, like the Baby Buddy Rattlin' Pacifier (*www.babybuddy.com*), feature a soft rattling sound. Baby Buddy also makes a musical pacifier that plays "Twinkle Twinkle Little Star" or "Rock-a-Bye Baby." Our opinion: Sound is nice, but not necessary.

Self-closing models. Keep-it-Kleen (Razbaby, $4.99) and AlwaysClean Pacifier (BébBéSounds, $3.99) have built-in covers that snap closed if the pacifier is dropped.

Banning the Binky

Between your child's first and second birthday, it's a good idea to wean him off the pacifier. Cold turkey is one possible method. Out of sight, out of mind. A more gradual strategy is to begin allowing the pacifier only at certain times, such as bed and naptime—and not during car rides or random moments during the day. Then, after a while, eliminate the pacifier at bed and naptime, too. You'll save on dental bills later because prolonged use of a pacifier can change the shape of your baby's growing jaw and palate. The sucking action can narrow the jaw in the wrong places and widen it in others. If pacifier use continues into the preschool years, there's a strong possibility that your child will need orthodontic treatment, Barna says.

There's another reason to ditch the pacifier even closer to the one-year mark. "When a child is sucking on a pacifier, the auditory tube in the middle ear actually opens, allowing bacteria that naturally reside in the mouth to pass through, which increases the chance of infection," Barna explains.

If your toddler wants something to suck on, Barna recommends graduating to a water-filled "sippy" cup with a collapsible rubber straw, rather than the rounded, plastic-spout style. The suction action required with a straw helps promote normal facial muscle development and won't lead to ear infections. It also helps children learn to drink from a cup because sucking through a straw and sipping through a cup use the same muscles. In general, using a sippy cup helps develop hand-eye coordination. But don't fill that spill-proof cup with juice, soda, iced tea,

SIPPY-CUP SAVVY

If your baby has graduated from pacifiers to sippy cups and likes her water chilled, get an insulated sippy cup. In our tests, we compared regular sippy cups from Evenflo, Gerber, and Playtex with their insulated counterparts. We paid about $3.50 to $5 for our insulated cups, which cost a little more than the regular ones. We chilled water in a refrigerator overnight, then quickly poured 8 ounces into each sippy cup, capped them, and monitored temperatures in the water. The verdict? The insulated cups kept their cool. After an hour, water in the insulated cups had warmed by about 10 degrees; it warmed by about 15 degrees in the regular cups. We think the insulated cups make sense if you want to keep your child's drink cooler.

lemonade, energy or sports drinks, or even milk between meals. They create acids in the child's mouth that can foster tooth decay.

Recommendations

If you decide to go the pacifier route, buy several in infant size, then buy more according to the manufacturer's age recommendations as your baby gets older. Try different brands and nipple shapes until you find one your baby likes (you'll know), but don't force your baby to use a pacifier if he doesn't want to. Some brands of newborn bottle sets come with a pacifier or two, so you might start there. Don't worry about buying the same brand of pacifier as the bottle your baby is using. Pacifier and bottle nipples may resemble each other, but they're not always exactly the same.

We recommend silicone over latex pacifiers because some babies can develop an allergy or sensitivity to latex. Silicone eliminates that potential problem and also tends to hold up longer. Over time, pacifiers can crack and tear. They can also become grainy instead of smooth. Check them carefully and often, and if you discover these problems, throw them away. Some manufacturers recommend replacing them every four weeks.

Use a pacifier between meals when you sense your baby needs something but isn't hungry. Don't sweeten the deal by dipping a pacifier in juice or anything sugary. If you want to dip it in something, use water. Giving a pacifier to a baby who wants food isn't a good idea, however.

PACIFIER SAFETY

To prevent choking, the Consumer Product Safety Commission requires that pacifiers be able to pass a "pull test" after being boiled and cooled six times. The pacifier must not come apart if the nipple is pulled away from the guard in any direction with a force of 10 pounds. The handle or ring must pass the same test. To verify that the pacifier's shield will not suffocate a child, CPSC requires that it pass a different pull test. With the pacifier placed in a test fixture, the nipple is pulled at a force of 2 pounds, which is held for 10 seconds. If the shield pulls completely through the test fixture, the pacifier fails.

Pacifiers sold with a ribbon, cord, string, yarn, or similar attachment must be labeled with this warning: "Do Not Tie Pacifier Around Child's Neck as It Presents a Strangulation Danger." Pacifiers have a tendency to gravitate to the floor or disappear when you need them most. Still, no matter how frustrated you get, take that warning seriously. Each year, the CPSC receives reports of infants strangling on pacifier cords or ribbons tied around their necks. A baby can catch a pacifier cord on crib posts, doorknobs, and many other objects when you're not looking. It takes only a second for a serious accident to occur.

It can make a baby so distraught that he may have trouble calming down enough to eat.

Once you settle on a brand/type, buy several so you don't waste time scouring the house for that precious pacifier—or running to the 24-hour pharmacy to get your baby's favorite brand and model in the middle of the night. Keep two in the diaper bag—it's nice to have an extra in case you drop one or your baby spits it out onto the floor. And if you're traveling together, make sure your spouse is armed with one, too. If you're near a drinking fountain or a restroom, give your baby's pacifier a quick rinse-and-dry before giving it to him. Disperse several in key locations—the baby's car seat, near the changing table, by the rocking chair—so you always know where they are.

Before you use a new pacifier, boil it for five minutes to remove any chemical residue. After that, wash your baby's pacifiers often with warm soapy water by hand or in the dishwasher and squeeze the bulb to remove excess water. Frequent washing is particularly important for pacifiers used by babies younger than 6 months, whose immune systems are especially immature.

Play Yards

These updated versions of the playpen can be handy for your home or when you travel. Play yards provide babies with an enclosed place for playing or napping.

Many play yards include an elevated changing table or changing table insert, an organizer for diapers and baby wipes, and a bassinet—perhaps even a mattress that vibrates to lull babies to sleep. Some play yards have extras to entertain your baby with a mobile, a detachable toy bar, or an entertainment center that features music, nature sounds, and/or dancing lights, some activated by remote control.

How necessary is a play yard? You can certainly live without one. But a play yard can fill a need you may not know you have until you start using it. Of course, a play yard gives your baby a place to play. Some play yards come with a changing table insert, saving you from having to run up and down stairs for every diaper or quick clothes change. Although a full-size crib is the safest place for your baby to doze, a play yard with a bassinet attachment can double as a portable crib.

Most play yards originally were designed for portability— to fit through a door, be moved from one room to another, or folded up to fit in the trunk of your car. Many

P-Q-R-S

are a standard rectangular size, usually 28x40 inches. But the latest versions, like restaurant portion sizes, have gotten bigger. Some play yards are now 30½ inches wide, which is the same as a standard-size door, so scooting them from room to room in the set-up position may be a tight squeeze, if not impossible. Still, many manufacturers also make *travel* play yards, which are designed to move. They roll on wheels and fold easily and compactly into their own tote that resembles a short golf bag for vacations, business trips, and jaunts to Grandma's. A basic play yard weighs around 23 pounds without the bassinet and changing station; over 33 pounds with them. Travel play yards, though, tend to be smaller (around 23 inches wide) and light (around 20 pounds) because they're not loaded with extras.

Play yard frames are made of metal tubing. Mesh on three or all four sides provides ventilation and allows you to keep an eye on your baby. Most models have hinges and lock buttons in the center of the top rails. To set up a play yard, pull the top rails up so they're locked, then push the floor down. To fold this design, pull the floor up, raise the top rails slightly while pressing the release buttons to unlatch and collapse the top rails. An alternate design from J. Mason eliminates the top-rail hinges altogether. To fold this play yard, loosen and remove the corner posts, then collapse the unit.

HOTEL CRIB VS. PLAY YARD

When you're traveling with your baby, you have two options: to use the hotel's crib or your own play yard as a temporary crib. Either is acceptable, provided they meet current safety standards. For the crib, check to make sure the mattress is firm and snug-fitting. You shouldn't be able to fit two fingers between the edge of the mattress and the crib side. You shouldn't be able to fit a soda can between the slats. There also shouldn't be any missing or protruding parts, screws or bolts, or high corner posts, which pose a strangulation hazard, or cutouts in the head or footboard. "We've found that lots of hotels don't have safe cribs," says Laura Reno, director of public affairs for First Candle/SIDS Alliance, in Baltimore. Your best bet may be to bring your play yard along in case the hotel's crib doesn't pass your inspection.

If all a hotel has to offer is a play yard, check it out. (These criteria also apply to your baby's play yard at home.) It should have mesh panels, which foster air flow, but a weave that's small (less than one-quarter-inch openings). Ask for another if the mesh is larger or has any tears, holes, or loose threads, or the top rail cover has tears or holes. The sides should lock securely (press on them to be sure), and the play yard should include a snug, tight-fitting mattress. Use only the mattress or pad provided by the manufacturer, and don't add a second mattress, pillow, comforter, or other soft bedding.

Shopping Secrets

Think about how you'll use your play yard. If it's going to function mostly as a playpen, you can probably go with a basic model, such as the Cosco Funsport ($40), which scored Very Good in our Ratings, on page 234, and skip the extras. A pair of lockable wheels or swivel casters on one end will make it easier to move from room to room. If you'll use it for travel, you'll want a play yard that's lightweight, folds quickly and compactly, and has its own carrying case. You may even want to roll the packed unit. A carrying bag that allows the play yard's own wheels to roll when it's packed is ideal. We found that feature on one product we tested, the Kolcraft Jeep Sahara Limited XT ($130).

If you plan to have your newborn take naps in the play yard as an off-site nursery, compare the bassinet options. Most play yards offer a full-size bassinet, which runs the entire length and width of the play yard. Some feature a rocking cradle with a canopy that fits into the top half of the play yard; the changing table insert occupies the other half. Some models have a canopy to help shield your baby from sun and wind, which can be helpful if you plan to take the play yard outside.

Know when to fold 'em. Some manufacturers claim their play yards can be folded in less than a minute, with "push-button" convenience. See for yourself by practicing on the floor models in a store, if you can. Ease of folding and set-up are especially important if you'll be traveling with the play yard and assembling/disassembling it often.

Select the play yard yourself. Play yards are popular shower gifts; if you're planning to include one on your registry list, select the model yourself and consider the features you'll need.

Go with a model that has storage compartments. Make sure they attach to the outside so they're out of your baby's reach.

Be sure to check the floor pad. It should be one that the manufacturer supplied for the model. It should also be no more than 1 inch thick, snug-fitting, and firm enough to protect your baby from falling or rolling into the loose mesh pocket that can form between the edge of the floor panel and side of the play yard (a suffocation hazard). We judged safer the models that have slots on the floor that allow the mattress's Velcro strips to be inserted and secured on the outside of the play yard, making it difficult for a baby or toddler to lift the mattress and possibly become entrapped under it. Avoid

CERTIFICATION

models with a mattress that attaches to the bottom of a play yard with Velcro pads that a child can access from the inside.

Think about "the look." The trend in play yards is to feature fabric that blends into the décor of your home. Evenflo, for example, makes play yards (and matching travel systems, swings, and high chairs) in lush Italian fabrics in gender-specific color selections, such as pink polka dot with coordinating plaid. But you'll also find collections in toffee, mocha, and eggplant, and patterns with names like "Wedgewood" (blue plaid and solid blue) and "Carlton" (red check and red plaid).

Check the production date and packaging. Buy the play yard with the most recent date. Make sure the model has a certification sticker from the JPMA indicating that it meets the current voluntary standard for play yards.

What's Available

The major brands, in alphabetical order, are Baby Trend (*www.babytrend.com*), Chicco (*www.chiccousa.com*), Combi (*www.combi-intl.com*), Evenflo (*www.evenflo.com*), Fisher-Price (*www.fisher-price.com*), Graco (*www.gracobaby.com*), Kolcraft (*www.kolcraft.com*), J. Mason (*www.jmason.com*), Safety 1st (*www.safety1st.com*), and Simplicity for Children (*www.simplicityforchildren.com*). Play yards range from $40 for the most basic to $130 for premium models.

Features to Consider

Removable bassinet. This gives newborns a place to nap. If you have older children or plan to use this play yard for your next baby, too, look for a bassinet that is secured to the play yard in a way that older children can't tamper with. Some of the units we tested had bassinets that attached to the play yard with easily disengaged bars or by bars and exposed plastic clips. Older siblings could easily outwit these fasteners, which could cause the bassinet to fall to the play yard floor. But one play yard we tested, the Evenflo Baby Go Portable ($70), had bassinet clips that are covered by the bassinet's fabric flaps that snap on the play yard, hiding the clips from view. It was judged safe.

Look for a design that's easy to use. Stop using the bassinet when your baby reaches the manufacturer's recommended weight limit (typically 15 pounds) or can sit up, pull up, or roll over.

Canopy. Many play yards with bassinets have a canopy to shade your baby from harsh light. Some canopies have attached toys that act as a mobile.

Carrying case. Most cases are fabric bags that all the components of the play yard fit into. The four sections of the folded-up floor provide support for the bag by surrounding the unit's other components. A carrying case with a shoulder strap can make life easier. One tested play yard had the added convenience of rolling while folded.

Changing station. Most attach to the top of the top rail, though some are suspended from the side and can be rotated down to hang at the side of the play yard. When using a changing table, always keep your hand on your baby and use the safety straps. One unit we tested, the Graco Pack 'n' Play 9952CLO, didn't have a restraining strap. We think you should avoid such models. Remove the changing station or flip it out of the way once your baby is in the play yard itself to avoid potentially fatal entrapment between the station and the yard's top rail.

Foldability. If you'll be traveling often with your baby, you'll want a play yard that folds and reassembles easily.

Storage. Some models provide storage for toys and other baby items in zippered side pockets, hook-on fabric storage pouches, and clip-on parent organizer bags. They should be big enough to actually

. . . .

Double the fun

The twin birth rate has risen by 70 percent since 1980, according to the National Center for Health Statistics in Hyattsville, Md., and retailers are striving to accommodate parents of twins. The Graco Pack 'n Play Playard 9999SOU ($199.99, www.gracobaby.com), for example, features cozy twin bassinets so two babies can nap side by side. The play space is meant for only one child, though, which is something to consider. What will you do with your other baby at play time?

WHAT NOT TO BUY: A USED PLAY YARD

For safety's sake, don't use a hand-me-down or garage-sale play yard. Buy a new model that meets the current voluntary safety standard, which addresses design problems of earlier models. Older models may have a top-rail hinge that can collapse, forming a steep, V-shaped angle that puts children at risk of being trapped or strangled.

The Consumer Product Safety Commission has recalled models that pose a rail-collapse hazard. If your child uses a play yard at a day-care facility, in a hotel, or at someone else's home, be sure it's a recent model.

hold something. Look for a model with storage compartments that attach to the outside so they're out of your baby's reach.

Toys, music, lights. Some play yards feature a mobile with suspended hanging toys or a detachable toy gym that can also be used with the bassinet mattress on the floor as a separate play mat for tummy time. These are a bonus, as are entertainment centers with music, soothing sounds, and lights, which will contribute to the price. They usually require C or AA batteries (not included). Toys may not be necessary if you intend to use your play yard as just a portable nursery. But if you use a play yard as a mobile activity center, toys and sound effects can be helpful, though you can always add your own.

Wheels or casters. A pair of lockable wheels or swivel casters on one end make moving the play yard easier. Make sure the wheels lock. Some designs can be rolled when folded. That's a definite plus.

Recommendations

Look for a new play yard that's certified by the JPMA, one that offers the best combination of useful features, such as an attachable bassinet where a newborn can nap, a diaper-changing station, and a parent organizer pouch. A pair of lockable wheels or swivel casters on one end will make it easier to move the play yard. Keep safety in mind. Be sure to check the floor pad: It should be no more than 1 inch thick and snug-fitting. If you have a play yard with a diaper-changing station or attachable bassinet, don't place your baby under either attachment while they're in place. Though some play yards come with two bassinets for twins, the playing area is designed to be used by only one child at a time.

If you use a play yard for overnight sleeping, keep in mind that the mattress pad is thin for a reason: to prevent a child from becoming wedged between the pad and the sides. Never add extra mattresses or

PLAY YARD SAFETY ROUNDUP

Although the voluntary standard for play yards has been revised and toughened a number of times since requirements were added in 1997 for automatically locking top rails and in 1999 for latch-strength, this equipment was still responsible for 1,300 injuries to children under the age of 5 in 2005, according to the CPSC. So you still need to be vigilant when using a play yard. To keep your baby safe, here's what you can do:

* Read and follow all safety precautions in the owner's manual (and on the play yard itself).
* Always follow the manufacturer's instructions for assembly, and double check that all latching features and hinges on the play yard are in place and secure. Never leave your baby in a play yard with the sides down.
* Don't put two or more babies in a play yard that's designed only for one.
* Stop using the bassinet feature when your baby either reaches the manufacturer's recommended weight limit, or can sit up, pull up, or roll over (at about 3 months old and 15 pounds).
* Stop using the play yard once your baby has reached the maximum height and weight recommendations, usually 35 inches and 30 pounds.
* Choose a play yard with mesh holes smaller than one-quarter inch. Those that are JPMA certified will meet this recommendation.
* Inspect your play yard regularly and stop using it if the mesh sides or vinyl- or fabric-covered rails get torn or punctured, or any rivets on the rails begin to protrude. Don't use a play yard with broken hinges.
* Remove the changing-station or bassinet insert when your baby is playing in the play yard. A baby's neck can get trapped between the side rail and the insert.
* Don't tie any items across the top or corner of the play yard or hang toys from the sides with strings or cords. These can be a strangulation hazard.
* Don't add a second mattress to the bassinet, or pillows, comforters, or toys.
* Buy a portable bassinet sheet that's tight-fitting—in other words, one that's designed for play yards. Never use a sheet made for a crib mattress or twin or other size bed.
* If you use the bassinet, place your baby to sleep on her back, as you would in a full-size crib.
* Never leave your baby unattended in a play yard, which means your baby should always be in view, even when she's sleeping in the bassinet.
* When you're using a play yard's changing table, always keep a hand on your baby and use the safety harness.
* Don't place a play yard near stoves, fireplaces, campfires, or sources of heat and wind.
* Stop using a play yard if it is damaged. Don't try to patch holes in the mesh with tape, for example.
* Don't place a play yard near a window where your baby can reach cords from window blinds or curtains. They're a strangulation hazard.
* When your baby can pull to a standing position, remove large toys and other objects that can serve as a stepping stool for climbing out of the play yard.

padding, and don't use blankets or other types of soft bedding, which pose a suffocation hazard. Instead, layer your baby for warmth with an onesie or T-shirt and a footed sleeper or wearable sleeper sack. Stop using a play yard when your child attempts to climb out or when he reaches the height and weight limits (typically 35 inches and 30 pounds). Stop using the bassinet attachment when your baby reaches 3 months or 15 pounds or can sit up, pull up, or roll over.

Ratings • Play Yards

Excellent Very good Good Fair Poor

In performance order.

Key number	Brand & model	Price Paid	Overall score (0–100, P F G VG E)	Safety	Ease of use	Portability	Bassinet
1	**Baby Trend** Nursery Center	130	82	⊖	○	⊖	⊖
2	**Evenflo** Baby Go Portable	70	79	⊖	⊖	⊖	○
3	**Kolcraft** Jeep Sahara Limited XT	130	73	⊖	⊖	⊖	⊖
4	**Graco** Pack 'n Play 9350 JNG	60	72	⊖	⊖	⊖	⊖
5	**Cosco** Funsport	40	71	⊖	⊖	◐	NA
6	**Fisher-Price** Aquarium	100	59	⊖	⊖	⊖	⊖
7	**Kolcraft** Contours 3-in-1 Travel	100	58	⊖	⊖	○	◐
8	**Graco** Pack 'n Play 9952 CLO	130	32	◐	⊖	⊖	○

Guide to the Ratings

The models are listed in order of overall performance based on safety tests and convenience judgments. **Safety** is our evaluation of mattress attachment, bassinet and changing table safety. **Ease of use** assesses ease of setup and closure, ease of use of the latch, and ease of mattress attachment. **Portability** is based on our assessment of how easy it is to pack and carry the packed play yard. **Price** is approximate retail.

CHAPTER

28

Rocking Chairs & Gliders

I f you've considered buying a rocking chair but aren't sure you'll use it, or are turned off by the grandmotherly image, think again.

Babies and rocking chairs go together like macaroni and cheese. The rocking motion of the chair will add to the soothing effect your baby feels when being held, and there's nothing better for you for quick catnaps, those 3 a.m. feedings, and snuggling in to read to your little one.

Basic hardwood rocking chairs have been around for ages. A glider is an updated version that's designed to slide forward and backward rather than rock in an arc. Some also swivel. Most gliders come with cushions. An ottoman you can prop your feet on is also available as a stand-alone item and is purely optional, so don't feel like you're missing out if you skip it. Some ottomans are stationary while others glide back and forth with their matching gliders.

P-Q-R-S

Shopping Secrets

Test it in the store. This is an item you don't want to research solely on the Internet (although you can certainly buy online if you know what you're getting). Sit in the chair and rock or glide away. That's the best way to tell if a chair's seat fits your bottom and if it's comfortable.

Determine the model, then finish, fabric, and whether or not you want an ottoman. Making your buying decisions in that order may make shopping easier. If you're looking for a glider, here are some basic questions that can help you find the right model for your needs: Do you want it to recline? Swivel? Do you want a traditional look, or sleigh-style? Then focus on finish (white, natural, maple, and cherry are common finishes), then fabric, and so on.

Go for a darker color. Stay away from natural beige or pastel fabrics. Furniture fabric can appear soiled from just normal wear and tear. And, of course, washable fabrics are a plus.

Check under the seat. "You want to make sure the fabric underneath the seat cushion has springs attached to it," says Seth Berger, director of operations of Kids Home Furnishings, a baby-to-teen furniture store, in Stamford, Conn. You may find four small springs that secure a bottom piece of fabric to the chair frame. That's good. The underbelly of the seat shouldn't be just fabric glued to a frame. You won't have much support or shock absorption.

Ask about warranties. If you choose a glider, you'll want to know if the bearings, which run the gliding mechanism, have a warranty. They take the brunt of a person's weight over time. Ten years is a good warranty length, although a lifetime warranty is better (although that's not the case for all baby products).

Get a rocker or glider with a generously wide seat and arms that won't hem you in. Both these features are especially important if you plan to use a nursing pillow (a Boppy). And with a baby on board, you'll need the room. Practice in the store with a display-model nursing pillow or your baby to make sure you're both a good fit in the chair. Well-padded arm rests on a glider may be all you need to support and comfortably feed your baby, negating the need for a Boppy.

Choose a glider that locks in place if you have a toddler or if you have only a newborn now but plan to have more than one child. You don't want to be gliding when you're feeding your newborn if there's a curious toddler underfoot; little fingers can get caught in the gliding mechanism. You'll also want to lock it to keep your toddler safe when you're not around.

What's Available

The major brands of rocking chairs and gliders, in alphabetical order, are: Angel Line (*www.angelline.com*), Best Chairs (*www.bestchairs.com*),

---

Gliders 101

FEATURES TO LOOK FOR:
- Solid wood construction.
- Cushions that won't lump and that are covered in woven fabrics that won't fray.
- High padded back for support, padded arms, and dense-foam seat cushions.
- Springs underneath the seat for support.
- Smooth gliding mechanism.
- Mechanism bearings with a warranty.
- Locking mechanism.
- Recline option.

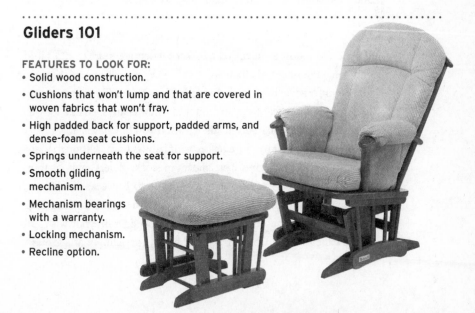

GLIDER IN DISGUISE

Although you may be rocking with your baby well into the toddler years, rocking chairs and gliders tend to have a limited use. Once your baby goes to sleep without rocking, you may find yourself sitting in the chair less and less—at least until the next baby comes along. Many manufacturers make gliders that are fully upholstered to look like a bedroom chair or one that might warm the corner of a living room. That's something else to consider when choosing the fabric for your glider—how it might look in the living room or a bedroom later.

Dutailier (*www.dutailier.com*), Foundations (*www.foundations.com*), Shermag (*www.sher mag.com*), and Storkcraft (*www.storkcraft.com*). Rocking chairs and gliders generally range from $150 to $400. You'll pay even more for gliders in custom fabrics and classic, spindle rocking chairs, which are available at high-end retailers such as Posh Tots *(www.poshtots.com)* In general, a higher price tag reflects solid wood construction. In gliders, you'll probably get more durable, cushier cushions; a higher-quality gliding system; a spring-supported seat; and a positional lock you can use to keep it from gliding. Some gliders even recline, which can come in handy for re-energizing catnaps. Although you get what you pay for, you don't have to go whole hog. There's quality and solid construction in the midrange, as well.

Recommendations

If in doubt, choose a glider over a rocker. Gliders are more comfortable, and you'll use one more than you think. They also dominate the market, so you'll have more to choose from. Secondhand is an option, but look for the same features you'd want in a new chair, such as a locking mechanism, and make sure it still works. If you buy new, allow plenty of time for the chair to arrive before your baby is born. Although many baby Web sites and stores have gliders in stock, gliders with custom-fabric cushions have to be ordered. Allow up to 10 weeks for delivery. Minimal assembly may be required. A glider can feel like a splurge, but if you're having a baby shower, why not put a glider on your wish list? It's an expensive item, but friends and family may chip in as a group.

CHAPTER
29

Shopping-cart Covers

S hopping-cart covers—decorative fabric or disposable plastic covers that fit over the seat of a shopping cart—are designed to shield children 6 months to 3 years of age from illness-causing germs innocently transferred to the cart by other shoppers, or by children who've touched or gnawed the handle or sat in the seat with a leaky diaper.

Cart covers have been around for a few years, but now, due to growing demand, they've really come into the mainstream. Much of their appeal stems from the general protectiveness you feel as a parent. The last thing you want is for your baby to get sick; even a stuffy nose can make him miserable. A cart cover can protect him from some of the bacteria and viruses he's exposed to every day.

Still, as fashionable as these products have become, you shouldn't consider them a must-have. There is no evidence that they reduce the incidence of colds and flu, and getting sick when you're a kid is part of the job description. "We all enter this world with an inexperienced immune system," says Charles Shubin, M.D., director of pediatrics at Mercy FamilyCare in Baltimore. Slowly, children strengthen their immune systems by battling germs, viruses, and other organisms.

Shopping-cart covers are part of the growing "germ defense" niche in the baby product industry. Besides cart covers, you'll now find disposable changing pads, toilet seat covers, disposable placemats, and combination bibs/placemats designed to help keep little hands on—not under—the table when you're dining on the go.

Even if shopping-cart covers cut down the number of infections your child picks up, simple hand-washing would suffice, says Amy Guiot, M.D., a pediatrician with Cincinnati Children's Hospital and Medical Center in Ohio. "There are certainly germs on shopping carts, but as long as you wash your child's hands with hand sanitizer or a disposable baby wipe in the car, or wash them when you get home, you've accomplished the same thing. In fact, diligent hand washing is one of the most effective things parents can do, even themselves, to keep everybody healthy." And these days, many supermarkets supply sanitizing wipes so you can give the cart handle and seat a quick cleaning when you walk in. In our opinion, that's another reason to put shopping-cart covers in the "optional" category.

Shopping Secrets

Think about where you'll use the cover. Shopping carts come in different sizes and shapes. If you decide you need one, be sure the one you buy suits the type of cart you'll use most often. Some brands specify right on the package which type of carts they fit. But if they don't, ask the salesperson for specifics, such as: "Does this shopping-cart cover fit the double-seater cart at Costco?" (Some cart covers are oversize; they're made for the double-seaters found at warehouse clubs.) Keep your receipt and know the store's return policy just in case it doesn't work out.

Check for coverage. If your main concern is "germ defense," look for a cart cover that encases the entire seating area—the handlebar, sides, back, and front.

Consider comfort. Cleanliness aside, shopping-cart covers can make for a cozy ride. If that's important to you, look for a deluxe model, which usually has extra cushioning and maybe even an attachable pillow.

SAFER SHOPPING

To prevent shopping-cart injuries from falls and tipovers, the American Academy of Pediatrics (AAP) recommends that parents avoid putting kids in shopping carts entirely by:

- Leaving your child home with another adult on your grocery shopping days.
- Having your child walk once he gets older.
- Having another adult come with you to watch your baby while you shop.
- Using a stroller, wagon, or soft carrier instead of a shopping cart.
- Food shopping online so you don't have to trek to the store with your baby.

If food shopping with your children can't be avoided and you decide to use a shopping cart, the Consumer Product Safety Commission recommends that parents always use seatbelts to restrain their child in the cart's seat.

The AAP also issues these guidelines. DON'T:

- Leave your child alone in the shopping cart.
- Let your child stand up in a shopping cart.
- Place an infant carrier on top of the shopping cart.
- Let your child ride in the cart basket.
- Let your child ride or climb on the sides or front of the cart.
- Let older children push the cart when there's another child in it.

Look for a safety belt. According to the American Academy of Pediatrics, in 2005 (the most recent statistics available), more than 24,000 children were treated in U.S. hospital emergency rooms for shopping-cart related injuries; more than 93 percent of those children were under age 5. Shopping carts are among the leading causes of head injuries to young children. Most injuries occurred when a child fell out of a shopping-cart seat, the cart tipped over, the child became trapped in the cart, or the child fell while riding on the outside of the cart. Most often, these young climbers fall out of the cart because the safety restraint was missing or not used. Since the cart cover you buy probably will override the built-in safety belt on the shopping-cart seat, be sure to buy a cover that has its own durable safety belt—one that's easy to use, so you'll be more likely to strap your baby in every time.

Check for ease. Before you buy, find out how the cover attaches to the cart—with Velcro, a buckle, or elastic. Since inserting a cart cover while holding your baby will be a challenge, you'll want to be able to do it quickly with one hand. Some brands claim their covers can be installed in 30 seconds. Read the instructions before you buy. Once you buy the cover, try it out at home so you'll know exactly what to do in the store. The cover also should be easy to store in your car.

What's Available

Shopping-cart covers run from basic to high-end, ranging in price from $9.99 (for a three-pack of disposable cart covers) to $65 for double-seater fabric covers with added features. Major brands are, in alphabetical order: Baby a la cart (*www.babyalacart.com*), Buggy Baggs (*www.buggybaggs.com)*, Cart Comforter by Little Peanuts Products (*www.cartcomforter.com*), Clean Shopper by Baby Ease (*www.cleanshopper.com*), Floppy Seat (*www.floppyseat.com*), and Infantino (*www.infantino.com*). You can also order custom-made cart covers online with such extras as monogramming or squeakers for baby-amusing sound effects.

Features to Consider

Versatility. Some cart covers have attached plush toys; side pockets for storing sippy cups, your cell phone, keys, and coupons; and loops for attaching toys and teethers. Some convert to a play mat or diaper bag, or can be used on high chairs, park swings, public strollers, or even as an emergency changing pad. You can pay more for these extras, so consider how much you'll use them before you buy.

Fabric. Patterns run the gamut from toile, plaid, and paisley to animal prints, florals, and popular cartoon character motifs. Machine-washable materials are standard, though some fabrics can only be wiped clean. Some covers offer extra long leg flaps to prevent pinching.

Safety belts. You'll find two basic safety belt/strap options: a cover that features one detachable strap that threads through the back of the seat to secure the baby to the cart, and a cover that features two straps, one to secure your baby to the cart and one to secure the cover to the cart.

Padding. Higher-end covers have plush, thick batting to give babies a luxurious ride. Lower-end models have quilted cotton fabric without batting.

Pillow. Covers at the high end have a pillow at the handlebar so a baby can rest his head.

Bag/tote. When not in use, some cart covers fold into a duffel-shape diaper bag with one large compartment for diapers, wipes, toys, and snacks. Others roll up and become their own carrying bag. Some have a separate, vinyl carrying case. Shopping-cart covers are just one more thing to carry, so choose a cover that has the portable system you think you'll use most often. Keep in mind that cars have their own colonies of germs. Though a cart cover may protect your baby

BOOST YOUR CHILD'S IMMUNITY

Besides hand-washing, which guards against spreading germs, here are healthy habits that can strengthen your child's developing immune system:

Breast-feed your baby. As mentioned in the "Breast Pumps" chapter, "Breast is best." There is strong evidence that nursing decreases the incidence and severity of ear and respiratory-tract infections, diarrhea, meningitis, and urinary-tract infections. Some studies suggest that nursing may also help lower the risk of Sudden Infant Death Syndrome (SIDS). Others suggest lower rates of diabetes, certain forms of cancer, obesity, high cholesterol, and asthma in older children and adults who were breast-fed as infants. Colostrum—the thin yellow "premilk" that flows from breasts during the first several days after birth—is especially rich in disease-fighting antibodies, says Charles Shubin, M.D., director of pediatrics at Mercy FamilyCare in Baltimore. The AAP recommends that moms exclusively breast-feed for a baby's first six months, if possible.

Log in sleep time. Studies show that sleep deprivation can make adults more susceptible to illness by reducing natural killer cells, immune-system weapons that attack microbes and cancer cells. The same is true for children, says Kathi J. Kemper, M.D., professor of general pediatrics at Wake Forest University School of Medicine in Winston-Salem, N.C. Children in day care are particularly at risk for sleep deprivation because all the activity can make it difficult for them to nap. How much sleep do kids need? A newborn may need up to 18 hours of crib time a day; toddlers require 12 to 13 hours, and preschoolers need about 10 hours. "If your child can't or won't take naps during the day, try to put her to bed earlier," says Kemper.

Banish secondhand smoke. If you or your spouse smokes, quit. According to the U.S. Surgeon General, secondhand cigarette smoke contains more than 250 chemicals known to be toxic or cancer causing. Babies and kids are especially vulnerable to the harmful effects of secondhand smoke because their bodies are developing. Secondhand smoke increases a child's risk of SIDS and ear and respiratory infections, such as pneumonia. There's no safe level of secondhand smoke exposure. Designating a smoking area in your home, for example, is like having a nonchlorinated section of a swimming pool (impossible). If you absolutely can't quit smoking, you can reduce your child's health risks by smoking only outside the house and making your car a smoke-free zone. (Smoking with the window open doesn't eliminate second-hand smoke exposure.) Also, ask others not to smoke around your child. For advice on quitting, call 1-800-QUIT-NOW.

Don't pressure your pediatrician. Urging your pediatrician to write a prescription for an antibiotic whenever your child has a cold, the flu, or a sore throat is a bad idea. Antibiotics treat only illnesses caused by bacteria, "but the majority of childhood illnesses are caused by viruses," says Howard Bauchner, M.D., a professor of pediatrics and public health at the Boston University School of Medicine. Studies show, however, that many pediatricians prescribe antibiotics at the urging of parents who mistakenly think it can't hurt. It can. Strains of antibiotic-resistant bacteria have flourished as a result, and a simple ear infection is more difficult to cure if it's caused by stubborn bacteria that don't respond to standard treatment. Whenever your child's pediatrician wants to prescribe an antibiotic, make sure she isn't prescribing it solely because she thinks you want it. "I strongly encourage parents to say, 'Do you think it's really necessary?' " Bauchner says.

from germs when you're shopping, just tossing the cart cover in the back or trunk of your car when it's not in use will wipe out the benefits.

Recommendations

A shopping-cart cover isn't necessary to protect your baby from bacteria and viruses. In our opinion, this product is purely optional. What has been proven to guard against spreading germs is ordinary hand-washing, so help your baby wash her hands often with soap and water, hand sanitizer or disposable baby wipes. Pay particular attention to her hygiene before and after each meal and after she plays outside, handles pets, blows her nose, uses the bathroom, and arrives home from day care, or anyplace else, for that matter. When you're out, carry disposable wipes or hand sanitizer with you for quick cleanups.

If you decide to get a shopping-cart cover, buy one with a safety belt and use the belt every time you shop. If germ protection is your main concern, go with a basic, low-end model that offers 100 percent cart seat coverage (no exposed metal or plastic).

30

Soft Infant Carriers

P-Q-R-S

Babies love and need to be held, and carriers are a great, hands-free way to keep your baby close and cozy, whether you're on the go or doing odd jobs around the house. And each step you take may help jiggle your baby to sleep. In a sense, you wear your baby, which may make him feel secure and ease any fussiness. Some carriers even allow easy and discreet nursing. If you like using a carrier (and your baby likes it, too—and that's important), you may even be able to postpone buying a stroller for a few months, until your baby can sit up.

There are two basic types of soft infant carriers. A strap-on model holds a baby in an upright position; an infant faces in and an older baby faces out or in. The carrier consists of a padded fabric pouch with leg holes attached to an adult shoulder and waist belt, which supports the baby. A sling—also called a wrap—is your other option. It consists of a length of fabric you wear over one shoulder and around your waist. With a marsupial feel to it, a sling forms a comfy, portable nest for an infant. Some slings can also be worn on your hip.

Most strap-on carriers and slings specify a maximum weight limit, but you'll probably find your baby will be too heavy to carry comfortably before he reaches the limit. "Both slings and soft infant carriers can pull your body weight forward, which isn't a natural carrying position," says Anne Coffman, a physical therapist from New Berlin, Wis., a member of the American Physical Therapy Association, and mother of two. You may want to graduate to a backpack carrier, which provides more structural support, by the time your baby can sit up, or around the 20-pound mark. Carrying a load on your back puts less stress on your body. "Make the change before it gets uncomfortable," says Coffman. "If you wait too long, you're asking for muscle strain."

There are pluses and minuses to both types of carriers, which we'll discuss throughout this chapter. For information on backpacks, see the "Backpack Carriers" chapter, page 57.

Strap-on Strategies

Strap-on carriers are designed for babies weighing 7 or 8 pounds to 26 pounds, depending on the brand, but there are exceptions. Weego (*www.weego.com*) makes the Weego Baby Carrier, which can be used for full-term babies who weigh as little as 6 pounds, and the Weego Preemie, for babies who weigh as little as 3½ pounds. Expecting twins? The same company also makes a strap-on carrier for two; both babies are carried together on your front, which sounds ambitious, but perhaps no more than navigating the supermarket or the mall with a double pram or stroller.

Strap-on models with leg openings big enough for a child to slip through have been subject to recalls. Some models now come with a seat insert for newborns to guard against that. Other models have straps or other ways to narrow the openings so they fit snugly around the legs. All the carriers in our tests on page 254, passed the leg openings test, which suggests this issue has been addressed by manufacturers. In any event, adjust leg openings to the smallest size that is comfortable for your child.

Pros: If both you and your spouse want to get in on the action, you can find one you both like. "The Baby Björn [a popular brand of strap-on carriers] is great because my husband wasn't comfortable wearing a sling," says Andrea Bledsoe from Fishers, Ind., the mother of a 6 month old. If you both want to use a strap-on carrier frequently, consider getting two—his and hers. To wear a strap-on successfully, you have to adjust the straps; so if you have two, you won't have to continually adjust the carrier when you trade back and forth.

Cons: Some infants don't like being carried in the upright position (and if they get upset, they're literally in your face about it). Some dislike any carrier that feels too confining around the head, which is necessary in the beginning months. Also, if your baby falls asleep in a strap-on carrier, you may feel stuck. "I couldn't get my baby out of the carrier and lay him down without waking him," says Jennifer Dulles Jansky from Broomfield, Colo., the mother of two. Most models have addressed that problem by modifying their design to include a side exit feature, which is a handy feature. (More on that later.)

Sling Savvy

Made of fabric (sometimes pleated or padded), some slings form an over-the-shoulder hammock for holding a young baby across your front in a semi-reclined position, as you'd naturally carry your baby and, like a strap-on carrier, frees your arms. Many claim they can be adjusted to tote a toddler up to 35 pounds. You can transport your child lying down or upright, facing in or out. Some slings can also be worn with your baby on your back or hip.

Pros: Like a strap-on carrier, a sling allows you to get around easily in spaces where a stroller can't go, such as an escalator at a shopping mall. You'll also fit better in cramped elevators. You may be surprised where you end up needing it. "I use a sling for grocery store trips because placing my daughter's car seat carrier on top of the shopping cart just didn't work," says Regina Haas from Dallas, Texas, the mother of a 9-month-old. "I'm only 5-foot-1, and I could barely see to steer the cart," she says.

Cons: Just as some babies don't like being carried upright in a strap-on, others don't feel comfortable being carried in a sling in a reclining position. Also, carrying your baby's weight diagonally in front may be uncomfortable, especially if you're petite and your baby is large. And one more thing: Extra-special care is needed with slings, since they generally aren't secure enough for activity more rigorous than leisurely

CERTIFICATION

To date, the Juvenile Products Manufacturers Association (JPMA) has certified seven brands of soft infant carriers, including Baby King, Dorel Juvenile Group (Safety 1st), The First Years, Kelty K.I.D.S., Kidsline, Kolcraft, and Maclaren. Certified soft infant carriers are in compliance with the voluntary American Society for Testing and Materials (ASTM) leg-opening requirements standard, which was created to minimize the risk of babies falling through leg openings. A warning label must also tell you how to adjust leg openings to accommodate your child. Certified carriers must also pass dynamic and static load tests, which push the limits on the amount of weight a carrier can safely support. They also have warning statements on the product and in the instruction booklet stating, for example, that small children can fall through a leg opening and that the product should be used only if your baby's weight is in a specific range, such as 8 to 26 pounds.

walking. If you want to pick up the pace, a strap-on carrier or a stroller is your best bet. Finally, our testers determined that some slings, such as The Ultimate Baby Wrap, have a steep learning curve for putting it on and using it properly. Don't buy a sling if you suspect that you won't have the patience for it.

Getting the Hang of It

You may feel a little awkward the first few times you use any type of infant carrier. You have to figure out how to put it on or wrap it around yourself and your baby (if you're using a sling). You have to adjust the straps or fabric so the carrier will fit your body comfortably. For maximum comfort with a sling, a baby should ride above your waist and below your bust line. Make fit adjustments before putting your baby in the carrier or sling. Mastering the adjustment of rings and folds so everything fits correctly takes time, even with clear, printed directions. But getting it right is critical to keeping your baby safe, since improper use can put your child at risk of injury. If your back or neck hurts from carrying most of a baby's weight on one side, give that shoulder a break and put the sling on with the strap on the other shoulder.

Last—and this is the fun part—you have to get your baby inside the carrier without provoking a fuss, then learn to trust the carrier and get used to the initially uneasy feeling of having your baby suspended. Our advice is to read the directions carefully, then practice. Some manufacturers recommend that you rehearse with a teddy bear or doll until all steps become natural. That's not a bad idea.

Learning how to move with a sling or strap-on carrier can take practice. You can't lean over too much, and your back, shoulders, and legs must adjust to the added weight. You'll also have to be mindful of your extra dimensions when you go through doorways and around corners so your baby won't bump into anything. Although many carriers are designed to adjust and "grow" with your baby, some parents complain of lower back pain with front carriers once their baby reaches about 20 pounds. A simple rule is to stop using a carrier when you sense you're approaching your own physical limits. You'll know.

Shopping Secrets

Decide if you're the type who'll use a soft carrier. "From the beginning, I knew that having my baby strapped to me was something that I'd be comfortable with and would prefer," says Regina Haas, who owns a strap-on Baby Björn for taking long walks because she says it's so sturdy. If you're not sure you'll use a strap-on carrier or sling, wait until after your baby is born before you buy one. If, for example, your baby constantly wants to be held, a soft infant carrier may be just the ticket for relieving your tired arms.

Better yet, borrow one first. Try on a friend's carrier to see if it is comfortable for you and how your baby fares in one.

By the same token, don't buy one secondhand. Strap-on carriers and slings have been subject to recalls, so buy new to ensure that you're carrying your baby safely. As recently as 2004, the Baby Björn Carrier Active, for example, was recalled because the back support buckle could detach from the shoulder straps, which could allow a baby to fall. That defect has since been addressed, but carriers sold from September 2003 to Aug. 15, 2004, could still be in circulation. We tested a newer version of the Baby Carrier Active and it rated Excellent overall.

To play it even safer, make sure any new carrier you're considering hasn't been subject to a recall. For the latest recall information, check the Consumer Product Safety Commission Web site at *www.cpsc.gov*. Send in the registration card so you will be alerted to any recalls.

Try on the floor model with your baby, if possible. But take another adult along to help, especially if you're not familiar with carriers and slings. Not all carriers and slings fit all builds. In our tests (page 254), the straps on the Baby Björn Active couldn't be tightened enough to accommodate the narrow shoulders and slim build of one of our testers, nor could the carrier fit a tester with a large frame. (It is still our top-rated soft infant carrier, however.) The Kelty K.I.D.S. Kangaroo and the Playtex Hip Hammock had straps that couldn't be adjusted to fit a large build. (Nonetheless, the Hip Hammock is our top-rated sling.) Doing a test-run in the store will give you a quick take on sizing and the features each carrier or sling offers.

Consider a framed carrier. This is an option when your baby can sit up unassisted (about 6 months and 16 pounds). These carriers are basically backpacks with a fabric baby seat and structured frame and generally can be used for children up to about 3 years old or 40 pounds.

Know you can return it. Some babies need time to adjust to an infant carrier; others never come around. Because your baby's verdict is unpredictable, keep your receipt and the packaging the carrier came in, and know the retailer's return policy. If you or your baby doesn't like the sling or strap-on carrier you select, take it back.

What's Available

The major brands of strap-on soft-carrier makers are, in alphabetical order, Baby Björn (*www.babybjorn.com*), Chicco (*www.chiccousa.com*), Evenflo Snugli (*www.even flo.com*), Infantino (*www.infantino.com*), Kelty K.I.D.S. (*www.keltykids.com*), Kidsline Body Glove carrier (*www.kidslineinc.com*), Kolcraft Jeep carriers (*www.kolcraft.com*), Maclaren (*www.maclaren baby.com*), Safety 1st (*www.safety1st.com*), and Weego (*www.weego.com*). Prices range from $15 for a very basic carrier to $120 for carriers with enhanced shoulder and back support.

The major brands of slings are, in alphabetical order, Ellaroo.com (*www.ellaroo.com*), Hotslings *www.hotslings.com*), Infantino (*www.infantino.com*), JJ Cole Collections/Premaxx baby carrier (*www.jjcoleusa .com*), Maya Wrap (*www.mayawrap.com*), Moby Wrap (*www.mobywrap .com*), the NoJo Baby Sling by Dr. Sears (available at *www.target.com* and *www.amazon.com*), Parents of Invention (*www.parentsofinvention.com*), Playtex (*www.playtexbaby.com*), and Ultimate Baby Wrap (*www.mommysthinkin.com*). Other hot sites for slings are *www.happyslings.com* and *www.theslingstation.com.* Prices range from $30 to $65 for lightly padded slings in designer fabric.

Features to Consider

Fabric. Slings and strap-on carriers are made of comfortable brushed cotton, stretchy T-shirt cotton interlock, corduroy, polyester and polyester blends, flannel-like materials, or meshy, moisture-resistant nylon, and come in fashionable colors and patterns. Carriers designed to be used in water may be made of neoprene—wet suit material. Slings and strap-on carriers should be completely washable.

Musical amenities. The latest models of strap-on carriers play music from the front pouch and serenade your baby with five nursery melodies (you'll find that feature in the Evenflo Snugli 4-in-1 Serenade Soft Carrier, *www.evenflo.com*).

Cup or bottle holders. Cup holders are now de rigueur in cars, and some strap-on carriers feature this extra so you or your baby can sip anywhere.

Fasteners. Carriers have a variety of buckles and fasteners for shoulder and waist straps and babies' seats. Snaps should be sturdy and require a lot of force to unfasten. Buckles that hold shoulder and waist straps should be easy to adjust and keep straps firmly fastened when the carrier is in use. Buckles and fasteners should be easy for an adult to use, but not so easy that a baby could undo them, and should fasten tightly, but not close in way that they could pinch your fingers. If they do, your baby could be pinched, too. And you might not properly secure the buckles when using the carrier for fear of being pinched, which isn't safe either. Several carriers we tested, the Infantino 6 in One Rider, the Infantino Smart Rider, the Kelty K.I.D.S. Kangaroo, and the Snugli Comfort Vent by Evenflo, rated somewhat lower because the buckles posed a pinching concern for panelists (some did get pinched).

Lumbar support. Well-made carriers may have a special padded waist strap that helps distribute a baby's weight from your shoulders to your hips and pelvic area. This is a definite comfort advantage. The latest models of strap-on carriers feature a massaging lumbar support pad that vibrates, which is nice but not necessary. When you're shopping, try on a floor model and fasten the belt/waist strap to see if it's long enough and neither too high nor too low when the carrier is in place. Padding should be firm, not mushy. Our tests show that two carriers, the Baby Björn Active and the Jeep 2-in-1, have especially good back support.

Shoulder straps. Shoulder-strap padding should be firm and wide so the straps won't dig in. Straps should be positioned so they won't slip off your shoulders or chafe your neck, and they should be adjustable while you're carrying your baby.

Side-vent insets. Babies can get sweaty in an infant carrier. To help keep them cool, some carriers have a panel of meshy material designed to promote air flow, or side insets that can be unzipped or unbuttoned to serve the same purpose. Look for either of those features if you'll be having a summer baby or you live in a warm climate.

Side entry. Some strap-on models, such as the Snugli Classic from Evenflo ($15), have a single side-entry buckle that allows you to remove your baby from the side instead of from the top. Like most carriers we tested, the Snugli Comfort Vent by Evenflo ($20) has dual side-entry buckles so you can get your baby out from either side. That exit strategy may be a good idea if you want to move your sleeping baby to a crib without waking him.

Pacifier and toy loops and storage pockets. These are handy for the essentials.

Recommendations

There are parents who like soft infant carriers and there are those who mostly leave their carriers hanging on a hook in the closet. Because it's impossible to predict how you or your baby will react to one, it doesn't pay to register for a soft infant carrier or buy it ahead of time. Wait to buy until your baby is born. Ideally, you've gotten a little practice with a friend's carrier. Still, bring your baby shopping with you and bring another adult along, to spot you as you try carriers out. Cross this product off your list if you plan to be active with your baby; for example, if you look forward to going on brisk walks in the park. If that's the case, a sling probably isn't the product for you.

COATS FOR INFANT CARRIERS

If you want to use your strap-on carrier outside in cooler months, consider getting a carrier cover (pictured on page 249), which slips over most brands of strap-on soft infant carriers so you don't have to stuff your bundled-up baby into a carrier or zip your coat around him. Infant carrier covers are made of high-tech materials like Thinsulate and/or polyester/nylon fleece blends. At the high end, you'll find faux mink and ultrasuede, imitation Persian lamb's wool, and denim paired with chenille. Popular brands include Baby Björn (*www.babybjorn.com*), Brookspond (*www.brookspond.com*), and Kiddopotamus *(www.kiddopotamus.com)*. They retail from $20 to $145.

If you decide to buy a carrier because you like the idea of keeping your baby close—and your baby is amenable—look for a comfortable, machine washable carrier that can be fitted for your torso, with sturdy, adjustable straps that secure your baby snugly, one that evenly distributes her weight and supports her head. Follow the manufacturer's instructions carefully to make sure you use the sling or carrier properly and be sure to send in the registration card so you can be notified in the event of a recall.

Check the carrier periodically for sharp edges, ripped seams, and missing, loose, or defective snaps, buckles, or rings. Think about how much you'll use it before you buy one. That will help you determine what to spend, though price isn't necessarily an indicator of quality. A low-priced version may be fine if you plan to use the carrier only occasionally. If you foresee long jaunts with your baby or expect to be using your carrier a lot around the house, consider a higher-end model, which may give you more support and be more comfortable. If you're uneasy about using your carrier—most parents are at first—load your baby into it over a soft surface, such as your bed or sofa.

Ratings • Soft Infant Carriers and Slings

	Excellent	Very good	Good	Fair	Poor
	⊖	⊖	○	◕	●

Within types, in performance order.

Key number	Brand & model	Price	Exterior material	Weight range (lbs)	Overall score	Safety	Ease of use	Comfort
					0 ···· 100 P F G VG E			
INFANT CARRIERS								
1	**Baby Bjorn** Active	$120	Cotton/Polyester	8 to 26	84	⊖	⊖	⊖
2	**Baby Bjorn** Original	80	Cotton	8 to 25	84	⊖	⊖	⊖
3	**Jeep** 2-in-1 by Kolcraft	40	Polyester	8 to 26	81	⊖	⊖	⊖
4	**Infantino** Smart Rider	50	Polyester	8 to 26	59	○	⊖	○
5	**Kelty K.I.D.S.** Kangaroo	80	Nylon	8 to 25	53	○	◕	○
6	**Snugli** Comfort Vent by Evenflo	20	Polyester Blend	7 to 26	48	○	⊖	◕
7	**Kelty K.I.D.S.** Wallaby	65	Cotton	8 to 25	35	◕	⊖	○
8	**Infantino** 6 in One Rider	40	Polyester/Cotton	8 to 35	28	○	●	◕
SLINGS								
9	**Playtex** Hip Hammock	40	Polyester	15 to 35	76	⊖	⊖	○
10	**Premaxx**	50	Cotton	up to 35	57	○	⊖	⊖
11	**Nojo** The Original	40	Cotton	up to 30	55	○	⊖	○
12	**The Ultimate Baby Wrap**	40	Cotton/Lycra	5 to 35	45	○	◕	○

Guide to the Ratings

The models are presented by type (soft infant carriers or slings) and are listed in order of performance. **Overall score** is based primarily on safety judgments, and judgments made by a small group of panelists for ease of use and comfort, using a lightweight baby doll and an 18-pound cloth test dummy. For the carriers, all models were evaluated in the front-carrier position. The slings were generally evaluated in the sling and in the hip position (depending on the model). **Safety** was assessed based on a variety of criteria, including modified versions of the two ASTM safety standards, potential for pinching, security of dolls in carriers and slings, and high potential for misuse. **Ease of use** considers many judgments, including how easy the directions were to follow, ease of getting carrier/sling on and off, ease of adjusting straps, buckles, and buttons, loading/unloading the doll and test dummy. **Comfort** considers the comfort of the person using the carrier or sling. **Price** is approximate retail.

Stationary Activity Centers

These all-in-one, molded-plastic play stations resemble walkers—but without the wheels, and that makes them a safer alternative to traditional wheeled walkers. Most activity centers have a circular frame with a rotating seat recessed in the center and a surrounding tray with attached toys. They can be used as soon as a baby begins to sit up independently (some starting at about 4 months and most by 6 months).

A stationary activity center keeps your baby relatively safe in one spot while you do other things, such as make dinner—and maybe even eat some of it, too. Most stationary activity centers adjust to three heights. Your baby will outgrow it when he's 30 to 32 inches tall or weighs 30 pounds; that's the maximum height and weight recommendation for most activity centers. You'll get the most use from this designated play space when your baby is between 6 and 16 months old. Children outgrow them when they become fairly confident toddlers.

CERTIFICATION

Four brands of activity centers bear the Juvenile Products Manufacturers Association (JPMA) certification seal that they meet the American Society for Testing and Materials (ASTM) standards: Dorel Juvenile Group (Safety 1st), Fisher-Price, Graco (Baby Einstein), and Kolcraft. Although JPMA certification can be an indication of a safer stationary activity center, in our tests, stationary activity centers that weren't JPMA-certified, such as the Evenflo Exersaucer SmartSteps Active Learning Center, scored Excellent for safety.

Shopping Secrets

Do your in-store research. The better stationary activity centers have a sturdy frame; no accessible sharp edges or hardware underneath or on top; comfortable, soft fabric edging on the sides and legs of the seat cushions; and well-designed, well-secured toys for little hands. The seat should swivel smoothly without any hitches, and there should be no gaps in the rim between the edge of the swivel mechanism and the tray. Such gaps could capture small fingers. If the activity center's bottom is a saucer, its flip-down braces, which prevent it from rocking, should be sturdy.

Look for an activity center that folds if you want the option of taking it with you when you travel or if you need the extra room. At least four we know of do, all these models from Evenflo: the Exersaucer SmartSteps Active Learning Center (a tested model), the Exersaucer Mega Active Learning Center, the Exersaucer Ultra 2-in-1 Active Learning Center, and the Exersaucer Triple Fun Active Learning Center. Practice collapsing display models in the store, if possible, to make sure the folding mechanism works well.

More isn't always better. Most activity centers offer activities that attract a baby's attention and promote her developing motor skills, including electronic toys, lights, sounds, songs, and a rotating seat. The most fully loaded we found, the Rockin' Jitter Buggy by Safety 1st, has a radio with three stations, a dial-and-chat electronic toy cell phone, 2-speed shifter (mock gear shift), honking horn, flashing blinker, jiggle start ignition, and springy seat.

One with fewer gadgets and toys, the Bright Starts Bounce Bounce Baby Activity Zone has only eight toys, plus mirror, lights, and sounds. Still, depending on the baby, that may be enough to keep her busy.

You'll pay more for a high-octane model, but more isn't always better. Although many babies enjoy a wide range of options, some find all that motion, sound, and light too stimulating. So go with an activity center with fewer bells and whistles—in other words, at the lower end of the price spectrum—if you suspect that your baby doesn't have a multitasking temperament, or if you'd rather use the activity center with some of your own toys, or primarily for eating.

What's Available

The major brands, in alphabetical order, are: Bright Starts (*www.bright starts.com*), Evenflo (*www.evenflo.com*), Fisher-Price (*www.fisher-price .com*), Graco (sold under the Baby Einstein license, *www.graco baby.com*), Kolcraft (some models also sold under the Sesame Beginnings brand, *www.kolcraft.com*), and Safety 1st (*www.safety1st .com*). Models come with a solid flat base or a rocking one; some become a walk-behind walker, although we don't recommend these because a baby could easily push one down the stairs. Prices range from about $40 to $100.

Features to Consider

Motion. Some activity centers offer merely a stationary seat. Others feature a seat that swivels 360 degrees, with springs that allow the unit to bounce when baby moves and create a rocking motion, which active babies may enjoy.

Stabilizers. These anchor the frame in a stationary position. They're a must to keep a rocking activity center from becoming too turbulent or if you want to feed your baby in her activity center. The stabilizers should seem sturdy. On one model we tested, the Graco Baby Einstein Discover and Play ($80), the stabilizers could release during use. The model otherwise rated highly, however.

Adjustable height. Many models offer legs that adjust to three

ACTIVITY CENTER SAFETY TIPS

Keep an eye out. Even though a stationary activity center can give you a chance to grab a bite (without a baby in your lap), take a quick shower, or check your e-mail, always keep your baby in view while he's in it.

• **Resist the urge to routinely park your baby.** Keeping your child in a stationary activity center for more than 30 minutes at a time can tax her naturally weak back and leg muscles.

• **Keep the activity center away from** hot surfaces, dangling appliance cords, window blind and curtain cords, stairs, sources of water such as a swimming pool, and anything else that might injure a child. Even though it is technically stationary, this play space can creep across the floor as your baby plays. Watch for movement and make sure your baby stays away from hazards.

• **Don't carry an activity center with your child in it.**

• **Place the product on level ground and make sure the legs are the same height.** The tray should be level. That's the best way to avoid tip-overs.

• **Follow the manufacturer's age or weight or height recommendations.** Don't use the activity center before your baby can sit up unassisted, and stop using it when your baby reaches the height or weight maximum. And, as a general rule, if your child can tip over the activity center by just leaning over the edge or can climb out of it, it's time to retire it.

heights, so the activity center can grow as your baby grows. The height of the play tray is the key. When the tray is at the proper height, your baby's feet will touch the floor, and her legs will be straight when she's seated. If your baby is on her tippy toes when she's seated, the tray is too high. If her knees are bent when she's seated, it's too low. You may have to adjust the legs (without your baby in it) every month or so, just to keep pace with your baby's growth.

Seat. More expensive models have cushy seat padding. Seat pads are often removable for machine washing, which is a plus. You might have to air-dry them, though. Check the care and maintenance requirements on the label or in the instruction manual.

Toys. All activity centers feature a play tray with attached interactive toys, such as a clicking or fun house mirror, a spinning stoplight, picture books, and bead toys along with lights, songs, sounds, and sometimes bilingual voices. To make these gizmos work, you'll need three AA or C batteries (not included), depending on the model. In general, more expensive models are loaded with exciting options and have lots of ways to bounce and rock so your baby feels like she's on the go. One activity center, the Intellitainer by Fisher-Price, which retails for $70, has a seat that slides back and forth and rotates 360 degrees. Babies can slide, spin, and turn the attached toys to activate a talking book, a singing school bus, a piano riff, and a trumpet solo, and learn letters, numbers, and colors.

Cup holder. A cup holder is part of the deal on many models, But during these early years, unlike during the soccer years or dance classes that may be ahead of you, your baby probably won't need to stay hydrated because of activity. Still, a little sippy cup action adds to the fun. But watch drinks around music and other buttons. If you've ever spilled a cup of coffee on your computer keyboard, you know liquids don't mix with electronics—even battery-powered ones.

Recommendations

Stationary activity centers with a solid, flat base are the most stable. Examine attached toys for size.

Although most babies enjoy being in these play spaces, some don't. If you can, have your baby test-drive a unit in the store or during play dates at other parents' homes to get a sense of how he fares. If you decide to buy one, look for an activity center with a thick, solid frame, no accessible sharp edges or sharp hardware underneath or on top, and comfortable, soft fabric edging on the sides and legs of the seat cushions. Also, the flip-down stabilizers, which may be available to prevent the saucer from rocking, should be sturdy. You shouldn't get the feeling that they could release during use.

Some activity centers come with lots of bells and whistles—and lots of parts. We counted 15 on one brand. You'll need a screwdriver and a good half an hour to assemble. Read the instructions beforehand and keep them for future reference. From time to time, check your baby's activity center for loose screws, worn parts, and torn material or stitching, and replace or repair as needed. You can usually order replacement parts from the manufacturer. Stop using a stationary activity center if it's damaged or broken.

Ratings • Stationary Activity Centers

In performance order.

Excellent Very good Good Fair Poor

Key number	Brand & model	Price	Status	Overall score		Safety	Ease of use
				0 100	P F G VG E		
	STATIONARY ACTIVITY CENTERS						
1	**Evenflo** Exersaucer SmartSteps Active Learning Center	$100		97		⊖	⊖
2	**Graco** Baby Einstein Discover and Play	80		71		⊖	⊖
3	**Kolcraft** Baby Sit & Step 2-in-1	80		24		◒	⊖

Guide to the Ratings

Overall score is based on lab tests assessing safety and ease of use. **Safety** reflects the security of the stabilizers and downgrading for converting into a walk-behind unit, which we consider to be unsafe. **Ease of use** is based on evaluations of assembly time, folding, ease of cleaning, adjustable seat height, and use of stabilizers. **Price** is approximate retail.

CHAPTER

32

Strollers

Having a new baby can be a walk in the park—with the right stroller, of course. In fact, a stroller is one of the most important pieces of baby gear you'll buy. And as your baby grows, you may end up with more than one. Many parents buy a traditional stroller for every day and a lighter-weight one for traveling. You may even want a more rugged stroller for jogging or simply negotiating uneven sidewalks and curbs. City streets are deceptively hard on strollers.

There are dozens of choices on the market, everything from the lightest-weight umbrella strollers to heavy-duty, midsized strollers, carriages, jogging strollers, and models designed to carry two or more children. For a newborn, you can find a basic frame with no stroller seat of its own that can support almost any infant car seat. Or, consider a fully reclining stroller with leg holes you can close, so your baby doesn't slip and get trapped.

Another option is a travel system, which consists of an infant car seat, a car-seat base for your car, and a stroller. Some jogging strollers, such as the Graco LeisureSport ($200), are sold as travel systems, and some strollers also function as travel systems by allowing you to attach an infant car seat. All Peg-Pérego strollers—the Pliko P3 Classico, GT3 Completo, Centro Completo, and Aria OH Classico—are designed to anchor a matching Peg-Pérego car seat, which is sold separately. Those strollers include a strap to attach other manufacturers' car seats to the stroller. When babies reach 6 months old or can sit up and control their head and neck movements, you can use the stroller alone, without the infant seat snapped in. The downside? Until then, you have to push your baby in both a stroller and a car seat, which can be unwieldy, depending on the circumstances, such as the terrain you're navigating.

A final option is a combo stroller—such as the Bugaboo Frog, Gecko, or Cameleon—which functions as both a carriage and a stroller. This stroller is a hybrid that consists of a stroller chassis with wheels that can be used with various manufacturers' car seats. It includes a removable bassinet, which converts it into a carriage, so your newborn baby can fully recline, and a removable stroller seat to use when your baby is ready to sit up.

Your stroller options are dizzying. Here's what you need to know to buy the right wheels for you and your baby.

Shopping Secrets

Select it yourself. Strollers are popular baby gifts and shower presents. Still, you should shop for a stroller yourself because you're the best judge of how you intend to use it—then register for it at a department or baby store if you want to receive it as a gift. If you receive a stroller you didn't select yourself, make sure you want to keep it. Strollers, like cars, are highly personal items. You'll probably use your stroller often, and your baby will spend a lot of time in it. You should love the one you end up with.

Let your lifestyle be your guide. City dwellers who rely on subways, buses, and cabs will need a lightweight but sturdy stroller that folds quickly and compactly. A travel system, for example, probably isn't your best bet. A stroller with sizeable, air-filled tires is recommended if you'll be going for long walks with your baby and your vehicle is big enough to accommodate it. Besides being more shock-absorbing, these strollers typically have cushier, more supportive seating. If you'll be strolling through snow, on unpaved roads, or on the beach or taking your baby to soccer games in the park, a stroller with large wheels is the way to go. Under those conditions, a stroller with small wheels may be difficult or impossible to push. If you're athletic, you might want an all-terrain or jogging stroller for walking or jogging workouts.

Don't go by price alone. As you'll find out when you're shopping, there's a wide price range among types and brands. What makes one stroller worth $100 and another $750? Several things drive up the price tag. Higher-end strollers are made of high-grade, lighter-weight aluminum, and are easier to lift in and out of a car. The seat is cushier, with more back support, and is likely to be made of high-quality fabric. And because they often feature large, shock-absorbing, swivel wheels, higher-end strollers are easier to push, especially over rough terrain, which includes anything from uneven sidewalks to sand and snow, so babies get a smoother ride.

Bigger-ticket strollers have such comfy amenities as adjustable handles, which can save your back if you're tall, and a reversible seat so your baby can face toward or away from you. They tend to be more durable, lasting from child to child. But that doesn't mean a lower-end stroller won't serve you well. A lot depends on where and how much you'll use the stroller. For infrequent travel or trips to the mall, a lower-end umbrella stroller (less than $100) may be all you need. But if you're going to be strolling more often and through all kinds of weather and conditions, consider spending more. Good-quality traditional strollers start at around $250.

That said, a higher price doesn't always mean higher quality. CONSUMER REPORTS' tests have shown that some economical strollers can perform as well as or better than models costing hundreds of dollars more. Even the most sophisticated models can have typical stroller flaws: malfunctioning wheels, frames that bend out of shape, locking mechanisms that fail, safety belts that come loose, or buckles that break.

Give it a test drive. Take the models you're considering for a spin in the store, even if you plan to buy online or expect to get a stroller as a gift. Compare maneuverability and practice opening and closing it—with one hand as well as two. See how easy it is to adjust the backrest, lift and carry the stroller, and apply the rear brakes. Make sure you can stand tall when you push the stroller and that your legs and feet don't hit the wheels as you walk.

If both you and your spouse will use the stroller, you should both try it out. Some models have adjustable handles, an important feature if one parent is taller than the other. If possible, take the floor model you're considering out to your car to be sure it will fit in your trunk when it's folded. Also, jiggle the stroller. The frame should feel solid, not loose.

Consider your baby's age. Newborns can't sit up, so they need a stroller that lets them lie on their backs for the first few months, or one that can hold an infant car seat. Don't use a traditional stroller that doesn't fully recline—including an umbrella-style stroller—until your child can sit up, usually at about 6 months of age.

If you buy a stroller that fully reclines for an infant, make sure it has a wall surrounding all sides above the retention space. In addition, you can use the cover or stroller boot the manufacturer sometimes supplies for the foot area/legholes so your baby can't possibly slip through, or use the bassinet that may come with the stroller.

Size up the storage. A stroller with a large shopping basket makes life easier for parents who get around town mostly on foot. If you opt for a model that reclines, make sure you can reach the basket if the seat back is fully reclined, or, if it's a travel system, when the infant car seat is in place.

Evaluate warranties and return policies. Most stroller manufacturers and retailers have warranties that cover poor workmanship and inherent flaws, but they won't necessarily take the unit back if it malfunctions. Manufacturers may refer you to the store for a replacement or insist that you ship the stroller back for repair—at your expense—leaving you stranded without baby wheels. Your best bet is to purchase the stroller from a store, catalog, or Web site that offers a 100 percent satisfaction guarantee.

Keep the packaging the stroller comes in until you're sure you want to keep the stroller and ask about a store's return policy (usually 30 days). It's not uncommon to buy a stroller many months in advance. If you're shopping that far ahead, you'll want to buy from a store with a flexible or long-term return policy.

Check certification. Somewhere on a stroller's frame or carton there should be a certification sticker showing that the stroller meets the minimum requirements of the American Society for Testing and Materials (ASTM) voluntary standard and that its manufacturer participates in the certification program administered by the Juvenile Products Manufacturers Association (JPMA). The key tests are for restraint system, brakes, leg openings, and locking mechanisms that prevent accidental folding, as well as for stability and the absence of sharp edges. The program is voluntary, and models from uncertified companies may be as safe as those from certified ones. But all things being equal, choose a certified model. Companies that are certified are: Baby Trend, Britax, Bugaboo, Delta Enterprise, Dorel Juvenile Group, Evenflo, Go-Go Babyz, Graco, Hauck Fun for Kids, J. Mason, Joovy, Kolcraft, Maclaren, Mia Moda, and Peg-Pérego.

What's Available

Major brands of single- and multi-seat strollers are, in alphabetical order, Baby Jogger (*www.babyjogger.com*), Baby Trend (*www.babytrend.com*), Bertini (*www.bertinistrollers.com*), Bob (*www.bobstrollers.com*), Britax (*www.britaxusa.net*), Bugaboo (*www.bugaboo.com*), Bumble Ride (*www.bumbleride.com*), Chicco (*www.chiccousa.com*), Combi (*www.combi-intl.com*), Dorel Juvenile Group (maker of Cosco, Eddie Bauer, and Safety 1st, *www.djgusa.com*), Evenflo (*www.evenflo.com*), Fisher-Price (*www.fisher-price.com*), GoGo Babyz (*www.gogobabyz.com*), Graco (*www.gracobaby.com*), Inglesina (*www.inglesina.com*), InStep (*www.instep.net*), Kolcraft (*www.kolcraft.com*), Maclaren (*www.maclarenbaby.com*), Mountain Buggy (*www.mountainbuggy.com*), Orbit (*www.orbitbaby.com*), Peg-Pérego (*www.pegperego.com*), Phil & Teds (*www.philandteds.com*), Rock Star Baby (*www.rockstarbaby.com*), Silver Cross (*www.silvercross.co.uk*), Stokke (*www.stokkeusa.com*), Stroll-Air

(*www.stroll-air.com*), Tike Tech (*www.tiketech.com*), Uppababy (*www*
.uppababy.com), and Zooper (*www.zooper.com*).

For Babies Younger Than 6 Months

Because newborns can't sit up without support, they can't ride in a
standard stroller, that is, one that doesn't fully recline. You'll find the
following basic choices for this age group:

Seat-carrier frames

These lightweight frames have no seat of their own. Instead, you
attach an infant car seat for strolling.

Pros: They're compact and convenient, also inexpensive because
your car seat does double duty. They let you smoothly get a sleeping
baby in and out of the car. When you move a baby in an infant car seat
to the stroller frame, you're less likely to wake her.

Cons: The car seat and the frame can no
longer be used as a stroller once your
child outgrows the seat (at about a year).

Price range: $30 to $90, for just
the frame.

Combo strollers

These are a combination carriage and
stroller. Before your baby can sit up, you can
use the stroller's bassinet, snap an infant car
seat into the stroller chassis, or, depending
on the model, fully recline the seat and
close the legholes. After that, use the stroller
seat attachment to wheel around your baby.

Pros: You can start using the stroller from
day one, and because it's designed for infants through
toddlers (to 40 pounds or so), you may not have to buy
more than one stroller.

As an alternative to a
dedicated stroller, you can
buy a frame that accepts
an infant car seat.

Cons: Combo strollers tend to be pricey. Bugaboo,
which is a popular brand of combo stroller, for
example, will run you from $680 (the Gecko model) to $880 (the
Cameleon). That price includes everything—the chassis, bassinet,
and reversible seat, which weigh a total of just 17 to 20 pounds,
plus a canopy, rain cover, tire pump and pressure gauge, bug net,

underseat bag for storage items, and maintenance kit. But you'll still need to buy a car seat.

Price range: $390 to $880.

Travel systems

These combine a stroller and an infant car seat; the baby is in the car seat snapped into the stroller until she can sit up, and then you use the stroller without the car seat, at right.

Pros: Like an infant seat with carrier frame, a travel system allows you to move a sleeping baby in the seat undisturbed from car to stroller. Some also can fully recline the seat, so you can use it as a carriage.

Cons: If you select the car seat first, you have to live with the stroller it works with (and vice versa). An alternative is to choose a stroller that can hold car seats from a number of manufacturers. You have to push around a car seat and a stroller, which can be bulky and unmanageable on stairs.

Price range: $130 to more than $600.

Carriages

These models provide sleeping space for infants. Some have large spoked wheels and compartments, or "carry cots," that can be removed and used as a bassinet.

Pros: They can be used for newborns and they're convenient for sleeping.

Cons: They're not very portable or user-friendly. If you get the kind with large, spoked wheels, it'll be nearly impossible to maneuver on public transportation, and you'll still need a car seat. Traditional prams, the kind that don't convert to a regular stroller, aren't very popular and few manufacturers produce them. If you want your baby to lie flat when strolling, consider a combo stroller.

Price range: From $135 to $370, or more.

Multiseat Strollers—Infants to Toddlers

Similar to other strollers, multiseat strollers give you a relatively efficient means of taking twins, triplets, or young siblings of different ages for a ride. Most companies that manufacture single strollers for one also make a version with two or more seats. Multiseaters offer the same features as strollers for a single rider, but are bigger. Options include strollers with a standing bench or small seat in the rear that lets a second child hitch a ride. Multiseat strollers usually come in one of two configurations, tandem or side-by-side.

Tandem models

These strollers have one seat directly behind the other. They're the same width as single-passenger strollers and easy to fit through doorways and get around enclosed spaces, such as retail stores. However, while the backseat can recline, the front one usually can't without limiting the space of the rear passenger. On some tandem strollers, you can set the seats so that the children face each other; others have a "stadium seat" that allows the child in back to see over the one in front.

Pros: Tandems easily go through standard doorways and fit through tight spots, such as an older apartment building with a narrow elevator door. A folded tandem takes up just a little more space than a folded standard midsized stroller. Many tandem models accept an infant car seat in one or both stroller seats, but check which brands of car seats are compatible before you buy.

Cons: Steering can be difficult, and it can be tricky getting over curbs. Some models have limited leg support and very little legroom for the rear passenger. They're often quite heavy, which can be difficult to manage if you're small.

Price range: $130 to $200 or more for double tandem strollers; tandem strollers for triplets, such as the Inglesina Trio Domino (there's not a lot to choose from), will cost you even more, in the range of $800.

Side-by-side models

The other configuration, side-by-sides have two seats attached to a single frame or a unit resembling two strollers bolted together. You can create your own side-by-side by joining two umbrella strollers with a set of screw-on brackets—available at baby discount chains and specialty stores. The features on side-by-side strollers are similar to those on single-passenger models. This type of stroller works best for children of about the same weight, such as twins. Each seat has an independent reclining mechanism.

Pros: A side-by-side model goes up curbs more easily than a tandem. Some side-by-side models accept an infant car seat, though some brands limit it to one seat only. That may be fine if you're shopping for a newborn and an older child. If you're shopping for infant twins and you want a side-by-side, look for one in which both seats recline, such as the Combi Twin Savvy Sport ($200), and use the infant boot that comes with the stroller for both seats.

Cons: If children of different weights ride in the stroller, it can veer to one side. Most side-by-side models can't be used with infant car seats. A folded side-by-side stroller typically requires twice as much space as the equivalent single-occupant version. Although manufacturers may claim that a stroller is slender enough to go through a standard doorway, it can be a tight squeeze, and the stroller may not fit through some doorways at all.

Price range: $120 (for lightweight models that don't accept an infant car seat) to more than $900 (for deluxe models with independent reversible seats with multiple reclining positions, and air-filled tires).

Down the Road

Stroller types appropriate for babies older than 6 months include:

Umbrella strollers

These are named for their curved, umbrella-like handles, and typically weigh less than 12 pounds. They may have a one-handed release for folding.

Pros: They're lightweight and convenient.

Cons: The compact size of umbrella strollers may cramp infants and toddlers, especially when they're dressed in heavy winter clothes. Because these strollers lack suspension and seat support, they don't provide a cushy ride.

Price range: $32 to $120.

Traditional strollers

This category runs the gamut from lightweight strollers to heavy-duty models that weigh 17 to 35 pounds. The heavy-duty strollers are somewhat bulky but stable, deep, and roomy. Higher-end models may have shock absorbers on all wheels as well. Many strollers have a two-step, one-handed release for folding.

Pros: Many are lightweight and convenient. They have more features than umbrella strollers, such as a snack tray and a roomy storage basket, and some may accommodate an infant car seat or fully recline and have a wall around all sides above the retention space, so it's possible to use this type of stroller from day one.

Cons: Heavier models are difficult to carry on public transportation and to lift into car trunks or minivan cargo areas. And you may still need a car seat. Small wheels don't perform well on uneven sidewalks or rough terrain. The compact size of lighter-weight models may cramp some toddlers, especially when they're dressed in heavy winter clothes.

Price range: $60 (lightweight strollers that are an upgrade from an umbrella stroller) to more than $1,000 (high-end traditional strollers).

All-terrain strollers

These three-wheel strollers or traditional-style strollers with larger air-filled tires let you push your child on a variety of surfaces, from mall floors to pavement and off-road. They have a rugged, outdoorsy look. Many all-terrains have bicycle-type air-filled tires, and larger wheels than a traditional stroller. The larger wheels make the stroller easier to push. All-terrain strollers have a three-wheel design that mimics jogging strollers, but check the user's manual to see if the manufacturer advises against using it for running. All have a front wheel that swivels for easier maneuvering on smoother surfaces but can be locked for use on rougher surfaces. Many all-terrains are unsuitable for babies under 6 months of age. A few exceptions: Maclaren MX3 (about $400) and the Phil & Teds e3 (about $380). One all-terrain that can accept an infant car seat using special separate adapters is the Zooper Boogie (about $360).

Pros: They're good for off-road use and provide a relatively smooth ride over rocks, potholes, or uneven sidewalks. Some all-terrain strollers can accommodate heavier children than other strollers can. Several companies offer double or triple all-terrain strollers with a total weight limit of up to 100 pounds or 150 pounds, respectively.

Cons: Three-wheel designs may be unstable when the rear wheels are rolled over a curb. Many all-terrains are not suitable for infants younger than 6 months. They are often large and heavy; some may require you to remove the front and/or rear wheel to fit in a car trunk. Air-filled tires can go flat and require reinflating with a bicycle pump or a gas-station hose.

Price range: $80 to more than $700.

TIPS FOR SAFER STROLLING

Learn how to operate your stroller before you use it. Read the instruction manual to get acquainted with it, and assemble it properly.

• Never leave your baby unattended in a stroller, especially when she's asleep.

• Use the safety belt or harness to restrain children from leaving the stroller and reduce the risk of a child causing it to tip over.

• To reduce the possibility of injuries, don't overload the stroller with a child heavier than the manufacturer's weight limit, and don't put more children in the stroller than its design allows.

• Don't jog with a stroller that's not a jogging stroller or an all-terrain stroller not recommended for jogging.

• Don't run with an infant younger than 6 months old in a jogging stroller. Some manufacturers advise you to wait until your baby is a year old and can be properly fitted with a bicycle helmet. That's not a bad idea.

• If you buy a combo stroller, which includes a bassinet and seat attachment, make sure you hear a "click" when installing these components to the stroller chassis, to ensure that each is installed properly. (Most combo strollers are designed this way.) Likewise, when installing an infant car seat to a stroller frame or to a travel system, make sure the seat is safely "locked" in by jiggling the seat to make sure it's secure, or listening for the audible click, if the seat is designed to provide one. Use the instruction manual as your guide for correct installation.

• Don't hang heavy bags on stroller handlebars. They can cause tipping.

• Make sure the frame locking mechanism is properly engaged to avoid collapse, and use the parking brake when you're stopped, especially on an incline.

• Keep your child away from the stroller when you're folding and unfolding it to avoid pinched fingers.

• Never use a pillow, folded quilt, or blanket as a mattress in a stroller or baby carriage, and don't add an extra mattress or cushioning to a carriage/pram bassinet. They're a suffocation risk.

• Don't use a stroller/pram bassinet as a car seat.

• Return the stroller warranty card so you can be notified of a recall, or sign up for the Consumer Product Safety Commission's e-mail subscription list at www.cpsc.gov/cpsclist.asp. Updated recall information will be sent directly to you via e-mail.

Jogging strollers

These three-wheel strollers with front hand brake, nonswivel or lockable front wheel for serious runners, and large, air-filled tires let you push your child while you run or jog. Larger wheels make it easier for the runner who's pushing, and the air in the tires helps provide a smoother ride for the little passenger. The long, high handlebar is designed to give running feet and legs more space to avoid bumping into the stroller's frame. A wrist strap should be attached to your wrist and the stroller at all times when you are running with a child in the stroller; this will give you some control and keep the stroller from getting away from you if you fall or trip. On some brands, the large front wheel is fixed and does not swivel; on others, it swivels but can be locked into place.

The appropriate minimum age for a child to ride in a jogging stroller is a matter of debate. Most manufacturers suggest a child should be 8 weeks or older, but our medical consultants say a baby should be at least 6 months, able to sit up, and have some head support to withstand the potentially jarring ride. Some jogging strollers are made to accommodate the youngest babies, however. Baby Jogger makes a bassinet/pram to work with its Baby Jogger City and Q-Series single strollers, so your baby can lie flat while you're logging the miles. The seat faces the rear of the stroller so you can see your baby at all times. But that doesn't mean you should sprint with your newborn; brisk walks are a better idea.

Pros: Jogging strollers can also be used for off-road walks. All jogging strollers tested scored Excellent for outdoor performance while running. Many jogging strollers have a longer life than traditional strollers, because they can accommodate heavier children. Several companies offer double or even triple strollers with total weight limits of 100 or 150 pounds, respectively.

Cons: The fixed (non-swiveling) front wheel is good for running, but can make maneuvering difficult. Some three-wheel designs may be unstable when the rear wheels are rolled over a curb, or if a child tries to climb into the stroller. Jogging strollers are often large and some are heavy; you may need to remove the wheel(s) to fit the stroller into your car trunk. Bicycle-type air filled tires can go flat and require reinflating with a bicycle pump or a gas-station hose.

Price range: $80 to more than $700.

Features to Consider

Restraint system. Get a model with a sturdy safety belt and crotch strap, which keep a baby or a toddler from slipping out. Most are made of thick nylon webbing. The Combi Cosmo ST, a small, light-weight stroller, the InStep RunAround, and the InStep RunAround LTD, both jogging strollers, scored lower for safety because they have a crotch strap that can be bypassed. According to ASTM safety standards, a crotch strap should be mandatory when the waist strap is in use. Look for buckles on the harness that are easy for you to operate but difficult for small hands to unfasten. If you're shopping with your baby, check the seat belt to make sure it's strong and durable, and fits snugly around your child. Some strollers have only waist and crotch straps, but many come with an adjustable five-point harness (two straps over the shoulders, two for the thighs, and a crotch strap), much like those found in car seats, which keep a baby from slipping or falling out if the stroller tips, or climbing out when you're not looking. The straps should be height-adjustable for proper fit, and securely anchored.

Wheels. The SUV syndrome has carried over into strollers with large wheels and a rugged, off-road appearance. The larger the wheels, the easier it is to negotiate curbs and rough surfaces. But big wheels eat up trunk space. Most strollers have double wheels on the front that swivel to make steering easier. Front wheels feature two positions: full swivel for smooth surfaces or locked in one forward-facing position for rough terrain. Some three-wheel strollers have a front wheel that doesn't swivel; these can be hard to maneuver. Misaligned and loose wheels are a chronic stroller problem. One sign of good construction is wheels that sit on the floor uniformly when a baby is inside. Pneumatic (air-filled) tires are relatively new in stroller design. You'll need a pump, which is not supplied with some models. Some manu-facturers have created wheel assemblies that can be completely slipped off the frame, which makes it easier to replace a damaged wheel, fix the tire, get it filled, and transport the stroller in compact spaces, such as the trunk of a car.

Leg holes. Carriages and strollers designed for newborns or young infants, which fully recline, must have leg holes that close so an infant can't slip through. Manufacturers use mesh or fabric shields or hinged, molded footrests that raise and clamp over the leg holes. According to the industry's voluntary standard, a stroller with leg holes that can't be closed shouldn't be able to fully recline, which is meant to prevent its use with a newborn.

Brakes. Check that any stroller you intend to buy has a good parking brake, one that's convenient to operate and locks one or two wheels. Parking brakes on two wheels provide an extra margin of safety. Some two-wheel parking brakes are activated in a single stroke by a bar in the rear of the stroller frame. Others require two actions and have foot-operated tabs above each rear wheel. When brakes are activated, plastic cogs engage with the sprockets of the rear wheels. Avoid models that can hurt your feet when you engage or disengage the brakes with light shoes or bare feet. In addition to parking brakes, most jogging strollers have bicycle-type hand-operated brakes—important to help you slow down when cruising at a fast clip. Some pricier jogging strollers have hand-operated brakes on the front or rear wheels.

Canopy. A canopy is a must-have for protecting your baby, especially in glaring sunlight or inclement weather. Canopies range from a simple fabric square strung between two wires to deep, pull-down versions that shield almost the entire front of the stroller. Reversible (or 180-degree travel) canopies protect the baby from sun or wind from ahead or behind. Some canopies have a clear plastic "peekaboo" window on top so you can keep an eye on your baby while you're strolling. The window (or viewing port) is a nice feature; you'll use it more than you'd think.

Handlebars. Handles may be padded, even thickly cushioned, on more expensive models. Adjustable handlebars can be extended or angled to accommodate people of different heights. Reversible handles can swing over the top of the stroller, then be locked into a front position so baby rides facing you. A single crossbar not only allows one-handed steering, if necessary, but may make the stroller more stable. Umbrella strollers and other models with two independent handles almost always require two hands to maneuver.

One-handed opening/folding mechanism. This is essential for when you need to open or fold the stroller with one hand while holding the baby with the other. The best strollers fold compactly in a matter of seconds.

Play tray. Strollers may have a tray where babies can play, keep snacks, or rest their hands. If the tray comes with attached toys, check their size and make sure they are securely fastened. Some strollers have been recalled because small parts on their play trays' toys pose a choking hazard. No toy part should be smaller than the diameter of a toilet-paper roll tube. To make it easier to get a squirming baby or toddler seated, the tray should be removable or swing open rather than be permanently attached to both sides. Instead of a tray, some models have a front bar to keep a baby restrained with the attached crotch strap.

Footrest. A footrest can help a child sit more comfortably without legs dangling, but many are too low to help any but the tallest toddlers. Make certain that the seat rim is soft and won't press uncomfortably into the back of your child's legs.

Cup holders/parent tray. Many strollers have a cup holder for you and one for the small passenger. They're a welcome feature for both. The parent tray is usually molded with a cup holder or compartment for keys, cell phone, and so on.

Boots. A few strollers have protective leg coverings, or "boots," made of a matching fabric that can snap over baby's legs for warmth. That's a feature to look for, especially if you live in a cold climate.

Shock absorbers. Air-filled tires or tires molded from foam can help give baby a smoother ride. So can shock absorbers—covered springs or rubber pads above the wheel assemblies. Softer suspension is a newer feature that offers a smoother ride, but a too-soft ride can come at the expense of steering control.

Fabric and upholstery. You'll want to be able to sponge off spills and splashes and launder the upholstery without worrying about shrinking, fading, or puckering. Look for a removable seat and laundry instructions, usually on an attached tag or on printed instructions inside the packaging.

Reflectors or reflective trim on fabric. Many strollers have this important safety feature. If yours doesn't, wear light-colored or reflective clothing so you can be seen on cloudy days. Even with a stroller with reflective trim, we don't suggest strolling near traffic in twilight or in the dark.

Large shopping basket. A roomy, easily accessible storage basket underneath the stroller makes errands with a baby much easier. Sizes of baskets vary. Choose one that's at least big enough to accommodate a diaper bag. When shopping for a stroller, press on the storage basket's floor—it shouldn't drag on the ground when loaded. Some strollers have storage pouches, with elastic top edges, in back. Don't hang heavy bags (including a hefty diaper bag or stroller diaper bag) on handle-bars. Follow manufacturers recommendations for all storage areas. The stroller can tip if overloaded.

Recommendations

Your first decision is which types of stroller you want to buy. You may want more than one—such as a traditional stroller and a lighter-weight model for traveling —though you might be able to get along fine with just one, depending on what you select as your main set of wheels.

Ratings • Traditional Strollers

	Excellent	Very good	Good	Fair	Poor
	⊖	⊖	○	⊖	●

Key number	Brand & model	Similar models	Price	Folded size	Weight (lbs.)	Overall score	Maneuverability	Ease of use	Safety	Durability
						0 .... 100 P F G VG E				
TRADITIONAL STROLLERS										
1	**Chicco** Cortina		$150	M	22	76	⊖	⊖	⊖	⊖
2	**Graco** Quattro Tour Deluxe	Graco Passage 531	150	M	27	74	⊖	⊖	⊖	⊖
3	**Graco** Passage 540		90	M	20	71	⊖	⊖	⊖	⊖
4	**Safety** 1st Acella LX		65	S	20	66	○	⊖	⊖	⊖
5	**Evenflo** Aura Elite	Evenflo Aura Select	90	M	24	58	○	⊖	⊖	⊖
6	**Combi** Cosmo ST		60	S	11	39	⊖	⊖	○	●

Guide to the Ratings

Overall score is based primarily on performance (only all-terrain and jogging strollers), maneuverability (only traditional strollers and all-terrain strollers), ease of use, and safety. **Performance** is panelists' impression of ease of pushing and maneuvering on varied terrain while walking (all-terrain strollers) or running (jogging strollers). **Maneuverability** was assessed by trained staffers on how well the strollers maneuvered S-turns through cones, narrow sections, grass, dirt trails, uphill, downhill and steps while walking. **Ease of use** is primarily based on ease of safety harness use, folding and unfolding, adjusting backrest, lifting, carrying, and engaging wheel brakes. **Safety** for each stroller was assessed by testing for compliance with ASTM F 833-05a voluntary standard and a stability test designed by Consumers Union. Strollers that did not meet the standard or had relatively lower stability on an adjustable inclined plane were downgraded. **Durability** was assessed by rolling the strollers 19 miles over 150,000 bumps with a 40 pound bag in the seat, then each stroller was folded and unfolded 10 times to check for mechanical failure or unusual wear. **Price** is approximate retail for stroller.

Ratings • Jogging/All-Terrain Strollers

Within types, in performance order.

Key number	Brand & model	Price	Folded size	Weight (lbs.)	Not for running	Overall score (0–100) P F G VG E	Performance	Ease of use	Safety
	JOGGING designed for the serious runner, nonswivel front wheel makes indoor maneuvering difficult.								
1	**Dreamer Design** Rebound Jogger Lite	$220	L	30		79	⊖	⊖	⊖
2	**Jeep** Overland Limited	170	L	30		76	⊖	⊖	⊖
3	**Kelty** Speedster 16 Deluxe	335	M	24		76	⊖	⊖	⊖
4	**Baby Trend** Expedition	100	L	25		75	⊖	⊖	⊖
5	**Schwinn** Free Runner LT	190	L	22		70	⊖	⊖	○
6	**Baby Jogger** Performance Series	330	L	25		60	⊖	○	○
7	**InStep** Run Around	90	L	23		53	⊖	⊖	○
8	**InStep** Run Around LTD	100	L	25		46	⊖	⊖	○
	ALL TERRAIN 3-wheeled stroller with locking/unlocking swivel wheel for nimble maneuverability.								
9	**Mountain Buggy** Urban	430	M	24		73	⊖	⊖	○
10	**Maclaren** MX3	400	M	25		72	⊖	⊖	⊖
11	**BOB** Revolution	360	M	23		65	○	○	○
12	**InStep** Safari TT (Schwinn Safari TT)	135	L	28		62	○	⊖	○
13	**Phil & Ted's** e3	380	S	24		58	○	○	○
14	**Zooper** Boogie	360	M	31	●	48	⊖	⊖	⊖
15	**Dreamer Design** Manhattan lite	230	L	26		44	⊖	⊖	⊖
16	**Jeep Liberty** Limited Urban Terrain	140	M	29	●	39	⊖	⊖	○

Swings

A baby swing can work wonders, soothing a fussy baby, lulling her to sleep at night or nap time, or occupying her for a few minutes while you get things done nearby or grab a bite to eat. It also comes in handy if your baby needs to sleep in a semi-upright position because she has a cold or stuffy nose. A swing provides a gentle rhythmic motion, which babies are accustomed to from their months in the womb. If you're like countless parents, you may consider a swing a godsend, especially for calming a colicky newborn and de-frazzling your nerves.

Full-size baby swings designed for indoor use from birth to 25 or 30 pounds (depending on the model) typically consist of a seat suspended by a pair of arms attached to a frame with wide-standing, tubular-metal legs. Most swings move from front to back, though several models swing from side to side, cradle-style. Portable travel swings are popular with on-the-go parents. These swings sit low to the ground

P-Q-R-S

SWING SAFETY

- Never leave your baby unattended in a swing.
- Always use the safety harness provided.
- Never place a portable swing on an elevated surface.
- Don't let older children "push" your baby in the swing.
- Limit the amount of time your baby swings; we recommend no more than 30- minute intervals, even if your baby seems content. More swinging time can make some babies dizzy. If you're drowsy while your baby's swinging, turn off the swing before you fall asleep. You don't want to wake up and find that your baby has been swinging for hours.
- With multi-speed swings, start with the lowest setting—high settings may be too rough for your baby. Very young babies tend to prefer slower speeds; older babies often like a quicker pace.
- Always follow the manufacturer's age and weight specifications and assembly directions exactly.
- To prevent falls, stop using a traditional swing when your child attempts to climb out. Stop using a cradle swing when your baby can roll over or push up on his hands and knees.
- Don't transport your baby in a swing or use a portable swing as an infant carrier.

and are designed to be moved from room to room or stowed in the car for a trip to Grandma's. Most swings on the market today are battery-operated and driven by a motor that uses four C or D batteries, which may provide up to 200 hours of swinging time. AA batteries may be required, too, if the unit has accessories, such as a CD player. Such models emit a low churning noise with each swing, which can be soothing for some babies but may irritate others.

Only one model we know of, the Power Plus Swing by Fisher-Price, features a plug-in option, eliminating the constant need for batteries. Windup swing models are a relic in the marketplace; we don't know of any new models for sale. To make a windup model swing, you crank a handle at the top or side of the frame, which provides 20 to 30 minutes of movement. If you do have a wind-up swing (maybe you found one secondhand) and it stops working, don't try to remove the spring housing to fix it. The spring is under tension and could injure you if it's released.

Although windup and battery-powered swings are lightweight, they're cumbersome to move. Standard-size swings eat up a fair amount of room, so they may not be for you if floor space is scarce.

You'll use the swing the most in your baby's first few months of life. After that, you'll probably use it less, maybe even abandon it altogether (save it for your next baby) unless your baby is addicted to motion. Keep in mind that some babies don't like the rocking of a swing, no matter which type you buy, although they may change their mind after a few tries.

Shopping Secrets

If you can, try your baby in a friend or relative's swing first, to see if he likes it. Or take your baby to the store with you for test runs. Take along your own C and D batteries and try the floor models. Your baby's reactions may help you decide on a brand, or whether he's even a candidate for a swing in the first place.

Decide between a traditional swing or a portable. If you want the option of moving your swing from room to room often and taking it on road trips, or if you're short on living space, a travel swing may be right for you. Travel swings take up about as much space as a bouncy seat, and many have a sturdy carrying handle. The downside? Because you have to crouch down to put your baby in the swing and take her out again, using the swing can be uncomfortable, or impossible if you have a bad back or are recovering from a C-section. It also can be tricky to maneuver a squirmy baby into the swing from a sitting position.

If you choose a traditional swing, decide between side-to-side movement or front-to-back motion. Some swings, like Nature's Touch Baby Papasan Cradle Swing by Fisher-Price, move in both directions. Cradle-style swings recline so your baby can lie down for the ride, which newborns tend to prefer—but the useful life of these

nfant swing safety standards are continually being updated. To make sure that your baby is using the safest possible swing, buy new, not used. Older swings may not have an adequate restraint system, which can put your baby at risk of falling.

swings is shorter. As soon as your baby can push up on his hands and knees, he'll want to sit up and see out. That's when it's time to retire it.

Look for a five-point harness. Traditional swings are required to have a fixed restraint system, which may include a waist and crotch belt (three-point harness) that must be used together so that your baby can't slip out, or a passive crotch restraint and a waist belt, such as a tray with a crotch post and a waist belt. Some models feature an over-the-shoulder, five-point harness. This type of harness is best because it keeps your baby from climbing out of his seat and plunging to the ground, which can happen long before you think possible. Travel swings don't have a tray with a middle post, just a safety harness.

Consider comfort. Seating ranges from deep, padded, womb-like cradles to a wider chair with an adjustable infant head support. For the infancy stage, you'll want a seat that reclines or has an angled back because your baby won't be able to hold his head up. An infant head-rest is a bonus; it will help keep your baby's head positioned properly. If your baby will use the swing after 3 months of age (up to 25 or 30 pounds), look for a seat with an infant head support that's removable and that has several seatback positions. Older babies will want to sit upright and reach for the toys on the toy bar, if the swing has that feature. If the swing has a front tray, make sure it pivots from side to side, flips up, or is detachable. You'll have a much easier time sliding your older baby in and out of the seat with the tray out of the way.

Check the store's return policy. Try the swing within the time limits of the store's return policy (usually within 30 days), so you have the option of taking it back. Keep the receipt and the packaging. A noisy motor may be a deal-breaker for you.

What's Available

The major brands are, in alphabetical order: Cosco (available at *www.wal mart.com*), Evenflo (*www.evenflo.com*), Fisher-Price (*www.fisher-price .com*), Graco (*www.gracobaby.com*), J. Mason (*www.jmason.com*), Kolcraft (*www.kolcraft.com*), Safety 1st (*www.safety1st.com*), and Simplicity (*www.simplicityforchildren.com*). Prices range from $42 for a portable swing to $140 for traditional swings with multiple speeds and features.

Features to Consider

Frames. If you opt for a traditional swing, look for one with strong posts and a stance that's wide enough so it won't tip, even if your baby leans one way or another. It should also fold or dismantle easily for storage.

Easy access. Portable and traditional swings are available without a top crossbar, typically called an "open-top design." Pay attention to these models. This design can be easier to use because there's no top crossbar to clear. You have access to your baby from the top, instead of having to crouch down to wriggle your baby in, which can be a plus when you're just home from the hospital.

Seat cover. Look for plush padding that's machine-washable and a removable infant-head support.

Seat settings. A swing with at least three reclining positions can help you find the most soothing posture for your baby, which is important if your baby likes to nap while swinging. Some swings also feature adjustable seat height—a raised position for newborns, and a lower position for older, more active infants.

Speeds. Some battery-operated swings have up to eight speeds, but

WATCH OUT FOR RECALLS

The following companies make Juvenile Products Manufacturers Association-certified swings: Dorel Juvenile Group (Safety 1st), Fisher-Price, Graco, J. Mason, Kolcraft, and Simplicity. Swings are also covered by the federal safety standard for small parts. Some models of baby swings have been recalled in recent years. Problems have included loose screws on the swing's arm support that caused the seat to separate and drop to one side, a seat that wasn't properly attached, swing frames that weren't stable, frames or seats with sharp edges, harnesses that could entangle a child, and hazardous toys. One recalled model could be easily disassembled, resulting in a loose seat that flipped forward. For a list of baby swing recalls, go to the CPSC Web site, *www.cpsc.gov*.

more than four is overkill. The faster speeds may annoy rather than relax your baby. In general, start with the lowest setting, and see what your baby prefers.

Entertainment. Many swings come with mobiles, toy bars, or trays, which are options your baby may enjoy. Your baby may not be able to reach the toy bar at first or even want to until around 3 months. If you can attach your baby's own favorite toys, even better. Check that all toys are safely attached and have no small parts that could cause choking. Nice-but-not-necessary extras are a light display and sound (classical music, lullabies, and nature sounds) with volume control; storage baskets on the side for toys and accessories; and a remote control to activate the swinging action, music, or both. You'll need a supply of AAA and/or AA batteries to operate these features.

Recommendations

Look for a swing that has a sturdy, stable frame with strong posts and legs and a wide stance to prevent tipping. The bottom of the legs or frame should not protrude so far that you're likely to trip over them, however. Examine the seat. It should be well padded, washable, and have a crotch post with a waist belt (if it's not a travel version), or a secure three-point or five-point harness (five-point is better). It should also have a partially reclining position for snoozing, and a position for sitting up. If you buy a cradle-style model, make sure it's firmly mounted underneath; the cradle-to-frame connection shouldn't feel loose or flimsy. To find the safest swing possible, look for the Juvenile Products Manufacturer's Association certification seal, which means the model meets the latest American Society for Testing and Materials F2088 safety requirements. Give yourself a good half-hour to assemble the swing. Make sure it's stable by swinging it without your baby in it, pushing down on the seat a little to make sure it's secure.

Thermometers

Unfortunately, babies sometimes get sick, and a fundamental clue that things are amiss is a fever—a body temperature that's higher than normal. Most pediatricians consider any thermometer reading above 100.4°F a sign of fever. A fever can be alarming, but except in the case of heat stroke (a dangerous rise in body temperature caused by a sweltering environment, like a car with the windows rolled up in August), a fever by itself isn't an illness. It's the immune system's way of signaling that it's working to fight an infection.

Still, fever is often the first sign of illness, and your baby's temperature reading—coupled with your baby's other symptoms (if any)—will help your pediatrician diagnose why he has a fever. But accuracy is key. For babies under 3 months old, especially, every tenth of a degree counts. The difference between a temp of 100.3°F and 100.4°F, for example, can determine whether you stay home or take your baby to the emergency room. Any fever in this age group is typically considered an

T-U-V

WHAT TO DO WHEN YOUR BABY HAS A FEVER

When your baby has a fever and you're worried, call your doctor. Be prepared to report your baby's temp, the method you used to take your baby's temp, how long your baby has had a fever, and any other symptoms your baby has. Wait to give any child under age 2 acetaminophen (Tylenol) or any fever-reducing medication until your pediatrician gives the OK. Ibuprofen, for example, should not to be given to children under 6 months or who are vomiting or dehydrated. Don't use aspirin to treat your child's fever. It has been linked with side effects such as intestinal bleeding, and most seriously, Reye's Syndrome, a severe neurological disorder.

emergency. If your baby is under 4 weeks old, and has a fever of 100.4°F or greater, call your pediatrician immediately. A baby that young with a fever of 100.4°F or higher will most likely need to be hospitalized to rule out serious infection. For babies 4 weeks to 3 months old, it's still an emergency that needs prompt medical attention.

Rectal Thermometers: Tops for Temps

Due to the toxic risks of mercury, digital thermometers have replaced the glass thermometers you may have grown up with. In fact, if you have a mercury thermometer, get rid of it, advises the American Academy of Pediatrics (AAP). But don't just throw it away. Your doctor or local health department can tell you how to dispose of it properly.

Digital thermometers are easy to read and they don't expose your baby to the mercury that's in a glass thermometer, which is dangerous if the thermometer breaks. Get a digital thermometer that can be used rectally and orally (for later on). You can also take a baby's temperature by mouth, by ear, on the forehead, or under the arm, but the AAP considers rectal readings to be the most precise way to take a temperature in infants and children younger than 3. (With the model of forehead thermometer we tested, which required pressing a button and rolling the thermometer over a child's forehead, the results weren't precise.) After your baby's first birthday, your pediatrician may allow you to use a different temperature-taking method, so be sure to ask what's acceptable at that point, if you want to switch.

A popular option you'll see in stores and online is digital ear (tympanic) thermometers, which measure body temperature inside the ear. "They aren't recommended for young children because there are lots of chances for error," says Paul Horowitz, M.D., medical director of Pediatric Clinics Legacy Health System in Portland, Ore. We've found that you have to align them in the ear canal perfectly to be accurate. Temps taken orally, with a pacifier thermometer, may seem to be another way to go. But oral thermometers tend to be as much as 1°F lower than rectal thermometers and aren't considered as accurate for children under age 3.

EAR

Shopping Secrets

Check features. Simple as digital thermometers are, some have bells and whistles that you might find convenient—beeps that tell you when they're in the right spot or when they're finished, or soft or curved tips.

Price and performance don't necessarily correlate. Extrapolating from our recent tests of oral, ear, and forehead thermometers in 24 adults and 21 children ages 5 to 14, we found you don't always get what you pay for. Thermometers can be pricey, but the best cost less than $15.

FOREHEAD

Think long-term. Since you'll probably be changing temperature-taking methods soon, go with a digital thermometer that can be used rectally and orally.

Ask your pediatrician for a recommendation. Your pediatrician may have a preferred brand, so be sure to ask at your next visit.

ORAL

What's Available

Major brands of digital thermometers are, in alphabetical order: BD Digital (*www.bd.com*), Bébé Sounds (*www.bebesounds.com*), Omron

TEMPERATURE–WHAT'S "NORMAL?"

Contrary to popular belief, a normal temperature isn't exactly 98.6°F. That's because "normal" isn't the same all the time. In each of us, temperature fluctuates throughout the day, depending on our age, general health, activity, how much clothing we're wearing, and the time of day. Body temperature tends to be lower in the morning and higher between late afternoon and early evening. There's a "normal," healthy temperature range for everyone. For children, it can run between 98.6°F or so and 100.3°F. Most pediatricians consider any thermometer reading above 100.4°F a sign of a fever. Because accuracy can vary depending on the temperature-taking method you're using, mention whether you took your baby's temperature rectally or some other way. Your pediatrician probably will ask anyway.

(*www.omron.com*), Safety 1st (*www.safety 1st.com*), Summer Infant (*www.summer infant.com*), The First Years (*www.thefirst years.com*), and Vicks (*www.vicks.com*). Digital thermometers retail from $3.79 to $34.99. Digital thermometers are available at leading pharmacy and baby product sites such as *www.amazon.com*, *www.buybuybaby.com*, *www.cvs.com*, and *www.target.com*.

Features to Consider

Speed reading. When you're trying to take a wiggly baby's temperature, you don't have much time to get the job done. Some thermometers

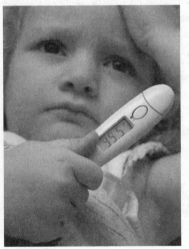

claim to display a reading in as fast as five seconds, but in our opinion, a reading in 20 to 60 seconds is fine.

Positioning gauge. To take the guesswork out of insertion, some rectal thermometers feature an indictor or design that makes it easy to know if the thermometer is positioned properly—a definite plus.

Sound effects. Thermometers that beep when they're done are useful; that way, you won't leave the thermometer in any longer than necessary.

Durability. Life with an under-the-weather baby is unpredictable. You'll want a digital

THERMOMETERS FOR THE FUTURE

At around age 4 or 5, when your child is old enough to hold a thermometer under his tongue, with his mouth closed, without biting, you can use an oral thermometer. In our recent test of eight oral, ear, and forehead thermometers in adults and children over age 5, the oral ones proved most accurate overall; a digital oral thermometer is the best choice for an adult or child over age 3. Besides the BD Digital Accu-Beep ($10), the Vicks Comfort-Flex ($13), and the Omron 20 Seconds Digital ($13) mentioned in our Ratings, which will last you beyond babyhood, the Vicks V920 oral (the only disposable thermometer we tested), $5 for 10, and the Timex oral (the only one that announces its results by speaking), $18, are other very good choices for preschoolers and the rest of the family.

TAKING YOUR BABY'S TEMPERATURE

If you're not comfortable taking your baby's temperature rectally, you're not alone. Most parents don't relish the thought. But most babies don't mind it as much as you'd think they would. Plus, many pediatricians consider a rectal temp the "gold standard" and insist you measure it that way. It gets easier with practice. Here are some pointers:

• Clean the end of the thermometer with soap and water or rubbing alcohol (whatever the instructions direct). Rinse it with cool water; don't use hot.

• Put a dab of petroleum jelly on the end and place your baby tummy-down on your lap or a firm surface. Hold him with your hand on his lower back. With your other hand, turn on the thermometer and insert it one-half to one inch (or to the length indicated on the thermometer) into your baby's bottom.

• Wait one minute, or until you hear the thermometer beep. Remove the thermometer and check the reading. Write the temperature down so you'll remember, in case your pediatrician or the nurse asks for it (she will).

thermometer that can withstand dropping, being submerged in water, even being gnawed on by your little one.

Brains. Some thermometers "remember" the last temperature read. That can be useful, especially in the middle of the night when you're sleep-deprived and trying to determine in what direction your baby's fever is going.

Recommendations

For your baby's first thermometer, go with an inexpensive digital model that can be used rectally, and later, orally. Look for an LCD display that's easy to read and a start button that's easy to press. But don't be swayed by digital thermometers that claim to take a reading in an instant. A reading in 20 to 60 seconds is sufficient.

Ratings • Thermometers

Which type of fever thermometer is best? We asked 24 adults and 21 children ages 5 to 14 to test eight oral, ear, and forehead thermometers and found:

• The oral ones proved best overall.

• Price and performance don't correlate. The best cost less than $15. A $40 children's ear thermometer was only fair.

• Simple as thermometers are, some have bells and whistles that can be convenient—beeps that tell you when they're in the right spot or when they're finished, or soft or curved tips.

We based our Ratings primarily on precision, or how widely the thermometers' results varied from those of our control, the Geratherm Mercury-free Oral thermometer, the accuracy of which we verified.

The bottom line. A digital oral thermometer is the best choice for an adult or a child over age 3. The best in our tests was the BD Digital Accu-Beep, $10, which beeps when it's properly located under the tongue. Its only disadvantage is that it takes about a minute to provide a readout. Very good choices that deliver the temperature in less than 30 seconds are Vicks Comfort-Flex, which has a soft tip, and Omron 20 Seconds Digital. Both cost $13.

The top three have a signal to indicate when they're done and a lifetime warranty. They can be used to take temperatures rectally and under the arm as well as orally. Rectal temperatures are generally considered most accurate for younger children. Oral temperatures tend to be as much as 1° F lower than rectal.

Ear thermometers work in just one second but were more precise than oral thermometers, perhaps because proper alignment in the ear canal can be tricky. With the forehead thermometer we tested, the Exergen, you press a button as you slide the probe across the forehead, then release the button and read the temperature. It cost $50, wasn't especially precise, and broke when we dropped it (no others did).

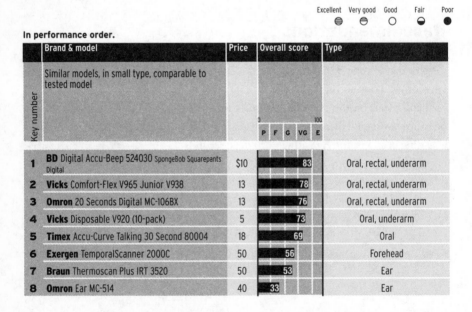

Excellent ⊖ Very good ⊖ Good ○ Fair ◑ Poor ●

In performance order.

Key number	Brand & model	Price	Overall score	Type
	Similar models, in small type, comparable to tested model		0 ⎯⎯ 100 P F G VG E	
1	**BD** Digital Accu-Beep 524030 SpongeBob Squarepants Digital	$10	83	Oral, rectal, underarm
2	**Vicks** Comfort-Flex V965 Junior V938	13	78	Oral, rectal, underarm
3	**Omron** 20 Seconds Digital MC-106BX	13	76	Oral, rectal, underarm
4	**Vicks** Disposable V920 (10-pack)	5	73	Oral, underarm
5	**Timex** Accu-Curve Talking 30 Second 80004	18	69	Oral
6	**Exergen** TemporalScanner 2000C	50	56	Forehead
7	**Braun** Thermoscan Plus IRT 3520	50	53	Ear
8	**Omron** Ear MC-514	40	33	Ear

CHAPTER

35

Toys

Your baby may look like he's simply having fun when he coos at his rattle or tries his hand at stacking "donuts." But make no mistake—what looks like playtime to us is work to babies, and toys are the tools for getting the job done.

Playing helps develop a baby's social, emotional, language, intellectual, and problem-solving skills, says Marilyn Segal, Ph.D., dean emeritus and director of the professional development program at Mailman Segal Institute for Early Childhood Studies at Nova Southeastern University in Fort Lauderdale, Fla. Batting at a mobile, giving a musical ball a shove, or transferring a rattle from one hand to another helps babies learn about the world. Such play also helps them connect sight, sound, touch, taste, and smell to objects; to recognize shapes, patterns, and colors; develop hand-eye coordination and memory; and to bond with you and others. "It's how your baby learns, and so much more," Segal says.

When you choose toys and activities that enhance your child's development, you're speaking your baby's language and helping him foster cognitive and social skills he can build on. But don't give toys all the credit. You're a key player. "The

T-U-V

most important toy is the parent and other caregivers because babies crave one-on-one social interaction and need the security it provides," says Segal. The right toy, though, can make key developmental stages more fun—for your child and for you. Here are some ideas about age-appropriate toys for your baby—and what you can do to play up their important lessons. Note: Retail prices vary widely, so the prices listed here may not match those in the store. Age recommendations are those of the manufacturer. (CONSUMER REPORTS has not tested these particular products, however.)

Newborn and Up: Shake, Rattle, and Manipulate

Babies are born with natural curiosity and gather information about the world through their senses. "The more of the five senses a particular toy commands, the more rewarding and appealing it is," says Sally Goldberg, Ph.D., program developer/director of the Center for Successful Children in Scottsdale, Ariz., and author of "Baby and Toddler Learning Fun." Babies enjoy looking at the world around them—lights, shapes, patterns, and colors. At around 3 months, they begin to swipe at objects and may try to reach for them.

Suggested Toys: Rattles and play keys with high-contrast colors

TIPS FOR TOY SAFETY

Keep toys intended for older children away from your baby.
• Look for warning labels on a toy's package. If the label suggests that the toy may pose a choking hazard, don't give that toy to a child under 3.
• Only buy toys deemed appropriate for the age of your child. Don't assume your little Einstein is ahead of the curve or that buying more advanced toys will enhance your child's development. Age grading relates to the safety of the toy as well as its play value.
• Check all toys for breakage and potential hazards each time you give them to your baby. If they can't be repaired, throw them away.
• Keep all balloons and broken balloon pieces away from your baby; they're a major choking hazard.
• Keep toys out of your baby's crib, and when your baby can begin to push up on his hands and knees (about 6 months), remove all mobiles.
• Never place an activity gym in a crib or playpen. Never add strings or ties to the gym.
• Keep all small round or oval objects, including coins, balls, and marbles, away from your baby. Use a common cardboard tube from a roll of toilet paper to screen out choking hazards. Any part small enough to pass easily through the tube is a hazard.

that make interesting noises, such as the Sassy Smiley Face Rattle ($8.99, birth and up) or Sassy's Classical Keys ($5.99, 6 months and up), and musical crib mobiles with bright, primary-color objects or patterns that stimulate your baby's sense of sight, such as Fisher-Price's Miracles & Milestones Mix & Match Musical Mobile ($35, birth and up). Keep toys out of the crib. However, mobiles can be suspended near or above the crib as long as they're safely mounted. Remove the mobile when your baby can push up on his hands and knees, at about 6 months.

Babies can see bright colors and shapes of rattles and play keys (for babies under 4 months, the toy should be any combination of red, black and white—the colors this age group sees best), feel their smooth or nubby texture, hear their rattling or clinking sound, and mouth them, which stimulates brain development. In the best rattles, the source of noise is visible so your baby can see the beads inside and link sound with sight. That helps babies learn about cause and effect—if they shake a rattle or keys, they make a sound.

Game Plan: Mold your newborn's fingers around a rattle or key ring and have him shake it or help him make the sound. Play is parent-driven for up to 6 months; after that, your baby takes over. Shake a rattle or toy keys at various points in your baby's sight lines so he'll enjoy the surprise of hearing the toy's sound from different angles. Have your baby grab for toys with either hand to help develop both sides of his brain; sometimes present toys on his right side, sometimes on his left. While some babies may start reaching for items at 3 months, the norm is more like 4 to 6 months. However, your baby probably won't show true hand dominance until about 18 months to 2 years, and many children remain ambidextrous until 3 to 5 years old.

You can also try tracking: hold a toy 6 to 12 inches from your baby's face, which is where babies 4 months and under see it best, with your baby sitting in your lap or lying down, and move it side to side slowly. This technique helps visual development and later hand-eye coordination. Later on, you can take turns playing with the rattle to instill the idea of taking turns and sharing, which your child will understand at about age 3.

4 to 10 Months: Gym Time

By now, babies can now reach for and grasp objects, move them from one hand to the other, and play with their feet. They'll search for the source of sounds.

Suggested Toys: A take-off on overhead mobiles, activity gyms such as the Baby Einstein Discovering Water Activity Gym by Kids II ($69.99, birth and up), Tiny Love's Gymini Deluxe Noah's Ark ($49.99, birth to 10 months), and the Fisher-Price Rainforest Melodies & Lights Deluxe Gym ($60, birth and up), feature charming, brightly colored floor and hanging detachable toys that make sounds, play music, and have tantalizing textures; some may include unbreakable, embedded mirrors, a definite plus. "Babies love to look at their own image," says Goldberg. Like rattles and play keys, activity gyms help babies explore their environment through their senses of sound, touch, sight, and taste. Their fine-motor skills get a tune-up when they bat, reach, and grab for toys. And if you place your baby in a gym on his tummy ("tummy time"), you'll help develop his posture and neck strength, a prerequisite for crawling and other physical skills. Babies of this age also tend to enjoy soft balls with sounds inside, musical toys, washable baby books, and toys with flaps or lids that can be opened and closed. They'll still be fascinated with rattles, and the more their pick-up skills develop, the more they'll reach for and play with them.

Game Plan: If your baby doesn't like tummy time (some babies don't initially), distract him with the gym's lights, music, and crinkle toys until he gets used to it. Take turns scrunching the crinkle toys and helping him squeeze the toys that beep. Detach his favorite toys and have him reach for them, either when he's lying down or supported by you or a Boppy, a horseshoe-shaped infant-support pillow. At first, your baby might just make general movements in the direction of a specific object, but eventually, he'll be able to reach out and pull objects to him.

9 Months and Up: The Nesting (and Stacking) Instinct Kicks In

Starting at about 9 months, babies play by shaking, banging, throwing, and dropping toys. They enjoy searching for hidden objects, taking objects out of containers, and poking their fingers into holes. Your baby will be able to grasp objects with her fingers and put one object

SAFETY STANDARDS

The Consumer Product Safety Commission regulates toys sold in the U.S., and toys must meet certain federal safety standards. For example, they must have acceptably low levels of lead in paint. They must not have sharp surfaces or points. Toys meant for children under 3 years may not have small parts, such as small balls or marbles, that could pose a choking, ingestion, or inhalation hazard. Other items on the safety checklist: no pinching parts; no small wires that could poke through; no strings, cords, or necklaces that could trap a baby's neck. Toys must not exceed flammability limits and they must contain no hazardous chemicals.

Teethers and squeeze toys must be large enough not to pose choking hazards. The same goes for rattles, which also must be designed so they can't separate into small pieces. Labels on crib gyms and mobiles must warn parents to remove them when a baby can push up on his hands and knees (about 6 months).

In recent years, the CPSC has recalled numerous toys for various reasons—rattles with seams that opened during use, releasing a bell or small beads (choking hazards), as well as toy phones with push buttons and antenna that could detach (also a choking hazard). If you've had a bad experience with a toy, call the CPSC at 800-638-2772 or log on to *www.cpsc.gov/talk.html*. Your call may lead to a recall.

on top of or into another, such as a ball into a box. At around age 1, he'll also start trying to put shapes through their designated slots on a shape sorter and by 15 to 18 months, he'll have the hand-eye coordination to ace the feat.

Stacking and nesting are another way babies develop eye-hand coordination and learn about spatial relationships—how things fit inside and on top of one another. Stacking and nesting also help babies develop the fine-motor skills of grasping and releasing, and the visual ability to align one object with another. Sorting helps babies understand the relationship among objects—how they fit together and spatially relate to one another and how they differ in size and shape. "It lays the groundwork for organizing and categorizing, which are basic mathematical concepts," says Goldberg.

Suggested Toys: Lightweight balls; nesting and stacking blocks or cups with rounded edges, such as the Stack & Smile Crocodile by Fisher-Price ($14.99, 12 months to 2 years); pop-up toys that require sliding, toggling, pulling, and turning, such as Brilliant Basics Bobble & Giggle Pals by Fisher-Price ($10.00, 9 months and up; requires three AA alkaline batteries, not included); squeeze and bath toys such as

THE BUZZ ON HIGH-TECH TOYS

Step into any baby store and you'll see that a generation of microchip-based toys is beeping, jingling, vibrating, flashing, and wailing its way into the nursery. Stimulating, tech-driven kid products aren't new, of course. What's newsworthy is the range of such offerings for babies—from an infant-size "interactive play center" that entertains with microchip-powered songs, sounds, and flashing lights to stuffed animals that sing and vibrate when you press their paws.

High-tech baby products can stimulate and entertain the older diaper crowd, but the chips inside aren't likely to add value for very young children. As for those electronic toys that claim to stimulate infant development or creativity, researchers say there's no credible supporting evidence regarding their long-term effects. "If it's a new toy, then for an hour or so, they're a little more alert and involved," says Jerome Kagan, a research professor emeritus of psychology at Harvard University. "But you wouldn't want to make profound predictions," such as, 'If my baby plays with electronic toys, he'll be smarter.' "

Says Kagan, the typical American household already provides enough sensory stimulation to make such toys unnecessary. "We should view the toys like an ice-cream cone," he says. "It's a brief source of pleasure that vanishes quickly."

Children will get far more meaningful stimulation from the sounds of the people, animals, and objects around them, notes Jane M. Healy, an educational psychologist in Vail, Colo., and author of "Your Child's Growing Mind." There's also a need for quiet time, when the brain consolidates what it has learned. "If there's nothing that's entertaining, it gives the brain time and space to learn to manage itself," Healy says.

Sassy's Snap & Squirt Sea Creatures ($7.99, 6 months and up); soft dolls, puppets, and baby books; musical toys, such as the Billy Bear in the Box by International Playthings ($21.99, 12 months and up); toy telephones and push-pull playthings, such as the Playskool Wheel Pals Chaser Chuck & Townee Vehicles by Hasbro ($5.99, 12 months and up).

Game Plan: Play with your child with shape-sorting toys and puzzles and hide another toy inside a nesting block to see if your baby can find it. "That adds the element of surprise and builds on the concept of object permanence," says Goldberg. You can enrich the experience by helping balance the block creation when it gets too high or even just commenting, "Oh, what a big tower!"

"Talking to young children as you're playing helps them assimilate words and concepts," says Jay Cerio, Ph.D., professor and chair of the division of school psychology at Alfred University in Alfred, N.Y.. Even though your child may not say his first words until 12 to 18 months, he's taking it all in.

Ages 1 to 2: Babies Get Their Fill

Playtime can get messy starting at age 1, when children begin to take an interest in emptying, transferring, and rearranging their environment. Turn your back and you're likely to find your toddler emptying the salt shaker, overturning the dog's dish, or upending the baby wipes. Filling and dumping are organizing skills that help your toddler experience how things work and relate to each other. They also enhance hand-eye coordination and teach basic spatial concepts like "in" and "out." Starting around 12 months, your baby may also begin walking.

Suggested Toys: Those that encourage your child's budding ambulatory skills, such as the Fisher-Price Laugh & Learn Baby Grand Piano ($44.99, 9 to 36 months) or the Little Tikes Wide Tracker Activity Walker ($21.99, 6 months to 3 years).

Game Plan: Encourage your baby's cruising confidence with plenty of praise as he pushes his way across carpeted or hardwood floors. Bath time is a good time to encourage filling and dumping by adding spoons, a plastic pitcher, measuring cups, and bath toys, such as Funny Face Bath Beakers by International Playthings Inc. ($9.99, 12 months and up) to the mix so your child can fill and pour without a mess.

There are literally hundreds of toys to choose from. Browse stores, catalogs, and Web sites. You can also get an idea of the toys your child might like by noticing what toys he gravitates to on play dates and at day care, and by asking other parents who have children of similar ages.

Shopping Secrets

Look for the manufacturer's recommended age range. It's on the front of the toy package—take it seriously. A toy labeled for children over age 3 is definitely not suitable for younger children. More than a friendly hint, an age recommendation can alert you to a choking hazard, the presence of small parts, and other dangers. If you're buying a toy for a child over 3 years old who has a younger sibling, remember that the younger child probably will find a way to get the toy.

Cheap, poorly constructed toys are no bargain. Flimsy plastic toys—the kind sometimes sold in drugstores, airports, and dollar stores—often have dangerous sharp edges or small parts that can break off easily.

Used toys, especially solid, molded-plastic ones, can be a great buy. Thrift stores, consignment shops, and yard and garage sales often have toys in excellent condition. But carefully check every toy to see that it's well made and safe, and wash it before giving it to your child. Babies experience much of their world through sucking, so expect that most toys will go straight to their mouths.

What's Available

Major brands of toys for newborns, infants, and toddlers are, in alphabetical order: Baby Einstein (*www.babyeinstein.com*), Bright Starts (*www.brightstarts.com*), Edushape (*www.edushape.com*), Fisher-Price (*www.fisher-price.com*), Infantino (*www.infantino.com*), International Playthings Inc. (*www.intplay.com*), Kids II (*www.kidsii.com*), LeapFrog (*www.leapfrog.com*), Learning Curve, which includes Lamaze, (*www.learningcurve.com*), Little Tikes (*www.littletikes.com*), Manhattan Toy (*www.manhattantoy.com*), Munchkin (*www.munchkin.com*), Neurosmith (*www.smallworldtoys.com*), Playskool (Hasbro, *www.hasbro.com*), Sassy (*www.sassybaby.com*), Small World Toys (*www.smallworldtoys.com*), The First Years (*www.thefirstyears.com*), Tiny Love (*www.tinylove.com*), and Vtech (*www.vtechkids.com*). Prices typically range from $4.99 for basic toys, such as rattles and baby books, to $70 or more for deluxe activity mats and stationary activity centers. For information on stationary activity centers, see page 255. For information on plush or stuffed toys, see "Zebras & Other Stuffed Animals," chapter, page 305.

Recommendations

When toy shopping, follow the manufacturer's age recommendations displayed on the package. Although you may think that a more "advanced" toy will present a welcome challenge, it could be a source of frustration if it is inappropriate for your baby's stage of development. It also may be unsafe. A stuffed toy, for example, that's labeled for a child over age 3 could have eyes that are potential choking hazards for a younger child.

The small-parts regulations ban toys made for children under age 3 that have, or could produce, small parts; for example, a toy bar or rattle that breaks, releasing fragments. But sometimes age recommendations can be difficult to find (or nonexistent). You can test an item for safe size by doing the toilet-paper-tube test: If the toy is

WHICH BATTERIES ARE BEST FOR TOYS AND BABY GEAR?

You may not go through as many batteries as diapers during your baby's first couple of years, but it will seem pretty close. Batteries usually aren't included when you buy toys and baby gear with music, lights, vibration, or sound effects, and some toys or baby products may require more than one size battery. Because not every battery is right for every job, here's a rundown of what to consider before your next visit to the battery aisle.

Buy rechargeable batteries for high-use items. For gear with a high power drain, such as an infant swing, or for toys and devices you use often, rechargeable batteries are much more economical than disposables, even after you factor in the cost of a $30 to $50 recharger, because the batteries can be recharged hundreds of times. Our tests show that rechargeable nickel metal hydride (NiMH) batteries perform better than rechargeable alkalines for such gear. But NiMH cells discharge when they're not in use, so they're not the best choice for battery-powered devices that often sit idle, such as a remote control.

Have disposables batteries on hand. Even if you plan to use rechargeables, it's a good idea to keep disposable batteries on hand as a backup. Among disposables, lithium batteries are best for digital cameras; the least expensive high-scoring alkalines are fine for everything else. Don't bother with nickel oxy-hydroxide cells.

Be wary of false savings. Disposable batteries are supposed to last a long time in storage—lithium cells for more than 10 years and alkalines for roughly seven—so you can buy in bulk and not worry when you need emergency juice. But be careful: Store-brand disposable batteries were less expensive in bulk, but we found that name-brand batteries were sometimes pricier per battery in the large pack. Bottom line: Scrutinize unit-price labels.

Follow manufacturer recommendations. No disposable battery is a deal if the toy or baby products manufacturer recommends another type. Be cautious of knock-off brands such as Dinacell, which may seem like a great value. Some have been defective.

See our Ratings of disposable AA batteries, next page.

small enough to pass through the tube, it's too small for a baby to play with. Look for anything that could be bitten or chewed off, such as hard, sewn-on parts like eyes, buttons, or wheels, and soft, small pieces, such as strings, ribbons, and stuffed animals' ears. All can be choking hazards.

Ratings • Disposable AA Batteries

To assess AA batteries, our tests, which conform to industry standards, simulate two situations: battery use in a typical digital camera: a high-current draw and then a low draw in cycles over a 5-minute period with a 55-minute break between periods, and battery use in a CD player that's on for two hours and off for six hours before that cycle is repeated. Although these tests aren't specific to toys and baby gear, they can give you an idea of how the tested batteries may perform in the battery-operated toys and baby gear you purchase.

Excellent ⊖ Very good ⊖ Good ○ Fair ◐ Poor ●

Within types, in performance order.

Brand & model	Price [1]	Digital camera Performance	Digital camera Cost per 50 photos [2]	CD player Performance	CD player Cost per hr. [2]
LITHIUM Best for cameras and other gear that draw a lot of power.					
Energizer e2	$2.35	Very good	$0.38	Very good	$0.38
PREMIUM ALKALINE Better for products with a low or medium power draw.					
Energizer e2 Titanium	1.02	Good	0.82	Very good	0.24
Duracell Ultra	1.11	Good	0.92	Very good	0.26
NICKEL Oxy-hydroxide OK but there are better choices for all gear.					
Duracell Power Pix	1.46	Good	0.82	Good	0.40
Panasonic Oxyride	0.85	Good	0.46	Good	0.24
REGULAR ALKALINE Best value for gear with a low or medium power draw.					
Kirkland Signature (Costco)	0.20 [3]	Fair	0.24	Very good	0.04
Duracell CopperTop	0.87	Fair	1.04	Very good	0.20
Rite Aid	0.87	Fair	1.08	Very good	0.22
Energizer Max	0.80	Fair	0.94	Good	0.20
CVS	0.87	Fair	1.16	Good	0.22
Diehard (Sears)	0.75	Fair	0.88	Good	0.20
Radio Shack Enercell	1.00	Good	0.94	Good	0.26
Rayovac Maximum Plus	0.39	Fair	0.44	Good	0.10
Walgreens	0.75	Fair	0.98	Good	0.22
Panasonic Digital	0.44	Fair	0.46	Fair	0.11
Panasonic Plus	0.22	Fair	0.28	Fair	0.06

[1] Per cell in 4-pack. Price is approximate retail. [2] Based on 2 batteries. [3] Smallest size is 48-pack.

CHAPTER

36

Walkers

A traditional walker, consisting of a molded plastic or metal frame with a suspended center seat and wheels attached to the base, gives a baby a quick way to get around before he can walk. Most are designed for a child of 4 to 16 months —or whenever a child begins to walk, usually around a year old. Don't use a walker once your baby can walk unassisted.

Walkers can keep a child away from certain dangers or let him follow you around the house—but they also raise concerns about safety and a child's normal development. Despite the name, a walker doesn't help a baby acquire walking skills. Walkers can strengthen lower leg muscles, but not the upper leg and hip muscles your baby will use most. Studies have shown that walkers may even delay a baby's desire to walk unassisted because he can scoot around too easily. More important, some walkers pose a significant risk of injury. Old-style walkers can fall down stairs or steps. They can turn over when their wheels get snagged, or roll up against hot stoves and heaters.

W-X-Y-Z

Outdoors, they can fall off decks and patios, over curbs, and into swimming pools. Many accidents involving walkers occur despite the presence of safety gates—either because the gates were closed incorrectly or they didn't hold up against the impact of the walker.

A second-generation voluntary safety standard was issued for walkers in 1997 to protect against stairway falls. According to this standard, walkers must have a bottom friction strip made of rubberized material to stop the walker if its wheels drop away at the edge of a step. Walker-related incidents have declined since the 1997 standard was introduced. The Consumer Product Safety Commission (CPSC) estimates that in 1992, walkers were involved in 25,700 injuries to children younger than 15 months who were treated in hospital emergency rooms. In 2003 (the latest government data), the number dropped to 3,200 such injuries, an 88 percent reduction.

Despite these promising statistics, the American Academy of Pediatrics urges parents not to use traditional baby walkers, and even recommended the U.S. government ban wheeled walkers. Since April 2004, the Canadian government has prohibited new and used baby walkers from being advertised, sold, or imported. However, baby walkers that don't conform to the nationally recognized stair-fall safety standard continue to be manufactured in the U.S. and abroad. The CPSC has put manufacturers, importers, and retailers of baby walkers on notice, urging them to continually review their product line to make sure all walkers they sell comply with the standard. Any walker they sell that doesn't meet this voluntary safety standard is considered defective and will be recalled from the marketplace. We agree that walkers can pose a safety hazard—even those that meet the safety standard—and believe there are plenty of safer alternatives, including stationary activity centers.

Shopping Secrets

Safety first. Select a model with a wheelbase that's longer and wider than the frame of the walker to ensure stability.

Practice collapsing display models in the store. Make sure the folding mechanism works well. In our tests, some models, such as the Safety 1st Grip 'N' Go ($40), pinched a finger when it was unfolded.

Don't buy a walk-behind walker. Some walkers, such as the Kolcraft Tiny Steps 2-in-1 Activity Walker #14570 ($60), can be converted to a walk-behind walker; once they're able, babies have the option of scooting around on foot by pushing the walker from behind.

We consider walk-behind units dangerous because a baby could push the walker down stairs. Avoid these models or simply don't convert them into walk-behind mode.

Take your baby with you. When you're shopping, make sure his feet can touch the ground on the seat's lowest setting.

Examine attachments. Look for small toys or parts that can break off or screws that can loosen. Toys and parts should be firmly attached.

What's Available

The major brands of traditional, wheeled baby walkers are, in alphabetical order, Baby Trend (*www.babytrend.com*), Delta Enterprise (*www.deltaenterprise.com*), Dream on Me *(www.dreamonme.com)*, Kolcraft (*www.kolcraft.com*), and Safety 1st (*www.safety1st.com*).

Also called "mobile entertainers" or "mobile activity centers," walkers are usually rectangular, but come in different shapes, such as a small car. Many have optional toy bars and toys, with or without sound and lights, and sometimes a mock steering wheel. Some also have a large snack tray with cup holder. Prices range from $30 to $80.

Features to Consider

Foldability. Some models fold flat for easy storage, a convenience if you live in a small space or plan to travel to Grandma's with your child's walker in tow.

Friction strips. They touch the floor when the wheels fall away on stairs or uneven pavement, making it difficult for a baby to push the walker farther. Most walkers that meet the voluntary safety standard have friction strips, but that's not a fail-safe design.

Parking stand. This allows the wheels to be lifted off the floor to limit a baby's scooting. Or look for a walker with wheels that lock.

Seat. Some seat covers can be removed and are machine washable. Seat height can be raised or lowered, using a locking mechanism located under the front tray, slots in the base of the walker, or adjusters on the seat.

Toys. Most walkers have rimmed trays, often with toys attached, some of which are equipped with lights and/or electronic sound effects. Infants under 4 months or so may not pay attention to toys at first.

Recommendations

Even with friction strips, a conventional walker isn't 100 percent safe. Consider a stationary activity center instead. One walker we can recommend is the top-rated Bright Starts Around We Go because it is attached to an anchored activity station, limiting its area of use.

We rated the The Kolcraft Tiny Steps 2-in-1 model #14565 Not Acceptable because it failed the American Society for Testing and Materials (ASTM) test for prevention of falls down stairs, and have urged the manufacturer and the CPSC to recall it. This Kolcraft model, discontinued but still available in stores, is certified by the Juvenile Products Manufacturers Association (JPMA) to meet the ASTM safety standard. A JPMA certification, however, is not an indicator of a safer infant walker.

Walkers do poorly on carpet, so reconsider if your house doesn't have hardwood, tile, or linoleum flooring. Babies on wheels can be surprisingly swift. When your baby is in walker mode, keep a close eye on your now-mobile baby.

Other precautions: Use a walker only in a room that doesn't have access to stairs leading down, and block access to stairs and the outside while the walker is in use. Clear objects off tables, counter, and stovetops that a baby in a walker might be able to reach. Make sure any springs and hinges on the walker have protective coverings. Finally, don't carry a walker with your baby in it. It's too easy for you to trip.

Ratings • Walkers

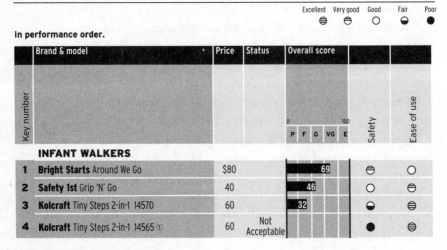

In performance order.

Key number	Brand & model	Price	Status	Overall score	Safety	Ease of use
	INFANT WALKERS					
1	**Bright Starts** Around We Go	$80		69	◒	○
2	**Safety 1st** Grip 'N' Go	40		46	○	◒
3	**Kolcraft** Tiny Steps 2-in-1 14570	60		32	◔	◒
4	**Kolcraft** Tiny Steps 2-in-1 14565 [1]	60	Not Acceptable		●	◒

Excellent ◒ Very good ◒ Good ○ Fair ◔ Poor ●

Guide to the Ratings

The **overall score** is based on lab tests assessing safety and ease of use. **Safety** reflects the security of the wheel locks and downgrading for converting into a walk-behind unit, not having an anchoring system limiting area of use, and failure to prevent falls down stairs. **Ease of use** is based on evaluations of assembly time, folding, ease of cleaning, adjustable seat height, and use of wheel locks.
[1] The Kolcraft Tiny Steps 2-in-1 14565 failed ASTM standards for prevention of falls down stairs.

CHAPTER

37

Zebras

& Other Stuffed Animals

A fter your baby's born—or even before—your home is likely to resemble a zoo of stuffed animals. Although your baby probably won't show an interest in a stuffed animal at first, this plush toy is likely to become his first friend. Stuffed animals can help your baby to make sense of the world; to discover how something feels, sounds, looks, and tastes. He can see its bright colors and shape, feel its smooth or nubby texture, hear its rattling sound or music, and mouth its fur—sensory stimulation that pave the way for brain development. Down the road, into the toddler and preschool years, a favorite stuffed toy can become an essential companion at bedtime.

Consider yourself warned: You're likely to spend hours in the toy store looking for just the right stuffed kitty, bear, alligator, or puppy. You may also find yourself back at the store searching for the twin of a beloved stuffed animal that has been lost.

Shopping Secrets

Stuffed toys are disarming because they're so squishy and cuddly, but they can pose safety hazards. When buying stuffed animals or introducing them to your baby, follow these guidelines.

Buy plush toys according to manufacturer's age recommendations. This helps ensure the ones you choose are safe and user-friendly. Plush toys meant for kids age 3+ may have small parts, such as eyes that are glued rather than sewn on, which can be a choking hazard for babies. Keep stuffed animals out of the crib.

Make sure toys are washable and bite-proof. The label on the product gives care and cleaning advice. Many are just surface washable. In our opinion, that's not good enough. Lightly pull on fur to be sure it won't shed and fray. Fur is not specifically covered by federal small-parts regulations, but it can still cause choking. Dyes should be colorfast.

Choose soft toys. Buy animals with the softest plush rather than those with scratchy fur. Nubby surfaces for teething are a plus.

Pick toys with contrasting or bright colors, and noises. A stuffed zebra or Dalmatian is likely to evoke more of a reaction from your baby than a cute pastel bunny. Stuffed toys with securely embedded, unbreakable mirrors tend to be a hit with the youngest set since children that age are naturally enamored of their own image. Squeaky, rattling, or jingly stuffed toys, or those that reward baby with a song (or a "moo" or a "baa") if he pulls, pushes, or jiggles them, provide an element of surprise and will be more entertaining than those toys that are simply cuddly.

What's Available

Major brands of plush toys for babies are, in alphabetical order: Aurora World (*www.auroragift.com*), Dakin (available at specialty retailers and online at sites such as *www.takeastroll.com/lovie.htm*), Eden (available at *www.amazon.com*), Fisher-Price (*www.fisher-price.com*), Gund (*www.gund.com*), Kaloo (*www.kaloo.com*), Manhattan Toy (*www.manhattantoy.com*), Mary Meyer (*www.marymeyer.com*), The First Years (*www.thefirstyears.com*), and Ty (*www.ty.com*). Prices generally range from $8 to $40, depending on the size and whether extras like music come with the deal.

Keeping Baby Safe
Childproofing Your Home

Before you know it, your baby will be highly mobile— and into everything. That's why it's a good idea to make your home a safety zone well before your baby starts crawling. Besides taking such common-sense measures as locking up guns and keeping matches and hazardous chemicals out of reach, installing special childproofing equipment early on is a prudent step. (You'll have time to get acquainted with it before it has to do its job.) Many of the accidents that injure or kill more than 2.5 million children age 4 and under in the United States each year could be prevented if adults took time to safeguard their homes.

You can childproof your home yourself or hire a childproofing service. Either way, you'll want to keep the preventive measures we outline in this section in place until they're no longer needed or effective. For instance, a safety gate's useful life ends when the child is about age 2 or big enough to climb over it. And a toilet lock probably won't be necessary beyond 3. Other measures, such as having locks on cabinets to thwart access to off-limits items, may not be needed when your child shows some judgment, maybe by age 4 or 5. And then again, much of the basic safety advice we mention in this section will kick in when your child is a toddler and will remain relevant well past the pre-school years. But childproofing isn't something you do once and then you're done. It's a constant process, especially when your baby becomes a toddler. In fact, a study in Pediatrics, the journal of the American Academy of Pediatrics (AAP) showed that childhood injuries peaked at 15 to 17 months of age.

Still, it's not realistic to be vigilant every single moment. "You're human. You will get distracted," says Robert Sege, M.D., Ph.D., chief of the Division of General Pediatrics and Adolescent Medicine at Tufts-New England Medical Center in Boston. Instead, think one step ahead and try to minimize the dangers in your child's environment. The room-by-room guide that follows can make your home safer—for your child and for you.

Kitchen

Cabinets, cupboards, and drawers

Anything that might be harmful to a child should be stashed in drawers, cupboards, or cabinets equipped with child-resistant safety latches. This list includes all kitchen cleaners; plastic wrap, food storage bags, and food-wrap dispenser boxes with a serrated edge; knives, scissors, corkscrews, and other sharp objects; refrigerator magnets or small kitchen knick-knacks; and liquor.

The best among the three combination drawer/door locks we tested was the KidCo Swivel Cabinet & Drawer Lock, $4 for four. It has a plastic base with a latching arm that mounts inside the door or drawer, a catch that mounts to the door or frame with screws, and is invisible from the out-

Cleaners in beverage-type bottles are a potential hazard

Some all-purpose cleaners sold in clear, beverage-style bottles are orange, blue, green, or purple and even smell fruity. It's easy for young children to mistake them for fruit juice, and unfortunately these cleaners don't have child-resistant caps, nor are they required to have them. So use locks or safety latches, and lock up cleaners, detergent, bleach, and other harmful products. Keep all chemicals in their original containers; never transfer them to soda bottles or other beverage containers. Labels often give important first-aid information.

side. It's easy to install inside a cabinet (it can't be used on metal cabinets) but harder to install in a drawer. It can be disabled by rotating the latching arm so it doesn't catch, an advantage in a home where children live only part-time such as a grandparent's house, but a disadvantage otherwise.

For center-opening cabinet doors with knobs or loop handles, the Safety 1st Model 00110 Cabinet Slide Lock, $1.99, was our top choice among four models tested. It can help keep kids up to about 5 years old out of cabinets where poisonous chemicals or sharp objects might be stored, but after that age they're likely to figure out how to defeat it.

CONSUMER REPORTS periodically puts childproofing products to the test. For the most recent product ratings of hundreds of household products, take advantage of your free 30-day subscription to Consumer Reports online. Go to *www.ConsumerReports.org/BabyOffer*.

Hot beverages

Get into the habit of drinking hot beverages from a travel mug to avoid spills. Use placemats instead of a tablecloth so little hands don't pull the tablecloth off the table—and your coffee with it.

Fire extinguishers

Keep a box of baking soda near the stove to extinguish grease fires. Purchase a small fire extinguisher and mount it nearby, out of kids' reach. Familiarize yourself with its use.

Kitchen access

When you cook, use a gate for the kitchen or keep your baby in a play yard, swing, or high chair—in view, but out of harm's way.

Kitchen stepstool

Keep your kitchen stepstool in a closet when you're not using it to prevent your little one from climbing into trouble.

Microwave ovens

Decide on an alternative to a microwave oven to warm bottles of breast milk or formula or heat jars of baby food. Holding bottles under warm tap water should do the trick. A microwave can create hot spots in the milk or food that can burn a baby's mouth and throat. It may also cause jars, bottles, and nurser liners to explode.

Small appliances

To prevent your baby from tugging down small appliances—including coffeemakers, food processors, and toaster ovens—wrap up and fasten cords out of reach with twist ties or rubber bands, or tape cords to the wall with masking tape. Push electric coffeemakers and teakettles away from counter edges.

Stove

Pull off front stove knobs and store them safely until it's time to cook. You can also buy childproof knob covers. When possible, cook on the back burners, and always turn all pot handles toward the back of the cooktop. We tested the Safety

1st Stove Knob Cover, $5.99 for a set of five. These covers work on stoves, usually gas, with knobs on the front. They didn't fit on all stove knobs and were difficult to use, but they were effective. Simply removing the stove knobs is equally effective.

Baby's room

Broken parts

Check all baby equipment frequently for broken parts or malfunctioning hardware. Stop using anything, particularly a crib, if it has broken or missing parts.

Crib

A crib is the safest place for your baby to nap or sleep. (For more on crib safety, see the "Cribs" chapter, page 127.) Place the crib well away from wall hangings, toys, windows, window blinds, curtains, and other furniture so that an adventurous baby can't reach anything dangerous. But once your child attempts to climb out of the crib, for her own safety, consider using a bed with child railings or putting the mattress on the floor.

Crib bedding

Be sure that the crib mattress is firm, that there are no gaps between the mattress and the sides of the crib, and that the mattress cover and sheets fit snugly. Soft bedding—pillows, padded bumpers, quilts, and comforters—is a suffocation hazard for infants, so keep those items out of the crib. Instead, dress your baby warmly enough for comfort. If you use a lightweight blanket, it should be pulled up no farther than a baby's waist and tucked securely under the sides and bottom of the mattress. For more information on crib bedding safety, see the "Crib Bedding" chapter, page 143.

Floor and carpet

Position furniture and toys so you'll have a clear path when you enter the room at night. Any area rug or throw rug should have a nonskid backing or, better yet, be secured with double-faced tape, so no edges stick up.

Furniture

Avoid high chests or tables. Bolt bookcases and chests to the wall so they won't tip if a child climbs on them. Furniture straps secure a piece of furniture to the wall to prevent it from tipping or toppling over when a child grabs on to balance himself or tries to climb. Toppling furniture can cause broken bones, bruising, and death from suffocation. If installed properly, furniture straps are effective protection up to about age 4 or 5. For more on furniture straps and preventing furniture tipovers, see "Changing Tables & Dressers," page 111.

Paint and other fumes

Allow time for fumes from new paint, wallpaper, drapes, and carpeting to subside before your baby comes home. Paint the nursery at least a week before the baby's arrival. When possible, use a paint that is low in volatile organic compounds, which may be irritating to a baby (and to some adults). To reduce fumes, air out new furniture and anything made of plastic or particleboard.

Toy chests

Don't store toys in wooden chests with lids that can slam or automatically latch shut when closed, and hurt a child or cause suffocation. Chests designed specifically for holding toys have hinges or lid supports that will hold the lid open in any position to prevent such accidents. Open shelves or crates are safer and make it easier to find toys. Or look for a chest without a lid, or one that has ventilation holes that won't be blocked if the chest is placed against the wall, so a child can breathe if she gets trapped inside, or one that leaves a space between the lid and the sides of the chest to allow ventilation when closed.

Soft toys and mobiles

Keep soft toys out of the crib. They're a suffocation hazard for young babies and can be used as stepping stools for climbing out. If you buy a crib mobile, hang it out of your baby's reach. A mobile should be taken down when your baby can push up on her hands and knees, at about 6 months. For more soft-toy safety tips, see "Zebras & Other Stuffed Animals," page 305.

- -

Basements, driveways, garages

Door to house

Install a lock on the door leading outside or to the garage. Consider a self-locking "Dutch door" that allows you to pass groceries into the house without letting your toddler out.

Driveway blind zones

Always make sure children are safely out of the way before backing your car out of the driveway. Some vehicles are now available with an optional rear-view video camera that shows the driveway in an in-dash display. See the "Autos" chapter, page 29, for more details and for other car safety tips.

Garage-door openers

Test an electric garage-door opener's sensitivity by placing a 2-inch-high block of wood on the floor in the door's path. If the door doesn't reverse direction and go up, don't use the garage door opener. Open and close the door manually, or replace the garage-door opener. In addition to reversing when they come in contact with something, new openers are equipped with optical sensors that prevent the garage door from closing if a child or anything else gets in the way.

Hazardous substances

Store matches, antifreeze, charcoal lighter fluid, windshield wiper fluid, gasoline, and oil as you would medicine—in their original containers, out of your child's sight and reach in a locked cabinet. Dilute any antifreeze spills by hosing them off. Antifreeze can contain ethylene glycol, a toxic chemical that smells and tastes sweet. It's particularly hazardous to children or pets that may lick it off driveways and garage floors (it happens).

Laundry supplies

Stash detergent, bleach, and other laundry essentials in a locked cupboard. Keep all chemicals in their original containers; never transfer them to soda bottles or other beverage containers.

Ride-on toys

Don't purchase a riding toy until you're certain your child is mature enough to use it safely. Attach a tall flag on the back of a tricycle so it's visible to motorists. The lower it is to the ground, the safer a wheeled toy is. Always supervise a child when riding. Be sure your child has a safe riding area, where she can navigate without the risk of going into traffic, down steep hills, on steps, or into driveways. If there's no safe place to ride, use a riding toy only for visits to the park. To keep children away from the garage, store tricycles and ride-on toys in the house.

Stairs

To prevent falls down basement stairs, install a lock as high as you can reach on both the front and back of the basement door. Make sure stairs are well lit and keep all clutter and toys off steps.

Water heater

Reduce the setting of your hot-water heater to 120° F. An infant's skin burns much more easily than an adult's.

Workbench

Make your workbench off-limits, whether you're working there or not. Lock up power tools and all small or sharp objects.

Bathroom

Bathroom doors

Keep bathroom doors securely closed or blocked with a gate. You may also want to cover the inside door lock with duct tape to keep your baby from locking you out. Install doorknobs that have a hole on the outside through which you can push a thin rod or screwdriver to disengage the lock in case your baby gets locked inside the bathroom.

Bathtub and water safety

When using a baby bathtub, always keep a hand on your baby. Never use a bath seat or bath ring; there have been numerous reports of babies drowning in them when their parents turned their backs, even for a moment. Never leave the room to answer the phone when your child is taking a bath—let your answering machine take your calls. You don't want any distractions during bath time. Before you use your regular bathtub for bathing a toddler, attach rubber strips to the surface to prevent slipping. Get a cover for the bathtub's spout to protect your child from its heat-conducting metal and hard edges. A bonus: Many come in fun animal shapes. For more on bath tub safety, see the "Bathtubs" chapter, page 65.

Diaper pail

If you soak cloth diapers, make sure the diaper pail has a tamper-proof lid with a solid locking device to eliminate a drowning hazard. If you use deodorizing tablets, store them out of reach of children. Some can be poisonous if ingested.

Electrical devices

Store all electrical devices, such as curling irons and hair dryers, in a high cupboard outside the bathroom.

Medicines

Keep medicines away from bedside tables and install a lock on the medicine cabinet well out of your child's reach. You can also store medications in a childproof, locked box kept on a high shelf outside the bathroom. Put vitamin supplements out of reach, too—iron pills and vitamins containing iron are leading child poisoners. Choose child-resistant packaging for prescription and over-the-counter drugs and vitamin supplements. Never keep medicines inside a purse in containers without childproof caps. Store visitors' handbags out of reach, such as on a high shelf. You never know. They might contain pill bottles without these caps, or small items that could be choking hazards. Discard expired drugs in their child-resistant packaging; don't just empty the contents in the garbage.

Toilet lid

Toilets pose a risk of drowning to curious infants and toddlers, so install a device to lock the lid of the adult toilet to keep your baby out. We tested the KidCo Toilet Seat Lock, $15, which installs in about 10 minutes. A spring-loaded arm swings out over the toilet lid when it's closed and locks in place. But, of course, adults have to remember to close the lid. Children older than 3 or 4 will probably learn how to overcome it, and the lock may not be as effective on padded toilet seats or unconventional toilets.

Decks, porches, yard

Backyard play equipment

Don't assume play equipment is safe simply because it's made for children. Supervise your child constantly;

toddlers don't understand heights, their own limitations, or the pendulum effect of swings. Put infants and toddlers between the ages of 9 months and 3 years in specially designed bucket swings with sides, backs, and crotch and waist restraints. Look for smooth edges and surfaces with no ragged seams or corners, and no nooks or crannies that could trap a child's fingers. Don't allow toddlers to use a regular swing until their feet firmly touch the ground and you're sure they're mature and strong enough to hold on without losing their balance when leaning backward.

Doors leading outside

Install a latch high on the back door. Firmly lock sliding patio doors, and secure them with a bar in the track.

Lawn & garden equipment

Keep your tot indoors whenever you use a lawn mower, string trimmer, snow blower, power mower, hedge trimmer, or other outdoor equipment. It's too dangerous for your toddler to be your little helper. Pour fuel into this equipment while outdoors, not in the garage, where fumes could become a hazard or ignite.

Pools, ponds, and hot tubs

Completely enclose pools with a four-sided fence and a self-locking gate (required under most building codes and by many insurance companies before they'll issue a policy), as well as hot tubs. Drain and securely cover the pool during the off-season, and cover the hot tub when it's not in use. Pool alarms raise an alert if people enter the water when they're not supposed to, but some are prone to false alarms. And in our tests, only two of six alarms worked well. They were the Poolguard PGRM-AG for above-ground pools ($140) and the Poolguard PGRM-2 for in-ground pools ($225). Four were rated Not Acceptable. But even effective alarms are no substitute for fencing a pool and latching doors and gates, says Julie Gilchrist, M.D., an epidemiologist at the federal Centers for Disease Control and Prevention.

Porch or deck railing

The spaces between the balusters on a railing or a porch or deck should be less than 3 inches. If they're wider than that (to check, see if you can pass a soda can through), install a railing guard made of mesh or plastic.

Swing sets

Make sure your backyard play set has a soft surface underneath it. It should have a layer of ground cover like wood chips, mulch, or pea gravel at least 9 inches deep extending from the equipment 6 feet in all directions. Lawn grass may seem cushy, but it's not.

Water containers and kiddie pools

Empty all outdoor containers of water—including 5-gallon and smaller buckets, insulated coolers, and wading pools—after use. They're a formidable hazard for small children who can drown in as little as an inch of water. Store them upside down, preferably indoors. If you have a large inflatable pool and can't dump the water every day, enclose it with a fence; it's the best protection against drowning, which is the second leading cause of accidental death in children under age 5. Simply covering a pool can be hazardous; children trying to move the cover have become entangled and drowned.

Living room or den

Fireplaces, wood-burning stoves, and radiators

If you have a fireplace, wood-burning stove, or steam radiators, teach your toddler to respect the warnings "Hot!" and "Don't touch!" Never leave a child in the room alone with a heat source, even if she seems safely enclosed in a play yard or bouncy seat. Consider a fireproof safety railing around the woodstove or fireplace, and always use a fireplace screen. If your fireplace has a glass enclosure, keep your child from touching it. Put fireproof padding around sharp edges on raised hearths.

Glass doors and objects

Put large stickers on sliding glass doors to keep your child from crawling, walking, or running into them. Remove vases and other knickknacks

your child could break, fall on, or swallow.

Houseplants

Give away poisonous houseplants (dumbcane, dieffenbacia, philodendrons, calla lilies, mistletoe, and hyacinths, to name a few), or ask friends to take care of them until your child is older. Keep all remaining plants well trimmed, so a child can't reach them.

TVs, VCRs, DVD players

Childhood injuries and deaths from falling television sets are a growing problem, according to Consumer Product Safety Commission statistics. The TV, VCR, and DVD player should be placed out of your child's reach. Secure them on a wall-mounted stand or on a shelf fastened to the wall. For more on preventing TV tipovers, see the "Changing Tables & Dressers" chapter, page 111.

General safety

Area rugs

Secure all area rugs or throw rugs with foam carpet backing or double-sided tape. To protect children who are just learning to walk from stumbling, be sure no edges or corners curl up.

Balloons

Don't let your child play with an inflated, deflated, or popped toy balloon. The material poses a choking hazard. "Popped latex balloons are the biggest single nonfood choking hazard that parents overlook," says Dr. Sege of Tufts-New England Medical Center. They're particularly dangerous because they conform to the shape of a child's airway, which makes them difficult to dislodge, and they can easily go in farther as a child inhales, he says. Put packages of unused balloons safely out of reach.

Bug spray

Avoid using bug sprays, carpet cleaners, and air fresheners where babies spend a lot of time crawling around. Keep spray cans in locked cabinets.

Charger packs

Unplug charger packs for cell phones and laptop computers when they're not in use. "The charger pack is a live wire if it's plugged into the wall, but not into your cell phone or laptop, and your baby can get quite a shock, if not worse, if he puts the wire in his mouth," says Rick Levinton, owner of Precious Baby Protectors, a home childproofing service in Houston. If you keep forgetting to unplug your charger pack, find an outlet in a high, out-of-reach location, and do all charging from there.

Doors

Consider buying doorknob covers, which can be squeezed open only by an adult hand.

Electrical outlets

Block unused electrical outlets with safety covers that screw into the outlet. Small outlet plugs that don't screw in can be dangerous because exploring babies can remove them and put them in their mouths.

For the over-the-outlet electrical outlet cover plates, we rated Mommy's Helper Safe-Plate Safety Outlet Cover, $4, effective in limiting the risk of injury to children up to about 4½ years old. The plastic plate has a spring-loaded sliding outlet cover to prevent injury. The device is easy to install and requires only a single screw. Foam backing helps keep it in place.

The KidCo S200 Decora Outlet Cover, $5, was another good choice among wall-mounted, over-the-outlet type cover plates. We also liked the Safety 1st Outlet Cover with Cord Shortener, $4. The socket and the coiled-up electrical cords are enclosed in a plastic cover to prevent injury. The device is designed to work only with outlets that have a center screw. It provides added protection against entanglement in the cords by taking up extra slack. Drawbacks: It can be difficult even for an adult to open and, in general, it isn't advisable to coil up power cords, because they can heat up. The label advises it not be used for appliances drawing 600 watts or more, or for extension cords supporting more than one appliance.

Among the individual plug-type outlet covers (the simplest type), the

Mommy's Helper Outlet Plugs Individual Outlet Caps, $1 for 12, was rated best of its type. The plugs were big enough that they didn't pose a choking hazard, fit snugly, and were easily visible. Their drawback: Children as young as 4 may be able to pull them out of the socket once they develop some manual dexterity, though removing them requires some effort. Directions suggest that adults remove them using a fingernail or non-metallic tool.

Elevated spaces

Anything that raises your baby up off the ground—a changing table, a framed backpack carrier, or a high chair, for example—can cause an injury. Make sure these items have safety belts and use them. Don't put a car seat or bouncer seat on a counter or table when your baby is in it.

Emergency numbers

Make a list of emergency telephone numbers, including those of your baby's doctor-to-be and the toll-free poison-control center (1-800-222-1222), as well as all contact numbers for family members. Post an easy-to-read copy of the list next to each telephone, and be sure to go over emergency procedures with baby-sitters and other caregivers before you leave the house.

If you believe your child has swallowed, inhaled, or handled something poisonous, call the Poison Control Center immediately. You'll be connected with a nurse, physician, or pharmacist at your local poison center who is specially trained in recognizing and treating poisoning. "Do this instead of heading directly to a hospital emergency room or calling 911—you'll get the fastest advice on how to handle the situation," says Rose Ann Soloway, RN, clinical toxicologist for National Capital Poison Center in Washington. And don't administer any remedy on your own. Don't use syrup of ipecac, for example, to induce vomiting. The AAP advises against it.

Extension cords

Purchase extension cords equipped with locking plug covers. If your house is overloaded with extension cords, talk to an electrician about having additional outlets installed.

Fire and carbon monoxide protection

Install a smoke alarm and a carbon monoxide detector in key locations on each floor of your home, such as inside bedrooms. If they require batteries, change the batteries when you set your clocks to standard time each fall. Check the detectors every other week to make sure the batteries are good. Place all matches and lighters on a high surface or in a locked drawer or cabinet. Formulate an escape plan. Finally, place large street address numbers at the entrance to your driveway or on the front door for firefighters, police officers, and other emergency workers to see easily.

Hazardous gaps

Beware of gaps that babies can get stuck in, such as the leg openings of strollers or baby carriers, the space between the seat and tray of a high chair, the area between the slats of a crib or cradle, or that between a gate and the floor.

Heavy furniture

Bolt or bracket bookcases and other heavy furniture, such as dressers, wall units or armoires, to the wall to prevent tipping if a toddler decides to climb on them. For more on preventing furniture tipovers, see the "Changing Tables & Dressers" chapter, page 111.

Helmets

When your baby gets to be toddler and preschool age, get her into the habit of wearing a helmet when riding a tricycle or bicycle. Choose a helmet with a label that states that the helmet meets the Consumer Product Safety Commission's mandatory safety standard. Have your child try on different sizes to make sure you've got the right one. Your child should be able to see and hear well; the chin strap should be easy to fasten and release; and the helmet should fit comfortably under the chin without chafing. See our Ratings in the "Bicycle-mounted Child Seats & Trailers" chapter, page 73.

Household cleaners and deodorizers

Assess household cleaning products. Cleaning ingredients such as ammonia can irritate a baby's nose and throat.

Fragrances can irritate a baby's sensitive skin and respiratory passages and can even trigger allergic reactions, so you may want to skip floral or citrus scents once your baby arrives. Avoid using plug-in or aerosol room deodorizers as well.

Irons

Put your baby safely in a swing, bouncer seat, or play yard whenever you iron, and don't leave an unattended baby and an iron in a room together.

Lead in tap water and furniture finishes

Have your home's tap water tested for lead and, if needed, purchase an effective water-purification system. Besides having possibly malfunctioning parts, heirloom furniture, such as cribs and chests, may have been coated with lead-containing paints, lacquers, or varnishes. All new cribs have very low and, therefore safe, levels. You can check antique finishes with a lead-testing kit. If you detect lead in a piece of furniture, put it in storage until your baby gets older.

New clothes and bedding

Launder all new baby clothes and bedding in a fragrance-free detergent once or twice to remove chemicals. Don't use liquid fabric softener or dryer sheets; the fragrance may irritate your baby's skin and respiratory system. Liquid softener may also reduce the absorbency of cloth diapers.

Night-lights

Night-lights at floor level attract crawling babies and toddlers to sockets. Place a night-light in a socket out of your baby's reach, install a dimmer switch for the room's lighting fixture, or use a lamp with a low-wattage bulb.

Old refrigerators

If you're discarding an old refrigerator, always remove the doors and store the unit facedown while awaiting pickup. Children can become trapped and suffocate inside a discarded refrigerator if the door closes.

Parked cars

There are many reasons you should never leave a little one alone in a parked car. Here's one: Even with windows cracked open, interior temperatures can rise almost 20 degrees Fahrenheit within the first 10 minutes on a hot day. Anyone left inside is at risk for serious heat-related illness or death, and heat affects children more quickly and severely. And remember to keep parked cars locked so children can't play in them. Kids who accidentally lock themselves in won't be able to unlock the doors.

Pets

Consider obedience training for your pet to ensure safe, controlled behavior around your baby. Talk to a trainer about easy ways to introduce your baby into a home with pets. Buy a tall gate or special pet gate to keep your dog in the kitchen or other safe area when appro-

priate. Move your cat's litter box to a spot that you know your toddler won't be able to reach.

Plastic bags

Plastic bags are suffocation hazards. Keep plastic garbage bags, laundry bags, food storage or grocery bags, and bags used in packaging everything from dry cleaning to electronics on a high shelf or in a locked cupboard. Tie a plastic bag in knots before throwing it out.

Product registration

Mail in registration cards that come with baby products so you can be notified about recalls. Follow manufacturers' age or weight guidelines in using products. Keep product instruction manuals in an easy-to-find location.

Railings

If railings on staircases, balconies or decks are spaced more than 3 inches apart (and many will be, especially in older houses), install railing guards made of mesh or clear plastic to prevent your child from getting stuck.

Sharp corners

Add padding to the sharp corners of coffee, TV, and bedside tables, desks, file cabinets, and the like, or consider storing them during your baby's first few years.

Small parts, edges, and hinges

Pick up clutter, such as batteries, paper clips, staples, and coins. Keep purses out of reach, and stash an older sibling's toys with small parts away from your baby. Inspect your home for all dangerously small objects and keep them out of your baby's reach. Anything small enough to fit through the tube of a toilet-paper roll (about 1¾ inches in diameter) could pose a choking hazard. Also, thoroughly check toys, strollers, high chairs, play yards, gates, and so on to see that they're free of sharp edges or points and potentially dangerous hinges.

Smoking

Ban smoking indoors or anywhere around an infant, such as in the car. Secondhand smoke has been associated with Sudden Infant Death Syndrome and baby respiratory ailments.

Stairways

Install pressure-mounted gates at the bottom of each staircase and hardware-mounted gates at the top. Never use a pressure gate at the top of stairs—no matter how much you want to avoid drilling holes into your woodwork. Also, choose a gate with a straight top edge and rigid vertical filler bars or a mesh screen. Avoid gates with horizontal slats or vertical slats that are spaced far enough for a child's foot to fit, or similarly tempting footholds; they're an invitation for a child to climb. If you choose a model with mesh panels, look for mesh holes of less than one-quarter inch—wide-holed mesh could entrap little fingers. To reduce the risk of falls, keep the barriers up until your child is at least 2 years old. Safety gates that meet the latest safety standards display a certification seal from the Juvenile Products Manufacturers Association. Look for it on the frame or packaging. For more information, see the "Gates" chapter, page 187.

Windows

Keep your baby away from open windows. Window screens aren't strong enough to stop a child from falling out. If you live in a high-rise, or in a house with second or third stories that have windows low enough for your child to reach, purchase window guards from a hardware or home-supply store and install them according to the manufacturer's instructions. Also keep in mind that cords from draperies or blinds can entangle a baby. Cut looped cords in half to form two strings. You can also roll cords up and tie them with rubber bands or twist ties, or mount a cleat (hook) high out of the child's reach to secure the excess cord. Or choose window treatments that don't use cords.

Medication Use In Children

Contents

General Information page 322

In this section you'll find the important information you need to know before giving any medication to your child, including how to administer various medications, some important questions to ask your pharmacist, how to prevent accidental poisoning in children, and how to prepare for your family's medication needs in an emergency.

Over-the-Counter Pain Relievers and Fever Reducers page 335

Read this section before giving pain relievers or fever reducers to your child. You'll find general tips about giving those medications as well as specific information about acetaminophen and ibuprofen, two of the medications most commonly given to young children.

Childhood Immunizations page 342

This section stresses the importance of childhood immunization and provides specific information that you should discuss with your child's doctor before your child is immunized. Included are potential side effects of certain vaccines and what to do if they occur. At the end of the section you'll find the recommended immunization schedule for children ages newborn to 6 years in the U.S.

GENERAL INFORMATION

The following general information is provided to help you safely use medications for your child. Always read the specific information that comes with each of your child's prescription medications and any medications you buy without a prescription.

If you have questions about any medication prescribed or recommended for your child or how to use it, you should always talk to your child's doctor, a pharmacist, or other health-care professional.

What should I tell the doctor and pharmacist before giving this medication to my child?

Tell the doctor and pharmacist if your child is allergic to any medications, dyes, or other substances, including any foods, such as eggs. Because some medications are sweetened with aspartame (Nutrasweet), tell the doctor if your child has phenylketonuria (PKU), a rare inherited disease.

Tell the doctor and pharmacist what prescription and over-the-counter medications (OTC, nonprescription), vitamins, nutritional supplements, and herbal products your child is taking or what you plan to give to them. Remember, even occasional use of some OTC medications such as fever reducers, pain relievers, antacids, cold products, and laxatives could effect other medications your child is taking.

Tell the doctor if your child has or has had any diseases or conditions. Sometimes the doctor may want to know if anyone else in your family has had a particular disease or disorder.

If your child is having surgery, tell the doctor whether he is taking any medications, vitamins, nutritional supplements, or herbal products because some can affect blood clotting and others can interact with anesthetic agents.

Ask the pharmacist or doctor for a copy of the manufacturer's information for the patient or get it from the Food and Drug Administration's Web site, at *www.fda.gov*. Be sure to read this information carefully and discuss any questions you may have with your child's doctor or pharmacist.

How should I give this medication to my child?

Follow the directions on prescription labels and on OTC drug labels carefully, and ask your child's doctor or pharmacist to explain any part you do not understand.

Use OTC medications only if there are age- or weight-specific directions on the label for your child or if your doctor or pharmacist provides specific instructions.

Read each label carefully each time you give the medication to your child.

If your child is taking medication on a regular basis, administer it at about the same time(s) every day according to dosing instructions. If necessary, use calendars or timers that remind you which medications to give when. It may help to give medication at a certain point in your child's daily routines such as brushing teeth or before a certain meal.

If your child is taking a medication that is given only as needed (such as fever-reducing or pain medications), do not give the child more than the recommended amount for each dose or for the total number of doses for each day.

Give the medication to your child exactly as directed. Do not give more or less, or give it more often than prescribed by the doctor or directed by the labeling on the package.

Give the medicine to your child for as long as the doctor has told you. Do not stop the medication just because your child's symptoms disappear or he begins to feel better unless told to do so. For OTC medications, carefully make sure to give your child the dose recommended for their age or weight.

Bring all the medications and supplements (including those prescribed by other doctors) or a complete record of them to your child's doctor for review at regular checkups.

If your child receives certain medications regularly, be sure to refill them on time so that he won't miss any doses.

Tell the doctor or pharmacist if you notice a change in the appearance (color, shape, size) of a medication that was refilled, unless an explanation has been given by your child's doctor or the pharmacist.

Do not give medications to your child where there is not enough light to read the label. If you can't see well, you could give the wrong medication or dose.

You may need to give some medications with food or meals to get the best effect or to reduce side effects in your child's stomach. Other medications may need to be given on an empty stomach to achieve the best effect. Ask your doctor or pharmacist whether your child's medication should be given on a full or an empty stomach.

If your child has trouble taking one form of medication, such as a tablet, ask your pharmacist or doctor whether it is available in another form (chewable tablet, liquid, rapidly dissolving tablet, or suppository) that he can take more easily.

If your child does not want to take the medication because of the taste, talk to the pharmacist or your child's doctor. Flavoring can sometimes be added to liquid medications to improve the taste. Or find out whether it is possible for the medication to be added to certain soft foods, such as applesauce or pudding, or to beverages to allow the child to take the medication more easily, but always ask your child's pharmacist first.

The taste of some liquid medicines may be improved with refrigeration, but ask your pharmacist whether it is okay to refrigerate your child's medicine. Be careful not to freeze it.

Shake the liquid or suspension containers well before each use to mix the contents evenly.

Always use the measuring device provided with liquid medications or ask the pharmacist to give you one. You should never use kitchen spoons because they can vary in size and may hold too much or too little medication. Ask the doctor or pharmacist if you are uncertain how much liquid medication you are to give to your child. Listed below are several types of measuring devices that may come with liquid medications or that can be provided by your pharmacist.

Oral syringes (without needles) and droppers: These are useful when giving liquid medications to infants. After drawing up the amount of medication that your child's doctor has prescribed, squirt the liquid between your child's tongue and the side of the mouth. Avoid squirting the medication directly onto the back of the throat as it can cause the child to gag and spit out the medicine. Always remove the plastic cap that comes with some oral syringes before giving the medication to your child. Be sure to throw the cap in the trash, as it is a choking hazard for infants and young children if put into the child's mouth. Clean this device thoroughly in warm water after each use.

Dosing spoons: This is a spoon on the end of a measuring device and works well for children who are old enough to drink from a cup. The child can hold the measuring "handle" and drink the medication directly into her mouth. Clean this device thoroughly in warm water after each use

Medication cups: Be sure to use only the cup that comes with the medication, and do not use it to measure other medications because the markings on the cup may be specific for that medicine. To measure the correct amount of medication to give to your child, pour the liquid up to the correct marking on the cup as seen at eye level on a flat surface. Clean this device thoroughly in warm water after each use.

How to Use Special Dosage Forms

Here are instructions with pictures showing the best way to give several types of medication that are placed into your child's eye(s), ear(s), nose, or rectum. These descriptions are for general information only; always follow the specific instructions that come with the medication.

How to Use Eye Ointments

If your child is very young and/or uncooperative, it is best to have someone else gently hold the child while you put the ointment into the child's eye. If this is not possible, sit on the floor and hold your child's head face up between your legs so that you can apply the medication with both hands.

1 Wash your hands thoroughly with soap and water.

2 Don't touch the tip of the tube against your child's eye or anything else—the medication and its container must be kept clean.

3 Holding the tube between your thumb and forefinger, place it as near to your child's eyelid as possible without touching it.

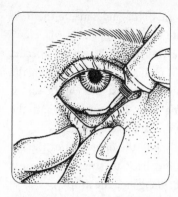

4 Brace the remaining fingers of that hand against your child's face.

5 Tilt your child's head forward slightly.

6 With your index finger, pull the lower eyelid down to form a pocket.

7 Squeeze a ribbon of ointment into the pocket made by the lower eyelid.

8 Tell your child to blink his eyes gently and then close them for 1 to 2 minutes.

9 With a tissue, wipe any excess ointment or gel from the eyelids and lashes.

10 Repeat steps 3 to 9 if the ointment is also to be placed in the other eye.

11 With another clean tissue, wipe the tip of the tube clean.

12 Replace and tighten the cap right away and store it as directed.

13 Wash your hands to remove any medication.

How to Use Eyedrops

If your child is very young and/or uncooperative, it is best to have someone else to gently hold the child while you put the drops into the child's eye. If this is not possible, you can sit on the floor and hold your child's head face up between your legs so that you can apply the medication with both hands.

1 Wash your hands thoroughly with soap and water.

2 Check the dropper tip to make sure that it is not chipped or cracked. Don't touch the dropper tip against your child's eye or anything else—eyedrops and droppers must be kept clean.

3 Have your child tilt his head back, then pull down the lower lid of the eye with your index finger to form a pocket.

4 Hold the dropper (tip down) with the

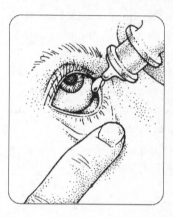

other hand, as close to the eye as possible without touching it.

5 Brace the remaining fingers of that hand against your child's face.

6 Gently squeeze the dropper so that the correct number of drops falls into the pocket made by the lower eyelid.

7 Have your child close his eyes for 2 to 3 minutes. Wipe any excess liquid on the face with a tissue.

8 Repeat steps 3 to 7 if the drops are also to be placed in the other eye.

9 Replace and tighten the cap right away and store it as directed. Do not wipe or rinse the dropper tip.

10 Wash your hands to remove any medication.

How to Use Eardrops

If your child is very young and/or uncooperative, it is best to have someone else gently hold the child while you put the drops into the child's ear.

1 Gently clean your child's ear with a damp facecloth and then dry the ear.

2 Wash your hands thoroughly with soap and water.

3 Warm the drops to near body temperature by holding the container in your hand for a few minutes.

4 If the drops are a cloudy suspension, shake the bottle well for 10 seconds.

5 Check the dropper tip to make sure that it is not chipped or cracked.

6 If the dropper is attached to the cap of the eardrop bottle, turn the bottle

upside down to allow the drops to drip into the dropper.

7 If the eardrop bottle came with a regular cap, and you are using a separate dropper, place the tip of the dropper

inside the bottle and squeeze the bulb gently to fill the dropper.

8 Have your child tilt up the affected ear or lie on his side. Avoid touching the dropper tip against the child's ear or anything else. The eardrops and the dropper must be kept clean.

9 Gently pull the outer rim of the ear down and back to straighten the ear canal before giving the drops.

10 Place the correct amount in the ear. Then tug gently on the ear to allow the drops to run in.

11 Keep the ear tilted up for a few minutes. Tell your child that his ear may feel a little full, but he should not put his fingers in his ear.

12 Replace and tighten the cap or dropper right away and store it as directed.

13 Wash your hands to remove any medication.

How to Use Nose Drops

Have your child blow her nose, if she can, or wipe her nose gently.

1 Wash your hands thoroughly with soap and water.

2 Check the dropper tip to make sure it is not chipped or cracked.

3 Don't touch the dropper tip against your child's nose or anything else. The nose drops and the dropper must be kept clean.

4 Have your child tilt her head as far back as possible, or have her lie on your lap and hang her head over the edge.

5 Place the drops into your child's nose.

6 Have the child remain in this position for a few minutes.

7 Clean the dropper tip thoroughly under running warm water. Cap the bottle right away and store it as directed.

8 Wash your hands to remove any medication.

How to Use Rectal Suppositories

If your child is very young and/or unco-operative, it is best to have someone else gently hold him while you insert the suppository.

1 Wash your hands thoroughly with soap and water.

2 If the suppository is soft, hold it under cool water to harden it before removing the wrapper.

3 Remove the wrapper, if present.

4 If you were told to use half of the sup-pository, cut it lengthwise with a clean, single-edge razor blade.

5 Put on a finger cot or disposable glove, if desired (available at a pharmacy).

6 Lubricate the suppository tip with a water-soluble lubricant such as K-Y Jelly,

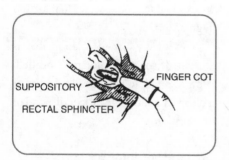

SUPPOSITORY
FINGER COT
RECTAL SPHINCTER

not petroleum jelly (such as Vaseline). If you do not have this lubricant, moisten the rectal area with cool tap water.

7 Have your child lie on her side with the lower leg straight and the upper leg bent forward toward her stomach.

8 Lift the upper buttock to expose the rectal area.

9 Insert the suppository, pointed end first, with your finger until it passes the muscular sphincter (opening) of the rectum, about ½ to 1 inch in infants and young children. If not inserted past this sphincter, the suppository may pop out.

10 Hold the buttocks together for a few seconds.

11 Have the child remain lying down for about 15 minutes to make sure the suppository stays in.

12 Discard used materials out of reach of children and pets and wash your hands thoroughly.

What special dietary instruc-tions should my child follow while taking this medication?

Unless the doctor tells you otherwise, have your child eat a normal diet. Tell the doctor if your child is following a special diet because some medications may contain other ingredients that could affect the diet.

Some medications should not be taken with certain foods or beverages, such as grapefruit or grapefruit juice. Ask the pharmacist or doctor.

What should I do if I forget to give a dose?

Review the specific information provided with the medication. Generally, give the missed dose as soon as you remember it.

However, if it is almost time for the next dose, skip the missed dose and continue the regular dosing schedule. Do not give a double dose to make up for a missed one.

If your child is using a cream, lotion, ointment, or gel, apply the missed dose as soon as you remember it. However, if it is almost time for the next dose, skip the missed dose and continue the regular dosing schedule. Do not apply extra cream, lotion, ointment, or gel to make up for a missed dose.

What side effects can this medication cause?

Medications may cause side effects, some serious. Learn what to do about them before your child starts taking the medication. If he experiences any serious side effects, call his doctor immediately.

Some medications may cause long-term risks when given to children. Talk to your child's doctor or pharmacist about all the risks and benefits of any medication your child is taking.

If your child experiences a serious side effect, you or your doctor may send a report to the Food and Drug Administration's (FDA) MedWatch Adverse Event Reporting program online at www.fda.gov/MedWatch/report or by phone at 800-332-1088.

For information on reporting serious side effects of a vaccine, see "What Should You Do If Your Child Has a Reaction?" on page 345.

How should I store this medication?

Keep the medication in the container it came in, tightly closed, and out of reach of children and pets.

Store it at room temperature and away from excess heat and moisture (not in the bathroom) unless the pharmacist or doctor told you to store it some other way.

Some medications have to be stored under special conditions, such as in a refrigerator or freezer. In general, don't freeze liquid medications that you are told to store in a refrigerator. Check with the pharmacist or doctor to find out how you should store your child's medication.

Keep each family member's medications separate from one another's so that you do not mistakenly take or give someone else's medicine.

Remove the cotton plug if there is one in the container. The cotton will attract moisture into the container if left in place after opening.

Do not leave your child's medication in a car for long periods of time. It may be exposed to temperatures that are too high or too low.

Throw away any medication that is outdated or no longer needed. However, talk to your child's doctor or pharmacist about the proper disposal of medication.

What other information should I know about my child's medication?

Always know the generic and/or brand (trade) name of your child's medication. Ask the pharmacist or child's doctor if you are unsure which is which.

Keep a list of all the medications your child is taking, including the name, dose, how often you give the medication, and the doctor who prescribed it.

Keep all appointments with your child's doctor and the laboratory. Your child's doctor sometimes may order certain lab tests to check your child's response to medication.

Before any laboratory test, tell your child's doctor and the laboratory personnel what medications or supplements your child is taking.

Do not give your child's medication to anyone else, including family members who may have the same symptoms or complaints.

Ask your pharmacist any questions you have about refilling your child's prescription. Some prescriptions are not refillable and the doctor will need to write another prescription if your child is to continue this medication.

Ask your pharmacist any questions you have about OTC medications. Tell your pharmacist what other medications, vitamins, nutritional supplements, and herbal products your child is taking. Always read the information on the package and check the list of ingredients to make sure that you are not giving your child more than one product that contains the same medication.

If you receive sample medications from your child's doctor, ask whether the new medicine will interact with any medications, vitamins, nutritional supplements, or herbal products that your child is already taking. You should always receive written instructions on how to give any sample medication; specifically, how many times a day it should be taken or for how long. Never rely on your memory of what your child's doctor or her staff told you.

Generic and Brand-Name Drugs

What is the difference between generic and brand-name drugs?

Prescription drugs come in basic forms—generic and brand-name drugs. Generic drugs are copies of brand-name products on which patents have expired. A generic drug has *exactly* the same active ingredient(s) as the brand-name drug it copies. The main differences are price and how the medications look. Generics are much less expensive and by law are not allowed to look exactly like the brands they copy; the may be a different color and/or shape. Certain inactive ingredients, colors, or flavors may be different in the generic drug.

Are generic drugs as strong as brand-name drugs?

Many people believe that because generics have been around longer, they are not as potent or effective as newer competing brand-name drugs. The truth is that the vast majority of generics continue to be useful medicines even years after their approval, and many remain the preferred first-line treatment even after newer brand-name competitor medicines emerge. Currently, about half of all prescriptions written in the U.S. are for generic drugs.

Are generic drugs as safe as brand-name drugs?

The Food and Drug Administration (FDA) requires that generic drugs be just as safe as brand-name drugs. The FDA applies the same set of strict rules to generics as to brand-name drugs. Both must meet the same specifications for their ingredients and manufacturing process. The FDA requires generics to have the same quality, strength, purity, and chemical stability and to work the same way in the body. Both types of medications are followed for their safety over time.

Because of U.S. patent laws, generic drugs usually come on the market about 12 to 15 years after the brand-name drugs they copy were first approved.

It is not uncommon for doctors and drug companies to find problems with new brand-name drugs that come to light only after they are approved. That's because even though new drugs undergo years of study to prove they are safe and effective, those studies may have involved only several thousand people; once a drug is used by millions of people, new problems can and sometimes do become known. Therefore, because they have been used

for a longer period of time by many more people, generics drugs may actually be safer than newer brand-name drugs.

How do I know if a generic drug is available for the brand-name drug that my child is prescribed?

Not all medications have a generic counterpart because brand-name drugs generally are protected by a patent for more than a decade. When the patent expires, other drug companies can manufacture generic versions of the drugs, but those generic versions first must be tested and approved by the FDA before they become available to patients.

Ask your pharmacist or child's doctor whether there are generic drugs available for the medication(s) your child is taking. Most states allow pharmacists to substitute the generic version of a drug when a doctor has written a prescription for the brand-name drug. But in many states, the pharmacist must ask the consumer's permission to make the switch. Sometimes the consumer may be uncertain about making this change because he is afraid that he will get a drug his trusted doctor did not intend. If a pharmacist suggests substituting a generic drug when your child's prescription is being filled, you can call the doctor if you are concerned about this switch.

Talk to your child's doctor about a new prescription when it is being written in his or her office. Ask whether the prescription is for a brand-name or generic drug, and learn why your doctor has prescribed one or the other. If you pay for your medicines out-of-pocket because you lack insurance coverage for drugs, ask the doctor whether there is a less expensive generic drug that will work for your child. Even if you have insurance that covers your child's prescription medicines, the amount of your out-of-pocket co-pay may be much higher than you would pay with a less expensive generic.

Pharmacist Q & A

What basic items should be stored in a home first aid kit?

• Antiseptics, first-aid ointments, hydrogen peroxide, and various sizes of bandages to treat cuts and scrapes. Gauze, adhesive tape, elastic bandages, and round-tipped scissors.

• Calamine lotion and hydrocortisone cream.

• Acetaminophen, aspirin, and ibuprofen for relief of fever and aches and pains. Aspirin should not be used to treat flu symptoms or be given to children or teenagers.

• Oral hydration solution (such as Pedialyte) for children with severe diarrhea and/or vomiting.

• An oral syringe or measuring device to give medications to children.

• Thermometer (rectal for babies under 1 year).

• Activated charcoal (an antidote for certain poisonings).

Ipecac syrup is no longer recommended for inducing vomiting as a home treatment for poisonings. Discard any ipecac syrup you have in your home.

All the items listed above should be well out of reach of young children.

Does it matter where medications are stored?

Yes, it does. Prescription medications should never be stored in a bathroom because heat and humidity can change the medication and/or decrease its potency. Most medicines should be stored in a childproof area and be kept at room temperature and away from sunlight. Some medications must be refrigerated. Check with your pharmacist or doctor if you are not sure how to properly store a medication.

Should you pay attention to the expiration date on medications?

Yes. Expired medicines often don't work as well, and can even be harmful. To make sure that you or someone in your family doesn't accidentally take an out-of-date medication, you should be sure to clean out your medicine cabinet every year and properly dispose of:

• Any medication that is past the expiration date on the label.

• Any medication that has changed color, smells, or has formed a residue.

• Any liquid that looks cloudy or has

thickened. Any container with cracks or leaks.
• Aspirin or acetaminophen that is crumbly or smells strange.
• Hydrogen peroxide that no longer bubbles when applied to the skin.

How should I dispose of medications that my family no longer needs or are expired?

The disposal of medication is a complex issue. Throwing the medication into the trash can be risky because of the potential for children or pets to find and eat it. The trash will most likely be taken to a landfill and will find its way into the water supply. Unwanted medication that is flushed down a toilet or sink can also wind up in the water supply. A better solution is to return the unwanted medication to your pharmacy or to your doctor for proper disposal as hazardous waste material.

What concerns should I have about taking medications if I am pregnant or breast-feeding?

Tell your doctor if you are pregnant or plan to become pregnant because some medications may harm your unborn child. This is especially important during the first few weeks when fetal organs are forming. If you become pregnant while taking any medication, call your doctor.

Tell your doctor if you are breast-feeding or intend to breast-feed. Many medications pass into your breast milk and can harm your baby.

Medication Safety

Preventing Medication Errors

Babies and children are at particular risk if they're given the wrong medication, or if they get the wrong dose of the right medicine. Medication errors not only delay treatment for the real problem, but they also can cause harmful side effects or even death.

Medication errors can happen when names of medicine look or sound like another—a problem that can be caused by poor penmanship in doctors' prescriptions, sloppy pronunciation, faulty memory, and hard-to-read labels. A report on medication errors by the National Academy of Sciences found that up to 25 percent of all errors reported were due to confusion caused by drugs with similar names.

Babies and children are at a higher risk than adults for two main reasons. First, their lower body weight makes them less tolerant of a wrong medication or variations in a medication's dosage. This can be a special concern when a medicine—prescription or over-the-counter—is delivered with a dropper or a spoon because the measurement is less exact.

Second, a medication's side effects may be harder to recognize in a child. An adult can tell you if something is wrong, but a child may simply cry, and a caregiver may dismiss those cries as colic, a tantrum, or discomfort due to illness. A child may not yet speak or have the vocabulary to express what's bothering him .

Some strategies for protecting your child

When your child's doctor prescribes a medication, ask her to print the name for you and even spell it aloud. If it's a brand-name medicine, make note of the generic name as well.

Ask the doctor to briefly note the medication's intended purpose on the prescription form. That will enable the pharmacist to double-check the name against that purpose.

When refilling your child's prescription, if you spot a difference in the color of the liquid or the color, size, or shape of the pills, tell your pharmacist immediately. In many cases that will be all right because generic versions of the same drug usually appear different. However, an error may have occurred in filling the prescription, so it's always best to ask.

Don't leave the pharmacist's counter until you've checked that your child's name is on the prescription label and verified that the label indicates the correct medication.

Choose OTC medications by their active ingredients, not by brand name. Drug manufacturers often use well-established brand names to launch a series of related—but different—products that may contain different active ingredients.

Know the intended therapeutic effects as well as potential adverse effects of the medication. Once your child starts taking the drug, be alert to any unexpected effects, which could signal a mix-up.

Maintain a complete list of all the medications your child takes, prescription and OTC, including dosages as well as brand and generic names. Update the list regularly, and take it with you whenever you visit your doctor or pharmacy.

For a list of soundalike or look-alike drugs, go to the Web sites for the Institute for Safe Medication Practices, at *www.ismp.org*, or the United States Pharmacopeia, at *www.usp.org*. For additional information on medication safety and efficacy, go to *www .ConsumerReports.org/health*.

. . . .
Poison Prevention

Did you know that many of the creative methods parents and caregivers use to get children to take their medicine can actually contribute to accidental poisonings? A recent consumer survey found that almost half of parents and caregivers said they had pretended to take their child's medication, or called it candy to convince the child to take it. These methods are extremely dangerous and could lead to an overdose.

The Centers for Disease Control and Prevention (CDC) report that approximately 9 of 10 accidental poisonings occur in the home. Sixty percent of those victims are children younger than age 6, and close to half of the poisonings in children of this age group involve a misuse of medicines.

Every parent, caregiver, and grandparent should use these safety tips to prevent accidental poisonings:

• Don't take medications in the presence of children, as they often try to imitate adults.

• Don't refer to medicine as candy.

• Use child-resistant closures on medicine and other products. Use of those closures has greatly decreased accidental poisonings of children. If you find it hard to open such closures, ask your pharmacist for an easier-to-open cap. Keep such containers securely stored in a place that a child cannot reach.

• Keep all medications (prescription and nonprescription) in their original child-resistant containers.

• Always turn on the light when giving or taking medicine.

• Check medications periodically for expiration dates. If the medication is not dated, consider it expired six months after purchase.

• Don't put medications in open trash containers in the kitchen or bathroom because adult medications can be deadly to small children and pets.

• Be aware that multivitamins, particularly ones containing iron, can be poisonous if taken in large doses. Children are especially susceptible to adverse effects from vitamin overdosing.

Be aware the medication (transdermal) patches that you apply to your skin may be poisonous if chewed or swallowed by children or pets. When the patch is removed from your skin, some medication remains on the patch. Do not throw away medication patches in trash cans that are within reach of children and pets.

In case of overdose, call your local poison control center at 800-222-1222. If a child has collapsed or is not breathing, immediately call local emergency services at 911.

Emergency Preparedness and Medications

Families should be aware of their medication needs as they prepare for any emergency, including weather-related emergencies such as flooding and hurricanes. Following these tips can help you be ready:

• Keep in your wallet a list of all the medications your family members take (include drug name(s), strength, dosage form, and regimen).

• Store three to five days worth of medications.

• Include any medications used to stabilize an existing medical condition or keep a condition from worsening or resulting in hospitalization, such as medications for asthma, seizures, cardiovascular disorders, diabetes, psychiatric conditions, HIV/AIDS, and thyroid disorders. Carry these with you, if possible, in a purse or briefcase in labeled containers.

• Don't store medications in areas that

are susceptible to extreme heat, cold, or humidity, such as a car or bathroom. Temperature and moisture can decrease the effectiveness of the medication.

• Use child-resistant containers and keep your purse or briefcase secure. Rotate those medications whenever you get the prescriptions refilled to make sure they are used before their expiration date.

• Refill prescriptions for family members while there is still at least a 5- to 7-day supply. Keep in mind that some sources, such as mail-order pharmacies, have a longer lead time to refill.

• If your child takes medications on a regular basis, ask his school about its emergency preparedness plans.

• If a family member is being treated with a complex medication regimen, talk to your doctor or pharmacist to create appropriate emergency preparation plans. Such regimens include injectable medications, including those delivered by pumps (insulin, analgesics, chemotherapy, parental nutrition), medications delivered by a nebulizer (antibiotics, bronchodilators), and dialysis.

OTC PAIN RELIEVERS AND FEVER REDUCERS

As a parent of an infant or young child, you may need to give OTC products such as acetaminophen (Genapap, Liquiprin, Tylenol, and others) or ibuprofen (Advil, Motrin, and others) to control pain or fever in your child as instructed by your child's doctor.

Although those products have been used safely and effectively for many years, they can cause problems when not used according to label instructions or as directed by your child's doctor. For instance, taking more acetaminophen than recommended can cause serious liver damage.

Some situations that can result in the wrong doses being given to children include:

Giving the wrong children's product. For instance, using the acetaminophen infant concentrated drops (80 mg/0.8 mL), instead of the less concentrated children's suspension (160 mg/5 mL) can result in giving the child three times the dose of medicine. Acetaminophen junior-strength dissolvable or chewable tablets also contain twice as much medication as regular-strength children's dissolvable or chewable tablets.

Giving the adult product to a child instead of the age-appropriate children's product. Most adult products contain too much medication for children younger than 12 years of age, or under 6 years for regular-strength (325 mg) acetaminophen.

Giving the wrong amount of medication for the child's weight. Check your child's weight, as it can change quickly in growing infants and toddlers.

Using the wrong measuring device to give the medication. If you use a device that did not come with the product or one recommended by your pharmacist, you may give too much (or too little) medication.

The following general advice is provided to help you use OTC pain relievers and fever reducers safely in your child. Information about using acetaminophen and ibuprofen in infants and children is provided on pages 337 and 339.

Important Tips for Giving Pain Relievers and Fever Reducers

Give the appropriate product for your child. Pain relievers and fever reducers come in different forms, including drops, liquid, and dissolvable or chewable tablets, to help you give the medication to the child in the easiest manner and at the correct dose. For example, because it is difficult to get liquid medications into an infant's mouth, concentrated infant drops are made so that a smaller amount of liquid is needed for each dose.

Carefully follow the age and weight limit recommendations for dosage that are provided on the package. If the label states not to give to children under a certain age, check with your doctor before giving the medication. You still may be able to give the medication to your child, but only according to the doctor's instructions. If you ever are not sure about what dosage to give, be sure to ask your doctor or pharmacist.

Always use the measuring device that comes with the specific product. For instance, use only the dropper provided with the concentrated infant drops and do not use any other measuring device such as a spoon or cup to measure the dose for your baby.

Acetaminophen is also available in combination with other medicines in over 600 OTC products and prescription medications, especially many cold, cough, and flu preparations. Read the label carefully so that you do not give your child two products that contain acetaminophen at the same time.

Do not give your child a medication for a longer period of time than stated on the product label or as recommended by your child's doctor.

Write down the dates and time of all doses that you or other caregivers give to your child. By keeping a record, you can be sure that the medication is given at the right time according to the directions on the package label or the instructions given to you by your child's doctor.

Do not give aspirin to children younger than 19, unless instructed by your child's doctor. This is especially important if your child has the flu or chicken pox because he could develop a very serious condition known as Reye's Syndrome. Check the label on all medications you are giving to your child, because aspirin (or an aspirin-like salicylate) may be included with other medications. Some products that contain aspirin are Alka-Seltzer, some Excedrin products, and Pepto-Bismol (contains an aspirin-like medication, bismuth subsalicylate). If a full list of ingredients isn't on the label, don't give the medicine to your child before checking with your doctor or pharmacist.

Children have been poisoned by accidentally swallowing pain relievers and fever reducers. It is important that those medicines be stored out of reach of children in a container with a safety cap. Call your poison control center at 800-222-1222 immediately if you suspect your child has mistakenly swallowed acetaminophen or aspirin.

Acetaminophen
(a see´ta min' oh fen)
Brand Names:
FeverAll, Genapap, Liquiprin, Tylenol, others

Why is this medicine used?
Acetaminophen is used to relieve mild to moderate pain of headaches, muscle aches, colds and sore throats, toothaches, and reactions to vaccinations (shots), and to reduce fever. Acetaminophen is in a class of medications called analgesics (pain relievers) and antipyretics (fever reducers). It works by changing the way the body senses pain and by cooling the body.

How should I give this medicine to my child?
Acetaminophen comes as a chewable tablet, suspension or solution (liquid), drops (concentrated liquid), and orally disintegrating tablet (that dissolves quickly in the mouth), for infants and children to take by mouth, with or without food. Acetaminophen also comes as a rectal suppository.

Follow the directions on the package carefully, and ask your child's doctor or pharmacist to explain anything you do not understand. Give acetaminophen exactly as directed. Children and infants may be given acetaminophen every 4 hours as needed for pain or fever, but should not be given more than five times in 24 hours.

Do not give more or less or give more often than directed on the package label or as directed by your child's doctor.

Giving your child more than the recommended amount or more than one product containing acetaminophen may cause liver damage.

If you are giving acetaminophen to your child, check the chart on the package to find out how much medication your child needs. If you know how much your child weighs, give the dose that matches that weight on the chart. If you don't know your child's weight, give the dose that matches your child's age. Ask your child's doctor if you don't know how much medication to give your child.

Tell your child to place the orally disintegrating tablet in her mouth and allow the tablet to dissolve or to chew it before swallowing.

Shake the suspension and drops well before each use to mix the medication evenly. Use the measuring cup provided by the manufacturer to measure each dose of the solution or suspension, and use the dosing device (dropper) provided to measure each dose of the drops. Use the dropper to slowly release the drops directly into the child's mouth near the inner cheek. Do not mix the drops with baby formula.

Stop giving acetaminophen to your child and call the doctor if your child develops new symptoms, including redness or swelling, or if her pain lasts for longer than five days or fever gets worse or lasts longer than three days.

Do not give acetaminophen to a child who has a sore throat that is severe or does not go away, or that occurs along with fever, headache, rash, nausea, or vomiting. Call your child's doctor right away because those symptoms may be signs of a more serious condition.

What special precautions should I follow when giving this medication to my child?

Tell your child's doctor and pharmacist if he is allergic to acetaminophen, any other medications, or any of the ingredients in the product. Ask your pharmacist or check the label on the package for a list of the inactive ingredients.

Tell your child's doctor and pharmacist what prescription and nonprescription medications, vitamins, nutritional supplements, or herbal products your child is taking.

Do not give your child two or more products that contain acetaminophen at the same time because of the risk of overdose and liver damage.

Read the package label carefully to make sure that it is the right product for the age of the child. Acetaminophen products for adults and older children may contain too much medication for a younger child. Drops used in infants are more concentrated (much more medicine in each drop) than liquids made for older children.

Tell your doctor if your child has any serious medical conditions.

If your child has phenylketonuria (an inherited condition that requires a special diet to prevent mental retardation), you should know that some brands of the chewable tablets may be sweetened with aspartame (Nutrasweet) that forms phenylalanine.

What should I do if I forget to give a dose?

This medication is usually given on an as-needed basis. If your doctor has told you to give acetaminophen regularly to your child, give the missed dose as soon as you remember it. However, if it is almost time for the next dose, skip the missed dose and continue your child's regular dosing schedule. Do not give a double dose to make up for a missed one because high doses of acetaminophen may damage your child's liver.

What side effects should I watch for in my child?

Acetaminophen can cause side effects.

Some side effects can be serious. If your child has any of the following symptoms, call his or her doctor immediately:

- Rash
- Hives
- Itching
- Swelling of the face, throat, tongue, lips, eyes, hands, feet, ankles, or lower legs
- Hoarseness
- Difficulty breathing or swallowing

Acetaminophen may cause other side effects. Call your child's doctor if any other unusual problems occur while your child is taking this medication.

What should I do in case of overdose?

In case of overdose, call your local poison control center at 800-222-1222. If your child has collapsed or is not breath-ing, call local emergency services at 911.

If your child takes or is given more than the recommended dose of acetaminophen, get medical help immediately, even if the child does not have any symptoms. Symptoms of overdose may include:

- Nausea
- Vomiting
- Loss of appetite
- Sweating
- Extreme tiredness
- Unusual bleeding or bruising
- Pain in the upper right part of the stomach
- Yellowing of the skin or eyes
- Flu-like symptoms

What storage conditions are needed for this medicine?

Keep this medication in the container it came in, tightly closed with a safety cap, and out of reach of children. Store it at room temperature and away from excess heat and moisture (not in the bathroom). Throw away any medication that is outdated or no longer needed. Talk to your pharmacist about the proper disposal of medication.

....

Ibuprofen
(eye byoo' proe fen)
Brand Names:
Advil, Motrin, others

Why is this medicine used?

Ibuprofen is used to reduce fever and to relieve mild pain from headaches, the common cold, and toothaches. Ibuprofen is in a class of medications called nonsteroidal anti-inflammatory medications (NSAIDS). It works by stopping the body's production of substances that cause pain, fever, and inflammation.

How should I give this medicine to my child?

Ibuprofen comes as a chewable tablet, suspension (liquid), and drops (concentrated liquid).

Follow the directions on the package label carefully, and ask your doctor or pharmacist to explain any part you do not understand. Children and infants usually may be given ibuprofen every 6 to 8 hours as needed for pain or fever, but not more than four times in 24 hours. Ibuprofen may be given with food or milk to prevent stomach upset. If your child is taking ibuprofen on a regular basis, you should give it at the same time(s) every day. Give ibuprofen exactly as directed. Do not give more or less or give it more often than is stated on the package label or as directed by your child's doctor.

The chewable tablets may cause a burning feeling in the mouth or throat. Have your child take the chewable tablets with food or water.

Shake the suspension and drops well before each use to mix the medication evenly. Use the measuring cup provided with the medication to measure each dose of the suspension, and use the dosing device (dropper) provided

to measure each dose of the drops.

Stop giving ibuprofen to your child and call the doctor if your child does not start to feel better after 24 hours of treatment. Also stop giving ibuprofen to your child and call the doctor if your child develops new symptoms, including redness or swelling, or your child's pain or fever gets worse or lasts longer than three days.

Do not give ibuprofen to a child with a sore throat that is severe or doesn't go away, or that occurs with fever, headache, upset stomach, or vomiting, unless you are told to do so by the doctor. Call the child's doctor right away if those symptoms develop because they may be signs of a more serious condition.

What special precautions should I follow when giving this medication to my child?

Tell your child's doctor and pharmacist if your child is allergic to ibuprofen, aspirin, or other NSAIDs; any other medications; or any of the inactive ingredients in the type of ibuprofen you plan to give to your child. Ask your pharmacist or check the label on the package for a list of the inactive ingredients.

Tell your child's doctor and pharmacist what prescription and nonprescription medications, vitamins, nutritional supplements, and herbal products your child is taking. Be sure to mention anticoagulants (blood thinners) such as warfarin (Coumadin); aspirin; other NSAIDS such as ketoprofen (Orudis KT, Actron) and naproxen (Aleve,

Naprosyn); or oral steroids such as dex-amethasone (Decadron, Dexone), methylprednisolone (Medrol), and prednisone (Deltasone). Your child's doctor may need to change the doses of medications or monitor more carefully for side effects.

Do not give your child ibuprofen with any other medication for pain unless your doctor tells you to do so.

Do not give your child two or more products that contain ibuprofen at the same time because of the risk of over-dose and stomach bleeding. Some nonprescription medications contain ibuprofen with other medications. Read the package labels or ask your child's doctor or pharmacist to be sure that you do not give more than one product that contains ibuprofen at the same time.

Tell your doctor if your child has or has ever had stomach problems such as heartburn, upset stomach, or pain; bleeding in the stomach or intestines, or other bleeding disorders; asthma, espe-cially if your child also has frequent stuffed or runny nose or nasal polyps (swelling of the inside of the nose); swelling of the hands, arms, feet, ankles, or lower legs; or liver or kidney disease. If you are giving ibuprofen to a child, tell the child's doctor if the child has not been drinking fluids or has lost a large amount of fluid from repeated vomit-ing or diarrhea.

If your child is having surgery, espe-cially cardiac surgery, tell the doctor that your child is taking ibuprofen.

If your child has phenylketonuria (an inherited condition that requires a spe-cial diet to prevent mental retardation), you should know that some brands of the chewable tablets may be sweetened with aspartame (Nutrasweet) that forms phenylalanine.

What should I do if I forget to give a dose?

If your child is taking ibuprofen on a regular basis, give the missed dose as soon as you remember it. However, if it is almost time for the next dose, skip the missed dose and continue the regu-lar dosing schedule. Do not give a dou-ble dose to make up for a missed one.

What side effects should I watch for in my child?

Ibuprofen may cause side effects. Tell your child's doctor if any of these symp-toms are severe or do not go away:

* Constipation
* Diarrhea
* Gas or bloating
* Dizziness
* Nervousness

Some side effects can be serious. If your child has any of the below symp-toms, call the doctor immediately. Do not give your child any more ibuprofen until you speak to the doctor.

* Stomach pain
* Vomiting a substance that is bloody or looks like coffee grounds
* Blood in the stool, or black and tarry stools
* Unexplained weight gain

- Fever
- Blisters
- Rash
- Itching
- Hives
- Swelling of the eyes, face, throat, arms, hands, feet, ankles, or lower legs
- Difficulty breathing or swallowing
- Hoarseness
- Excessive tiredness
- Pain in the upper right part of the stomach
- Upset stomach
- Loss of appetite
- Yellowing of the skin or eyes
- Flu-like symptoms
- Pale skin
- Fast heartbeat
- Cloudy, discolored, or bloody urine
- Back pain
- Difficult or painful urination
- Stiff neck
- Headache
- Confusion
- Aggression

Ibuprofen may cause other side effects. Call your child's doctor if any other unusual problems occur while your child is taking this medication.

How should I store this medicine?

Keep medication in the container it came in, tightly closed, and out of reach of children. Store it at room temperature, away from excess heat and moisture (not in the bathroom). Throw away outdated or unneeded medication. Talk to your pharmacist about proper disposal.

CHILDHOOD IMMUNIZATIONS

Importance of Childhood Immunization

One the most important ways to prevent disease in your children is to make sure they receive recommended childhood immunizations. Although many of the vaccine-preventable diseases rarely occur in the U.S. today, the viruses and bacteria that cause those diseases still exist. Infectious diseases caused by those pathogens can occur in children who are not protected by vaccines and the pathogens can cause serious diseases and sometimes long-term medical consequences for children who become infected.

Vaccines control many infectious diseases that were once common in this country, including polio, measles, diphtheria, pertussis (whooping cough), rubella (German measles), mumps, tetanus, *Haemophilus influenza* type b (Hib, once the most common cause of meningitis in children), and many other dangerous diseases.

Vaccines help prevent infectious diseases and save thousands of lives.

How Vaccines Work

Vaccines help your child's body to develop immunity (ability to fight diseases). Usually when bacteria or viruses enter the body, they start to multiply. Your child's immune system recognizes those pathogens as outside invaders and responds by making proteins called antibodies. Antibodies will help destroy the bacteria or viruses that are making your child sick. They can't act fast enough to prevent your child from becoming sick, but by eliminating the attacking bacteria or viruses, antibodies help your child get well.

Once these antibodies are produced in your child's body, they remain in her bloodstream for many years. Those antibodies protect your child from infections in the future, as they can destroy the bacteria or viruses before they have a chance to make her sick. Newborn babies may have immunity to some diseases because they have antibodies they got from their mothers; however, this immunity may last only a month to about a year.

Vaccines are made from the same bacteria or viruses (or parts of them) that cause disease. For example, measles vaccine is made from measles virus and Haemophilus influenzae type B (Hib) vaccine is made from parts of the Hib bacteria. But the pathogens in vaccines are either killed or weakened so that they won't make your child sick. Vaccines containing those attenuated (weakened) or inactivated (killed) bacteria or viruses are usually injected into your child's body, but sometimes are given by mouth or as a nasal spray. Your child's immune system reacts to the vaccine by making antibodies, the same as it would if it were being infected with the disease. The antibodies stay in your child's body, giving her immunity if she is exposed to the natural disease.

....

Parents' Questions about Immunization

How safe are vaccines?

Vaccines are very safe, but like any medication they can cause reactions. The vast majority of reactions that may occur in your child are mild, such as a sore arm where the shot is given or a slight fever. Serious reactions are very uncommon. Some are caused by the vaccine, but others are too rare to know whether they are caused by the vaccine or would have occurred anyway. Occasionally a child with allergies, such as to eggs, may have a severe allergy to part of a vaccine. While there is a very small risk (around one in a million) that a vaccine will trigger an allergic reaction, make sure your child's doctor knows about any allergies the child has had in the past.

Your doctor will discuss the risks with you before each immunization for your child, and will give you a Vaccine Information Statement (VIS), which describes the vaccine's benefits and risks. You can also review the information about precautions and side effects of individual vaccines on pages 348-360.

The important thing is that having your child immunized is generally much safer than leaving her open to the diseases the vaccines can prevent. Once thousands of children in the U.S. died each year from diseases that vaccines now can prevent. Two of the greatest success stories of vaccines are the worldwide elimination of smallpox disease and the eradication of polio in the U.S.

There is a lot of incorrect or misleading information about the safety of vaccines, so it is important for you to know that the source of any information about vaccines is a trusted one. Discuss any concerns you have with your child's doctor.

Do vaccines always work?

Most vaccinations that children receive provide immunity about 90 to 100 percent of the time. Occasionally, a child does not respond to certain vaccines, for reasons that aren't entirely understood. This is one reason why it is important for all children to be immunized. A child who does not respond to a vaccine has to depend on the immunity of others around him.

Why should I have my child immunized?

Immunizing your child not only helps to keep her from getting serious illnesses, but it also helps to protect the health of the community. Some children are too young to get certain vaccinations, such as the measles vaccine, which should not be given to children younger than 1 year. Other children cannot be vaccinated for medical reasons, such as children with leukemia or another type of cancer. It also helps to give protection to some

people who do not make an adequate immune response to vaccination or those who have just received a vaccine, but whose bodies have not yet developed immunity.

Why are vaccines given at such an early age?

The diseases vaccines prevent can occur at a very young age. Some diseases are far more serious or common among infants or young children. For example, children under 1 year old are the most affected by severe diseases such as bacterial meningitis caused by *Streptococcus pneumoniae* or *Haemophilus influenzae* type b bacteria. Of the children under 6 months of age who get pertussis, 72 percent must be hospitalized, and 84 percent of all deaths from pertussis are among children younger than 6 months.

What should I do to ease the pain and fear of vaccination?

Many children fear getting routine vaccinations and other shots, and studies have shown that several strategies can reduce that fear. Depending on the age of the child, many of these techniques can be used alone or in combination. Counting, listening to music, blowing soap bubbles, watching a video tape, or reading or telling a story can distract the child from the shot and anticipated pain. Getting the parent involved can reduce the parent's concern, which may improve the child's coping skills.

What if my child misses a dose of vaccine?

Talk to your child's doctor about a catch-up schedule. If immunizations have been delayed, your child can continue the series regardless of the time between doses. Vaccinations do not have to be repeated if there is a longer-than-recommended interval between doses.

What are preservatives and why are they added to vaccines?

Although the major ingredient of any vaccine is a killed or weakened form of the bacteria or virus that the vaccine is designed to prevent, some vaccines (mainly ones that come in vials that might be used several times) contain preservatives to prevent bacterial growth. Thimerosal is a preservative that contains a very small amount of mercury and was used for many decades in some vaccines.

In recent years, there has been concern about a possible connection between the amount of thimerosal given to children and developmental disorders such as autism, Attention Deficit Hyperactivity Disorder (ADHD), and delays in speech and language development. But there is not sufficient research evidence to support any such link.

However, because of concerns about the total amount of mercury that a child would be exposed to, given the total number of vaccines in the recommended childhood immunization schedule,

thimerosal has been removed from or reduced in those products. Some inactivated flu vaccines still contain this preservative, so you may want to ask your doctor about using a flu vaccine that is thimerosal-free.

What should you do if your child has a reaction?

Most children do not have reactions to vaccines or if they do, the reactions are usually minor, local reactions (pain, swelling, or redness at the injection site) or a mild fever. These go away within a day or two and don't normally require any special treatment. If your child shows symptoms of an allergic reaction (difficulty breathing, hoarseness or wheezing, hives, paleness, weakness, a fast heart beat, or dizziness) after getting vaccinations, or if he or she shows other unusual symptoms such as a high fever or behavioral changes, call a doctor or get the child emergency medical care right away.

Tell your doctor what happened, the date and time it happened, and when the vaccination was given.

If your child had a severe (life-threatening) allergic reaction to a dose of a vaccine, it is very likely he should not get another dose of that specific vaccine. If the severe allergic reaction was thought to be caused by an ingredient in the vaccine, he very likely should not get any other vaccine that contains that specific ingredient. Discuss with your child's doctor which vaccines can be given safely to your child if he had a serious allergic reaction to any vaccine.

Reporting Adverse Reactions

If your child has a serious vaccine-associated reaction, or even if you think a medical problem your child has might have been caused by a vaccine, report the problem. It is especially important to report any problem that happened after vaccination and resulted in hospitalization, disability, or death. The Vaccine Adverse Event Reporting System (VAERS) collects and reviews reports of suspected vaccine injuries. Generally, the doctor fills out a VAERS report and sends it to the program, but a parent can also file. You can get more information about VAERS from the toll-free information line at 800-822-7967, or go to the Web site at *www.vaers.hhs.gov.*

VAERS cannot prove that a vaccine caused a problem or provide medical advice, but it does provide important information to the Food and Drug Administration (FDA) and Centers for Disease Control and Prevention (CDC). Those agencies monitor the safety of the vaccine as it is given to millions of children and adults of various backgrounds and medical conditions. If it is reported a vaccine might be causing a problem, the CDC and FDA will investigate further to make sure that the benefits of using the vaccine continue to exceed the risks.

Should I keep a record of my child's vaccinations?

It is important for parents to maintain complete records of all vaccinations that their child has received. Some doctors keep these records, but often only for a few years. Families move, travel, and change health providers so a complete record often is not available from one source. Ask your doctor for an immunization record form. Have the form updated with the date and doctor's signature each time your child is vaccinated.

Parents can create an online computer record of their children's shots by using an Immunization Information Systems (IIS), also known as Immunization Registries. An IIS is useful for making sure that your child gets all of her immunizations on schedule, and for maintaining good records that you and your child's doctor can use, even when you move. State laws require that information in the IIS be kept confidential. To find your IIS, go to *www.cdc.gov/nip/registry.*

What vaccinations does my child need?

Because vaccines work best when they are given at certain ages, the CDC has developed a schedule. This schedule (see page 361) is reviewed and updated each year to determine which childhood immunizations are necessary and when they should be given. Your child's doctor will use those recommendations to determine the best time for your child to be vaccinated. In some cases, such as with preterm (premature) infants or children with a serious illness, your child's doctor may make changes to this schedule.

Travel

Your child may need additional vaccines if he will be traveling overseas. If you plan to travel, be sure to talk with your child's doctor when you begin to make travel plans so that these immunizations can be given before you leave.

If you have any questions or concerns about immunizations and your child, you should always talk to your child's doctor. For additional information about immunizations, visit the CDC's Web site, at *www.cdc.gov*.

The following information provides important facts that parents should know about each vaccine listed in the recommended immunization schedule.

Diphtheria, Tetanus, & Pertussis (whooping cough) (DTaP)

When should my child not get DTaP vaccine?
• If your child has ever had a life-threatening allergic reaction to a previous dose of DTaP
• If your child has had a brain or nervous system condition such as coma, decreased level of consciousness, or prolonged seizures within 7 days of a previous dose of DTaP
• If your child is allergic to latex

When should my child wait to get DTaP vaccine?
If your child is moderately or severely ill at the time the shot is scheduled, he should usually wait until he is well before getting DTaP vaccine. Check with your child's doctor to see whether he should wait.

Tell your child's doctor if the child has any of the following conditions.
The doctor may recommend that the child wait, not receive DTaP vaccine, or receive a vaccine that does not contain pertussis if he:
• Had a seizure (with or without a fever) within three days after a dose of DTaP
• Collapsed or was in shock, cried nonstop for three hours or more, or had a fever over 105°F within 48 hours after a dose of DTaP

• Has had Guillain-Barre Syndrome (GBS, a condition of paralysis and loss of reflexes)
• Has a history of central nervous system (brain) disease or seizures
• Has HIV/AIDS or another disease that affects the immune system
• Is being treated with medications that affect the immune system, such as steroids, for two weeks or longer
• Is receiving cancer treatment with X-rays or medications
• Has a bleeding disorder, such as hemophilia or low platelet count
• Is receiving an anticoagulant (blood thinner) medication such as warfarin (Coumadin)
• Has received an immune globulin
• Has had a reaction to any vaccine

What are the side effects of DTaP vaccine and what should I do if they occur?
Getting diphtheria, tetanus, or pertussis disease is much riskier than getting DTaP vaccine. However, a vaccine, like any medication, may cause serious problems, such as severe allergic reactions. The risk of DTaP vaccine causing serious harm, or death, is extremely small. Call your child's doctor if he has any unusual problems after receiving this vaccine.

Side Effects (Mild)	What should I do?
Fever (occurs more often with repeat vaccinations)	Give acetaminophen (Tylenol, others) or ibuprofen (Advil, Motrin, others) as directed by your child's doctor
Soreness, tenderness, redness, or swelling where the shot was given (occurs more often with repeat vaccinations)	Apply a clean, cool, wet washcloth over the sore area. Give acetaminophen (Tylenol, others) or ibuprofen (Advil, Motrin, others) for pain, as directed by your child's doctor. Call the doctor if the symptoms get worse or do not go away
Swelling of the entire arm or leg in which the shot was given, lasting for 1-7 days (occurs more often after the 4th or 5th dose of DTaP than with the earlier doses)	Call your child's doctor if the swelling gets worse or does not go away
Fussiness or restlessness (1-3 days after the shot)	Give acetaminophen (Tylenol, others) or ibuprofen (Advil, Motrin, others). Call your child's doctor if these symptoms get worse or do not go away
Vomiting, poor appetite, or tiredness (1-3 days after the shot)	Call your child's doctor if these symptoms get worse or do not go away
Side Effects (Moderate or Severe)	What should I do?
Nonstop crying for 3 hours or more	Call your doctor right away
Serious allergic reaction (difficulty breathing; hoarseness or wheezing; hives; swelling of the face, throat, tongue, lips, eyes, hands, or feet; paleness; weakness; fast heartbeat; or dizziness within a few minutes to a few hours after the shot)	Get emergency medical care for your child right away
High fever within 7 days after the shot	Call your child's doctor right away
Seizure (jerking, twitching, shaking, or staring) caused by fever within 7 days after the shot	Get emergency medical care for your child right away

Live Chicken Pox (Varicella) Vaccine

When should my child not get chicken pox vaccine? Your child should not get chicken pox vaccine if she has ever had a life-threatening allergic reaction to:
• A previous dose of chicken pox vaccine gelatin
• Neomycin (an antibiotic)

When should my child wait to get chicken pox vaccine? If your child is moderately or severely ill at the time the shot is scheduled, you should usually wait until she is well before getting chicken pox vaccine. Check with your child's doctor to see whether she should wait.

Tell your child's doctor if the child has any of the following conditions. The doctor may recommend that the child wait or not receive chicken pox vaccine. Ask the doctor for more information if your child:
• Has HIV/AIDS or another disease that affects the immune system
• Is being treated with medications that affect the immune system, such as steroids, for 2 weeks or longer
• Has any type of cancer
• Is receiving cancer treatment with X-rays or medications
• Has recently had a blood transfusion, immune globulin, or other blood products
• Has had a reaction to any vaccine

What are the side effects of chicken pox vaccine and what should I do if they occur? The chicken pox vaccine, like any medication, may cause serious problems, such as severe allergic reactions. The risk of chicken pox vaccine causing serious harm, or death, is extremely small. Getting chicken pox vaccine is much safer than getting chicken pox disease. Most children who get chicken pox vaccine do not have any problems with it. Chicken pox vaccine may cause other side effects. Call your child's doctor if she has any unusual problems after receiving this vaccine.

Side Effects (Mild)	What should I do?
Soreness, redness, or swelling where the shot was given	Apply a clean, cool, wet washcloth over the sore area. Give acetaminophen (Tylenol, others) or ibuprofen (Advil, Motrin, others) for pain, as directed by your child's doctor. Call the doctor if the symptoms get worse after 24 hours
Fever	Give acetaminophen (Tylenol, others) or ibuprofen (Advil, Motrin, others) as directed by your child's doctor. Do not give aspirin
Mild rash	Call your child's doctor if rash gets worse or does not go away
Side Effects (Moderate or Severe)	**What should I do?**
Unusual changes in behavior	Call your child's doctor
Serious allergic reaction (difficulty breathing; hoarseness or wheezing; hives; swelling of the face, tongue, lips, eyes, hands, or feet; weakness; fast heartbeat; or dizziness within a few minutes to a few hours after the shot)	Get emergency medical care for your child right away
High fever, usually within 1-6 weeks after the shot	Call your child's doctor right away
Seizure (jerking, twitching, shaking, or staring) caused by fever, usually within 1-6 weeks after the shot	Get emergency medical care for your child right away

Haemophilus Influenzae type b Vaccine (Hib)

When should my child not get Haemophilus Influenzae type b (Hib) vaccine? Your child should not get Hib vaccine if he has ever had a life-threatening allergic reaction to:
• A previous dose of Hib vaccine
• Latex (dry, natural rubber)

When should my child wait to get Hib vaccine? If your child is moderately or severely ill at the time the shot is scheduled, he should usually wait until he is well before getting Hib vaccine. Check with your child's doctor to see whether he should wait.

Tell your child's doctor if the child has any of the following conditions. The doctor may recommend that your child wait or not receive Hib vaccine. Ask your doctor for more information if your child:
• Has HIV/AIDS or another disease that affects the immune system
• Is being treated with medications that affect the immune system, such as steroids, for two weeks or longer
• Has any type of cancer
• Is receiving cancer treatment with X-rays or medications
• Has or has ever had a low platelet count (a blood disorder which may cause unusual bruising or bleeding)
• Is receiving an anticoagulant (blood thinner) medication such as warfarin (Coumadin)
• Has recently received an immune globulin
• Has had a reaction to any vaccine

What are the side effects from Hib vaccine and what should I do if they occur? A vaccine, like any medication, may cause serious problems, such as severe allergic reactions. The risk of Hib vaccine causing serious harm, or death, is extremely small. Most people who get Hib vaccine do not have any problems with it. Hib vaccine can cause other side effects. Call your child's doctor if he has any unusual problems after receiving this vaccine.

Side Effects (Mild)	What should I do?
Fever	Give acetaminophen (Tylenol, others) or ibuprofen (Advil, Motrin, others) as directed by your child's doctor
Redness, warmth, pain, firmness, skin discoloration, or swelling where the shot was given	Apply a clean, cool, wet washcloth over the sore area. Give acetaminophen (Tylenol, others) or ibuprofen (Advil, Motrin, others) for pain, as directed by your child's doctor. Call the doctor if these symptoms do not improve
Irritability	Call your child's doctor if this symptom gets worse or does not go away
Sleepiness	Call your child's doctor if this symptom gets worse or does not go away
Decreased appetite or diarrhea	Call your child's doctor if the symptoms get worse or do not go away
Side Effects (Moderate or Severe)	**What should I do?**
Unusual changes in behavior	Call your child's doctor
Serious allergic reaction (difficulty breathing; hoarseness or wheezing; hives; rash; itching; swelling of the face, throat, tongue, lips, eyes, hands, or feet; paleness; weakness; fast heartbeat; or dizziness within a few minutes to a few hours after the shot)	Get emergency medical care for your child right away
High fever	Call your child's doctor right away

Hepatitis A Vaccine

When should my child not get hepatitis A vaccine? Your child should not get hepatitis A vaccine if he has ever had a life-threatening allergic reaction to:
• A previous dose of hepatitis A vaccine
• Latex (dry, natural rubber)

When should my child wait to get hepatitis A vaccine? If your child is moderately or severely ill at the time the shot is scheduled, he should usually wait until he is well before getting hepatitis A vaccine. Check with your child's doctor to see whether he should wait.

Tell your child's doctor if the child has any of the following conditions. The doctor may recommend that the child wait or not receive hepatitis A vaccine. Ask the doctor for more information if your child:
• Has HIV/AIDS or another disease that affects the immune system
• Is being treated with medications that affect the immune system, such as steroids, for two weeks or longer
• Has any type of cancer
• Is receiving cancer treatment with X-rays or medications
• Has ever had a low platelet count (a blood disorder that may cause unusual bruising or bleeding)
• Has a bleeding disorder such as hemophilia
• Is receiving anticoagulant (blood thinner) medication such as warfarin (Coumadin)
• Has had a reaction to any vaccine

What are the side effects from hepatitis A vaccine and what should I do if they occur? A vaccine, like any medication, may cause serious problems, such as severe allergic reactions. The risk of hepatitis A vaccine causing serious harm, or death, is extremely small. Getting hepatitis A vaccine is much safer than getting the disease. Hepatitis A vaccine can cause other side effects. Call your child's doctor if he has any unusual problems after receiving this vaccine.

Side Effects (Mild)	What should I do?
Soreness, tenderness, redness, warmth, or swelling where the shot was given	Apply a clean, cool, wet washcloth over the sore area. Give acetaminophen (Tylenol, others) or ibuprofen (Advil, Motrin, others) for pain, as directed by your child's doctor. Call the doctor if the symptoms get worse or do not go away
Headache	Give acetaminophen (Tylenol, others) or ibuprofen (Advil, Motrin, others) as directed by your child's doctor
Vomiting, diarrhea, stomach pain, or decreased appetite	Call your child's doctor if the symptoms get worse or do not go away
Irritability or tiredness	Call your child's doctor if the symptoms get worse or do not go away
Runny nose, congestion, or cough	Call your child's doctor if the symptoms get worse or do not go away
Mild rash	Call your child's doctor if rash gets worse or does not go away
Side Effects (Moderate or Severe)	**What should I do?**
Unusual changes in behavior	Call your child's doctor
Serious allergic reaction (difficulty breathing; hoarseness or wheezing; hives; swelling of the face, throat, tongue, lips, eyes, hands, or feet; paleness; weakness; fast heartbeat; or dizziness within a few minutes to a few hours after the shot)	Get emergency medical care for your child right away
High fever	Call your child's doctor right away

Hepatitis B Vaccine

When should my child not get hepatitis B vaccine? Your child should not get hepatitis B vaccine if she has ever had a life-threatening allergic reaction to:
- A previous dose of hepatitis B vaccine
- Yeast (the kind used for baking)
- Latex (dry, natural rubber)

When should my child wait to get hepatitis B vaccine? If your child is moderately or severely ill at the time the shot is scheduled, she should usually wait until she is well before getting hepatitis B vaccine. Check with your child's doctor to see whether she should wait.

Tell your child's doctor if the child has any of the following conditions. The doctor may recommend that the child wait or not receive hepatitis B vaccine. Ask your doctor for more information if your child:
- Has or has had heart or lung disease
- Is being treated with medications that affect the immune system, such as steroids, for two weeks or longer
- Has HIV/AIDS or another disease that affects the immune system
- Has any type of cancer
- Has a bleeding disorder such as hemophilia or low platelet count
- Has had a reaction to any vaccine

What are the side effects from hepatitis B vaccine and what should I do if they occur? A vaccine, like any medication, may cause serious problems, such as severe allergic reactions. The risk of hepatitis B vaccine causing serious harm, or death, is extremely small. Getting hepatitis B vaccine is much safer than getting hepatitis B disease. Most people who get hepatitis B vaccine do not have any problems with it. Hepatitis B vaccine can cause other side effects. Call your child's doctor if she has any unusual problems after receiving this vaccine.

Side Effects (Mild)	What should I do?
Soreness, firmness, redness, swelling, itching, and/or warmth where the shot was given, lasting 1-2 days	Apply a clean, cool, wet washcloth over the sore area. Give acetaminophen (Tylenol, others) or ibuprofen (Advil, Motrin, others) for pain, as directed by your child's doctor. Call the doctor if the symptoms get worse or do not go away
Fever	Give acetaminophen (Tylenol, others) or ibuprofen (Advil, Motrin, others) as directed by your child's doctor
Tiredness, weakness, or irritability	Call your child's doctor if the symptoms get worse or do not go away
Nausea or decrease in appetite	Call your child's doctor if the symptoms get worse or do not go away
Headache	Give acetaminophen (Tylenol, others) or ibuprofen (Advil, Motrin, others) as directed by your child's doctor
Side Effects (Moderate or Severe)	**What should I do?**
Unusual changes in behavior	Call your child's doctor
Muscle or joint aches	Call your child's doctor
Serious allergic reaction (difficulty breathing; hoarseness or wheezing; hives; rash; itching; swelling of the face, throat, tongue, lips, eyes, hands, or feet; tingling; paleness; flushing; weakness; fast heartbeat; chest discomfort; dizziness; or blisters on the skin within a few minutes to a few hours after receiving the shot)	Get emergency medical care for your child right away
High fever	Call your child's doctor right away

Inactivated Influenza Vaccine

When should my child not get inactivated influenza vaccine? Your child should not get inactivated influenza vaccine if he has ever had:
• A life-threatening allergic reaction to a previous dose of inactivated influenza vaccine
• A life-threatening allergic reaction to eggs, egg products, or chicken
• Guillain-Barre syndrome (GBS, a condition of paralysis and loss of reflexes)

When should my child wait to get inactivated influenza vaccine? If your child is moderately or severely ill at the time the shot is scheduled, he should usually wait until he is well before getting inactivated influenza vaccine. Check with your child's doctor to see whether he should wait.

Tell your child's doctor if the child has any of the following conditions. The doctor may recommend that the child wait or not receive influenza vaccine. Ask your doctor for more information if your child:
• Has HIV/AIDS or another disease that affects the immune system
• Is being treated with medications that affect the immune system, such as steroids, for two weeks or longer
• Has any type of cancer

• Is receiving cancer treatment with X-rays or medications
• Has or has had a neurologic (brain) disorder
• Has a low platelet count (a blood disorder that may cause unusual bruising or bleeding)
• Has a bleeding disorder such as hemophilia
• Is receiving anticoagulant (blood thinner) medication such as warfarin (Coumadin)
• Has had a reaction to any vaccine

What are the side effects from inactivated influenza vaccine and what should I do if they occur? A vaccine, like any medication, may cause serious problems, such as severe allergic reactions. The risk of inactivated influenza vaccine causing serious harm, or death, is extremely small. The viruses in inactivated influenza vaccine have been killed, so someone cannot get influenza ("flu") from the vaccine. Any colds or other upper respiratory illnesses that may occur soon after getting this vaccine are just a coincidence. However, inactivated influenza vaccine can cause other side effects. Call your child's doctor if he has any unusual problems after receiving this vaccine.

Side Effects (Mild)	What should I do?
Fever (usually begins soon after shot and lasts 1-2 days)	Give acetaminophen (Tylenol, others) or ibuprofen (Advil, Motrin, others) as directed by your child's doctor
Muscle aches (usually begin soon after shot and last 1-2 days)	Give acetaminophen (Tylenol, others) or ibuprofen (Advil, Motrin, others) as directed by your child's doctor
Soreness, redness, pain, or swelling where the shot was given (usually begin soon after shot and last 1-2 days)	Apply a clean, cool, wet washcloth over the sore area. Give acetaminophen (Tylenol, others) or ibuprofen (Advil, Motrin, others) for pain, as directed by your child's doctor. Call the doctor if the symptoms get worse or do not go away
Rash	Call your child's doctor if rash gets worse or does not go away
Tiredness (usually begins soon after shot and lasts 1-2 days)	Call your child's doctor if this symptom gets worse or does not go away
Side Effects (Moderate or Severe)	**What should I do?**
Unusual changes in behavior	Call your child's doctor
Serious allergic reaction (difficulty breathing; hoarseness or wheezing; hives; swelling of the face, throat, tongue, lips, eyes, hands, or feet; paleness; weakness; fast heartbeat; or dizziness within a few hours after the shot)	Get emergency medical care for your child right away
High fever	Call your child's doctor right away

Live Intranasal Influenza Vaccine (LAIV)

When should my child not get live, attenuated (weakened) influenza vaccine?
Your child should not get LAIV if she has ever had a life-threatening allergic reaction to:
• A previous dose of influenza vaccine
• Eggs or egg products

When should my child wait to get LAIV?
If your child is moderately or severely ill at the time the shot is scheduled, she should usually wait until she is well before getting LAIV. Check with your child's doctor to see whether she should wait.

Tell your child's doctor if the child has any of the following conditions. The doctor may recommend that the child wait or not receive LAIV. Ask your doctor for more information if your child:
• Has HIV/AIDS or another disease that affects the immune system
• Is being treated with medications that affect the immune system, such as steroids, for two weeks or longer
• Has any type of cancer
• Is receiving cancer treatment with X-rays or medications

• Has had Guillain-Barré syndrome (GBS, a condition of paralysis and loss of reflexes)
• Has heart, lung, or kidney disease
• Has asthma, diabetes, anemia, or other blood diseases
• Is being treated with any nasal (in the nose) medications, aspirin or aspirin-containing products, or any antiviral medications to treat the flu
• Comes in close contact (in the same household) with anyone who has a weakened immune system
• Has had reaction to any vaccine

What are the side effects from LAIV and what should I do if they occur? A vaccine, like any medication, may cause serious problems, such as severe allergic reactions. However, the risk of a vaccine causing serious harm is extremely small. Live influenza vaccine viruses rarely spread from person to person, and if they do, they are not likely to cause illness. LAIV is made from weakened virus and does not cause influenza (flu). LAIV can cause other side effects. Call your child's doctor if she has any unusual problems after receiving this vaccine.

Side Effects (Mild)	What should I do?
Fever	Give acetaminophen (Tylenol, others) or ibuprofen (Advil, Motrin, others) as directed by your child's doctor
Headache, muscle aches, chills	Give acetaminophen (Tylenol, others) or ibuprofen (Advil, Motrin, others) as directed by your child's doctor
Stomach pain, vomiting, or diarrhea	Call your child's doctor if the symptoms get worse or do not go away
Runny nose, nasal congestion, sore throat, or cough	Call your child's doctor if the symptoms get worse or do not go away
Irritability, decreased activity, tiredness, or weakness	Call your child's doctor if the symptom get worse or do not go away
Side Effect (Moderate or Severe)	What should I do?
Unusual changes in behavior	Call your child's doctor
Serious allergic reaction (difficulty breathing; hoarseness or wheezing; rash; itching; hives; swelling of the face, throat, tongue, lips, eyes, hands, or feet; paleness; weakness; fast heartbeat; or dizziness within a few minutes to a few hours after the shot)	Get emergency medical care for your child right away
High fever	Call your child's doctor right away

Meningococcal Vaccine

When should my child not get meningococcal vaccine? Your child should not get meningococcal vaccine if he has ever had a life-threatening allergic reaction to:
• A previous dose of meningococcal vaccine
• Latex (dry, natural rubber)

When should my child wait to get meningococcal vaccine? If your child is moderately or severely ill at the time the shot is scheduled, he should usually wait until he is well before getting meningococcal vaccine. Check with your child's doctor to see whether he should wait.

Tell your child's doctor if the child has any of the following conditions. The doctor may recommend that the child wait or not receive meningococcal vaccine. Ask your doctor for more information if your child:
• Has HIV/AIDS or another disease that affects the immune system
• Is being treated with medications that affect the immune system, such as steroids, for two weeks or longer
• Has any type of cancer
• Is receiving cancer treatment with X-rays or medications
• Has had Guillain-Barré syndrome (GBS, a condition of paralysis and loss of reflexes)
• Has had a reaction to any vaccine

What are the side effects from meningococcal vaccine and what should I do if they occur? A vaccine, like any medication, may cause serious problems, such as severe allergic reactions. The risk of meningococcal vaccine causing serious harm, or death, is extremely small. Meningococcal vaccine can cause other side effects. Call your child's doctor if he has any unusual problems after receiving this vaccine.

Side Effects (Mild)	What should I do?
Fever, chills	Give acetaminophen (Tylenol, others) or ibuprofen (Advil, Motrin, others) as directed by your child's doctor
Redness, pain, swelling, or firmness where the shot was given, usually lasting 1-2 days	Apply a clean, cool, wet washcloth over the sore area. Give acetaminophen (Tylenol, others) or ibuprofen (Advil, Motrin, others) for pain, as directed by your child's doctor. Call the doctor if the symptoms get worse or do not go away
Headache	Give acetaminophen (Tylenol, others) or ibuprofen (Advil, Motrin, others) as directed by your child's doctor
Tiredness	Call your child's doctor if this symptom gets worse or does not go away
Side Effects (Moderate or Severe)	**What should I do?**
Unusual changes in behavior	Call your child's doctor
Serious allergic reaction (difficulty breathing; hoarseness or wheezing; hives; swelling of the face, throat, tongue, lips, eyes, hands, or feet; paleness; weakness; fast heartbeat; or dizziness within a few minutes to a few hours after the shot)	Get emergency medical care for your child right away
High fever	Call your child's doctor right away

Live Measles, Mumps & Rubella Vaccine (MMR)

When should my child not get MMR vaccine? Your child should not get MMR vaccine if she has ever had a life-threatening allergic reaction to:
- A previous dose of MMR vaccine
- Neomycin (an antibiotic)
- Gelatin
- Eggs

When should my child wait to get MMR vaccine? If your child is moderately or severely ill at the time the shot is scheduled, she should usually wait until she is well before getting MMR vaccine. Check with your child's doctor to see whether she should wait.

Tell your child's doctor if the child has any of the following conditions. The doctor may recommend that the child wait or not receive MMR vaccine. Ask your doctor for more information if your child:
- Has HIV/AIDS or another disease that affects the immune system
- Is being treated with medications that affect the immune system, such as steroids, for two weeks or longer
- Has any type of cancer
- Is receiving cancer treatment with X-rays or medications
- Has had a low platelet count (a blood disorder that may cause unusual bruising or bleeding)
- Has recently had a blood transfusion, immune globulin, or other blood products
- Has a history of seizures or any type of head or brain injury, or there is a family history of seizures
- Has had a reaction to any vaccine

What are the side effects from MMR vaccine and what should I do if they occur? A vaccine, like any medication, may cause serious problems, such as severe allergic reactions. The risk of MMR vaccine causing serious harm, or death, is extremely small. Getting MMR vaccine is much safer than getting any of these three diseases. Most children who get MMR vaccine do not have any problems with it. MMR vaccine can cause other side effects. Call your child's doctor if she has any unusual problems after receiving this vaccine.

Side Effects (Mild)	What should I do?
Fever	Give acetaminophen (Tylenol, others) or ibuprofen (Advil, Motrin, others) as directed by your child's doctor
Mild rash	Call your child's doctor if rash gets worse or does not go away
Swelling of the cheek or neck	Call your child's doctor if the swelling gets worse or does not go away
Side Effects (Moderate or Severe)	**What should I do?**
Unusual changes in behavior	Call your child's doctor
Serious allergic reaction (difficulty breathing; hoarseness or wheezing; hives; swelling of the face, tongue, lips, eyes, hands, or feet; paleness; weakness; fast heartbeat; or dizziness within a few minutes to a few hours after the shot)	Get emergency medical care for your child right away
High fever (usually within 1 or 2 weeks after the shot)	Call your child's doctor right away
Seizure (jerking, twitching, shaking, or staring) caused by fever	Get emergency medical care for your child right away
Unusual bleeding or bruising	Call your child's doctor right away. If severe, get emergency medical care for your child right away

Pneumococcal (conjugate) Vaccine

When should my child not get pneumococcal (conjugate) vaccine? Your child should not get pneumococcal (conjugate) vaccine if he has ever had a life-threatening allergic reaction to:
• A previous dose of pneumococcal vaccine
• A previous dose of diphtheria vaccine
• Latex (dry, natural rubber)

When should my child wait to get pneumococcal (conjugate) vaccine? If your child is moderately or severely ill at the time the shot is scheduled, he should usually wait until he is well before getting pneumococcal (conjugate) vaccine. Check with your child's doctor to see whether he should wait.

Tell your child's doctor if the child has any of the following conditions. The doctor may recommend that your child wait or not receive pneumococcal (conjugate) vaccine if he:
• Has HIV/AIDS or another disease that affects the immune system
• Is being treated with medications that affect the immune system, such as steroids, for two weeks or longer
• Has any type of cancer
• Is receiving cancer treatment with X-rays or medications
• Has or has ever had a low platelet count (a blood disorder that may cause unusual bruising or bleeding) or blood clotting disease
• Is receiving anticoagulant (blood thinner) medication such as warfarin (Coumadin)
• Has had a reaction to any vaccine

What are the side effects from pneumococcal (conjugate) vaccine and what should I do if they occur? A vaccine, like any medication, may cause serious problems, such as severe allergic reactions. The risk of pneumococcal vaccine causing serious harm, or death, is extremely small. Pneumococcal vaccine can cause other side effects. Call your child's doctor if he has any unusual problems after receiving this vaccine.

Side Effects (Mild)	What should I do?
Fever	Give acetaminophen (Tylenol, others) or ibuprofen (Advil, Motrin, other) as directed by your child's doctor
Redness, tenderness, pain, firmness, lump, or swelling where the shot was given	Apply a clean, cool, wet washcloth over the sore area. Give acetaminophen (Tylenol, others) or ibuprofen (Advil, Motrin, others) for pain, as directed by your child's doctor. Call the doctor if the symptoms get worse or do not go away
Fussiness, restlessness, or irritability	Give acetaminophen (Tylenol, others) or ibuprofen (Advil, Motrin, others) as directed by your child's doctor
Drowsiness	Call your child's doctor if this symptom gets worse or does not go away
Diarrhea, vomiting, or decreased appetite	Call your child's doctor if the symptoms get worse or do not go away
Side Effects (Moderate or Severe)	**What should I do?**
Unusual changes in behavior	Call your child's doctor
Serious allergic reaction (difficulty breathing; hoarseness or wheezing; hives; rash; itching; swelling of the face, throat, tongue, lips, eyes, hands, or feet; paleness; weakness; fast heartbeat; or dizziness within a few minutes to a few hours after the shot)	Get emergency medical care for your child right away
High fever	Call your child's doctor right away

Polio Vaccine (IPV)

When should my child not get polio vaccine? Your child should not get polio vaccine if she has ever had a life-threatening allergic reaction to:
• A previous dose of polio vaccine
• Neomycin, streptomycin, or polymyxin B (antibiotics)

When should my child wait to get polio vaccine? If your child is moderately or severely ill at the time the shot is scheduled, she should usually wait until she is well before getting polio vaccine. Check with your child's doctor to see whether she should wait.

Tell your child's doctor if the child has any of the following conditions. The doctor may recommend that the child wait or not receive polio vaccine. Ask your doctor for more information if your child:

• Has HIV/AIDS or another disease that affects the immune system
• Is being treated with medications that affect the immune system, such as steroids, for two weeks or longer
• Has any type of cancer
• Is receiving cancer treatment with X-rays or medications
• Has had a reaction to any vaccine

What are the side effects from polio vaccine and what should I do if they occur? A vaccine, like any medication, may cause serious problems, such as severe allergic reactions. The risk of polio vaccine causing serious harm, or death, is extremely small. Most children who get polio vaccine do not have any problems with it. Polio vaccine can cause other side effects. Call your child's doctor if she has any unusual problems after receiving this vaccine.

Side Effects (Mild)	What should I do?
Soreness, redness, swelling, or area of firmness where the shot was given	Apply a clean, cool, wet washcloth over the sore area. Give acetaminophen (Tylenol, others) or ibuprofen (Advil, Motrin, others) for pain, as directed by your child's doctor. Call the doctor if the symptoms get worse or do not go away
Fever	Give acetaminophen (Tylenol, others) or ibuprofen (Advil, Motrin, others) as directed by your child's doctor
Fussiness	Call your child's doctor if this symptom gets worse or does not go away
Tiredness	Call your child's doctor if this symptom gets worse or does not go away
Side Effect (Moderate or Severe)	**What should I do?**
Unusual changes in behavior	Call your child's doctor
Serious allergic reaction (difficulty breathing; hoarseness or wheezing; hives; swelling of the face, throat, tongue, lips, eyes, hands, or feet; paleness; weakness; fast heartbeat; or dizziness within a few minutes to a few hours after receiving the shot)	Get emergency medical care for your child right away
High fever	Call your child's doctor right away

I Live, Oral Rotavirus Vaccine

When should my child not get rotavirus vaccine? Your child should not get rotavirus vaccine if he has ever had a life-threatening allergic reaction to:
• A previous dose of rotavirus vaccine

When should my child wait to get rotavirus vaccine? If your child is moderately or severely ill (such as diarrhea or vomiting) at the time the shot is scheduled, he should usually wait until he is well before getting rotavirus vaccine. Check with your child's doctor to see whether he should wait.

Tell your child's doctor if the child has any of the following conditions. The doctor may recommend that the child wait or not receive rotavirus vaccine. Ask your doctor for more information if your child:
• Has any digestive problems, such as previous abdominal surgery, chronic diarrhea, or failure to thrive (difficulty gaining weight and/or growing according to average expected growth rate for child's age), or a bowel obstruction (intussusception)
• Has HIV/AIDS or another disease that affects the immune system
• Is being treated with medications that affect the immune system, such as steroids, for two weeks or longer
• Has any type of cancer
• Is receiving cancer treatment with X-rays or medications
• Recently had a blood transfusion, received immune globulin, or any other blood product
• Has had a reaction to any vaccine

What are the side effects from rotavirus vaccine and what should I do if they occur? A vaccine, like any medication, may cause serious problems, such as severe allergic reactions. The risk of rotavirus vaccine causing serious harm, or death, is extremely small. Rotavirus vaccine can cause other side effects. Call your child's doctor if he has any unusual problems after receiving this vaccine.

Side Effects (Mild)	What should I do?
Mild diarrhea or vomiting (within 7 days of getting the shot)	Call your child's doctor if these symptoms get worse or do not go away

Side Effect (Moderate or Severe)	What should I do?
Unusual changes in behavior	Call your child's doctor
Serious allergic reaction (difficulty breathing; hoarseness or wheezing; hives; swelling of the face, throat, lips, eyes, hands, or feet; paleness; weakness; a fast heart beat; or dizziness within a few minutes to a few hours after the shot)	Get emergency medical care for your child right away
High fever	Call your child's doctor right away

Recommended Immunization Schedule for Ages 0–6 Years UNITED STATES • 2007

Vaccine ▼ Age ▶	Birth	1 month	2 months	4 months	6 months	12 months	15 months	18 months	19–23 months	2–3 years	4–6 years
Hepatitis B[1]	HepB	HepB		see footnote 1	HepB				HepB Series		
Rotavirus			Rota	Rota	Rota						
Diphtheria, Tetanus, Pertussis			DTaP	DTaP	DTaP		DTaP				DTaP
Haemophilus Influenzae type b			Hib	Hib	Hib	Hib					
Pneumococcal[2]			PCV	PCV	PCV	PCV					
Inactivated Poliovirus			IPV	IPV		IPV					IPV
Influenza[3]						Influenza (Yearly)					
Measles, Mumps, Rubella						MMR					MMR
Varicella						Varicella					Varicella
Hepatitis A						HepA (2 doses)					
Meningococcal											

Legend:
- Range of recommended ages
- Catch-up immunization
- Certain high-risk groups

This schedule gives the recommended ages for routine administration of currently licensed childhood vaccines for children aged 0–6 years. The information is based on the 2007 recommendations by the Advisory Committee on Immunization Practices, the American Academy of Pediatrics, and the American Academy of Family Physicians. Additional information is available at www.cdc.gov/nip/recs/child -schedule.htm. Because these recommendations may change or new vaccines may become available, always check with your child's doctor for the most current immunization information.

Footnotes to table 1. Hepatitis B vaccine (4-month dose): When hepatitis B vaccine is given as a shot in combination with other vaccines, a dose at 4 months may be given. If hepatitis B vaccine is given alone, then a dose at 4 months is not needed. 2. Pneumococcal vaccine: Two types of pneumococcal vaccine are available. Pneumococcal conjugate vaccine (PCV) can be given to certain high-risk patients at ages 24–59 months and pneumococcal polysaccharide vaccine (PPV) can be given to children 2 years or older in certain high-risk groups. 3. Influenza vaccine: Two doses of influenza vaccine (as a shot or nasal spray) are recommended for children 9 years and younger who are receiving the vaccine for the first time.

Source: Recommended Immunization Schedule for Ages 0–6 Years – United States, 2007. AAP News. 2007; 28:21.

MEDICATION USE IN CHILDREN

Information about medications is constantly changing because of new research and knowledge from the ongoing use of each drug. The information about medications is often subject to interpretation and the uniqueness of each child and his medical condition. While care has been taken to ensure the accuracy of the information presented, the reader is advised that the authors, editors, reviewers, contributors, and publishers cannot be responsible that the information in this book remains up-to-date or for any errors or omissions or for any associated consequences. Because of the ever changing nature of drug information, decisions regarding your child's medications and medical care must be based on the judgment of his doctor.

If after reading and reviewing any information in this chapter or from other sources you have special concerns about the medications you are giving your child, talk to your child's doctor before you make any changes. Do not stop giving medication to your child without talking to your child's doctor, pharmacist, or other health-care provider.

Product Recalls

F ar too many products get into consumers' homes that are later the subject of a recall by the manufacturer due to safety problems. In 2006, the U.S. Consumer Product Safety Commission (CPSC) recalled 471 products for safety problems—a 10-year high. Many of those products were intended for kids. There are no pre-market testing requirements in the U.S. for juvenile products to ensure that products are safe before they are sold. Instead, the burden is placed on consumers to be attentive to recall notices that affect the baby products they own. Recalls on juvenile products in particular have a very poor response rate from consumers, perhaps because parents and caregivers are not made aware of all recalls that could affect their baby's safety.

Here are a few tips on what to do to make sure you are always in the know.

Fill out and mail product registration cards. These are required on child car seats, but optional on other juvenile products. You don't need to supply any personal information other than your address so the manufacturer can contact you.

Sign up for e-mail alerts for recalls. Go to *www.cpsc.gov/cpsclist.asp* and sign up for regular e-mail notices when recalls are announced.

Watch and read news reports. Some news organizations, including CONSUMER REPORTS, publicize the most serious product recalls. Read these notices regularly to make sure the products you own are not involved.

Check your current products. Many consumers, day-care centers, and secondhand stores may possess recalled products without knowing it. Products sold on auction Web sites such as eBay may never have been used but could still be the subject of a recall. You can check for recalls by going to *www.recalls.gov* and searching for your product by type, manufacturer, or description.

Report unsafe products. If you uncover a safety problem with a product you own, help protect other consumers by reporting the problem to the government, the manufacturer, and CONSUMER REPORTS.

• To report to the government, go to *www.recalls.gov*. You can also call the National Highway Traffic Safety Administration's toll-free hotline at 888-327-4236 for child safety seats, or the Consumer Product Safety Commission's toll-free hotline at 800-638-2772 for all other juvenile products.

• To report to the manufacturer, you can usually find the manufacturer's address on either the product's name plate, its instruction manual, or through a Web search. Keep a record of your correspondence.

• To report to CONSUMER REPORTS, go to Consumer.Reports.org and click on "Report a product safety problem." We use that information to conduct our own independent investigations and work to remove any unsafe products from the marketplace.

A

Activity Block Set
Adams Trail-a-Bike and Slipstream bicycle attachment
Anthem C Elite WSD bicycle helmets

B

Babi Italia/LaJobi Industries "Tiffany" and "Josephine" wooden cribs sold at Babies "R" Us stores
Baby Bjorn soft-fabric infant carrier
Baby Buzz'r interactive infant toy
Baby Connection Reef Rocker infant toy
Baby Trend "Passport" strollers sold at Babies "R" Us stores
Baby Trend Road Runner jogging strollers
Baby Trend "Trend Swing" infant swings sold at Toys 'R' Us stores
"Baby 2 Pack" pacifiers
Beech-Nut Table Time Chicken Dices toddler food
Betesh Group, The John Lennon musical crib mobiles
Bikepro baby walkers
Binky Newborn Orthodontic pacifiers
Bob Trailers Inc. Sport Utility Stroller and Sport Utility Stroller D'lux
Boston Billows maternity and nursing pillows
Brio "Curious George" monkey plush toy
Brio wooden clown stacking toy

Britax model E9022 convertible child safety seat
Britax Roundabout convertible child safety seat
Britax Super Elite child car seat

C

Carter's infant and child overalls
Century Fold-N-Go Care Centers
Century infant safety seats/carriers (various models)
Century Take 2, Travel Solutions, Pioneer, Travelite, and Pro Sport 4-in-1 Strollers
Child Guidance "Busy Baby Activity Tool Pliers" sold at Radio Shack
Children's furniture sold at Target stores
Cosco Arriva and Turnabout child safety seats/infant carriers
Cosco "Arriva" and "Turnabout" infant carrier/safety seats
Cosco Bungee Baby Jumpers
Cosco Geobuy Two Ways tandem strollers
Cosco model M tubular metal cribs
Cosco "Options5" high chair
Cosco Rock 'N Roller baby stroller

D

Delta Enterprise Corp portable wooden cribs

E

Electronic Light N' Learn activity gym
Evenflo Hike 'N Roll child carrier

Evenflo "Joyride" child safety seat/infant carrier
Evenflo On My Way Position Right child safety seat
Evenflo Snugli Front & Back Pack soft infant
   carriers
Evenflo Two-In-One booster car seat

F

First Alert True Fit child safety gate
First Team Sports "Guardian Junior" bicycle
   helmet
Fisher-Price 3-in-1 Cradle Swing with detachable
   carrier
Fisher-Price Bounce 'n Play Activity Dome
Fisher-Price Get Up & Go walker
Fisher-Price "Hop, Skip, Jumper" baby activity toy
Fisher-Price Intelli-Table toys
Fisher-Price Laugh & Learn Musical Learning Chair
Fisher-Price Safe Embrace convertible child safety
   seat
Fisher-Price Safe Embrace safety seats
Fisher-Price Smart Response infant swing
Fisher-Price "Sparkling Symphony" battery-
   powered spinning crib mobiles
Formula, infant, Mead Johnson Gentlease
   powdered formula
Francisca full-sized wooden cribs sold through
   J.C. Penney catalog

G

Gerry and Evenflo portable wood cribs
Gerry TrailTech backpack baby carrier
Graco and Children on the Go activity trays and
   bath sets with suction cups
Graco "Aspen 3-in-1" wood cribs with wood
   mattress support
Graco high chairs (various models)
Graco infant carriers and carrier/swings
Graco infant swings (various models)
Graco SnugRide infant carrier/safety seats
Graco SnugRide infant car seat and carrier
Graco SnugRide infant car seats equipped with
   base
Graco Stationary Entertainer children's activity
   toys
Graco Tot Wheels Entertainer Activity Center
   infant walker
Graco Travel Lite portable baby swing

H

Halcyon WaterSpring Dex Wipe Warmer electric
   heating pad for baby wipes
H-E-B Baby and Mom's Organic Choice baby-food
   brands
High chair recalled, Cosco "Options 5" high chair
Home Trends Kiddy Sling Chair sold at Wal-Mart

I

Infant formula, Mead Johnson Gentlease
   powdered formula
InStep and Healthrider brand single and double
   jogging strollers

J

J. Mason infant carrier

K

KB Toys Electronic Light N' Learn Activity Gym
Kelty K.I.D.S. Backpack child carriers
Kid Trax by Safety 1st battery-powered ride-on toy
   vehicles
Kids II "Bounce Bounce Baby!" door jumpers
Kids Line Inc. "Le Cradle" bassinet

Kids II Bouncer seats
Kolcraft LiteSport Stroller
Kolcraft Ranger and Ranger Quattro strollers
Kolcraft Tot Rider walkers
Kolcraft toy attachments on walkers sold under
   Tot Rider and Carter's names

L

L.L. Bean backpack child carrier Model AC25
L.L. Bean backpack child carrier Model W695
Lov's Decorated Orthodontic Pacifier

M

Mead Johnson Gentlease powdered infant formula
Minnie Mouse nautical outfits for infant and
   toddler girls
Mountain Buggy Urban Single and Urban Double
   jogging strollers
Mountain Buggy Urban Single, Urban Double, and
   Breeze strollers

N

Next Generation Pisces crib
Nike Little Air Jordan XIV infants' and children's
   sneakers

O

Oriental International Trading baby
   walkers
Oshkosh B'Gosh newborn girls garments

P

Peg Perego "Primo Viaggio" infant seats
Playtex Classic Patterns "Cherubs" and Soft
   Comfort latex pacifiers
Playtex Hip Hammock infant carrier
Portable wooden cribs
Precious Moments Tender Tails plush toys
Prince Lionheart electric baby-wipe warmer

S

Safety 1st and Beatrix Potter "Designer 22" infant
   seats/carriers
Safety 1st cabinet and drawer child-
   lockout latches
Safety 1st Fold-up booster seat
Schwinn Deluxe Bicycle Child Carriers
Similac Advance with Iron infant formula powder
Simmons "Little Folks" cribs
Snuggle Bear plush toy distributed as a premium
   with Snuggle fabric softener
"Sulley and Boo" plush dolls sold at The Disney
   Store

T

"The Baby Sitter" infant seat pad
The First Years liquid-filled teethers
Theraline "Big V" maternity and nursing pillows
Tommy Hilfiger white socks for infants and
   children
Trek Anthem C Elite bicycle helmets
Tropical fish and Rockin' Reptile Push 'n Pop toys
TSG "Metallic Gold". "Gloss Black", and
   "Foundation Blue" bicycle helmets

V

Various baby walkers
Various brands of foldable mesh-sided play
   yards/playpens

W

"Wiggly Giggler" baby rattles

Index